PERSPECTIVES ON THE CUSTOMARY INTERNATIONAL HUMANITARIAN LAW

The Study on *Customary International Humanitarian Law* by Jean-Marie Henckaerts and Louise Doswald-Beck (Cambridge University Press 2005) contains a unique collection of evidence of the practice of States and non-State actors in the field of international humanitarian law, together with the authors' assessment of that practice and their compilation of rules of customary law based on that assessment. The Study invites comment on its compilation of rules.

This book results from a year-long examination of the Study by a group of military lawyers, academics and practitioners, all with experience in international humanitarian law. The book discusses the Study, its methodology and its rules and provides a critical analysis of them. It adds its own contribution to scholarship on the interpretation and application of international humanitarian law.

ELIZABETH WILMSHURST is Associate Fellow, International Law, at Chatham House in London, and Visiting Professor at University College, London.
SUSAN BREAU is Reader in International Law at the School of Law, University of Surrey, and previously the Dorset Fellow in International Law at the British Institute of International and Comparative Law.

PERSPECTIVES ON THE ICRC STUDY ON CUSTOMARY INTERNATIONAL HUMANITARIAN LAW

EDITED BY
ELIZABETH WILMSHURST AND SUSAN BREAU

British Institute of
International and
Comparative Law

CHATHAM HOUSE

CAMBRIDGE
UNIVERSITY PRESS

CAMBRIDGE UNIVERSITY PRESS
Cambridge, New York, Melbourne, Madrid, Cape Town,
Singapore, São Paulo, Delhi, Tokyo, Mexico City

Cambridge University Press
The Edinburgh Building, Cambridge CB2 8RU, UK

Published in the United States of America by Cambridge University Press, New York

www.cambridge.org
Information on this title: www.cambridge.org/9781107402386

First published 2007
First paperback edition 2011

A catalogue record for this publication is available from the British Library

ISBN 978-0-521-88290-3 Hardback
ISBN 978-1-107-40238-6 Paperback

CONTENTS

PREFACE

The three volumes of *Customary International Humanitarian Law* by Jean-Marie Henckaerts and Louise Doswald-Beck (the Study) constitute a monumental work which has given rise to a huge amount of interest and discussion throughout the world. As is said in chapter§1 of the present book, all those associated with the preparation of the Study are to be congratulated: in focusing on the actual practice of States they have brought us closer to the heart of international humanitarian law. It is the unanimous view of the authors of this book that the Study represents a valuable work of great service to international humanitarian law. This book is intended as a complement to the Study – and as a compliment to it.

The book emerged from meetings of a group assembled to discuss the Study at the British Institute of International and Comparative Law during 2005/2006. Following a conference at Chatham House to launch the Study in the United Kingdom in April 2005,[1] it was decided that further discussion and analysis would be valuable and would also be in keeping with the spirit expressed by Yves Sandoz in his Foreword to the Study:

> [T]his study will have achieved its goal only if it is considered not as the end of a process but as a beginning. It reveals what has been accomplished but also what remains unclear and what remains to be done. . .[T]he study makes no claim to be the final word.

The discussion group was accordingly convened as a joint collaboration between the British Institute of International and Comparative Law and Chatham House. The meetings were attended by a number of academics and practitioners in international humanitarian law, largely from the United Kingdom. A representative of the ICRC attended every meeting and participated fully in the discussion.

---

[1] The proceedings of the conference are summarised at www.chathamhouse.org.uk/research/international_law/view/_/id/282/

The group took as its subject first, the methodology of the Study and secondly, a number of the principal Rules and groupings of Rules in the Study. At each session, following presentations by a principal speaker and a commentator, the subject was discussed by the participants. The principal speaker then wrote the relevant chapter of the book, expanding upon his or her presentation, as well as incorporating, as appropriate, the commentator's remarks and the substance of the discussion.

There was a precedent for the convening of a humanitarian law discussion group in London. From§1985–92, the British Institute of International and Comparative Law (BIICL) organised a discussion group to consider aspects of the 1977 Additional Protocols to the 1949 Geneva Conventions, and the 1980 United Nations Convention on Certain Conventional Weapons, the most recent humanitarian law treaties at that time. These meetings, involving academic specialists and practitioners from the British armed forces, the UK Foreign and Commonwealth Office and on occasion, the International Committee of the Red Cross (ICRC), played a valuable role in contributing to the process of reflection which eventually led to the United Kingdom's ratification of these treaties. The aim of the discussion group on the Study differed, of course, in that the Study represents not treaty law negotiated by States and open for ratification by them, but a proposed set of Rules put forward as having a legal status. The objective of the group, therefore, was to contribute to the discussion on the Rules; this involved consideration both of the formulation of the individual Rules and the manner in which they had been arrived at – the methodology of the Study.

Consequently, the present book aims to be a constructive comment with regard to both the methodology of the Study and the 'delivery' of the product of that methodology. The book also makes a scholarly contribution to international humanitarian law in general and, in particular, to the debate which the Study has occasioned.

The book starts, as the discussion group did, with introductory comments on the methodology used by the Study. With the extensive collection of evidence assembled in the Study's two Volumes of Practice, the Study presents a unique opportunity for discussion of the question of perennial interest to all international lawyers: how is international customary law formed? The first three chapters of the book consider the methodology described in the Introduction to the Study itself and the practical application of that methodology by the authors of the Study, including the sources of State practice which the authors have chosen and the way in which those sources have been treated.

The second part of the book deals with two subjects necessary for any examination of international humanitarian law: the status of armed conflicts and the status of combatants. Chapter 4 discusses the question of the existence of an armed conflict and its status as international or non-international; the chapter helps to fill a gap left by the Study, which does not address these important questions. The status of combatants, which runs as a theme through a number of the Rules, is discussed in chapter 5.

The third part of the book follows the order of the Study in addressing different groups of Rules: targeting, the natural environment, specific methods of warfare, weapons, fundamental guarantees, prisoners of war and displaced persons, and enforcement and implementation. Particular attention is paid to Rules considered likely to generate the most debate. There are some omissions; in particular Rules 109–117 concerned with the wounded, sick and shipwrecked were regarded as uncontroversial and an example of Rules where the authors of the Study have comprehensively encapsulated the law. Each chapter provides a context to the Rules it addresses, usually in the form of a discussion of the relevant treaty law, and reviews the Rules in the light of relevant State practice.

The concluding chapter draws together the different strands. It emphasises that the identification and formulation of rules of international customary law are matters of considerable difficulty, and they admit of different views. While not all of the contributors to this book would agree with all of the choices made by the authors of the Study in these respects, they agree that the Study has considerably advanced our understanding of the law. This book carries forward the debate.

Although each chapter of this book has been written after consultation with other participants of the group, each one remains the responsibility of the writer alone.

Grateful thanks are due to Michael Meyer of the British Red Cross who worked with us in planning both the discussion group and the book. Many thanks are due also to Agnieszka Jachec-Neale for her work at the British Institute of International and Comparative Law in organising the discussion group. The British Red Cross contributed financially to the organisation of the group, for which we express our sincere appreciation. Jean-Marie Henckaerts, Nils Melzer, Jelena Pejić, Jean-François Quéguiner, Lou Maresca, Stéphane Ojeda and Chris Harland from the ICRC travelled from Geneva to attend our discussion group and added invaluable observations within our deliberations.

Individual authors have had the benefit of assistance with their chapters; appreciation is extended to Adam Clark for his research assistance, and for their useful comments many thanks are extended to Group Captain Bill Boothby, Dr. Robert Cryer, Professor Guy Goodwin-Gill, Dr Stephanie Carvin, Dr Jenny Kuper, Professor Sir Adam Roberts and the staff of the ICRC mentioned above. We express our gratitude to Gill Wigglesworth and Maziar Jamnejad for their assistance in editing.

Elizabeth Wilmshurst
Susan C. Breau
February 2007

LIST OF CONTRIBUTORS

Daniel Bethlehem, Legal Adviser, Foreign and Commonwealth Office, formerly Director of Lauterpacht Centre for International Law, University of Cambridge, United Kingdom

Dr Susan C. Breau, School of Law, University of Surrey, United Kingdom

William Fenrick, Dalhousie University Law School, Canada

Charles Garraway, Associate Fellow, Chatham House, United Kingdom

Professor Steven Haines, Department of Politics and International Relations, Royal Holloway College, University of London, United Kingdom

Professor Françoise Hampson, Department of Law, University of Essex, United Kingdom

Dr Karen Hulme, Department of Law, University of Essex, United Kingdom

Agnieszka Jachec-Neale, Department of Law, University of Essex, United Kingdom

Jelena Pejić, Legal Adviser, International Committee of the Red Cross, Geneva, Switzerland

Professor Ryszard Piotrowicz, Department of Law, University of Wales, Aberystwyth, United Kingdom

Anthony P. V. Rogers, Yorke Distinguished Visiting Fellow of the Faculty of Law, University of Cambridge, Senior Fellow of the Lauterpacht

Centre for International Law, University of Cambridge, United Kingdom, former Director of Army Legal Services

Professor Michael N. Schmitt, Charles H. Stockton Professor, United States Naval War College

Professor Iain Scobbie, Sir Joseph Hotung Research Professor in Law, School of Oriental and African Studies, University of London, United Kingdom

David Turns, School of Law, University of Liverpool, United Kingdom

Elizabeth Wilmshurst, Associate Fellow, International Law, Chatham House, United Kingdom; Visiting Professor, University College, University of London, United Kingdom

TABLE OF CASES

International Criminal Tribunal for Rwanda

International Criminal Tribunal for the former Yugoslavia

Eritrea–Ethiopia Claims Commission/Arbitral Tribunal

Treaties and International Court Statutes

Declarations

ABBREVIATIONS

Additional Protocol I	Protocol Additional to the Geneva Conventions of 12 August 1949, and Relating to the Protection of Victims of International Armed Conflicts, 8 June 1977
Additional Protocol II	Protocol Additional to the Geneva Conventions of 12 August 1949, and Relating to the Protection of Victims of Non-International Armed Conflicts, 8 June 1977
ASIL	American Society of International Law
BFSP	British and Foreign State Papers
CCW	Convention on Prohibitions or Restrictions on the Use of Certain Conventional Weapons which May Be Deemed to Be Excessively Injurious or to Have Indiscriminate Effects (1980)
CoDH	Council of Europe Steering Committee for Human Rights
ECHR	European Convention on Human Rights
ECtHR	European Court of Human Rights
ECOSOC	United Nations Economic and Social Council
ENMOD Convention	United Nations Convention on the Prohibition of Military or Any Other Hostile Use of Environmental Modification Techniques (1976)
EWCA	England and Wales Court of Appeal
FARC	Fuerzas Armadas Revolucionarias de Colombia
GA	General Assembly
GC	Geneva Convention
HL	House of Lords (United Kingdom)
HRC	Human Rights Committee
HRW	Human Rights Watch
IACHR	Inter-American Commission on Human Rights
ICC	International Criminal Court

ICCPR	International Covenant on Civil and Political Rights
ICJ	International Court of Justice
ICJ Rep.	International Court of Justice Reports of Judgments, Advisory Opinions and Orders
ICRC	International Committee of the Red Cross and Red Crescent
ICTR	International Criminal Tribunal for Rwanda
ICTY	International Criminal Tribunal for the former Yugoslavia
IDF	Israel Defence Forces
IHL	International Humanitarian Law
IIHL	International Institute of Humanitarian Law
ILC	International Law Commission
ILM	International Legal Materials
ILR	International Law Reports
IMT	International Military Tribunal
ITLOS	International Tribunal for the Law of the Sea
LNTS	League of Nations Treaty Series
LRTWC	Law Reports of Trials of War Criminals
NATO	North Atlantic Treaty Organization
NEPA	National Environmental Policy Act
NIAC	Non-International Armed Conflict
OAS	Organization of American States
OIF	Operation Iraqi Freedom
PCIJ	Permanent Court of International Justice
POW	Prisoner of War
Recueil des Cours	*Recueil des Cours de l'Academie de Droit International de La Haye*
Rome Statute	Statute of the International Criminal Court, 17.07.1998
Study	*Customary International Humanitarian Law* Jean-Marie Henckaerts and Louise Doswald-Beck (Cambridge University Press, 2005)
UNCLOS	UN Convention on the Law of the Sea, 10.12.1982
UNHCR	United Nations High Commissioner for Refugees
UNPROFOR	United Nations Protection Force
UKTS	United Kingdom Treaty Series

UN	United Nations
UNTS	United Nations Treaty Series
YUN	Yearbook of the United Nations

PART 1

Setting the scene: Theoretical perspectives on
international law in the ICRC Study

The methodological framework of the Study

DANIEL BETHLEHEM*

1. Introduction

The Study on Customary International Humanitarian Law (the Study) took a decade to complete. By any standards, it is a significant contribution to the learning on, and the development of, international humanitarian law. Three volumes, 5,000 pages, 161 Rules and commentaries and supporting materials: it is a remarkable feat. All those associated with the preparation of the Study are to be congratulated. They have brought us closer to the heart of international humanitarian law – the actual practice of States.

In his foreword to the Study, Yves Sandoz observed as follows:

> The Study is a still photograph of reality, taken with great concern for absolute honesty, that is, without trying to make the law say what one wishes it would say. I am convinced that this is what lends the study international credibility. But though it represents the truest possible reflection of reality, the study makes no claim to be the final word. It is not all-encompassing – choices had to be made – and no-one is infallible. In the introduction to *De jure belli ac pacis*, Grotius says this to his readers: 'I beg and adjure all those into whose hands this work shall come, that they assume towards me the same liberty that I have assumed in passing upon the opinions and writings of others.' What better way to express the objectives of those who have carried out this study? May it be read, discussed and commented on. May it prompt renewed examination of international humanitarian law and the means of bringing about greater compliance and of developing the law. Perhaps it could even go beyond the subject of war and spur us to think about the value of the principles on which the law is based in order to build universal peace – the utopian imperative – in the century on which we have now embarked.[1]

---

* This chapter is a lightly edited version of a paper delivered at Chatham House in April 2005 in the author's then capacity as Director of the Lauterpacht Centre of International Law at the University of Cambridge. The views expressed are personal.
[1] Vol. I, xvii–xviii.

These are wise words, in every respect. The Study should indeed be a spur to further thinking about these issues.

Without detracting from this genuine appreciation, it is necessary and appropriate to draw attention to some important misgivings about the Study, as regards both methodology and the formulation of certain specific Rules. The purpose of doing so is not to detract from the utility of the Study, which is high. There is no doubt that the Study will be amongst the first texts consulted by both practitioners and academics confronted with issues of international humanitarian law. Rather, it is to place the Study in what the present author considers to be its appropriate analytical context. Had the Study been entitled 'State Practice and *Opinio Iuris* in the Interpretation and Application of International Humanitarian Law', many (although not all) of the difficulties identified below would be of lesser significance. The Study, however, is entitled simply 'Customary International Humanitarian Law'. And in this manner, as well as in its black-letter approach to the elucidation of Rules, which are almost invariably described as 'norms of customary international law', it has sought to take on the mantle of the Pictet commentaries to the Geneva Conventions, purporting implicitly to be a study of equivalent weight and authority in respect of customary international humanitarian law. In the author's view, this assessment is not warranted, for the reasons explained below.

2. The methodological framework

The framework for the comments that follow is not that of a military lawyer or a serviceman. There have been, and will no doubt be, many concerns expressed by military lawyers in the service of governments about this or that formulation of a rule. Where they are voiced seriously, such comments will have to be taken seriously, as customary international law reflects above all the practice of States and if a State challenges the assessment of practice that informs these volumes, that is a significant matter which will have to be met at the level of substance.

The focus of this chapter is different. It is that of a general international lawyer, engaged as a practitioner in cases before domestic and international tribunals which raise issues ranging from international humanitarian law and human rights law to State responsibility, treaty interpretation and the effect of treaty-based and customary international law rules within the municipal sphere. The focus is on legal method and the formulation of customary law rules, especially those which parallel equivalent rules found in treaties, and in the risks and advantages which are both inherent in any such exercise and are also evident specifically in this particular exercise.

A similar, though much smaller, initiative of trying to elucidate custom from an extensive patchwork of multilateral treaties was undertaken by the UNHCR four years ago in respect of certain core principles of international refugee law. In that exercise, in a joint Opinion (now published),[2] Sir Eli Lauterpacht QC and the present author were asked to consider whether the principle of *non-refoulement*, found in Article 33 of the 1951 Refugee Convention and, in similar terms, in a host of other treaties and international instruments, was a principle of customary international law and, if so, what was the scope and content of the customary rule. This exercise addressed *one* principle, deeply embedded in general international law, in respect of which there was extensive State practice. The analysis ran to 100 pages. There was annexed supporting material. The Opinion concluded that the principle was indeed a principle of customary international law. The analysis and the conclusion were the subject of detailed consideration by governmental and non-governmental experts. While the conclusion of customary status was generally endorsed by an Expert Roundtable organised by the UNHCR,[3] a number of the participants were cautious about the exercise and one or two notable scholars and others have since challenged the assessment and expressed hesitation about coming to such a conclusion in the abstract, detached from a concrete case.[4]

Having seen this process of divining custom from treaties in respect of one largely uncontroversial principle, the present author finds it is impossible to escape the nagging sense, in respect of the Study, that there are too many steps in the process of the crystallisation and of the formulation of the black letter customary rules that are insufficiently clear, even by reference to the two accompanying volumes of practice. Too much certainty is expressed in the affirmation of the customary status of the Rules as formulated. The formulation of each Rule is followed by a 'summary' which, almost without exception, asserts 'State practice establishes this rule as a norm of customary international law'. There are occasions in which this affirmation is followed by a statement noting ambiguity or controversy in respect of some element of the Rule, but the

---

[2] E. Lauterpacht and D. Bethlehem, 'The Scope and Content of the Principle of *non-refoulement*: Opinion', reproduced in E. Feller, U. Türk and F. Nicholson (eds.), *Refugee Protection in International Law* (Cambridge University Press, 2003), pp. 87 *et seq.*

[3] Feller, Türk and Nicholson (eds.), *ibid.*, pp. 178–179.

[4] See, for example, generally, J. Hathaway, *The Rights of Refugees Under International Law* (Cambridge University Press, 2005).

affirmation of customary status stands fast. François Bugnion, speaking
at the Chatham House conference organised to mark the publication of
the Study,[5] referred to the early development of customary international
humanitarian law as 'reflecting the requirements of the divinity'. As one
goes through the Study, and focuses on the methodology of divining and
formulating the individual Rules, one cannot help but feel that the exercise has something of an encyclical about it. Yet above all in the context of
the identification of customary international law, the credibility of the
law dictates that we must be able to see inside the black box.

This aspect is addressed further below illustratively by reference to a
number of the Rules. Before doing so, however, it is useful to take a
broader look at the exercise of identifying custom.

International humanitarian law, perhaps more than any other area of
international law, is heavily regulated by treaty. In his foreword to the
Study,[6] ICRC President Jakob Kellenberger referred to the Geneva Convention for the amelioration of the wounded and sick of 1864, which was
revised in 1906, 1929 and 1949. There are the Hague Conventions of 1899
and 1907, containing the Regulations respecting the laws and customs of
war on land. There is the subsequent body of Hague law concerning
weaponry and methods and means of warfare. There are the two 1977
Protocols additional to the 1949 Geneva Conventions. There is the Convention on Certain Conventional Weapons and its various protocols.
There is the Ottawa anti-personnel mines convention. And the list goes on.

In these circumstances of heavy regulation by treaty, the question
arises as to why it is useful and important to identify rules of customary
international law, and what are the dangers of doing so.

Kellenberger notes three reasons why customary international law
remains an important body of law despite the extensive reach of the
treaties. First, he notes that, while the 1949 Geneva Conventions enjoy
universal adherence today, the same is not yet the case for the other major
treaties in this field, notably the Additional Protocols of 1977. While
treaties bind only their parties, rules of customary international law bind
all States. Customary international law is therefore a means for achieving
the universal application of principles of international humanitarian law,
and notably of those enshrined in the Additional Protocols.

In this context, it is useful to identify the States that are not parties
to the Additional Protocols; they are the ones whose interests will be

[5] *The Law of Armed Conflict: Problems and Prospects*, Chatham House, 18–19 April 2005;
texts available at: www.chathamhouse.org.uk/research/international_law/papers/view/_/
id/282.   [6] Vol. I, ix–xi.

especially affected by the crystallisation of custom. States not parties to Additional Protocol I include: Iran, Iraq, Pakistan, India, Myanmar, Nepal, and most of the south-east Asian States – Philippines, Indonesia, Thailand, Malaysia; the United States is not a party, nor are Israel, Somalia, Sudan, Sri Lanka, Eritrea and Morocco. This is a 'Who's Who' of many of the States that have been engaged in conflicts over the past 30 years.

The second reason for the importance of custom noted by Kellenberger is that treaty-based international humanitarian law applicable to non-international armed conflicts falls short of meeting the protection needs arising from those conflicts. State practice, however, he suggests, affirms that many customary rules apply to all conflicts, whether international or non-international.

Third, Kellenberger notes that customary international law can help in the interpretation of treaty law.

Elements of these observations by Kellenberger are echoed in the Foreword by Judge Koroma,[7] of the International Court of Justice, and also in the Introduction by the authors of the Study.[8]

These are all important reasons in favour of identifying custom, but they carry with them a cautionary injunction, namely, that we must be hesitant about engaging in the crystallisation of custom simply with the object of remedying the defect of the non-participation by States in a treaty regime. If States have objections to particular treaty-based rules, those objections will subsist as regards the formulation of the rules in a customary format.

To Kellenberger's three reasons pointing to the importance of custom, three more may be added:

(a) customary international law may be self-executing and apply directly in the municipal sphere, whereas treaties may not;

(b) customary international law may supervene and prevail over an inconsistent rule in a treaty.[9] There is no hierarchy of sources of

---

[7] Vol. I, pp. xii–xiii.   [8] Vol. I, pp. xxv–li.

[9] The relationship between treaties and custom is complex, not simply for their interaction at the level of the derivation of customary rules – on which see further below p. 8 – but also when it comes to the interpretation of treaties. For example, Article 31(3)(c) of the Vienna Convention on the Law of Treaties 1969 provides, for certain purposes, that there shall be taken into account 'any relevant rules of international law applicable between the parties'. This principle is commonly relied upon to contend that a treaty rule must be interpreted and developed in the light of a subsequent rule of customary international law.

international law and, in principle, a recently formed rule of custom may prevail over an older, inconsistent treaty rule; and

(c) custom may be opposable beyond States, not only to armed opposition groups but also to other non-State actors and individuals.

There are, therefore, good reasons for engaging in a study of rules of customary international law in an area which is heavily marked by the imprint of treaties. But there are also dangers in doing so, and broader methodological concerns, and these need to be weighed in the balance. These dangers and concerns include at least the following.

(a) As regards methodology, there is the view, as expressed by Judge Sir Robert Jennings, dissenting in the *Nicaragua* case,[10] that it is difficult, if not impossible, to identify State practice relative to a rule of customary international law by a State party to a treaty of parallel application as all the relevant practice is in reality practice in the exercise of the treaty, not the customary rule.

(b) This leads to a wider issue, that of the greying of – the propensity towards a lack of clarity in – the process of rule formulation in international law. Traditionally, there are treaties and there is custom. Some interaction between the two is evident, as the Study points out,[11] but traditionally the areas of this interaction have been limited and usually achieved through the imprimatur of courts, as in the *North Sea Continental Shelf* cases[12] and the *Nicaragua* case. Outside of a judicial process, however, the exercise of deriving custom in an area heavily regulated by treaties, and by heavy reliance on these treaties, runs certain risks, for example, as regards legal certainty, the likely acceptance by States standing outside the treaty regime, compliance and enforcement by those States, and individual criminal responsibility.

(c) Particularly when heavy reliance is placed on treaties to which a number of States are not parties, initiatives to derive customary rules may be seen as an attempt to circumvent the requirement of express consent necessary for a State to be bound by the treaty-based rule.

(d) This may raise wider questions about treaty ratification in the future. Why should a State that is not now a party to the 1977 Additional Protocols ratify these treaties if the relevant principles therein

---

[10] *Case concerning Military and Paramilitary Activities in and against Nicaragua (Nicaragua v. United States of America)*, Merits, Judgment of 27 June 1986, *ICJ Rep.* 1986, 14.

[11] Vol. I, Introduction, at xlii–xlv.

[12] *North Sea Continental Shelf, Federal Republic of Germany v. Denmark; Federal Republic of Germany v. Netherlands*, Judgment of 20 February 1969, *ICJ Rep.* 1969, 3.

operate at the level of customary international law? Perversely, the articulation of customary rules which parallel those set out in a treaty may weaken rather than strengthen the potential for the universal application of the treaty.

(e) As customary international law is, in Judge Koroma's words (in his foreword to the Study), 'notoriously imprecise', we may find, particularly in the area of complex rules such as these, that the content of a customary rule may turn on the treaty-based formulation of the rule. This may be all well and good when the articulation of the customary rule mirrors the treaty-based formulation. If it does not, however, this may give rise to difficulties as regards interpretation and application.

(f) Finally, customary law, because of its imprecise nature, may be ill-suited to interpretation and application by municipal courts and as a foundation for individual criminal responsibility. This is one of the reasons why the establishment of the International Criminal Court was accompanied by a detailed articulation of written rules rather than simply by a *renvoi* to customary international law. It is also one of the reasons why the United Kingdom legislated for the prosecution of those accused for war crimes during the Second World War. Customary international law will not always be a sufficiently steady foundation from which to address individual criminal responsibility.

These points should not be over-stated. The issue is essentially simple. There are both advantages and disadvantages to the derivation of customary rules in an area which is heavily regulated by treaty. While, in the main, the exercise in which the ICRC was engaged in the Study maximises the advantages and minimises the risks associated with such an exercise, there are elements of the Study which give rise to a number of concerns.

The first concern is that, in key areas, the Study, in its formulation of the black-letter customary rules, is heavily contingent on the parallel treaty-based rules and notably on the provisions of Additional Protocol I. It is evident, of course, from the footnoted material accompanying the Rules, that the authors have looked at wider sources and the breadth of the exercise in which it engaged was both impressive and commendable. But there is no escaping the fact that, in very many critical areas, the customary formulation follows or draws heavily on the formulation in the Additional Protocol.

There are potential problems with this approach. In cases in which the customary formulation is simply that of the Additional Protocol – particularly when there are also questions about the weight of the other

source material relied upon – the risk is that the Study will be seen simply
as an attempt to get around the non-application of the treaty to certain
States. The difficulty is not avoided, however, if the customary formulation diverges from the treaty language without any apparent reason. In
such cases, questions may arise as to which formulation reflects the normative content of the Rule. This carries risks of uncertainty and perhaps
even of a lowering of standards of protection.

A second concern is that, although the statement of methodology set
out in the Introduction to the Study is generally sound, the rigorous
approach described therein is not always evident in the discussion and
evaluation of State practice and *opinio iuris*. So, for example, notwithstanding the reference in the Introduction to the importance of assessing
the 'density', that is, the weight, of relevant items of practice, there is
often little or no evidence that this is done. For example, resolutions of
the UN Commission for Human Rights seem to attract the same weight
as the legislation or policy statements of specially affected States. Little
account is taken of persistent objection, on the ground that some doubt is
said to exist about the validity of the doctrine. But custom, as in the case
of treaties, requires the consent of States. It is just that consent in the case
of custom is assessed differently; through practice or acquiescence.

A third concern is that, in some cases, the evidential source material
relied upon is either equivocal on its face as regards the Rule in question
or the quoted extracts are insufficient to allow weight to be placed upon it
reliably.

Fourth, following on from these comments, it is sometimes unclear why
the black-letter expression of the customary rule is formulated in the way
that it is. In some cases, the customary formulation is identical to the treaty
formulation. In other cases, there are what appear to be minor deviations
in formulation, although the reasons for, and import of, the deviations are
not explained. In yet other cases, the customary formulation departs
significantly from the treaty formulation. Again, however, the reason for,
and import of, the departure is not clear. In still other cases, there is a
propensity for the Study to take different elements of a single treaty-based
formulation and spread these across a number of customary rules and
commentaries. The attendant uncertainty about how one should read both
the customary rule and the 'supplanted' treaty rule is sometimes considerable, raising wider questions about standards of protection.

These general points of concern are illustrated by reference to a
number of tangible examples, including some prosaic ones and one or
two that may be more important.

Rules 23 and 24 address elements of the principle of distinction. Rule 23 states:[13] 'Each party to the conflict must, *to the extent feasible*, avoid locating military objectives within or near densely populated areas.'[14] Rule 24 then states:[15] 'Each party to the conflict must, *to the extent feasible*, remove civilian persons and objects under its control from the vicinity of military objectives.'[16] In support of these Rules, reference is made in the Commentary to Article 58(b) and 58(a), respectively, of Additional Protocol I as well as to provisions in Additional Protocol II, a large number of military manuals and official statements and reported practice. Reference to the national practice shows that different formulations are used, some of which track the language of Additional Protocol I and some of which do not. Reference to Article 58(a) and (b) of Additional Protocol I shows that the language of the customary formulation draws directly from the Additional Protocol language, although with one small difference. Article 58 of the Protocol requires the parties to a conflict to take precautions against the effects of attacks 'to the *maximum* extent feasible'.[17]

The reason for the omission of the word *maximum* from the customary formulation is unclear, as also is the significance, if any, of the omission. The omission might reflect the fact that some of the military manuals referred to also omit the word. The omission may not be significant; it is a relatively minor point. But, at least at first glance, it would seem that the customary formulation is weaker than the treaty formulation. Why? What are the implications for civilian protection? Which formulation is to be preferred?

Potentially more significant omissions are found in Rules 4 and 5, both also addressing the distinction between civilians and combatants.

Rule 4 states:[18] 'The armed forces of a party to the conflict consist of all organised armed forces, groups and units which are under a command responsible to that party for the conduct of its subordinates.' The Commentary refers notably to Article 43(1) of Additional Protocol I, as well as to military manuals and official statements and practice.

Reference to the national practice shows a range of different formulations. Article 43(1) of Additional Protocol I shows the antecedent of the customary rule formulation. It reads:

> The armed forces of a Party to a conflict consist of all organised armed forces, groups and units which are under a command responsible to that

---

[13] Vol. I, 71.   [14] Emphasis added.   [15] Vol. I, 74.   [16] Emphasis added.
[17] Emphasis added.   [18] Vol. I, 14.

> Party for the conduct of its subordinates, *even if that Party is represented by a government or an authority not recognised by an adverse Party. Such armed forces shall be subject to an internal disciplinary system which, inter alia, shall enforce compliance with the rules of international law applicable in armed conflict.*[19]

As will be apparent, the second part of the Protocol I formulation is missing from the customary formulation. The Commentary explains this by indicating that the customary formulation builds on earlier definitions of armed forces contained in the Hague Regulations and the Third Geneva Convention and further explains the omission of certain of the elements of the Hague Regulations, the Third Geneva Convention and Additional Protocol I definitions as being either addressed elsewhere in the Study or as being unnecessary. But, from a review of the other parts of the Study referred to, it is not at all clear that the omitted elements are either adequately addressed elsewhere or are unnecessary. Once again, one is left with a degree of uncertainty about the normative centre of gravity of the particular Rule.

The uncertainty is potentially more serious in the case of Rule 5. This states:[20] 'Civilians are persons who are not members of the armed forces. The civilian population comprises all persons who are civilians.' The Commentary refers to Article 50 of Additional Protocol I as well as to military manuals and reported practice.

Reference to this national material again shows different formulations. Article 50 of Additional Protocol I, which is headed 'Definition of civilian and civilian population', reads as follows:

1. A civilian is any person who does not belong to one of the categories of persons referred to in Article 4 A 1), 2), 3) and 6) of the Third Convention [detailing the principal categories of Prisoners of War] and in Article 43 of this Protocol [defining armed forces]. *In case of doubt whether a person is a civilian, that person shall be considered to be a civilian.*
2. The civilian population comprises all persons who are civilians.
3. *The presence within the civilian population of individuals who do not come within the definition of civilians does not deprive the population of its civilian character.*[21]

As will be evident, the definition of civilians and civilian population in Additional Protocol I is more elaborate than in the customary formulation, and in material respects. Although the elements of doubt about a

---

[19] Emphasis added.   [20] Vol. I, 17.   [21] Emphasis added.

person's civilian character and the presence of persons who are not civilians within the civilian population are addressed elsewhere in the Study, they do not feature in the definition and are dealt with far more equivocally in other sections. So, for example, reference is made to persons within the civilian population who do not come within the definition of civilians only in the commentary to Rule 6, which deals with the more problematical principle concerning civilians who take a direct part in hostilities.

The purpose here is not to dwell on the substantive issues raised by these divergent formulations, although they are of considerable importance. The significant points for present purposes are simply that (a) the reason for the omission from the customary law formulation of certain key elements of the Protocol I formulation are unclear, (b) the omissions are likely to give rise to considerable normative uncertainty, and (c) the omissions may undermine civilian protection rather than advance it.

Other chapters in this book illustrate these points by reference to other Rules, including those which address more controversial topics. For example, from a review of the supporting material contained in Volume II of the Study, it is not at all clear that the State practice and *opinio juris* cited can sustain the formulation of Rule 6, which concerns the limits on the protection of civilians who take a direct part in hostilities. This is an example of a customary law formulation which mirrors exactly the parallel treaty-based formulations, but in circumstances in which the national materials referred to are equivocal in their support of the customary law formulation. As is well known, the scope, interpretation and application of this principle has attracted particular controversy in recent years.[22]

The intention in raising these issues is not to undermine the edifice of the Study or to detract in any way from its importance. The Study is a remarkable endeavour and one that will greatly advance scholarship and debate, and ultimately compliance with, international humanitarian law. The essence of the present assessment can be summed up simply.

First, as a general matter, one should approach exercises of distilling customary international law in areas that are heavily regulated by treaty with caution. There are difficult methodological problems and questions of normative integrity to surmount. In some cases, one risks, inadvertently, diminishing rather than enhancing protection through such exercises.

---

[22] See, for example, Annex I to the September 2003 Report of the ICRC on *International Humanitarian Law and the Challenges of Contemporary Armed Conflicts.*

Second, the Study has the benefit of momentum that derives from the name, stature and authority of the ICRC. There will no doubt be many who would see it as the Pictet equivalent for customary international law. It would be a mistake to do so. Crystallising custom is not the same as interpreting a treaty. The exercise needs to be approached with considerably more circumspection.

Third, the pitfalls of the present exercise would be much reduced by a more deliberative approach to the formulation of the black-letter rules and a less affirmative approach to the underscoring of their customary status. As indicated at the outset, there is reason to be cautious about encyclical or black-box approaches to the crystallisation of custom. The Study is and should be the appropriate starting point in a review of State practice and *opinio iuris* relevant to the crystallisation of custom is clear. It is less evident that it is the last word on the subject.

The approach to customary international law in the Study

IAIN SCOBBIE

1. Introduction

The function of this chapter is not to evaluate the substantive merits of the customary rules formulated in the Study on customary international humanitarian law applicable in international and non-international armed conflicts. Rather it aims to evaluate the methodology underpinning it – in particular, the approach adopted to the question of custom formation – in order that its conceptual foundations may be tested and appraised. The structure of this chapter is quite straightforward. It starts by raising some general considerations regarding the reduction of customary law to a written text, essentially issues associated with the process of codification. A brief account of the methodology employed in the Study is then made in order to lay the basis for its evaluation. One of the principal questions addressed is whether the Study's methodology is as traditional as it claims to be: this necessitates an examination of the role of treaty practice in custom formation and the question of persistent objection. The final section is a critical appraisal of some aspects of the practice invoked by the Study. At the outset, however, it must be emphasised that a critical scrutiny of the Study's methodology does not necessarily undermine the validity of the substantive conclusions reached.

2. The question of codification

Perhaps the obvious analogies to the Study are the Harvard Drafts of the 1920s and 1930s[1] and the US Restatement of Foreign Relations

---

[1] For instance, the 1929 Harvard Law School draft Articles on 'The Law of Responsibility of States for Damage Done in their Territory to the Person or Property of Foreigners' (1929) 23 *American Journal of International Law* Supplement 131 and on 'Rights and Duties of Neutral States in Naval and Aerial War' (1939) 33 *American Journal of International Law* Supplement 167.

Law.[2] A more recent and more pertinent precursor is the International Institute of Humanitarian Law's *San Remo Manual* on naval warfare,[3] whose existence led to the decision not to include naval warfare in the ICRC Study on customary international humanitarian law.[4] The latter is, however, anointed with the prestige and authority of the ICRC, and it should be expected that it will assume the mantle of status and persuasion accorded to the ICRC commentaries on the Geneva Conventions[5] and Additional Protocols[6] because of its provenance and the wealth of practice it surveys.[7]

This does not detract from the fact, however, that the Study is fundamentally the work of a non-governmental institution. Unlike, for instance, the International Law Commission's 2001 Articles on the Responsibility of States for Internationally Wrongful Acts,[8] there was no formal governmental involvement in the evolution of the Study. Baxter argued that conventions prepared by the International Law Commission exert influence not simply because they represent the considered views of an expert group, but also because they are scrutinised by States and

[2] *Restatement of the Law, Third. The Foreign Relations Law of the United States, as Adopted and Promulgated by the American Law Institute at Washington, D C, May 14, 1986* (St Paul: American Law Institute Publishers, 1987).

[3] L. Doswald-Beck (ed.), *San Remo Manual on International Law Applicable to Armed Conflicts at Sea* (Cambridge University Press, 1995): an account of this Study's methodology is at pp. 61–69.

[4] See Study, Vol. I, Introduction, xxx.

[5] J. Pictet (ed.), *Commentary on the Geneva Conventions of 12 August 1949*, 4 volumes (Geneva, ICRC, 1952–1958).

[6] Y. Sandoz, C. Swinarski and B. Zimmermann (eds.), *Commentary on the Additional Protocols of 8 June 1977 to the Geneva Conventions of 12 August 1949* (Geneva: ICRC, 1987).

[7] For an account of the working methods which lie behind the Study, see Study, Introduction, xlv–li. It might be objected that the Study should not be associated with the ICRC inasmuch as Dr Kellenberger (the President of the ICRC), stated in the foreword that '[c]onsidering this report primarily as a work of scholarship, the ICRC respected the academic freedom both of the report's authors and of the experts consulted' (Study, ix at xi). This simply mirrors statements made in relation to the *Commentaries*: thus, the foreword common to the *Commentaries on the Geneva Conventions* stated '[a]lthough published by the International Committee, the Commentary is the personal work of its authors' (e.g., *Commentary to the First Convention* (1952) 7), and Hay (then President of the ICRC) stated in his foreword to the *Commentary on the Additional Protocols* (at xiii), that the ICRC 'allowed the authors their academic freedom, considering the Commentary above all as a scholarly work, and not as a work intended to disseminate the views of the ICRC'. Consequently, there is reason to expect that the Study will assume a status equal to that of the *Commentaries*.

[8] UN Doc. A/CN.4/L.602/Rev.1 (26 July 2001), formally adopted by the Commission on 9 August 2001.

adjusted to take account of their political demands in the final draft.[9] In contrast, the Study was overseen by a Steering Committee of academic experts in international humanitarian law.[10] Although governmental experts were also consulted at an advanced stage of the project when an executive summary was circulated for comment, this was done in their personal capacity.[11] Accordingly, while the Study is not an 'official' (State sponsored) codification of customary international humanitarian law, given the role and responsibilities of the ICRC in relation to international humanitarian law, it is undoubtedly a quasi-official codificatory text in a broad sense, inasmuch as it is an attempt to discern 'unwritten' rules and reduce them to an authoritative written form.

Some considerations are common to all codifications, such as the inevitability of progressive development through the elimination of ambiguity and discarding of anomalous cases, and the systemisation of a field of law.[12] At least on its face, the Study has avoided some of the common dangers of codification – for instance, it expressly states that it is not comprehensive, but has been selective on the issues it examined.[13] As Sandoz observes in his Foreword:

> The study is a still photograph of reality, taken with great concern for absolute honesty, that is, without trying to make the law say what one wishes it would say. I am convinced that this is what lends the study international credibility. But though it represents the truest possible reflection of reality, the study makes no claim to be the final word. It is not all-encompassing – *choices had to be made* – and no one is infallible.[14]

Accordingly, the reader is on notice that the Study does not address all the issues, far less contain all the answers. Customary law continues to exist outside its confines.

---

[9] R. Baxter, 'Multilateral Treaties as Evidence of Customary International Law' (1966) 41 *British Year Book of International Law* 275, at 292.

[10] See Study, Vol. I, Introduction, xlv and l–li.

[11] See Study, Vol. I, Introduction, xlviii.

[12] See, e.g., International Law Commission, *Report on the Work of its Forty-eighth Session 6 May–26 July 1996*, UN Doc. A/51/10 (1996), 86–87, paras. 157–158; K. Marek, 'Thoughts on Codification' (1971) 31 *Zeitschrift für ausländisches öffentliches Recht und Völkerrecht* 489, at 490–491; O. Schachter, 'Entangled Treaty and Custom', in Y. Dinstein (ed.), *International Law at a Time of Perplexity: Essays in Honour of Shabtai Rosenne* (Dordrecht: Martinus Nijhoff, 1989), pp. 717 and 721; H. Thirlway, *International Customary Law and Codification* (Leiden: Sijthoff, 1972), pp. 16–21; and C. de Visscher, 'La Codification du Droit International' (1925) 6 *Recueil des Cours* 327, at 380–384.

[13] See Study, Vol. I, Introduction, xxx–xxxi.

[14] Y. Sandoz, Foreword, in Study, xiv at xvii: emphasis added.

Indeed, by virtue of the Martens Clause,[15] first inserted into the pre-amble of 1899 Hague Convention II and since incorporated into other treaties relevant to the conduct of armed conflict, international humani-tarian law itself recognises that its treaties are not comprehensive and that, as a discipline, it cannot be insulated from developments occurring in other fields of international law. This relatively narrow interpretation of the clause finds solid support in State practice and judicial decisions.[16] Meron argues that the pleadings in the *Nuclear weapons* Advisory Opinion proceedings demonstrated that there was general agreement on this construction of the Martens clause while 'broader layers of interpre-tation inspired strong disagreement'.[17] Although the International Court acknowledged the continued relevance of the clause,[18] it 'did not resolve the principal controversies concerning its interpretation'.[19]

Given this uncertainty, it is perhaps surprising that the effect of the Martens Clause was not further addressed by this Study given the Clause's dynamic generative role in the law of armed conflict.[20] Its exclusion might indicate an underlying structural issue. Does the Study take an unduly

[15] On the Martens Clause, see: *Military and Paramilitary Activities in and Against Nicaragua (Nicaragua v. United States of America)*, Merits, Judgment of 27 June 1986, [1986] *ICJ Rep.* 14, pp. 113–114, para. 78 (hereafter *Nicaragua Merits* case); *Legality of the Threat or Use of Nuclear Weapons* Advisory Opinion of 8 July 1996 [1996] *ICJ Rep.* 66, p. 257, para. 78 and p. 259, para. 84 (hereafter *Nuclear Weapons* Advisory Opinion); *US v. Krupp* (1948) 15 Annual Digest 620 at 622; and *Prosecutor v. Kupreškic and others* (ICTY) Judgment of Trial Chamber, 14 January 2000, IT-95-16, paras. 525–527. For commentary on the clause, see A. Cassese, 'The Martens Clause: Half a Loaf or Simply Pie in the Sky?' (2000) 11 *European Journal of International Law* 187; Y. Dinstein, The Conduct of Hostilities under the Law of International Armed Conflict (Cambridge: Cambridge University Press, 2004), pp. 56–57; L. Green, The Contemporary Law of Armed Conflict (Manchester University Press, 2000, 2nd edn) pp. 17–18, 34 and 349; T. Meron, 'The Martens Clause, Principles of Humanity, and Dictates of Public Conscience' (2000) 94 *American Journal of International Law* 78; M. Sassòli and A. Bouvier, *Un Droit dans la Guerre?* (Geneva: ICRC, 2003), p. 145 *et seq.*; G. Schwarzenberger, *International Law as Applied by International Courts and Tribunals: Vol.II The Law of Armed Conflict* (London: Stevens, 1968), pp. 21–22; and R. Ticehurst, 'The Martens Clause and the Laws of Armed Conflict' (1997) 317 *International Review of the Red Cross* 125.
[16] The most extensive analysis is in Cassese, 'The Martens Clause' (note 15 above).
[17] Meron, 'The Martens Clause' (note 15 above), at 85.
[18] *Nuclear Weapons* Advisory Opinion, p. 257, para. 78 and 259, para. 84: see also *Nicaragua merits case*, pp. 113–114, para. 218.
[19] T. Meron, 'The Martens Clause' (note 15 above), at 87: see also Cassese, 'The Martens Clause' (note 15 above), at 210–211.
[20] The Martens Clause is expressly identified as a topic which 'could not be developed in sufficient detail for inclusion' in the Study, but which might be included in a future edition – see Study, Introduction, xxx. Henckearts informed the author that practice concerning the Martens Clause had been collected but an analysis of its customary

atomised view of the customary norms it identifies? Are they each seen as self-contained and separate from one another, rather than being integrated within the wider substantive network of the international legal system? In short, does the Study ignore the systemic location and the internal relationships between norms?[21] These considerations indicate that an examination of the Martens Clause as a dynamic element peculiar to the development of the law of armed conflict should have been addressed.

The Study does, however, take into account practice under environmental and human rights instruments, including those concerning refugees and displaced persons, where these are relevant. The relationship between these diverse areas of law is not, however, addressed in the Study which confines itself to noting that human rights law continues to apply during armed conflict under the express terms of human rights treaties themselves.[22] Further, in addressing human rights issues, the aim was not to provide an account of customary human rights law 'but in order to support, strengthen and clarify analogous principles of humanitarian law'.[23]

Given that the topic of the Study is the customary law of armed conflict, and the endeavour has been undertaken by a non-governmental institution without the active participation of States, special and additional factors are relevant to the process of codification. In the first place, because governments were not formally engaged in the formulation of the Rules contained in the Study, presumably there was no call to engage in the horse-trading and compromise that would have been inevitable had a diplomatic conference been convened to establish a list of customary rules or, as noted above, had the International Law Commission been charged with this task.[24] Although political compromise would, or should, have been excluded from this codificatory Study, no doubt good faith differences held by the participants in the drafting process regarding the precise content and formulation of specific customary rules must have been accommodated. Here the process is not transparent: the reader only has the text of the final Rules, a commentary upon each, and an

---

implications was omitted from the Study due to considerations of time (personal communication, December 2006).

[21] See J. Raz, *The Concept of a Legal System* (Oxford: Clarendon Press, 1980, 2nd edn).

[22] See Study, Introduction, xxx–xxxi: the general question of the continued relevance of multilateral treaties during an armed conflict is considered below.

[23] See Study, Vol. I, 299.

[24] Compare G. H. Aldrich, 'Customary International Humanitarian Law – an Interpretation on behalf of the International Committee of the Red Cross' (2005) 76 *British Yearbook of International Law* 503, at 507.

edited account of practice. Reading the Rules, at times, can be like reading the text of some pronouncements of the International Court where its legal reasoning lies submerged under a text which merely sets out its conclusions. The International Court, however, publishes the pleadings made before it, so one can (usually) examine the arguments and evidence which led to the judgment or advisory opinion and thus attempt to reconstruct the Court's reasoning. In contrast, Volume II of the Study presents the practice upon which the Rules are based, and which underpins the analysis contained in the commentaries to the Rules.[25] It has been claimed that this account of practice is incomplete,[26] but the reader does not have the resources available to make an independent evaluation.

The exclusion of States from the process may perhaps also have another implication. Schachter argued that willingness of States to treat the texts of codificatory conventions as customary arises, at least in part, from the bureaucratic aspect of codification. Legal advisers and government officials play an important role in the codification process by commenting on preparatory drafts of the convention and by participating in the conference which establishes its final text. Officials who subsequently have to ascertain and apply the law generally look to the convention for guidance because this is the product of a process in which they, or their colleagues, participated.[27] The need to search out and evaluate the practice on which the convention was based is short-circuited, and the convention takes on and accumulates a normative weight. It may be that States will be less ready to embrace the Study simply because they were not players in the process but, on the other hand, this consideration will not apply to non-governmental lawyers or, presumably, to domestic and international courts and tribunals. In particular, the International Criminal Tribunal for the Former Yugoslavia exercises jurisdiction *ratione materiae* on the basis of customary law because:

> the application of the principle *nullum crimen sine lege* requires that the
> international tribunal should apply rules of international humanitarian law

---

[25] 'Upon completion of the research, all practice gathered was summarised and consolidated into separate parts covering the different areas of the study . . . The chapters containing this consolidated practice were subsequently edited, supplemented and updated by a group of ICRC researchers, and are published in Volume II, "Practice"' – Study, Introduction, xlvii–xlviii.

[26] See W. H. Parks, 'The ICRC Customary Law Study: A Preliminary Assessment' (2005) 99 *Proceedings of the American Society of International Law* 208, at 211.

[27] Schachter, 'Entangled Treaty and Custom' (note 12 above), at 722, n.13. Compare Study, Introduction, xliii: 'the drafting of treaty norms helps to focus world legal opinion and has an undeniable influence on the subsequent behaviour and legal conviction of States.'

which are beyond any doubt part of customary law so that the problem of adherence of some but not all States to specific conventions does not arise.[28]

Further – and this could be an important factor in the reception of the Study and the normative weight it attains – according to de Visscher, codifications are an instrument for the diffusion of international law into public opinion which, in democratic societies, is a mechanism that may guarantee the observance of international law.[29] Customary rules are generally known only to a restricted circle of specialists, to whom their validity, proper formulation and exegesis are frequently matters of debate and controversy: codification presents proposed rules in a form accessible to non-specialists and makes them appear both definitive and authoritative. As national Red Cross and Red Crescent Societies have a duty to disseminate international humanitarian law,[30] within the Red Cross Movement there exists a standing mechanism for the diffusion and dissemination of the Study. If that can be mobilised behind the Study, through the pressure of informed public opinion, it might be more difficult for governments to disregard its Rules. At the very least, if a (democratic) State departed from the Study's Rules, it may be faced with the necessity of justifying its action to domestic political audiences, or even to the judiciary in those States where customary international law is automatically incorporated into domestic law. This point was not lost on the authors of the Study.[31]

Moreover, it is rational that the conditions in which international humanitarian law falls to be applied should have influenced the Study. It is intended to be instrumental inasmuch as it aims to formulate customary rules in order to provide a guide for future practice. Consequently,

---

[28] *Report of the Secretary-General pursuant to paragraph 2 of Security Council Resolution 808 (1993)*, UN Doc. S/25704 (3 May 1993), para. 34. Para. 35 of the Secretary-General's Report identifies treaties which are 'beyond doubt' part of customary law as being the 1949 Geneva Conventions, the 1907 Hague Regulations, the 1948 Genocide Convention and the 1945 London Charter of the International Criminal Tribunal. Although international humanitarian law and international criminal law are not coextensive, and violations of international humanitarian law need not give rise to criminal proceedings, Article 1 of the Yugoslav Tribunal's Statute confers upon it 'the power to prosecute persons responsible for serious violations of international humanitarian law'.

[29] De Visscher, 'La Codification du Droit International' (note 12 above) 327, at 399–401.

[30] H. Haug, *Humanity for All: the International Red Cross and Red Crescent Movement* (Berne: Henry Dunant Institute/Paul Haupt Publishers, 1993), p. 175.

[31] See Study, Introduction, xxx; but compare P. Rowe, 'The Effect on National Law of the Customary International Humanitarian Law Study' (2006) 11 *Journal of Conflict and Security Law* 165. The Study has already been invoked in cases before the Israel and United States Supreme Courts – see Wilmshurst, chapter 16, p. 410.

one might expect that the Study should not result in indeterminate expression and, indeed, the Study expressly acknowledges this consideration: 'A study on customary international humanitarian law may also be helpful in reducing the uncertainties and the scope for argument inherent in the concept of customary international law.'[32]

This gives reason to argue that the Study should result in reasonably straightforward rules insofar as this is possible, rather than more sophisticated norms which entail evaluation or discretion in order that they may be applied. It would be best if the normative content of the Rules lay in a definition of conduct 'purely in terms of externalized acts' which aims to promote determinacy and narrow the margin of appreciation on the part of the actor.[33] Because law is expressed in natural language, indeterminacy is undoubtedly inevitable,[34] but some rules are more resolute than others in their aim to eschew ambiguity. In international humanitarian law, a rule cast in terms of using equitable principles to achieve an equitable solution, akin to that employed by the International Court in cases of continental shelf delimitation,[35] would appear to be dysfunctional. A rule so formulated is an extreme example of what Franck terms a 'sophist' rule, a rule which is sensitive to the 'multi-layered complexity' of the matter in hand.[36] Lawyers would still be debating the conduct, and standard of conduct, entailed by such a rule in given circumstances long after the conflict itself was over. The convergence of international humanitarian and international criminal law gives an additional reason for simplicity. To respect the *nullum crimen sine lege* principle, a degree of clarity is required to enable those subject to the rules to know how to act within the law and thus avoid individual criminal responsibility.

---

[32] Study, Vol. I, Introduction, xxix.

[33] T. Franck, *The Power of Legitimacy among Nations* (New York: Oxford University Press, 1990), p. 67 *et seq.*, especially pp. 74–77 on the notion of 'idiot' and 'sophist' rules. Compare Posner's marginal approach to judicial decision making in matters of national security which is reliant on standards rather than rules – see R. Posner, *Not a Suicide Pact. The Constitution in a Time of National Emergency* (New York: Oxford University Press, 2006), pp. 31–41.

[34] See, for instance, C. Perelman, *Logique juridique: nouvelle rhetorique* (Paris: Dalloz, 1976), pp. 34–36, para. 24 and pp. 114–115, para. 56 bis.

[35] See, e.g., *Continental Shelf Case (Libya Arab Jamahiriya/Malta)* [1985] *ICJ Rep.*13, pp. 30–31, paras. 28–29.

[36] Franck, *The Power of Legitimacy* (note 33 above), p. 75.

2. The Study's exposition of the methodology employed

The Study was motivated in part by the realisation that, although there are numerous treaties in the field of international humanitarian law, there are barriers to their implementation in contemporary armed conflict, whether international or non-international. In the first place, States are only bound to apply treaties to which they are parties. The 1977 Additional Protocols were singled out for attention by the Study: Additional Protocol I has not been ratified by several States which have recently been participants in international armed conflicts.[37] Similarly, Additional Protocol II is applicable only in conflicts occurring in the territory of States parties, but this fails to cover several contemporary non-international conflicts. Secondly, there was a perceived need, or desire, to regulate non-international armed conflicts in greater detail, principally by an extension of rules applicable in international armed conflict: 'Common sense would suggest that such rules, and the limits they impose on the way war is waged, should be equally applicable in international and non-international armed conflicts.'[38]

The mechanics of custom formation is perhaps one of the most contested, yet fundamental, issues in contemporary international law. The Study's account of the concept of customary international law underlying its conclusions is almost telegraphically concise.[39] It relies principally on *dicta* of the International Court to construct its account of the process of custom formation, although it presents an incomplete and selective survey of the Court's rulings. As the template for its systemisation and codification of practice, the Study employed the International Law Association's *Final Report of the Committee on the Formation of Customary (General) International Law*[40], associated publications of

---

[37] Aldrich, 'Customary International Humanitarian Law' (note 24 above), argues that the failure of some key States to become parties to Additional Protocol I motivated the Study: see also Y. Dinstein, 'The ICRC Customary International Humanitarian Law Study' (2006) 36 *Israel Yearbook on Human Rights* 1 at 2.

[38] Study, Vol. I, Introduction, xxix: see xxviii–xxix generally. In contrast, Aldrich, 'Customary International Humanitarian Law' (note 24 above) is much more sceptical regarding this aspect of the Study, criticising its lack of 'analysis of the potential political implications for States engaged' in non-international armed conflicts and noting that they are often 'reluctant to accept rules that appear to restrict their actions in suppressing rebellions and will always oppose anything that appears to give rebels belligerent status'.

[39] See Study, Introduction, xxxi–xlv.

[40] International Law Association, *Final Report of the Committee on the Formation of Customary (General) International Law*, at 712: cited in Study, Vol. I, Introduction, xxxiii, n.18, xxxiv, n.20, xxxix, n.41, xl, n.42, and xli, n.45.

Mendelson[41] who acted as rapporteur of the Committee, and also
Kirgis's influential article *Custom on a Sliding Scale.*[42]

With the exception of the use of Kirgis's work, the notion of custom
formation that underpins the Study is ostensibly fairly traditional – a
point underlined by Meron.[43] It does not take into account contemporary
critical or revisionist accounts of custom formation.[44] The Study simply
affirms that the existence of a customary rule requires two elements, State
practice, and *opinio iuris,*[45] the belief that this practice is legally required,
prohibited or allowed. As the Study underlines, there is a malleability at
the heart of the custom formation process: are verbal acts, such as statements that certain acts are prohibited, State practice, or do they constitute *opinio iuris* because they express a State's legal opinion? Or can verbal
acts be both simultaneously? The Study thought that the need to draw a
strict line between practice and *opinio iuris* was generally unnecessary.

---

[41] M. Mendelson, 'The Formation of Customary International Law' (1999) 272 *Recueil des
Cours* 158, cited in Study, Volume 1, Introduction, xxxix, n.40. Other relevant works by
M. Mendelson are 'The Subjective Element in Customary International Law' (1995) 66
British Year Book of International Law 177, and his *Comments* presented at the Chatham
House conference, 'The Law of Armed Conflict: Problems and Prospects', held to mark
the publication of the Study on 18 April 2005, www.chathamhouse.org.uk/research/
international_law/papers/view/–/id/282 at 17–23.

[42] F. Kirgis, 'Custom on a Sliding Scale' (1987) 81 *American Journal of International Law* 146
cited in Study, Vol. I, Introduction, xlii, n.46.

[43] T. Meron, 'Revival of customary humanitarian law' (2005) 99 *American Journal of
International Law* 817.

[44] Contemporary doctrine is voluminous – see, for instance, M. Byers, *Custom, Power and
the Power of Rules: International Relations and Customary International Law* (Cambridge
University Press, 1999); M. Chinen, 'Game Theory and Customary International Law:
a Response to Professors Goldsmith and Posner' (2001) 23 *Michigan Journal of
International Law* 143; J. Goldsmith and E. Posner, 'A Theory of Customary International
Law' (1989) 66 *University of Chicago Law Review* 1113; J. Kammerhofer, 'The Uncertainty
in the Formal Sources of International Law: Customary International Law and Some of
its Problems' (2004) 15 *European Journal of International Law* 523; J. Kelly, 'The Twilight
of Customary International Law' (2000) 40 *Virginia Journal of International Law* 449;
A. Roberts, 'Traditional and Modern Approaches to Customary International Law: A
Reconciliation' (2001) 95 *American Journal of International Law* 757; and D. Vagts,
'International Relations Looks at Customary International Law: A Traditionalist's
Defence' (2004) 15 *European Journal of International Law* 1031.

[45] In passing, it is worth noting that in stressing the need for *opinio iuris* the Study parts
company from Mendelson's own academic view which effectively denies the need for
opinio iuris, although he concedes that this is a 'dissent from the prevailing ortho-
doxy' – M. Mendelson, *Comments* at note 41 above. For more detail see his 'The
Subjective Element in Customary International Law' (note 41 above), at 194–202,
204–207; and his 'The Formation of Customary International Law' (note 41 above),
at 245 *et seq.*

If practice was dense, *opinio iuris* was largely enfolded within it, and there was no need to demonstrate the two elements separately. *Opinio iuris* became significant where practice was ambiguous in order to determine whether a customary norm had emerged.[46]

Accordingly, the Study classifies both physical and verbal acts as State practice, while stressing that only official practice is relevant.[47] The latter category comprehends: 'military manuals, national legislation, national case-law, instructions to armed and security forces, military communiqués during war, diplomatic protests, opinions of official legal advisers, comments by governments on draft treaties, executive decisions and regulations, pleadings before international tribunals, statements in international organisations and at international conferences and government positions taken with respect to resolutions of international organisations'. The use of some of these materials, particularly instructions to armed forces, comments on draft treaties and pleadings, has been criticised.[48]

Further, while conceding that acts which are not made public do not contribute to the process of custom formation, because other States cannot react to them, the Study has nonetheless relied on communications made by States to the ICRC itself, despite the fact that these are often confidential. The underlying rationale is that State practice need not be communicated to the whole world to be pertinent to the custom formation process; it suffices that it is conveyed to at least one other State or competent international organisation. As the ICRC is charged with assisting in the implementation of international humanitarian law, and may take note of complaints of alleged breaches, it is a relevant organisation in this regard.[49] Similarly, because of its responsibilities in relation to international humanitarian law, the Study takes into account official ICRC statements as practice relevant to the formation of custom, as well as that of other international organisations. The latter includes the negotiation and adoption of resolutions, along with explanations of vote, as these are acts of States.[50] On the other hand, the practice of armed opposition groups, including their commitments to observe given rules of international humanitarian law, is ruled not to constitute State practice as such.

[46] Study, Vol. I, Introduction, xl–xli.
[47] Study, Vol. I, Introduction, xxxiii; but compare Dinstein, 'ICRC Customary International Law Study' (note 37 above), at 5–6.
[48] Study, Vol. I, Introduction, xxxii; for criticism, see, e.g., Aldrich, 'Customary International Humanitarian Law' (note 24 above), Dinstein, 'ICRC Customary International Law Study' (note 37 above), at 4 and Parks, 'ICRC Customary Law Study' (note 26 above), at 208–209.   [49] Study, Vol. I, Introduction, xxxiv.
[50] Study, Vol. I, Introduction, xxxv–xxxvi.

Although this may be evidence that certain rules are accepted as applicable in non-international armed conflict, 'its legal significance is unclear'.[51]

The methodology outlined by the Study, in general, stresses a traditional inductive approach to custom formation until the issue of ambiguous practice arises. To address this problem, it then invokes Kirgis's 'sliding scale' analysis. This claims that, in certain matters, the balance between State practice and *opinio iuris* may be modified to place weight on humanitarian considerations in a manner that lessens the need for practice.[52] In particular, the Study invokes Kirgis in support of the proposition that:

> It appears that international courts and tribunals on occasion conclude that a rule of customary international law exists when that rule is a desirable one for international peace and security or for the protection of the human person, provided that there is no important contrary *opinio juris*.[53]

Although the widespread ratification of the Geneva Conventions and Additional Protocols was taken into account in assessing custom,[54] the Study claims to have taken a 'cautious approach' to treaty participation which was assessed in relation to other elements of practice, especially that of non-party States. If their practice conformed to a treaty provision, then this was seen as important positive evidence of custom: conversely, their contrary practice was held to be important evidence that the provision did not have customary status. The practice of parties in their relations with non-parties was also seen to be significant. Despite placing apparently little weight on the practice of treaty parties, the Study expressly states that it did not limit itself to the practice of non-parties because, for instance, only to examine the practice of the thirty or so States that were not party to the Additional Protocols would not comply with the requirement that custom be based on widespread and representative practice.[55]

Further, the Study affirms the finding of the International Military Tribunal at Nuremberg that the 1907 Hague Regulations were customary; that of the International Court in the *Nicaragua* case that common

---

[51] Study, Vol. I, Introduction, xxxvi.

[52] Compare Schachter, 'Entangled Treaty and Custom' (note 12 above) at 731–732, 734.

[53] Study, Introduction, xlii.

[54] At the time the Study was written, the Geneva Conventions had been ratified by 192 States, Additional Protocol I by 162, and Additional Protocol II by 157 – Study, Volume I, Introduction, xliv. As of December 2006, the Geneva Conventions have 194 States parties; Additional Protocol I, 166; and Additional Protocol II, 162. The ICRC claims that this represents universal ratification of the Geneva Conventions – see J. A. Lavoyer, 'A Milestone for International Humanitarian Law' (22 August 2006), www.icrc.org/web/eng/siteeng0.nsf/html/geneva-conventions-statement-220906?opendocument.

[55] Study, Vol. I, Introduction, xliv.

Article 3 of the Geneva Conventions constituted 'elementary considerations of humanity' applicable in all armed conflicts; and its ruling in the *Nuclear Weapons* Advisory Opinion that the great majority of the provisions of the Geneva Convention are customary. Finally, it noted that there was general agreement that the definitions of crimes in the 1998 Rome Statute of the International Criminal Court are customary.[56]

In its account of the methodology employed, the Study asserts that its approach in assessing whether a given proposition was customary was 'a classic one', as delineated by the International Court in various cases, but 'in particular in the *North Sea Continental Shelf* cases'.[57] In reality, however, there appears to be a divergence between this rhetorical reaffirmation of the views set out in *North Sea Continental Shelf* and the less stringent methodology which actually appears to have been employed. Two principal methodological considerations account for this more relaxed attitude, namely, the Study's reliance on Kirgis's reformulation of the relationship between practice and *opinio iuris*, and its approach to the practice of States parties to relevant conventions. This is more redolent of the International Court's views in *Nicaragua* than *North Sea Continental Shelf*. These factors result in the Study adopting an approach to customary international law which is much less traditional than it claims.[58]

3. Kirgis' 'sliding scale'

The Study's invocation of Kirgis raises at least two specific issues. First, as a general matter, it points to notions of relative normativity.[59] This itself

---

[56] Study, Volume I, Introduction, xliv–xlv: see International Military Tribunal (Nuremberg) Judgment and Sentences, reprinted in (1947) 41 *American Journal of International Law* 172; *Nicaragua Merits* case, para. 218; and *Nuclear Weapons* Advisory Opinion, pp. 257–258, paras. 79–82 (reaffirmed, *Legal Consequences of the Construction of a Wall in the Occupied Palestinian Territory*, Advisory Opinion of 9 July 2004 [2004] *ICJ Rep.* 136, 199, para. 157). See also *Report of the Secretary-General pursuant to paragraph 2 of Security Council Resolution 808 (1993)*, UN Doc. S/25704 (3 May 1993), para. 35. For a critical account of the Study's reliance on aspects of the ICC Statute, see R. Cryer, 'Of Custom, Treaties, Scholars and the Gavel: The Influence of the International Criminal Tribunals on the ICRC Customary Law Study' (2006) 11 *Journal of Conflict and Security Law* 239, at 257–262.

[57] Study, Introduction, xxxii; *North Sea Continental Shelf* Cases *(Germany v. Denmark* and *Germany v. the Netherlands)* [1969] *ICJ Rep.* 3 – see in particular, pp. 37–45, paras. 60–79.

[58] Compare T. Meron, 'Revival of Customary Humanitarian Law' (2005) 99 *American Journal of International Law* 817 at 833.

[59] J. Beckett, 'Behind Relative Normativity: Rules and Process as Prerequisities of Law' (2001) 12 *European Journal of International Law* 627; Roberts, 'Traditional and Modern Approaches to Customary International Law: A Reconciliation' (note 44 above); D. Sheldon, 'International Law and "Relative Normativity"', in M. Evans, *International Law*

raises two questions: where does the notion of higher normativity which privileges *opinio iuris* at the expense of State practice come from, and how does it act to affect the balance between the two? As President Higgins has observed:

> I am not sure where one gets this notion of 'higher normativity', still less the suggestion that the requirements of practice do not operate in the normal way . . . To assert an immutable core of norms which remain constant regardless of the attitudes of states is at once to insist upon one's own personal values (rather than internationally shared values) and to rely essentially on natural law in doing so. This is a perfectly possible position, but it is not one I take.[60]

This position has merit. Reliance on essentially a natural law position raises not simply the question of which values are to be privileged, but also the specific content or variant of the values that are to be employed. Efforts could all too easily be deflected from a principled and technical assessment of practice and *opinio iuris* to a discourse aimed primarily at an exegesis of value.

The second concern is more specific: employing Kirgis's analysis may result in the elaboration of customary rules on the basis of a single or restricted array of practice. For example, Rogers qualifies as problematic the doctrinal claim that irregular combatants must not owe a duty of allegiance to the Detaining Power in order to qualify as privileged belligerents and thus benefit from prisoner of war status on capture. He claims this view is squarely based on a Privy Council case, *Public Prosecutor v. Koi*, which arose during the Malaysian insurgency in the 1960s, and on which it places too much weight.[61] The normative canonisation of propositions on the basis of restricted practice raises an obvious danger of the consolidation of norms whose implications have not been fully thought out or

Footnote 59 (*cont.*)

(Oxford University Press, 2006, 2nd edn) p. 159; J. Tasioulas, 'In Defence of Relative Normativity: Communitarian Values and the Nicaragua case' (1996) 16 *Oxford Journal of Legal Studies* 84; and P. Weil , 'Towards Relative Normativity?' (1983) 77 *American Journal of International Law* 413.

60 R. Higgins, *Problems and Process: International Law and How We Use It* (Oxford: Clarendon Press, 1994) p. 27. For an argument which expressly grounds obligations *erga omnes* in objective moral value, which has a decidedly theological twist, see M. Ragazzi, *The Concept of International Obligations Erga Omnes* (Oxford: Clarendon Press, 1997) pp. 182–187.

61 See chapter 5, pp. 107–108; see *Public Prosecutor v. Koi* [1968] AC 829; Y. Dinstein, *The Conduct of Hostilities under the Law of International Armed Conflict* (Cambridge University Press, 2004) pp. 36–37 and 40–41; and R. Baxter, 'The Privy Council on the Qualifications of Belligerents' (1969) 63 *American Journal of International Law* 290.

thought through. This is a general criticism of Kirgis' doctrine which the Study may well have avoided given the range of practice examined. Indeed, it affirms that: 'In some instances, it is not yet possible to find a rule of customary international law even though there is a clear majority practice in favour of the rule and such a rule is very desirable.'[62] Given this note of caution, one may wonder why the Study invoked Kirgis in the first place.

4. The move towards *Nicaragua*

The Study, while referring inter alia to various *dicta* in the *North Sea Continental Shelf* cases,[63] places principal emphasis on the International Court's proposition that 'even without the passage of any considerable period of time, a very widespread and representative participation in [a] convention might suffice of itself, provided it included that of States whose interests were specially affected,' to transform a conventional provision into 'a general rule of [customary] international law'.[64] It is perhaps telling that it passed over in silence the Court's assessment of the State practice in issue, taken pursuant to the 1958 Geneva Convention on the Continental Shelf:

> over half the States concerned, whether acting unilaterally or conjointly, were or shortly became parties to the Geneva Convention, and were therefore presumably, so far as they were concerned, acting actually or potentially in the application of the Convention. From their action no inference could legitimately be drawn as to the existence of a rule of customary international law in favour of the equidistance principle.[65]

Nevertheless, the Study took into account the practice of States parties to conclude that 'the great majority' of the provisions of the Geneva Conventions and Hague Regulations have customary status.[66]

As Meron notes, taking into account the practice of States parties to a treaty as well as that of non-party States constitutes a shift towards the Court's views of custom formation employed in the *Nicaragua* case[67]

---

[62] Study, Vol. I, Introduction, xlii.
[63] See Study, Vol. I, Introduction, xxxii, xxxvi, xxxviii, xli and xliii.
[64] *North Sea Continental Shelf* cases (note 57 above), p. 42, para. 73.
[65] *Ibid.*, p. 43, para. 76.   [66] Study, Vol. I, Introduction, xxx and xliv.
[67] T. Meron, 'Revival of customary humanitarian law' (note 58 above) at 833. It should be noted that the methodology employed in the *Nicaragua Merits* case was expressly rejected by the International Law Association, 'Final report of the Committee on the formation of customary (general) international law' (note 40 above), at 141 which observed that this aspect of the case has been 'severely criticised' and that, moreover, 'the parties in that case were broadly agreed that . . . the main treaty provisions were also part of customary law'.

where it ruled that it was bound to take into account the UN Charter and
that of the Organisation of American States, to which the United States
was party, 'in ascertaining the content of the customary international law
which the United States is also alleged to have infringed'.[68] It should be
recalled, however, that this did not entail an automatic translation of
treaty provisions into customary rules:

> apart from the treaty commitments binding the Parties to the rules in
> question, there are various instances of their having expressed recognition
> of the validity thereof as customary international law in other ways. It is
> therefore in the light of this "subjective element" – the expression used by
> the Court in its 1969 Judgment in the *North Sea Continental Shelf* cases
> (*ICJ Reports 1969*, p.44) – that the Court has to appraise the relevant
> practice.[69]

Accordingly, the Court proceeded to seek collateral evidence for the existence of customary norms which, moreover, the parties to the case had
expressly agreed existed in parallel to their treaty commitments.

This issue is insufficiently developed in the discussion of the Study's
methodology. There appears to be too easy an elision from the fact of
widespread participation in the Geneva Conventions and Additional
Protocols to the normative conclusion of customary status. A belief in the
ease of normative mutation is, however, not peculiar to the Study: in particular, the identification by the International Court of the specific rules
of international humanitarian law which it thinks are 'intransgressible'
has hardly been candid. The Court did not enumerate these rules in
either the *Legal Consequences of the Construction of a Wall* Advisory
Opinion or in the *Nuclear Weapons* Advisory Opinion. In the latter, it
simply opined:

> It is undoubtedly because a great many rules of international humanitarian
> law applicable in armed conflict are so fundamental to the respect of the
> human person and 'elementary considerations of humanity' as the Court
> put it in its Judgment of 9 April 1949 in the *Corfu Channel* case (*ICJ
> Reports, 1949*, p.22), that Hague and Geneva Conventions have enjoyed a
> broad accession. Further these fundamental rules are to be observed by all
> States whether or not they have ratified the conventions that contain them,

Footnote 67 (*cont.*)
  Mendelson has been equally critical in his academic writings: see M. Mendelson, 'The
  International Court of Justice and the Sources of International Law', in V. Lowe and M.
  Fitzmaurice (eds.), *Fifty Years of the International Court of Justice: Essays in Honour of Sir
  Robert Jennings* (Cambridge University Press, 1996), pp. 67–71, 77–79 and 86–87.
  [68] *Nicaragua Merits* case, p. 97, para. 183.   [69] *Ibid.*, p. 98, para. 185.

THE APPROACH TO CUSTOMARY INTERNATIONAL LAW

because they constitute intransgressible principles of international customary law.[70]

The Study takes this as an authoritative ruling,[71] although it is apparent that in these proceedings the Court would have had neither the reason nor the opportunity to examine whether there existed *opinio iuris* and practice sufficient to support this conclusion in relation to many, if not most, provisions of the Geneva Conventions. The question posed in the advisory opinion focused on means and methods of warfare: unlike the Hague Regulations, the Conventions do not regulate this issue. Similarly, as Meron points out, in the *Nicaragua* case the Court completely failed to scrutinise whether practice and *opinio iuris* validated its finding of the customary status of common Articles 1 and 3 of the Geneva Conventions.[72]

Although Schachter has noted that there is an increasing tendency by both governments and international lawyers to view multilateral treaty provisions as customary,[73] the International Court has rejected the existence of a legal presumption to this effect. Even in the *Nicaragua* case, although the parties were agreed on the existence of customary norms parallel to their treaty commitments, the International Court nonetheless thought it necessary to validate this hypothesis.[74] It also adopted this approach in the *Tunisia/Libya Continental Shelf* case and *Libya/Malta Continental Shelf* case.[75] Accordingly, there is reason to recur to the more articulate and stringent requirements of *North Sea Continental Shelf* as the baseline to determine the normative impact of participation in multilateral treaties on customary international law. This is consonant with the

---

[70] *Nuclear Weapons* Advisory Opinion, p. 257, para. 79.

[71] Study, Vol. I, Introduction, xliv.

[72] T. Meron, 'Revival of customary humanitarian law' (note 58 above) at 819, and see also his 'The Geneva Conventions as Customary Law' (1987) 81 *American Journal of International Law* 348 and *Human Rights and Humanitarian Norms as Customary Law* (Oxford, Clarendon Press, 1989), pp. 25–37: see *Nicaragua Merits* case, pp. 113–115, paras. 218–220. Compare G. Mettraux, *International Crimes and the* ad hoc *Tribunals* (Oxford University Press, 2005), pp. 14–16 identifying a similar tendency in the Yugoslav and Rwanda Tribunals – p. 15, 'many a Chamber of the *ad hoc* Tribunals has been too ready to brand norms as customary, without giving any reason or citing any authority for that conclusion'.

[73] Schachter, 'Entangled Treaty and Custom' (note 12 above), see also S. Rosenne, *Developments in the Law of Treaties 1945–1986* (Cambridge University Press, 1989), p. 124.

[74] *Nicaragua Merits* case, p. 98, paras. 184–185: compare International Law Association, 'Final Report of the Committee on the Formation of Customary (General) International Law' note 40 above, at 757–765.

[75] See *Continental Shelf Case (Tunisia/Libyan Arab Jamahiriya)* [1982] *ICJ Rep.*18 p. 38, para. 24, and *Continental Shelf* case *(Libya Arab Jamahiriya/Malta)* [1985] *ICJ Rep.*13 pp. 29–30, para. 27.

view expressed in the International Law Association Report upon which the Study purports to rely.

5. The normative significance of the practice of States parties to treaties

The Geneva Conventions achieved universal State participation on 2 August 2006 with the accession of Montenegro. Does this automatically entail that their provisions have a presumptive customary status? The authors of the Study appear to think so. In their headnote to the digest of practice associated with Chapter 33, which deals with combatants and prisoner of war status, they state:

> The treatment of captured combatants entitled to prisoner-of-war status is regulated by the Third Geneva Convention. Practice pertaining thereto is not examined in detail in this study because the Third Geneva Convention is considered to be part of customary international law.[76]

This assumes that all provisions of Convention III necessarily must 'at all events potentially, be of a fundamentally norm-creating character such as could be regarded as forming the basis of general rule of law'.[77] Could this be reasonably claimed of, for example, the provision in Article 119 which provides that, on repatriation, each prisoner of war is entitled to carry 25kg of personal effects and baggage, or the Article 26 duty to permit prisoners the use of tobacco? Moreover, as the Study itself acknowledges, some provisions of Convention III have been overtaken by subsequent practice, for example, Article 118 on the release and repatriation of prisoners of war.[78]

The assumption that universal participation in a convention inescapably transmutes its provisions into customary law cannot lightly be accepted. In *North Sea Continental Shelf,* while conceding that widespread participation in a treaty could in itself transform a conventional rule into a rule of general customary law,[79] the International Court was categorical that where action is taken in pursuit of a treaty commitment 'no inference could legitimately be drawn as to the existence of a rule of customary international law'.[80] This position was effectively reaffirmed

---

[76] Study, Vol. II, Part II, 2537; compare R. Baxter, 'Treaties and Custom' (1970) 129 *Recueil des Cours* 27, at 96.   [77] *North Sea Continental Shelf* cases, p. 42, para. 72.
[78] See Study, Vol. 1, 455, commentary to Rule 128; see further Jachec-Neale, chapter 12, pp. 333–335.   [79] *North Sea Continental Shelf* cases, p. 42, para. 73.
[80] *North Sea Continental Shelf* cases, p. 43, para. 76.

by the Court in *Nicaragua* where it sought collateral evidence of *opinio iuris* to establish the existence of parallel custom.

The search for an indication that practice has an autonomous normative weight which contributes to the formation of custom, and is not simply the fulfilment of a treaty commitment, undoubtedly avoids some of the conceptual difficulties identified by the Baxter paradox, namely that:

> As the number of parties to a treaty increases, it becomes more difficult to demonstrate what is the state of customary international law *dehors* the treaty . . . As the express acceptance of the treaty increases, the number of States not parties whose practice is relevant diminishes. There will be less scope for the development of international law *dehors* the treaty.[81]

Nevertheless, it may be asked whether the Study begs the question through its reliance on the practice of States parties to the relevant conventions, and in particular that of parties to the Additional Protocols. The Study states that, in assessing the normative status of their provisions, it did not confine itself to the examination of the practice of the thirty or so non-party States because this would not comply with the requirement that custom be based on widespread and representative practice.[82] Surely this is circular, masking an assumption that customary norms should conform to the provisions of the Protocols, and thus privileging the views of States parties who are, in any case, bound conventionally. As the International Court observed in *North Sea Continental Shelf*:

> In principle, when a number of States, including the one whose conduct is invoked, and those invoking it, have drawn up a convention specifically providing for a particular method by which the intention to become bound by the régime of the convention is to be manifested – namely by the carrying out of certain prescribed formalities (ratification, accession), it is not lightly to be presumed that a State which has not carried out these formalities, though at all times fully able and entitled to do so, has nevertheless somehow become bound in another way.[83]

The acts of non-party States which dissent from the provisions of the Protocols may constitute representative practice, and the expression of *opinio iuris*, outside the confines of the treaty. These could indicate that

---

[81] Baxter, 'Treaties and Custom' (note 76 above), at 73, see also 64 and 96: compare T. Meron, 'Revival of customary humanitarian law' (note 58 above) at 833, and his *Humanitarian Norms* (note 72 above) 50–57; and Schachter, 'Entangled Treaty and Custom' (note 12 above), 725.

[82] Study, Vol. I, Introduction, xliv: see also T. Meron, 'Revival of customary humanitarian law' (note 58 above) at 833.   [83] *North Sea Continental Shelf* cases, p. 25, para. 28.

States are divided on what the law requires, to the extent that neither uniform practice nor *opinio iuris* exists,[84] and thus that customary law has not crystallised around the Protocols' provisions. The approach adopted by the Study appears to reverse the burden of proof of customary law, making the Protocols presumptively customary as opposed to merely conventional.[85]

In turn, this raises a related issue, namely the doctrine of persistent objection upon which the Study purportedly expresses no opinion, partly on the basis that some authorities 'doubt the continued validity of this doctrine'[86] although it was endorsed in the International Law Association's Report.[87] Are the authorities doubting the continued existence of persistent objection publicists or States? The Study simply does not consider whether, in principle, States not party to Additional Protocol I could qualify as persistent objectors to any supervening customary law arising from its provisions. Can States be expected to accept as customary that which they have rejected as a conventional obligation?

Despite the agnosticism regarding persistent objection expressed by the Study, it expressly invokes the doctrine in relation to Rule 45 which provides:

> The use of methods or means of warfare that are intended, or may be expected, to cause widespread, long-term and severe damage to the natural environment is prohibited. Destruction of the natural environment may not be used as a weapon.

The Study comments:

> State practice establishes this rule as a norm of customary international law applicable in international, and arguably also in non-international, armed conflict. It appears that the United States is a 'persistent objector' to the first part of this rule. In addition, France, the United Kingdom and the United States are persistent objectors with regard to the application of the first part of this rule to the use of nuclear weapons.[88]

---

[84] See *Nuclear Weapons* Advisory Opinion, p. 254, para. 67.

[85] See Dinstein, 'ICRC Customary International Humanitarian Law Study' (note 37 above), at 10–11.   [86] Study, Vol. I, Introduction, xxxix.

[87] See International Law Association, 'Final Report of the Committee on the Formation of Customary (General) International Law' (note 40 above), at 738–740; and Mendelson, 'Formation of Customary International Law' (note 41 above), at 227–244. On the doctrine, compare J. Charney, 'The Persistent Objector Rule and the Development of Customary International Law' (1985) 56 *British Year Book of International Law* 1 and T. Stein, 'The Approach of a Different Drummer: The Principle of the Persistent Objector in International Law' (1985) 26 *Harvard Journal of International Law* 457.

[88] Study, Vol. 1, 151, commentary to Rule 45.

The Commentary to Rule 45 notes that it stems from Article 35.3[89] and 55.1[90] of Additional Protocol I which were innovative when adopted, although subsequent practice indicates that this prohibition has become customary.[91] It continues, however, that some practice casts doubt on this conclusion, effectively that of France, the United Kingdom and the United States,[92] and also that the International Court did not consider Articles 35.3 and 55.1 to be customary in the *Nuclear Weapons* Advisory Opinion.[93]

The United States is not a party to Additional Protocol I and, on balance, its recorded practice indicates that it does not consider the prohibition to be customary:[94] accordingly, in regard to this Rule, it qualifies as a persistent objector *tout court*. On the other hand, although France and the United Kingdom are parties to Additional Protocol I, each made a reservation to Articles 35.3 and 55 on ratification.[95] Their national military manuals nevertheless acknowledge the prohibition on means and methods of warfare which are intended or may be expected to cause widespread, long-term and severe damage to the natural environment.[96] Both, however, have expressly stated that these Articles do not have customary status[97] and moreover do not apply to the use of nuclear weapons.[98] The Study concludes that they are persistent objectors to the application of the first part of Rule 45 to nuclear weapons as their practice is deemed consistent on this point.[99]

---

[89] Article 35.3 provides: 'It is prohibited to employ means or methods of warfare which are intended, or may be expected, to cause widespread, long-term and severe damage to the natural environment.'

[90] Article 55.1 provides: 'Care shall be taken in warfare to protect the natural environment against widespread, long-term and severe damage. This protection includes a prohibition of the use of methods or means of warfare which are intended or may be expected to cause such damage to the natural environment and thereby to prejudice the health or survival of the population.'

[91] For a summary of supporting practice, see Study, Vol. 1, 151–153, commentary to Rule 45: for the digest of practice, see Study, Vol. II, Part 1, 876–912. This is not the place to consider substantive issues regarding Rule 45: for an analysis, see Hulme, chapter 8.

[92] Study, Vol. 1, 153–155, Commentary to Rule 45.

[93] Study, Vol. 1, 153–154, Commentary to Rule 45: and *Nuclear Weapons* Advisory Opinion, p. 242, para. 31.

[94] See, in particular, Study, Vol. II, Part 1, 878, §153, 891, §244, 894–895, §263–264 and 896, §267–269: but compare 882–883, §185–186.

[95] Study, Vol. II, Part 1, 877, §147 (France) and §149 (United Kingdom).

[96] Study, Vol. II, Part 1, 880, §170 (France) and 882, §184 (United Kingdom).

[97] Study, Vol. II, Part 1, 878, §152 (France) and 894, §262 (United Kingdom).

[98] See paragraph 2 of France's reservation, deposited on 11 April 2001, and paragraph (a) of the United Kingdom's declaration, deposited on 28 January 1998 – see www.icrc.org/ihl.nsf/WebSign?ReadForm&id=470&ps=P ; and also Study, Vol. II, Part 1, 882, §184 and 894, §262 (United Kingdom).

[99] Study, Vol. 1, 151 and 154–155, Commentary to Rule 45.

One may, however, wonder whether in relation to nuclear weapons these States are truly persistent objectors, or whether the practice of France, the United Kingdom and the United States, as States 'specially affected' in the matter of nuclear weapons, demonstrates a fragmentation of practice which precludes the emergence of a customary norm.[100] The latter conclusion appears more consonant with the approach adopted elsewhere in the Study: for instance, in relation to the prohibition on blinding laser weapons, it classified States involved in their development as 'specially affected States' whose practice had an especial weight in the process of custom formation.[101] A consistent application of the Study's methodology should indicate that no customary prohibition equivalent to Rule 45 applies to the use of nuclear weapons – 'if "specially affected States" do not accept the practice, it cannot mature into a rule of customary international law'.[102]

Moreover, the Study does not deem France and the United Kingdom to be persistent objectors to Rule 45 as a whole, despite their clear statements denying customary status to the underlying provisions of Additional Protocol I. The Study appears to rely on the restatement of the prohibition in their military manuals as sufficient to disrupt their persistent objection – but without indicating how these statements are evidence of an autonomous *opinio iuris* as opposed to the fulfilment of a treaty commitment. In the case of France, the manual relied upon was promulgated in the same year as it ratified Additional Protocol I: one might expect some caution in viewing this as anything other than the declaration of its obligations under the Additional Protocol.[103] On the other hand, the United Kingdom 'manual' employed was issued in 1981, but it did not ratify the Protocol until 1998. This perhaps provides a surer foundation to claim that it is evidence of autonomous *opinio iuris*, but the use of this document as State practice has given rise to a controversy which is representative of wider concerns.

6. The identification of practice

In the *Fisheries* case, the International Court of Justice decisively indicated that State practice relevant to the custom formation process could

---

[100] *Contra* Study, Vol. 1, 154–155, commentary to Rule 45: the three States are identified as 'specially affected' in the matter of nuclear weapons at 154.

[101] See Study, Vol. I, Introduction, xxxviii, and also commentary to Rule 86 at 292–296, and Study, Vol. II, Part 1, 1961–1982: compare Parks, 'ICRC Customary Law Study' (note 26 above), at 211–212.

[102] Study, Vol. I, Introduction, xxxviii: see also Dinstein, 'ICRC Customary International Humanitarian Law Study' (note 37 above), at 13–14; Hulme, chapter 8, p. 233; and, generally, Hampson, chapter 3, pp. 68–71.

[103] See *North Sea Continental Shelf* cases, p. 43, para. 76.

lie in verbal, as opposed to physical, acts. Following the promulgation of Norwegian legislation delimiting its fisheries zone in 1935, the United Kingdom protested and suggested recourse to the Permanent Court of International Justice. Pending resolution of this dispute, Norway stated that it would deal leniently with foreign fishing vessels which breached its legislation but in 1948, because no agreement had been reached, it abandoned this policy and a considerable number of United Kingdom trawlers were arrested and condemned. The United Kingdom then instituted proceedings before the International Court.[104] In his dissenting opinion, Judge Read argued that Norway could not base its claim on its legislation alone. In the absence of enforcement, this could not amount to practice:

> Customary international law is the generalization of the practice of States. This cannot be established by citing cases where coastal States have made extensive claims, but have not maintained their claims by the actual assertion of sovereignty over trespassing foreign ships . . . The only convincing evidence of State practice is to be found in seizures, where the coastal State asserts its sovereignty over the waters in question by arresting a foreign ship and by maintaining its position in the course of diplomatic negotiation and international arbitration.[105]

Obviously the Court thought otherwise. Accordingly, in principle, the Study's use of essentially verbal acts in the construction of its Rules is unimpeachable. This has, however, been subject to criticism. For instance, Parks argues that the Study 'focuses on statements to the exclusion of acts and relies only on a government's words rather than deeds. Yet, war is the ultimate test of law. Government-authorized actions in war speak louder than peacetime government statements'.[106]

Leaving to one side, for the moment, the nature of the statements upon which the Study relied, the claim that battlefield practice should be seen as paramount is not without difficulty, particularly if this departs from views previously expressed by a State. Surely a peacetime assessment of what the law requires is more considered, precisely because it is detached from the pressures of conflict? An emphasis on battlefield practice is akin to Judge Read's view on the nature of State practice, yet he required that this be maintained in subsequent international actions, such as diplomatic exchanges. Departure from the initial peacetime position thus requires

---

[104] See *Fisheries* case (*United Kingdom v. Norway*) [1951] *ICJ Rep.* 116, pp. 124–125.
[105] *Ibid.*, dissenting opinion of Judge Read, p. 191.
[106] Parks, 'ICRC Customary Law Study' (note 26 above), at 210; compare Dinstein, 'ICRC Customary International Humanitarian Law Study' (note 37 above), at 6.

justification,[107] because the State in question is acting contrary to the view it has previously held out as lawful. An analogy may be drawn here with the International Court's view of unilateral statements in the *Nuclear Tests* cases which, in certain circumstances, were seen as giving rise to binding obligations.[108] As the Court also observed in these cases, it cannot be assumed that States will act in breach of commitments they have undertaken,[109] upon which other States may rely.[110] If a State's battlefield behaviour differs from its earlier views, in the absence of justification, how can a principled departure from its earlier position be distinguished from its violation? No doubt other States may react to battlefield practice which becomes public, but will this practice be known with sufficient objectivity and adequate detail for a principled assessment?

Further, the normative weight of some of the material employed in the construction of the Study has been criticised. For example, objections have been raised to the use of materials which have an official State provenance, but which are seen as inappropriate. Two considerations underpin this objection. It has been claimed that rules of engagement and military manuals may be informed by factors which are not legal, for instance by political and operational issues, and that accordingly instructions issued to armed forces should not blindly be relied upon without further analysis.[111] It has also been claimed that some manuals cited are essentially training manuals, produced administratively but which do not reflect, or reflect fully, the official governmental position on international humanitarian law. Three documents in particular have been claimed to have less than official status – an Israeli manual, which is claimed to be a training document which has been claimed to have 'no binding or even authoritative

---

[107] Compare Perelman's principle of inertia: this simply refers to the presumption that an attitude adopted in the past will subsist and may be relied upon, because change requires justification: see C. Perelman and L. Olbrechts-Tyteca, *The New Rhetoric: A Treatise on Argumentation* (University of Notre Dame Press, 1969) pp. 105–107, §27: for commentary, R. Alexy *A Theory of Legal Argumentation: The Theory of Rational Discourse as Theory of Legal Justification* (Oxford: Clarendon Press, 1989) pp. 171–173.

[108] *Nuclear Tests* cases (*Australia v. France*; *New Zealand v. France*) [1974] *ICJ Rep.*1974, 253 and 457: see the *Australia v. France* judgment pp. 269–270, paras. 50–51.

[109] *Ibid., Australia v. France* judgment, p. 272, para. 60. This presumption is a long-standing feature of the Court's jurisprudence – see, e.g., *Certain German interests in Polish Upper Silesia* case: Merits Judgment, PCIJ, Ser.A, No.7 (1926) 30.

[110] *Nuclear Tests* cases, *Australia v. France* judgment, p. 269, para. 51.

[111] For wider criticism along these lines, see Parks, 'ICRC Customary Law Study' (note 26 above), at 208–209. This criticism is elaborated in his *Asymmetries and the Identification of Legitimate Military Objectives*, which is to be published in W. von Heinegg (ed.), *Humanitarian Law: New Challenges* (Berlin: Springer, 2007). See also Schmitt, chapter 6, p. 134.

standing';[112] a 1981 UK manual, officially entitled *A Soldier's Guide to the Law of Armed Conflict*, which has been characterised as 'a training document which is no more than basically trying to keep soldiers on the straight and narrow';[113] and a German manual which, it has been alleged, assimilated international and non-international armed conflict on a number of issues as the result of one official's view as a matter of policy, from which no normative conclusions should be drawn.[114] A more general objection along these lines has been expressed by Aldrich:

> This study [cites] . . . official statements, such as the remarks by the Deputy Legal Advisor of the United States Department of State at a 1987 meeting in Washington DC, as well as public reports or statements by military officials or agencies of many other States that give some indication of official attitudes with respect to how hostilities have been or should be conducted. But such materials, while helpful, fall short of defining with any precision the extent of contemporary State acceptance of or probable State agreement with the proposed rules of customary international humanitarian law made by this study.[115]

These considerations raise a point of principle. Can States dissociate themselves from purportedly official statements to disavow that they express either its practice or *opinio iuris*?[116]

---

[112] Dinstein, 'ICRC Customary International Humanitarian Law Study' (note 37 above), at 6. The Study cites two Israeli documents, the 1986 *Law of War Booklet* (e.g., Study, Volume II, Part 1, 103, §726) and the 1998 *Manual on the Laws of War* (e.g., *ibid.*, 948, para. 253). Professor Dinstein disparages the use of both by the Study.

[113] Statement of C. Garraway, BIICL/RIIA International Law Workshop, 11 October 2005. That this document was not the official UK military manual is clear from the preface to UK Ministry of Defence, *The Manual of the Law of Armed Conflict* (Oxford University Press, 2004), vii: see also Dinstein, 'ICRC Customary International Humanitarian Law Study' (note 37 above), at 7.

[114] Intervention by Professor W. Heintschel von Heinegg, April 2005 Chatham House conference: this intervention does not appear in the published record of the conference.

[115] Aldrich, 'Customary International Humanitarian Law' (note 24 above), at 507. The remarks to which Aldrich refers were published as M. Matheson, 'The United States Position on the Relation of Customary Law to the 1977 Protocols Additional to the Geneva Conventions of 1949' (1986) 2 *American University Journal of International Law and Politics* 419. As Cryer points out, 'Of Custom, Treaties, Scholars and the Gavel' (note 56 above), this is the most frequently cited publication drawn from an academic source in the Study's digest of practice.

[116] The Appeals Chamber of the Yugoslav Tribunal, in its Decision on the Defence Motion for Interlocutory Appeal on Jurisdiction in *Prosecutor v. Tadić* (2 October 1995) appears to have taken the view that military manuals were principally instances of State practice, IT-94-1-AR72; paras. 130–131.

In the *Cumaraswamy* advisory opinion, the International Court ruled that, 'According to a well-established rule of international law, the conduct of any organ of a State must be regarded as an act of that State. This rule . . . is of a customary character'. The Court noted that this rule was reflected in draft Article 6 of the Draft Articles on State Responsibility which had been adopted provisionally by the International Law Commission.[117] This became Article 4.1 of the International Law Commission's 2001 Articles on Responsibility of States for Internationally Wrongful Acts, which provides:

> The conduct of any State organ shall be considered an act of that State under international law, whether the organ exercises legislative, executive judicial or any other functions, whatever position it holds in the organisation of the State, and whatever its character as an organ of the central government or territorial unit of the State.[118]

It is settled law that responsibility attaches to the acts of officials regardless of their position in the national hierarchy, providing that they act in their official capacity.[119] Accordingly, it is difficult to see how States may disavow, without further ado, statements and official documents emanating from its functionaries, however lowly, providing they are acting in an official capacity at the time. A State could, of course, give reasons why an ostensibly official statement should be disregarded – for instance, that it was not consonant with the body of its settled practice – but otherwise the presumption must be that acts of officials are acts of State.

The criticism that the Study did not properly evaluate its primary sources, however, merely points to a wider issue. At times it is clear that the Study demonstrates a lack of discernment in its assessment of practice. This is apparent in its general treatment of whether multilateral treaties which

---

[117] *Difference relating to Immunity from Legal Process of a Special Rapporteur of the Commission on Human Rights*, Advisory Opinion of 29 April 1999 [1999] *ICJ Rep.* 62, p. 87, para. 62. Draft article 6 provided: 'The conduct of an organ of the State shall be considered as an act of that State under international law, whether that organ belongs to the constituent, legislative, executive, judicial or other power, whether its functions are of an international or an internal character, and whether it holds a superior or a subordinated position in the organization of the State' (*Yearbook of the International Law Commission*, 1973, Volume II, 193).

[118] For the International Law Commission's commentary on Article 4, see *Report of the International Law Commission: Fifty-third Session*, A/56/10 (2001), http://untreaty.un.org/ilc/reports/2001/2001report.htm, 29 at 84–92 (accessed 29 January 2007); and also J. Crawford, *The International Law Commission's Articles on State Responsibility: Introduction, Text and Commentaries* (Cambridge University Press, 2002) pp. 94–99.

[119] See *Commentary to Article 4, para.7, International Law Commission's Articles on State Responsibility*, at 87–88; and Crawford (note 118 above) p. 96.

do not deal with international humanitarian law continue to bind the contesting States during an international armed conflict where this matter is not expressly regulated by the treaty concerned.[120] This issue arises particularly in connection with chapter 14 of the Study which examines armed conflict and the natural environment.[121] The Study claims that there is insufficient uniformity of opinion on whether environmental law treaties continue to apply in armed conflict and, although this was not directly addressed in the *Nuclear Weapons* Advisory Opinion, the four States that did consider the matter in their submissions – France, the Solomon Islands, the United Kingdom and the United States[122] – expressed different views.[123] France claimed that multilateral environmental law treaties were not applicable in armed conflict, whereas the Solomon Islands claimed that, failing contrary express stipulation, they did apply. The United Kingdom claimed that environmental law treaties were concluded principally to protect the environment in time of peace, and that armed conflict and particularly nuclear weapons were not mentioned in their texts and 'scarcely alluded to' during negotiations. The United States adopted a similar position, but claimed that even if the treaties applied during an armed conflict, they did not proscribe the use of nuclear weapons.

The validity of these claims is simply not addressed by the Study. Although the question of the impact of armed conflict on treaty relationships is currently under consideration by the International Law Commission,[124] there is substantial authority to support the proposition

---

[120] This issue was expressly excluded from the ambit of the 1969 Vienna Convention on the Law of Treaties, Article 73 of which provides: 'The provisions of the present Convention shall not prejudge any question that may arise in regard to a treaty from a succession of States or from the international responsibility of a State or from the outbreak of hostilities between States.'

[121] For a substantive analysis of Chapter 14, see Hulme, chapter 8, *passim*. The impact of armed conflict on treaty relationships in the text is confined to international armed conflict principally because two of the three Rules set out in Chapter 14 (Rules 44 and 45) are said only 'arguably' to apply to non-international armed conflict. The specific case of human rights treaties, which frequently contain derogation clauses, is dealt with by Hampson, chapter 3.

[122] Study, Vol. II, Part 1, 862, §89; 865, §103; 866, §107 and §108 respectively.

[123] Study, Vol. 1, 151, Commentary to Rule 44.

[124] See I. Brownlie, *First Report on the Effects of Armed Conflicts on Treaties*, A/CN.4/552 (21 April 2005); International Law Commission, *Report of the International Law Commission: Fifty-seventh Session*, A/60/10 (2005); Brownlie I, *Second Report on the Effects of Armed Conflicts on Treaties*, UN Doc. A/CN.4/570 (16 June 2006); and Memorandum by the Secretariat, *The Effect of Armed Conflict on Treaties: An Examination of Practice and Doctrine*, A/CN.4/550 (1 February 2005), 44, para. 108 *et seq.*, and *Corrigenda 1 and 2*, A/CN.4/550/Corr.1 (3 June 2005) and A/CN.4/550/Corr.2 (7 November 2005).

that, in general, the outbreak of hostilities at most only suspends the operation of a multilateral treaty in relations between the opposing States:

> the existence of a state of war between some of the parties to [non-political
> multilateral] treaties did not *ipso facto* abrogate them, although it is
> realised that, as a practical matter, certain of the provisions might have
> been inoperative. The view of the [United States] Government is that the
> effect of the war on such treaties was only to terminate or suspend their
> execution as between opposing belligerents, and that, in the absence
> of special reasons for a contrary view, they remained in force between
> co-belligerents, between belligerents and neutral parties, and between
> neutral parties.[125]

Other authorities similarly indicate that the extent to which the provisions of a multilateral convention are suspended by war between belligerents depends on its subject matter. For instance, the Italian Court of
Cassation in *Società Fornaci di Stazzano v. Rancillo* suggested that treaties
which deal with private law matters are not affected by war:

> the continuing validity of those treaties is generally recognized *bello pendente*
> which, by their nature, by reason of the interests which they protect and by
> reason of the upheaval which would be caused by their unexpected cessation,
> are not considered incompatible with a state of war (such as conventions of
> private international law, labour conventions, conventions dealing with the
> enforcement of judgments, bankruptcy, and the legal status of aliens).[126]

This is supported in the practice of other States, such as France,[127]
whereas Dutch courts have adopted a modified position, holding that

---

[125] See M. Whiteman, *Digest of International Law* (Washington, Department of State, 1970),
Vol. 14, pp. 508–509: letter dated 29 January 1948 from the Legal Adviser, the Department
of State (Gross). See also, for instance, *Herzum v. van den Borst* (1955, District Court of
Roermond, the Netherlands) 22 *International Law Reports* 900; *Trademark Registration
Case* (1967, Federal Patent Court, Federal Republic of Germany) 59 *International Law
Reports* 490; *Landificio Branditex v. Società Azais e Vidal* (1971, Court of Cassation, Italy)
71 *International Law Reports* 595; *Masinimport v. Scottish Mechanical Light Industries Ltd*
(1976, Court of Session, Scotland) 1976 Session Cases 102, 74 *International Law Reports*
559 – see 564 in particular; and, less directly, *Re-application of a Treaty Case* (1973,
Supreme Court, Austria) 77 *International Law Reports* 440. The *Hecht case* (1941,
Supreme Court, the Netherlands) 11 *Annual Digest* 242 is less clear stating, in relation to
the 1905 Hague Convention on Civil Procedure, 'as a consequence of the outbreak of war
between the Netherlands and Germany, the said Treaty has ceased to operate between
them'. It is not apparent whether the Court intended to indicate that the treaty had been
abrogated or simply suspended as a result of the war.
[126] *Società Fornaci di Stazzano v. Rancillo* (1957) 24 *International Law Reports* 890 at 892.
[127] See *CAMAT v. Scagni* (1946, Court of Appeal of Ager, France) 13 *Annual Digest* 232.

provisions of multilateral private law treaties should only be suspended during wartime if they become unenforceable.[128] Moreover, the District Court of Rotterdam in the *Golden River* case ruled:

> A multilateral treaty such as the [1868] Revised Convention of Mannheim, which was not concluded in contemplation of war, was indeed suspended as between Holland and Germany as from May 1940, but only in so far and as long as its provisions had in fact become inapplicable. The concept of factual inapplicability must be interpreted restrictively and must, therefore, be limited to the period during which it was impossible to apply the provisions of the Convention properly.[129]

This extensive view has not been adopted in all Dutch cases,[130] but it does point to the view expressed in the Secretariat memorandum specifically in relation to environmental law treaties that, failing express stipulation, the continued applicability of provisions between belligerents depends upon whether they are compatible with the prosecution of hostilities.[131]

Nevertheless, in principle, general international law dictates that the existence of an armed conflict between parties to a multilateral treaty does not alter their treaty relations with neutral contracting parties.[132] This appears to have been ignored in the claims made during the *Nuclear*

---

[128] See *In re Utermöhlen* (1948, Court of Cassation) 16 *Annual Digest* 380; *Guardianship (Holland)* case (1950, Cantonal Court of the Hague) 17 *International Law Reports* 357. *Utermöhlen* reversed previous Dutch cases in which it was held that multilateral private law treaties were wholly suspended during wartime: see *Hecht*, 11 *Annual Digest* 242; *Gehrmann and Maatje van der Have v. Registrar* (1947, Middelburg District Court) 14 *Annual Digest* 176; *In re Anna K (German subject)* (1946, District Court of Rotterdam) 14 *Annual Digest* 177.

[129] *The Golden River v. The Wilhelmina* (1950, District Court of Rotterdam) 17 *International Law Reports* 354 at 355. See also *In re Holzwarth Gasturbinen AG (Patent Office Appellate Division)* 17 *International Law Reports* 356.

[130] See *Nederlandsche Spoorwegen v. Stichting Nederlandsche Groenten en Fruitcentrale* (1948, Court of Appeal of Amsterdam) 15 *Annual Digest* 439; *Nederlandsche Rijnvaartvereeniging v. Damco Scheepvaart Maatschappij* (1954, District Court of Rotterdam) 21 *International Law Reports* 276; *Gevato v. Deutsche Bank* (1952, District Court of Rotterdam) 19 *International Law Reports* 29 at 30; *Herzum v. van den Borst* (1955, District Court of Roermond) 22 *International Law Reports* 900; *In re Swane* (1958, Supreme Court) 26 *International Law Reports* 577.

[131] A/CN.4/550, 36, para. 59: compare the commentaries to draft Article 7.2.e, Brownlie, *First Report* (note 124 above); International Law Commission, *Report of the International Law Commission: Fifty-seventh Session*, (note 124 above), pp. 29–30, paras. 89–91; Brownlie, *Second Report* (note 124 above), p. 10, para. 34 and p. 12, para. 39.

[132] See *Enforcement of Foreign Judgments (Switzerland)* case, 18 *International Law Reports* 574; *Telefunken v. NV Philips* (1952, Federal Tribunal, Switzerland) 19 *International Law Reports* 557.

Weapons Advisory Opinion proceedings that, in the absence of express stipulation, belligerents are not bound to apply multilateral environmental law treaties to which they are party during an international armed conflict. Rather than assess the authority to be placed on these statements, the Study decontextualised them as if the exigencies of armed conflict released belligerents from the performance of obligations which are not specifically derived from international humanitarian law. It may be that the decision not to investigate the implications of the Martens Clause placed limitations on the Study's ability to engage in a normative assessment of practice, but this example is symptomatic of a tendency to take statements at their face value rather than scrutinise their normative significance.[133]

One final aspect of 'official' practice deserves comment. Although the International Court in the *Legal Consequences of the Construction of a Wall* Advisory Opinion laid weight on the views of the ICRC regarding the interpretation of Geneva Convention IV,[134] it must be questioned whether it was appropriate to take into account confidential communications made to the ICRC as evidence of State practice. Although, as the *Nicaragua* case reminds us, treaties and custom are different when it comes to matters of interpretation,[135] the International Court has excluded confidential *travaux préparatoires* as pertinent to the interpretation of treaties.[136] If confidential material cannot give rise to legitimate expectations regarding the interpretation of existing texts, because not all the parties to the case were participants in the drafting of the text, can it be said that confidential communications to which other States cannot react are relevant to the generation of general customary law?

Generally, Dinstein has complained that the practice relied upon in constructing the Study is indiscriminate, including materials which do not constitute State practice as such, for instance, reports of UN committees which 'can never contribute directly through their own practice to

---

[133] For a similar criticism in relation to the Study's treatment of reprisals, see D. Fleck, 'International Accountability for Violations of *ius in bello*: the Impact of the ICRC Study on Customary International Humanitarian Law' (2006) 11 *Journal of Conflict and Security Law* 179, at 186.

[134] *Legal Consequences of the Construction of a Wall* Advisory Opinion (note 56 above), pp. 175–176, para. 97.   [135] *Nicaragua Merits* case, p. 95, para. 178.

[136] See *Jurisdiction of the European Commission of the Danube* Advisory Opinion, PCIJ, Ser.B, No.14 (1927) 32 and *Territorial Jurisdiction of the International Commission of the Oder* case, PCIJ, Ser.A, No.23 (1929) 8, and *Order of August 20th, 1929* (Annex 3 to the judgment): see also A. McNair, *The Law of Treaties* (Oxford: Clarendon Press, 1961) 420–421; and D. Sandifer *Evidence before International Tribunals* (Charlottesville: University Press of Virginia, rev: edn, 1975) pp. 378–379.

the creation of customary norms'.[137] Hampson echoes this point in relation to the Study's use of statements made by human rights bodies. As she comments, the use of this material requires acceptance of the view that either this non-State practice is accepted as proof of custom and/or that these statements can give rise to practice where the State affected by the pronouncement does not object.[138] One may wonder how the failure to react to a non-binding instrument can give rise to a claim of acquiescence which might be relevant to the custom-formation process. This is not to say that the use of non-State materials is necessarily illegitimate in uncovering and establishing the existence of customary rules, but are these not better seen as secondary, rather than primary, evidence of State practice?

This criticism may, however, be misplaced, although it clearly arises from the way in which the Study presents its digest of practice in Volume II. Henckaerts has observed[139] that only some of the practice detailed in Volume II was taken into account in formulating the Rules contained in Volume I, namely that identified in the commentaries to the Rules. In particular, materials emanating from non-governmental organisations were not used to support any Rules, and although ICRC statements were cited in support of some conclusions, they were never used to tip the balance in favour of a customary rule that would not otherwise exist. In the light of methodological criticisms the Study has attracted, this should have been made clear in the Study itself.

Finally, despite the assimilation of international and non-international armed conflicts, the Study claims not to have relied on the practice of armed opposition groups. The digest of practice, nevertheless, contains numerous references to statements made by insurgents. On the whole, these groups are not identified and the statements appear to have been drawn from the ICRC's archives which, moreover, one assumes were hitherto confidential.[140] Although the Study categorised the legal significance of insurgent practice as unclear,[141] in the *Tadic* case[142] the Yugoslav

---

[137] Y. Dinstein, 22 June 2005 statement to US Naval War College Annual International Law Conference; see also his 'The ICRC Customary International Humanitarian Law Study' (note 37 above), at 5–6.

[138] Hampson, chapter 11, p. 297; see also Hulme, chapter 8, 228.

[139] Personal communication to author, December 2006.

[140] For instance, see Study, Vol. II, Part 1, 161, §194 and §195; 171, §263; 200, §460; 450, §184; 479, §173; 574, §830; 870–871, §124; 1075, §458; and 1114, §752 and §754. This is a random and incomplete sampling.   [141] Study, Vol. I, Introduction, xxxvi.

[142] See *Prosecutor v. Tadić*, Decision on the Defence Motion for Interlocutory Appeal on Jurisdiction, Appeals Chamber (note 116 above), paras. 102–103, 107 and at 108, 'In addition to the behaviour of belligerent States, Governments and insurgents, other

Tribunal's Appeal Chamber took it into account in constructing the customary international humanitarian law applicable in non-international conflicts. It has also been argued that, because they have a restricted international personality under international humanitarian law,[143] the practice of insurgent groups is relevant to the custom formation process. It is better, nonetheless, that the Study did not employ this practice in constructing its Rules.

Assuming, *arguendo*, that insurgent practice is relevant to the custom formation process, one must first identify which insurgent groups may participate in this process. When, for instance, is an insurgent group significant enough to count? Further, Rule 149 of the Study, which fundamentally sets out rules of attribution of conduct for the purposes of the law of State responsibility rather than a norm of international humanitarian law as such, provides:

> A State is responsible for violations of international humanitarian law attributable to it, including:
>> (c) violations committed by persons or groups acting in fact on its instructions, or under its direction and control; and
>> (d) violations committed by private persons or groups which it acknowledges and adopts as its own conduct.[144]

This is a corollary of Rule 139[145] which provides that parties to a conflict must respect and ensure respect for international humanitarian law by its armed forces and other persons or groups acting on its instructions or under its direction and control. Consequently the actions of insurgent groups which are attributable to a State amount to practice of that State rather than that of an autonomous sub-State entity.

Despite the *Tadić* decision, the practice of insurgent groups for which no State bears responsibility could, of course, be dismissed on the basis that this is simply not State practice. *Tadić*, however, illustrates the difficulties inherent in placing normative weight on insurgent practice: the judgment only cited practice in support of the proposition the

Footnote 142 (*cont.*)
    factors have been instrumental in bringing about the formation of the customary rules at issue.'
[143] See P. Kidd, 'Can armed opposition groups participate in the customary process?', unpublished: I am grateful to Jean-Marie Henckaerts for bringing this article to my attention. See also M. Sassoli 'Transnational Armed Groups and International Humanitarian Law' (2006) 38–42, www.hpcr.org/pdfs/OccasionalPaper6.pdf.
[144] Study, Vol. 1, 530, Commentary to Rule 149.
[145] Study, Vol. 1, 495, Commentary to Rule 139, at 496.

Chamber wished to uphold. If account is taken of insurgent practice which is consonant with State practice on international humanitarian law, should insurgents' contrary practice be given equal weight to disrupt the formation of custom? The weight to be accorded to insurgent practice potentially implicates complex doctrinal issues which, moreover, have an acute political dimension. The Study was sensible not to become embroiled in this issue.

7. Some concluding observations

It is premature to speculate upon the influence the Study will exert. It is undoubtedly an impressive document, based upon a methodology that is more stringent than some commentators have alleged. Some crucial issues, however, remain unanswered. The Introduction to the Study declares:

> The general opinion is that violations of international humanitarian law are not due to the inadequacy of the rules, but rather to a lack of willingness to respect them, to a lack of means to enforce them and to uncertainty as to their application in some circumstances, but also to ignorance of the rules on the part of political leaders, commanders, combatants and the general public.[146]

While the Study may act as an instrument for the dissemination of international humanitarian law and thus overcome ignorance, it is nonetheless true that the Study is a source of more rules. Moreover, being customary,[147] these rules have a different normative basis from the conventional obligations which have previously characterised international humanitarian law. As the International Court observed in the *Nicaragua* case:

> There are a number of reasons for considering that, even if two norms belonging to two sources of international law appear identical in content,

---

[146] Study, Vol. I, Introduction, xxvii.

[147] The customary rules identified by the Study are the 161 numbered propositions it contains, but not the accompanying Commentaries to these Rules. Nevertheless, the Commentaries may be used to clarify the application of these Rules – J. M. Henckaerts, 'Customary International Humanitarian Law – a rejoinder to Judge Aldrich' (2005) 76 *British Yearbook of International Law* 525 at 527–528. A note to this effect will be included in subsequent printings of the Study (Henckaerts, personal communication to author, December 2006). The relationship between the Rules and Commentaries has attracted some criticism – see, for instance, Cryer, 'Of Custom, Treaties, Scholars and the Gavel' (note 56 above), at 262–263; Hampson, chapter 11, p. 296; Garraway, chapter 15, p. 384; and Wilmshurst, chapter 16, pp. 405–408 and 411.

and even if the States in question are bound by these rules both on the level of treaty-law and on that of customary international law, these retain a separate existence . . . Rules which are identical in treaty law and in customary international law are also distinguishable by reference to the methods of interpretation and application.[148]

A question converse to that of the role of treaties in the formation of custom thus arises: what is the role of customary international law in the application of treaties? What is the relationship between norms drawn from these different sources of international law which deal with the same substantive issues? In his foreword to the Study, Kellenberger notes that customary international law can aid in the interpretation of treaty provisions which, moreover, must be interpreted in good faith and with due regard for all relevant rules of international law.[149] This simply begs the question.

Commentators have noted that while the formulation of some Rules mirrors that contained in a parallel conventional obligation, others differ, sometimes significantly.[150] De Visscher argued that codification can have the aim of unifying the law where customary practice is diverse or there is a contradiction between custom and the written law.[151] To the extent to which the formulation of the customary Rules diverge from corresponding treaty provisions, does the Study amount to a dysfunctional codification? As Schachter points out, treaties and custom are not merely alternative sources of international law, but are also competitive.[152] Where customary and conventional rules deal with the same substantive issue but impose different obligations, which should prevail?[153] Presumptively, it seems apparent that if not all the parties to the conflict were parties to the relevant convention then the customary rule should take preference because only it binds those not party to the treaty. This view has an obvious utility in relation to non-international conflicts in particular as it provides a mechanism to impose international humanitarian law on non-State actors.

[148] *Nicaragua Merits* case p. 95, para. 178.
[149] Kellenberger, Study, Vol. 1, Foreword, x: see Article 31.3.c of the 1969 Vienna Convention on the Law of Treaties.
[150] For instance, Aldrich, 'Customary International Humanitarian Law' (note 24 above), at 507; Bethlehem, chapter 1, 8–12; and Schmitt, chapter 6, *passim.*
[151] De Visscher, 'La Codification du Droit International' (note 12 above), p. 380.
[152] Schachter (note 12 above), p. 720.
[153] For an overview of the issues implicated in this question, see, N. Kontou, *The Termination and Revision of Treaties in the Light of New Customary International Law* (Oxford: Clarendon Press, 1994) pp. 19–36.

On the other hand, if all the parties to the conflict are parties to the governing convention, then do the principles of *pacta sunt servanda* and *lex specialis* dictate that the conventional formulation of the obligation applies to the exclusion of the customary? Or does the doctrine of *lex posterior* require application of the customary norm? Further, suppose the parties to a conflict decide, *inter se*, to apply a customary rule which is ostensibly less stringent than their corresponding obligation under either the Geneva Conventions or Additional Protocols. Does this trigger the duty of third States which are parties to the treaty in question under common Article 1 to 'ensure respect'? Or, in the light of the International Court's pronouncements on 'intransgressible principles', their right to invoke responsibility under Article 48 of the International Law Commission's 2001 Articles on State responsibility regarding obligations owed to the international community as a whole? These are complex doctrinal questions which are not answered simply by the affirmation that treaties must be interpreted in the light of any relevant rules of customary international law.

Other areas of customary law in relation to the Study

FRANÇOISE HAMPSON

1. Introduction

When seeking to determine what material to include in a study of customary international humanitarian law, the authors have to decide on the extent to which other areas of law may be relevant. There is a real risk of confusion between two discrete issues: to what extent does a rule of non-international humanitarian law remain applicable during the existence of fighting (fact), and to what extent and in what manner does a rule of applicable non-international humanitarian law interact with a rule of international humanitarian law (law)?[1] The first question concerns only the rule of international law from a field other than international humanitarian law. The second concerns the relationship between two bodies of rules. This chapter seeks to examine whether areas of law other than international humanitarian law should have been included in a study of customary international humanitarian law and, if so, the extent to and manner in which they were to be considered. The first section considers international law in factual situations of armed conflict, taking into account the mandate given to the ICRC by the Red Cross Conference.[2] The second section considers whether customary international law is one

---

[1] By non-international humanitarian law is meant something other than humanitarian law, rather than the rules applicable in non-international armed conflict. The term international humanitarian law will be used throughout, on account of the use of the phrase in the mandate and title of the Study. It will be used to include both rules on the protection of victims of war (Geneva law) and rules on the conduct of hostilities (Hague law).

[2] Study, Vol. 1, xxvii. The ICRC was asked to produce 'a report on customary rules of IHL'. It is difficult to see how the raw data in a compilation of evidence of state practice could constitute a 'report'. If a 'report' requires the evaluation of evidence, then general criticisms based on the fact that the ICRC did not simply produce the raw data would appear to be misconceived. In that case, it is possible to disagree with the status the authors assigned to certain types of evidence (e.g. military manuals) or to disagree with their conclusion as to whether there is sufficient evidence to establish the existence of a particular rule but it is inappropriate to object to the existence of Volume I: Rules. They were *required* to produce such a document.

amorphous body of rules or whether it can be compartmentalised by subject matter and the implications of the distinction. The third section considers one particular area of law, human rights law, and its potential relevance to a study of customary international humanitarian law. The conclusion seeks to evaluate the extent and appropriateness of the reliance on areas of law other than international humanitarian law and evidence about international humanitarian law derived from non-international humanitarian law sources.

International law and situations of conflict

Most of the rules of international law do not refer or relate to situations of conflict. That raises the question of the extent to which they remain applicable in such situations.

It is perhaps helpful to distinguish between two different *types* of rules, although the two categories overlap. Some rules relate to the international legal system as such. They determine which entities constitute international actors and the implications of such a status, as well as establishing the sources of legal obligation for such entities. They are rules which enable an international legal system to exist and are rules about the system *qua* system. For convenience such rules will be called constitutive, to reflect their role in establishing an international legal order. This category includes rules dealing with sources of international law, sovereignty, personality, recognition, jurisdiction, immunities and state responsibility. *Prima facie*, there is no reason why the applicability or application of such rules should be affected by the outbreak of fighting within or between members of the international community. An obvious exception would be the status of a party to a conflict which seeks or claims statehood. A study of customary international humanitarian law might be expected to take such constitutive rules and their application for granted. The only issue which would need to be addressed is the relationship between international humanitarian law and the status of the parties to the conflict.[3]

The other type of rule is one which is applicable to the conduct of an entity vis-à-vis other entities, rather than the international legal system

---

[3] The applicability of international humanitarian law (IHL) does not affect the status of parties of a conflict but the fear of legitimising a party often appears to be behind a claim that IHL is not applicable, particularly in non-international conflicts. A separate issue *within* IHL is the status of an individual as civilian or combatant. In the case of combatant status, such a determination depends, in part, on the status of the party on behalf of whom the individual fights.

as such. Such rules may, for convenience, be labelled 'material', although that should not be thought to call into question the materiality of the first category of rule. Examples of such fields of international law include environmental law, trade law, the law of the sea and human rights law. The applicability and application of a rule in one of these fields may well be affected by the outbreak of fighting. That might be as the result of the operation of a rule about field X where the rule derives from that field. For example, a rule of the law of sea might modify normally applicable passage rights in situations of conflict.[4] It might equally be the result of the operation of a rule about field X where the rule derives from a different field. For example, hypothetically, it could be the case that in time of armed conflict all trade agreements should be suspended between parties of the conflict. Such a rule might derive not from international trade law but rather from international security law. In neither case would the interference in the applicability or application of the normal rule be the result of a rule of international humanitarian law as such.

The question of the continued applicability of peace-time rules in relation to treaty law is well-discussed in the literature.[5] The issues are not identical to those which arise in relation to the continued applicability of customary law. First, treaties are, almost by definition, compartmentalised as far as their content is concerned. They are about one or more things and not about others. Second, they are only applicable to the parties to the treaties. In both the case of treaties with limited participation and also those which are potentially universal, a key question is who are the parties, as opposed to what the treaty is about. The second issue is irrelevant in the customary law. It binds everyone.[6] Nevertheless, the issue of the extent to which customary law norms remain applicable during conflict is a legitimate question and one which, in general terms at least, appears to be barely touched on in the

---

[4] This is purely given as a hypothetical example. War at sea is not within the scope of the Study, not least on account of the existence of the San Remo manual; L. Doswald-Beck (ed.), *San Remo Manual on International Law applicable to Armed Conflicts at Sea* (Cambridge University Press, 1995).

[5] A. McNair and A. Watts, *The Legal Effects of War* (Cambridge University Press, 4th edn, 1967); *Oppenheim's International Law, Vol.II: Disputes, War and Neutrality* (London: Longmans, 6th edn, 1940); ILC, First Report on the Effects of Armed Conflicts on Treaties (I. Brownlie, Special Rapporteur), A/CN.4/552, 21 April 2005; ILC, The Effect of Armed Conflict on Treaties: An Examination of Practice and Doctrine, Memorandum by the Secretariat, A/CN.4/550, 1 February 2005.

[6] With regard to the possible exception of a persistent objector, see further below.

literature.[7] The Study *could* have looked at the question, but *should* it have done so?

The mandate given to the ICRC was not for a study of the customary rules applicable during conflict. It was confined to customary rules of international humanitarian law and not of international law generally.[8] The test is not whether a rule is one of international law which remains applicable in the factual situations of conflict but rather whether a rule is part of the body of rules expressly designed to regulate armed conflicts. Whilst the distinction is theoretically clear-cut, in practice there may be some overlap. A rule may belong simultaneously to two or more areas of law. Rules on the passage of warships during periods of conflict may be part of the law of the sea, neutrality law and part of international humanitarian law. Similarly, the rule that 'widespread, long-term and severe' environmental damage is to be avoided may be both a rule of environmental law and a rule of international humanitarian law.[9] So long as a rule forms part of international humanitarian law, it should be included, even if it also forms part of another area of international law.

There are areas of law linked situationally, if not necessarily legally, to armed conflicts. The two most obvious examples are the rules on the resort to armed force (*ius ad bellum*) and the rules on neutrality.[10] Whilst occasional passing reference, at least to the existence of rules on neutrality, might be legitimate, where relevant, any detailed examination of such rules would have been outside the scope of the mandate, because the neutral power is not a party to the conflict.

If the mandated scope of the Study was to be confined to rules specifically designed to apply in situations of conflict to the parties to such a conflict, then this would appear to preclude the examination of any areas other than international humanitarian law, unless a rule exists simultaneously in two or more fields of law or came within human rights law.[11] In the view of this author, the ICRC was not mandated to examine all

---

[7] Specific issues, particularly rules which may be characterised as forming part of both IHL and some other area, may be discussed: e.g. passage rights at sea during conflict.

[8] Study, Vol. 1, xxvii and text at note 2.

[9] K. Hulme, *War Torn Environment: Interpreting the Legal Threshold*, (The Hague: Martinus Nijhoff, 2004); see also chapter 8 below.

[10] Neutrality law does not just address the situation of the neutral power but has a range of implications for the fighting parties. It affects where they can do certain things and against whom certain measures may or may not be taken.

[11] For the explanation of why human rights law is not an exception to the general principle, see the third section below.

customary rules applicable during armed conflict. The authors cannot therefore be reproached for not having done so.

Customary law and compartmentalisation

The previous section addressed the relevance of legal rules which are outside the corpus of international humanitarian law but which may remain applicable in conflict situations. This section addresses the different issue of what is meant by international humanitarian law under customary law. If the first section was about areas outside a boundary, the second seeks to determine where the boundary in question lies.

a. The compartmentalisation of rules

The boundaries of the material scope of international humanitarian law are less of a problem when examining treaty law. The reason why the rule, referred to above, regarding environmental damage can be said to be a rule of international humanitarian law is because it is contained in what is indubitably an international humanitarian law treaty. When examining customary law, the question is whether there is only one amorphous body of customary law, consisting of the totality of customary law rules, or whether there are discrete areas of customary law, such as customary environmental law, customary human rights law and customary international humanitarian law. In mandating a study of customary international humanitarian law, the Red Cross Conference must have thought the concept meant something but that is hardly sufficient to answer the question.[12] Does such compartmentalisation exist and, if so, what difference does it make?

The International Law Commission has briefly examined the problem of the alleged fragmentation of international law, albeit in a different context.[13] The question may be framed in the following terms: is public international law one train with different carriages or different trains? It is easy to see why it was thought necessary to ask the question but the one question rapidly gives way to several separate questions, to which the answers appear to be relatively straightforward. The author has the impression that the pressure to ask the question arose out of certain

---

[12] Since the Red Cross Conference includes representatives of States, the resolution may be evidence of State practice to the effect that such compartmentalisation exists.

[13] See generally, ILC, Report of the Study Group on Fragmentation of International Law: Difficulties arising from the Diversification and Expansion of International Law, A/CN.4/L676, 29 July 2005.

positions taken by some human rights lawyers but the statements of other experts in particular fields of international law may also have played their part. Some human rights lawyers may be thought to believe that certain rules of international law applicable throughout that system of law are not applicable to human rights law. So, for example, one sometimes sees attempts to argue that non-State actors are directly bound, as a matter of international law, by human rights law.[14] Another example is the claim that reservations incompatible with the objects and purposes of a human rights treaty can simply be severed.[15] It is necessary to distinguish, in this context, between two different arguments. It may be argued that a generally applicable rule is not applicable in a particular context. This is simply a claim that there exists an exception which, if anything, reinforces the generally applicability of the normal rule. That argument is to be contrasted with a claim that, in a particular legal field, there is no generally applicable rule or that the exception is the rule. It is not clear into which of these categories come the claims made for human rights law. Generally speaking, there is nothing in the practice of States or that of human rights judicial or quasi-judicial bodies to support the notion that human rights law is *per se* not subject to generally applicable rules of international law. They appear to treat human rights law as part of general public international law. Certain States have occasionally sought to claim that non-State actors in their jurisdiction should be held responsible for human rights violations.[16] This has usually been in a quasi-political context, where their principal preoccupation appeared to be excusing or establishing their own lack of responsibility for their own human rights violations. It is far from clear whether they understood or accepted the implications of their assertions.[17] What is clear is that such statements

---

[14] They may clearly be bound indirectly, or horizontally, as a result of the implementation by a State of its own obligations. It is also clear in practice, if theory has yet to provide a completely satisfactory explanation, that they are directly bound by international criminal law.

[15] Human Rights Committee, General Comment No.24, CCPR/C/21/Rev.1/Add.6, 4 November 1994, para. 18. How, as a matter of general principle, a State can be bound by a provision which it has expressly rejected or limited is unclear and seems at odds with any notion of state sovereignty. That said, it is not clear what an independent monitoring body should do faced with an incompatible reservation. See generally, the reports of the Rapporteur of the ILC on Reservations to Treaties (Professor Alain Pellet), which deal with the generality of treaties, and Sub-Commission on the Promotion and Protection of Human Rights, Final Working Paper on Reservation to Human Rights Treaties, E/CN.4/Sub.2/2004/42, 19 July 2004.

[16] On occasion, Turkey, Peru and Colombia, amongst others, have made such claims.

[17] If human rights law is based on the relationship between an individual and the authorities exercising power, there may be an assumption that the individual owes some measure of

have been opposed by other States, notably members of the Western Group, on legal, rather than political, grounds. It is submitted that there is no significant evidence to suggest that there exist areas of international law outside the generally applicable rules regarding who or what has legal personality, sources of international law and the rules of treaty law. That is not to say that, with regard to certain specific issues, there may not be exceptions to the generally applicable rules. If this view is correct, it suggests that international law is one train with many carriages, rather than different trains.

It does not necessarily follow from such a determination that one cannot refer to specific areas of customary law, such as the law of the sea. It does, however, affect the status of such terminology. It means that the label is simply a tool of convenience and a descriptive label. It is not a way of indicating legally distinct areas of customary law. This leaves open the possibility not merely that a specific rule may exist in more than one area but also that there may be significant degrees of overlap between different areas. It suggests that there are not rigid barriers between different areas of international law.

The issue of overlapping boundaries can be illustrated with an example. If, during the course of an armed conflict, State A uses a weapon with allegedly serious impact on the environment and if State A has not ratified any of the relevant treaties, the conduct of the State will have to be evaluated in the light of customary law. There is not one single customary rule which would enable one to reach a conclusion as to the lawfulness of State A's action. It would be necessary to examine the interplay between two possible customary notions. First, it would be necessary to determine whether there are customary rules in the field of international humanitarian law regulating weapons use by reference to the impact on the environment. If so, it would be necessary to identify notions of customary environmental law to determine how one sets about evaluating environmental harm, since humanitarian law is probably not of a nature to contain quasi-scientific criteria on how to measure environmental impact.

This suggests that a label such as customary international humanitarian law is both legitimate and meaningful but it is no more than a tool of

Footnote 17 (cont.)

loyalty to those authorities, to the extent of accepting the legal character of rules they promulgate. Such authorities could legitimately punish attempts to overthrow them. Does Colombia, for example, really accept that the FARC can legitimately criminalise opposition to itself on the part of individuals living in areas under their control?

convenience. Whilst the core of the area so described may be clear, it would not be surprising if it had fuzzy boundaries. That would simply be a reflection of the fact that reasonable people may disagree. It would not be of legal significance.

In these circumstances, it might have been helpful if the authors of the Study had set out more clearly at the outset what they see as the boundaries of international humanitarian law. Instead, two distinct notions of the boundaries appear to be present. First, the close link between the Rules and the provisions of treaty law suggest that the test was that any activity regulated by a treaty generally regarded as an international humanitarian law treaty was to be regarded as potentially within the field of customary international humanitarian law. This might result in the inclusion of rules on anti-personnel mines but the exclusion of rules on biological weapons.[18] On the other hand, the Study includes some issues not generally regulated by the *ius in bello*, such as the right to return of refugees and displaced persons.[19] The objection is not, or not necessarily, to the inclusion of such a rule but to the lack of an explanation regarding the criteria for inclusion in the concept of humanitarian law. The inclusions may be more controversial than the exclusions. It is submitted that a *ius post bellum* issue can legitimately be regarded as part of international humanitarian law where the rule is seeking to undo the consequences of an unlawful act which is generally recognised as forming part of the *ius in bello*. In other words, the justification for inclusion is not the rule itself but the prior violation of a different rule. The significance, in this context, of a right to return is not that right in and of itself but rather the previous violation of a rule prohibiting forced displacement. It is submitted that, if there is a problem in this regard in the Study, it is not attributable to what is included but rather to the lack of explanation. That could easily be rectified by the addition of a few lines in the introduction and/or in the relevant chapters in the next edition.

b. Compartmentalisation of evidence

A separate but related issue to the one previously discussed concerns the possible compartmentalisation of evidence of customary law. The problem

---

[18] Some authors appear to treat rules regarding weapons of mass destruction as not forming part of the laws of war, presumably partly because they are negotiated very differently. A. Roberts and R. Guelff, *Documents on the Laws of War* (Oxford University Press, 3rd edn, 2000) for example, does not include such treaty texts. This author thinks the distinction unhelpful, to the extent to which general principles on weapons use are applicable to the use of any weapon. [19] See chapter 13.

relates to possible limitations regarding the types of sources which can be relied upon when seeking evidence of state practice and *opinio iuris*. There are two distinct aspects to the issue. The first is whether the practice or evidence of *opinio iuris* has to be *about* humanitarian law. The second is whether the practice or evidence of *opinio iuris* has to be generated in a *forum* specifically addressing humanitarian law. In order to constitute evidence regarding an area of customary international law, it would seem to be self-evident that the practice has to be about or relating to that area. If not, it could not be relevant as evidence, unless it related to a rule found in two or more areas of international law. So, for example, evidence of practice relating to straight baselines for the measurement of territorial sea is not capable of constituting evidence about humanitarian law, unless the practice expressly relates to the use of straight baselines in situations of conflict.

The second aspect of the issue is of far greater significance. Where State A objects to the use of poisonous gas by State B against part of State B's civilian population on the grounds that such use is unlawful, should the weight to be attached to the statement as evidence of *opinio iuris* be affected by whether the statement was made in a human rights forum, before a body of general competence such as the General Assembly or Security Council or in a humanitarian law forum, such as a Red Cross Conference? It is suggested that the particular forum makes no difference to the weight to be attached to the evidence. What matters is whether the speaker can speak on behalf of the State and whether the pronouncement contains evidence of what the State believes to be a generally applicable legal rule. There is a significant difference between a simple objection by State A to the conduct of State B, without giving reasons, and an objection based on the alleged unlawfulness of the conduct. Without entering more generally into the controversy about what material can constitute evidence of State practice, it is submitted that evidence of State practice and *opinio iuris* in the field of international humanitarian law is not restricted to evidence generated exclusively from humanitarian law fora.

The coexistence of international humanitarian law and human rights law

In the first section of this chapter, it was suggested that there might be one area of non-international law which a study of international humanitarian law needed to take into account – human rights law. This might be viewed as an exception to the general rule that areas of international law other than humanitarian law were not within the purview of the study. It is suggested, however, that the inclusion of human rights law may equally plausibly be seen as an application of the principle that the study is limited to rules expressly applicable in situations of conflict.

a. Whether human rights law is expressly designed to apply in situations of conflict

In the first wave of academic interest in the 1970s regarding the relationship between the two bodies of rules, the assumption was made that human rights law principally related to peacetime and only strayed into situations of conflict almost by accident. It is probably not without significance that the authors of such views were generally better known as experts in the field of the law of 'armed conflict', rather than human rights law.[20] It may be time for a re-examination of that assumption. Owing to the greater certainty regarding the content of human rights treaty law, human rights conventions will be used in the initial consideration of the argument. It is recognised that, theoretically, customary human rights law may be significantly different from human rights treaty law and that will be examined separately. Human rights law appears to consist of undertakings given by States to other States and natural and legal persons within their jurisdiction with regard to how the State will treat the latter. The obligations are not reciprocal obligations between States in the usual sense but there must be some obligation vis-à-vis other States, for otherwise the obligations would presumably not be contained in treaties or considered to be part of public international law.[21] The

---

[20] For example, W.K. Suter, 'An Enquiry into the Meaning of the Phrase 'Human Rights in Armed Conflicts' (1976) XV (3–4) *Revue de Droit Pénal Militaire et de Droit de la Guerre* 393; H. Meyrowitz, 'Le Droit de la Guerre et les droits de l'homme' (1972) 5 *Revue du Droit Public et de la Science Politique en France et à l'Etranger* 1059; G. Draper, 'The Relationship between the Human Rights Regime and the Law of Armed Conflict' (1971) 1 *Israel Yearbook on Human Rights* 191.

[21] In *France, Norway, Denmark, Sweden, the Netherlands v. Turkey*, 9940-44/82, Admissibility Decision of 6 December 1983, the European Commission of Human Rights stated, 'The Commission finds that the general principle of reciprocity in international law and the rule, stated in Article 21, para. I of the Vienna Convention on the Law of Treaties, concerning bilateral relations under a multilateral treaty do not apply to the obligations under the European Convention on Human Rights, which are "essentially of an objective character, being designed rather to protect the fundamental rights of individual human beings from infringement by any of the High Contracting parties than to create subjective and reciprocal rights for the High Contracting Parties themselves"' (*Austria v. Italy*, Yearbook 4, p. 116, at p. 140). The European Court of Human Rights (at para. 239 of its judgment in *Ireland v. United Kingdom*, 5310/71, Judgment of 18 January 1978), has similarly referred to the 'objective obligations' created by the Convention over a network of mutual, bilateral undertakings (para. 39).

phrase 'collective guarantee' is sometimes used to describe the arrangement but that appears to describe, rather than to analyse, the particular nature of inter-State guarantees in this field.[22]

The key question in this context concerns the substance of the undertakings. They may be principally about peacetime with any leakage into conflict being exceptional and limited. Support for such a view might be thought to be found in the fact that only one provision in the human rights treaties of general application appears to address conflict situations: the derogation provision. By treaties of general application is meant treaties which address a range of rights in relation to the population at large, such as the International Covenant on Civil and Political Rights, the European Convention on Human Rights, the American Convention on Human Rights and the African Charter on Human and Peoples' Rights.[23] It is submitted that this approach puts form above substance and seriously distorts the meaning of the provisions contained in human rights treaties. It may also be a peculiarly euro- or western-centric view of the treaties. Those societies have experienced the fewest conflicts over the past forty years and have got used to human rights, meaning human rights in peacetime because that has been the prevailing condition. Much of Africa, on the other hand, may have greater experience, as aspiration if not reality, of human rights during situations of conflict than in peacetime. Those who approach human rights law as only exceptionally applying in situations of conflict often appear to slip into the assumption, perhaps inevitably, that any rights not expressly characterised as non-derogable are wholly inapplicable during conflict.

It is submitted that this is a serious misreading of human rights treaties. They are far more subtle than suggested by such an approach. First, in many cases, they do not define a right in abstract terms. They define a protected interest and provide the tools to permit a determination of whether the interest has been violated in a particular situation. Many of the protected interests, or at least their exercise, may be limited

---

[22] It is clearly not the same notion of collective as 'collective security' or 'collective self-defence', where it is used to describe a response which is collective, rather than a guarantee.

[23] The African Charter contains no express provision on derogation but the Commission has interpreted the text as though an analogous provision were present. Similarly, the Covenant on Economic, Social and Cultural Rights also contains no derogation provisions. The treaties of limited application either concern a limited range of rights, such as the Convention Against Torture and the Convention on the Elimination of Racial Discrimination, or address a limited group in the population, such as the Convention on the Elimination of Discrimination Against Women or the Convention on the Rights of the Child.

on defined grounds, provided that the limitation is both necessary and proportionate. It is only by examining the interplay between the protected interest and the permitted limitations that one can determine what is the right at issue. Limitations are more likely to be necessary in situations of political disturbance than peacetime and in war than situations of political disturbance. The structure of 'rights' such as privacy, freedom to manifest religious belief, freedom of speech and freedom of association does not require that situations be labelled as peace or war. They permit an appropriate evaluation at any point along the spectrum. Even in the case of 'rights' not structured in this way, room is expressly provided for a flexible evaluation. The International Covenant on Civil and Political Rights prohibits *arbitrary* deprivation of life and *arbitrary* detention.[24] What is arbitrary depends on the circumstances. That does not mean that the definition of arbitrary is itself arbitrary. It is rather that objective criteria have to be applied to a wide variety of factual situations. A killing judged to be arbitrary in a policing context in peacetime may well not be arbitrary in war. Internment or the administrative detention of persons said to pose a threat to national security may be arbitrary in peacetime but not in war.[25] Even in the case of 'rights' which, on their face, are more clear-cut, there may be areas of flexibility. Whilst some of the elements of a fair trial are set out in the treaty texts, the concept of a fair trial is itself flexible. The only absolute right is the prohibition of torture, cruel, inhuman or degrading treatment or punishment and even that requires a definition of each of the terms. Interestingly, the one absolute prohibition is also prohibited in situations of both international and non-international conflict under international humanitarian law.

On this analysis, the significance of the derogation clause is, first, that it injects an even greater degree of flexibility in the case of certain protected interests in situations of conflict and, second, that it prevents the modification of non-derogable interests. It certainly does not establish

---

[24] International Covenant on Civil and Political Rights, Articles 6 and 9.

[25] It is not clear whether administrative detention is prohibited by the notion of arbitrary detention. If it is, then States would probably be able to legitimise the practice by derogating on condition that they could show a genuine situation of emergency and the necessity and proportionality of the measure. The situation in relation to the European Convention on Human Rights is somewhat different. The equivalent articles (Articles 2 and 5) do not prohibit by reference to arbitrariness but rather set out the only circumstances in which a person may be lawfully deprived of life and the only circumstances in which a person can be detained. This reduces the flexibility available, unless a State chooses to derogate. The American and African texts resemble the International Covenant on Civil and Political Rights, rather than the European Convention on Human Rights.

that human rights law is not intended to apply during armed conflict. On the contrary, it expressly provides that human rights law is to remain applicable in such situations and makes that possible by modifying the scope, not eliminating, the scope of certain provision. Lest this be thought to be the wild ramblings of 'un droits de l'hommiste', it is worth examining the view of judicial and quasi-judicial bodies.[26]

Every human rights body under the treaties referred to above has applied the treaty in question in situations in which it is at least arguable that common Article 3 of the Geneva Conventions was applicable.[27] It should, however, be noted that in many cases the State in question denied, at least internationally, that it was dealing with anything other than criminal or terrorist activity.[28] They might therefore be regarded as estopped from denying the applicability of human rights law. That has not, however, always been the case. There have been situations in which States appear to have accepted the applicability of common Article 3 but the human rights body still applied human rights law, possibly taking into account international humanitarian law.[29] Whilst situations of inter-national conflict have come before human rights bodies less often than non-international conflicts, even there human rights bodies have applied human rights law, at least with regard to the acts of a belligerent occupant or the acts of those for whom it is internationally responsible.[30] The Human Rights Committee has addressed generally the extent to which

[26] The phrase is used by Alain Pellet to describe those who place human rights law and human rights concerns on a higher plane than any other considerations of international law.

[27] For example, the Human Rights Committee has dealt with cases from Colombia, the Inter-American Court of Human Rights has dealt with cases involving Colombia, Peru and Guatemala and the European Court of Human Rights has dealt with cases from south-east Turkey and Chechnya.

[28] Turkey denied and the Russian Federation denies, in international fora at least, that common Article 3 was applicable to the situations in their respective countries. In the case of Russia, the Constitutional Court held that Protocol II of 1977 was applicable to the first Chechen war; European Commission for Democracy through Law of the Council of Europe, CDL-INF (96) 1.

[29] Colombia and El Salvador appear to have accepted that the situations in their respective countries at the relevant times came within Additional Protocol II of 1977 but do not appear to have relied on international humanitarian law before human rights bodies.

[30] Loizidou v. Turkey, 15318/89, Preliminary Objections Judgment of 18 December 1996 [1996] ECHR 70, perhaps more surprisingly, Ilascu and others v. Moldova and the Russian Federation, 48787/99, Judgment of 8 July 2004 [2004] ECHR 318. The monitoring bodies under the two Covenants have only addressed the issue in the context of a State party report, for example regarding Israel in relation to the Occupied Territories and, at the relevant time, Lebanon. Turkey appears not yet to have reported to the Human Rights Committee.

human rights law remains applicable in armed conflict and the geographical scope of applicability in General Comments 29 and 31.[31] General
Comment 29 confirms the approach set out above. The existence of an
armed conflict does not extinguish a derogable right. It might be argued
of a human rights body, 'They would say that, wouldn't they?' That is
hardly true of the International Court of Justice. That Court has the
advantage of being able to apply any applicable law, unlike human rights
bodies whose mandate restricts them to findings of violation of human
rights law, even if they can take international humanitarian law into
account. The International Court of Justice could have relied exclusively
on international humanitarian law when addressing situations of conflict. In fact, the International Court of Justice has done the opposite. In
the Advisory Opinion on *Nuclear Weapons*, it spoke very generally about
the continued applicability of human rights law in situations of conflict
and referred to international humanitarian law as the *lex specialis*.[32] That
might have been thought to suggest that the special or particular rule displaced the general rule. The International Court of Justice clarified its
position in the Advisory Opinion on the *Legal Consequences of the
Construction of a Wall in the Occupied Palestinian Territory*.[33] The Court
stated that it,

> considers that the protection offered by human rights conventions does
> not cease in case of armed conflict, save through the effect of provisions for
> derogation of the kind to be found in Article 4 of the International
> Covenant on Civil and Political Rights. As regards the relationship between
> international humanitarian law and human rights law, there are thus three
> possible situations: some rights may be exclusively matters of international
> humanitarian law; others may be exclusively matters of human rights law;
> yet others may be matters of both these branches of international law. In
> order to answer the question put to it, the Court will have to take into con-
> sideration both these branches of international law, namely human rights
> law and, as *lex specialis*, international humanitarian law.[34]

It is noteworthy, first, that it is not the fact of conflict or the applicability
of international humanitarian law that may have the effect of modifying
the scope of human rights obligations, but only a derogation and, second,

---

[31] CCPR/C/21/Rev.1/Add.11, 31 August 2001 and CCPR/C/21/Rev.1/Add.13, 26 May 2004.
[32] *Legality of the Threat or Use of Nuclear Weapons*, Advisory Opinion of 8 July 1996 [1996]
  ICJ Rep. 66; on *lex specialis* see further below.
[33] *Legal Consequences of the Construction of a Wall in the Occupied Palestinian Territory*, ICJ
  Advisory Opinion of 9 July 2004 [2004] *ICJ Rep.* 36.   [34] *Ibid*, para., 106.

that the Court did not suggest that only non-derogable rights are applicable in situations of conflict.[35] The International Court of Justice applied its analysis by expressing the Opinion that Israel was in breach of various human rights provisions, including potentially derogable human rights. The Court has applied the same analysis more recently in a contentious case. In the *Congo* case, the Court did not limit its finding of human rights violations to areas of the Congo where the Ugandan forces were held to be an occupying power. The Court found violations of human rights law in areas where Uganda did not exercise that type of control. They did so on the basis of the control Uganda exercised, or should have exercised, over its armed forces. Furthermore, the Court did not limit itself to human rights violations which were also violations of the rules on the protection of victims of the conflict. It found violations of human rights law where the act in question also violated the rules on the means and methods of combat.[36]

It is submitted that the Court's judgment makes it clear that human rights law is not peacetime law. It is designed to be applicable, albeit in different ways, in all circumstances, including armed conflict. Unlike other areas of customary law, which are not generally relevant to the Study because the rules are not designed to apply in situations of conflict, human rights law is designed to apply in such situations. Human rights law is not an exception to the general exclusion of other areas of law. It is to be included by virtue of the application of the test that would include

[35] It is submitted that the first implication is problematic, at least in cases where the applicability of international humanitarian law is not in doubt. If State A and State B are the parties to an international armed conflict and State A detains some of State B's soldiers, can they be detained as prisoners of war (POW)? Article 9 of the ICCPR, by referring to arbitrary detention, may give the HRC the flexibility to include detention as a POW as legitimate. Would the HRC be able to use international humanitarian law to determine the duration of detention on such a ground, if the State had not derogated? The problem is much more acute in the case of the European Convention on Human Rights. Article 5 lists the only permitted grounds of detention. They do not include detention as a POW. If the State fails to derogate and if the scope of a right cannot be modified without derogation, then detention as a POW would appear to be unlawful. It is submitted that where a State has not derogated but relies on an authority to detain which would be legitimate had it derogated and where that authority comes from another branch of international law applicable in the circumstances, the Court should take into account that branch of law. Detention of POWs in an international armed conflict would then be lawful, but the State might be found in breach of its obligation to notify the relevant authorities of the derogation and the measures taken pursuant to that derogation.

[36] *Armed Activities on the Territory of the Congo* (*Democratic Republic of the Congo v. Uganda*), Judgment of 19 December 2005, para. 219.

anything expressly designed to be applicable in situations of armed conflict. The Study not only could, but was required to, take human rights law into account.

The preceding analysis has been based on the provisions of human rights treaty law. The mandate for the Study was limited to customary law and did not include the question of the extent to which a State remained bound by its treaty obligations. This raises the question of the existence and scope of customary human rights law obligations and the way in which any such rules are formulated. The first difficulty lies in determining the relationship between United Nations Charter human rights law and customary human rights law. It is possible to identify certain norms, or at least certain mandates relating to certain norms, which have some measure of authority in relation to all States. The authority of a thematic Special Rapporteur extends to all States, at least all States members of the United Nations. Does this mean that the subject matter of the mandate, such as torture or summary, arbitrary or extra-judicial execution, is a principle of customary human rights law or is the authority of the norm distinct from the authority of the mandate-holder? Is the authority of the mandate-holder derived solely from his or her institutional authority, provided by the Commission, ECOSOC and the General Assembly or occasionally the Secretary-General? There may be a significant overlap between customary law and Charter law, in the case of the two mandates cited. In other areas, such as the effects of economic reform policies and foreign debt on the full enjoyment of human rights or the adverse effects of the illicit movement and dumping of toxic and dangerous products and wastes on the enjoyment of human rights, it is difficult to argue that there is a simple equation between the existence of a mandate held by a Special Rapporteur or Independent Expert and the existence of a customary law norm. It is suggested that the only way to determine the existence of a customary norm of human rights law is by applying the usual principles for the establishment of a customary law rule. There is a need for a study, like the customary international humanitarian law study, in the field of human rights law. In the meantime, all that can be suggested here is that there may be principles of customary human rights law.

What is more important is to determine whether possible principles of customary human rights law apply, possibly in a modified way, throughout the peace-war spectrum. Certain Special Rapporteurs – such as those on torture, on summary, arbitrary or extra-judicial execution, on the right to health and the right to adequate housing – routinely address the matter of concern to them in the context of conflict situations, as do the Special Representatives of the Secretary-General on internally displaced persons and human rights defenders and the Working Groups on arbitrary detention and enforced or involuntary disappearances. Generally speaking, States have not appeared to dispute their jurisdiction on the specific basis that the norm was not applicable in situations of conflict or where international humanitarian law was applicable.[37] It is likely that some of the norms contained in these mandates are strong contenders for customary law status. It may be tentatively concluded that customary human rights law probably operates in a broadly similar way to conventional human rights law. Since the formal procedure of derogation does not exist in customary law, one must assume that the scope of certain rights may be affected solely by the situation. It would seem likely that any conventional non-derogable norm would also be non-derogable in customary law. There would seem to be nothing in customary human rights law to displace the earlier conclusion that human rights law is expressly designed to apply in all circumstances, including conflict, and that it therefore had to be taken into account in a study of customary international humanitarian law.

Before considering the use of human rights law actually made by the authors of the ICRC Study, it is necessary to consider two specific issues. The first concerns the significance of the *lex specialis* character of international humanitarian law and the second whether a State can opt out of the applicability of human rights law in situations of conflict.

b. Lex specialis

As seen above, the International Court of Justice has suggested that, in situations of conflict, international humanitarian law is the *lex specialis*.[38] This may have implications for the application of human rights law, if not its applicability. In the light of the Court's subsequent case-law, it is not altogether clear what is meant by the expression. The full expression is *lex specialis derogat legi generali*. It is not clear whether this means only that the special prevails over the general or whether it means that it actually displaces it. The phrase suggests that a particular type of situation will be regulated by the rules generally applicable to such a situation but that, if in fact the particular situation comes within a sub-category, it will be regulated by any rules applicable to that sub-category. So, for example, a

---

[37] For the attitude of the United States and Israel, see the discussion below of persistent objection.
[38] See generally, N. Prud'homme, '*Lex specialis*: Oversimplifying a More Complex and Multifaceted Relationship?', forthcoming (on file with author).

lease of commercial premises will give rise to a normal landlord and tenant relationship but if there are special rules applicable to the leasing of commercial properties, not only will they be applicable but they will take priority over general landlord and tenant rules. This example suggests that the special will generally be a sub-set of the general, rather than a different body of general law. The issue of the relationship between international humanitarian law and human rights law is rather different. It is more akin to establishing the boundaries between contract and tort law or between tort law and crime. The position becomes clearer if one applies the principle not to the applica*bility* of human rights law but only to its applica*tion*. This appears to be the implication of the International Court of Justice's Advisory Opinion on the *Legal Consequences of a Wall*, in which the Court found both the International Covenant on Civil and Political Rights and the International Covenant on Economic, Social and Cultural Rights to be applicable. If it is accepted that both humanitarian law and human rights law may be simultaneously applicable, there is a need for a principle which will ensure at the minimum that the application of the two sets of rules will not lead to conflicting results and ideally that the fit between the two sets of rules will be as close as possible. That could be achieved by saying that one area of law should be interpreted in the light of the other. Such a principle would mean that conflict would be avoided but only where both bodies of rules contain a rule addressing the same issue. So, for example, if priority is given to international humanitarian law rules regulating the conduct of hostilities, the detailed rules of international humanitarian law on when a death is unlawful would be used to determine what constitutes an arbitrary killing. Not only would the intentional killing of civilians be arbitrary but so would be the targeting of a military objective in circumstances in which the death of a disproportionate number of civilians was foreseeable. This would have no effect on the 'normal' interpretation of arbitrary in a policing context.[39] Such a principle would, however, appear to be of no assistance where

[39] It would still leave the potentially difficult and sensitive question for the Human Rights Committee of determining when to press the international humanitarian law button. In genuinely borderline cases of possible non-international conflict, it might be acceptable to pay particular attention to the attitude of the State. If it plausibly claimed that humanitarian law was not applicable, it would be estopped from disputing the applicability of the normal policing standard. That is not likely to be satisfactory, particularly if the *lex specialis* principle should trigger the application of international humanitarian law as a matter of law, when it is clear that some form of humanitarian law is applicable. Examples of such difficulties would be the outbreak of organised fighting in occupied territory and the targeted assassination of individuals who pose a threat to civilians in the jurisdiction

international humanitarian law contains no equivalent of a human rights norm. International humanitarian law does not, for example, address the right to marry. This presumably means, according to the International Court of Justice, that the human rights norm remains applicable during conflict and that its application would be determined by whatever limitations are attached to the interest, together with those arising out of derogation, if relevant.

It is to be regretted that the International Court of Justice did not spell out its reasoning in the Advisory Opinion on the *Legal Consequences of a Wall* and the judgment in the *Congo* case. In the former the Court confirmed both the *lex specialis* character of international humanitarian law and the continued applicability of human rights law but simply asserted the existence of certain violations of human rights law, without explaining how international humanitarian law modified its interpretation of the scope of human rights law, if it in fact did so. Similarly, in the *Congo* case, the Court simply found violations of Protocol I of 1977 and Article 6 of the Covenant on Civil and Political Rights, without explaining whether the latter finding was dependent on the former.

It will be assumed for the purposes of this chapter that the *lex specialis* principle relates to the application and not the applicability of human rights law in situations of conflict. It will further be assumed that the principle requires that human rights law norms generally be interpreted in the light of relevant norms of international humanitarian law.

c. Persistent objection to the applicability of human rights law

The second issue is whether a State can opt out of the simultaneous applicability of international humanitarian law and human rights law. This assumes that, unless it can and does opt out, a State may find itself obliged to apply both simultaneously. Generally speaking, the only way in which a State can avoid being bound by a principle of customary law is if it is a persistent objector.[40] The reason for including a consideration of

---

Footnote 39 (*cont.*)
of the State but who are located outside the State and whom the territorial State refuses to hand over for trial. It should be noted that the ICJ has only referred to the *lex specialis* of international humanitarian law when dealing with international armed conflicts. It has not said whether the same principle would apply in non-international armed conflicts. There is a real risk that such application would have the effect of reducing the current level of protection under human rights law.

[40] In the case of treaty law, a State can opt out by not ratifying the treaty. It nevertheless has to take care to object lest the norm to which it objects over time acquires the status of customary law, notwithstanding its origin in a treaty provision. See generally, Scobbie, Chapter 2.

the issue here is that two States, Israel and the United States, have repeatedly asserted that human rights law ceases to be applicable when international humanitarian law is applicable.[41] This raises a variety of discrete issues. The first is whether, in fact, those States have been persistent in their objection. That will not be pursued further here, beyond noting that erratic objection is insufficient. Since the objecting State is seeking to depart from the normal rule, the burden of proof would appear to be on the objector to establish persistence.

The next issue is whether there are any limits to the principles to which a State can object. Given the content of the rules on *ius cogens*, it seems likely that a State cannot be a persistent objector to what is agreed to be a rule of *ius cogens*. Whether a State can be a persistent objector to the *ius cogens* rules themselves is beyond the scope of this chapter. That still leaves the question of whether there exist rules of international law of such a character as to preclude the applicability of the persistent objector principle. Arming rebels in another State is a form of intervention.[42] Could a State be a persistent objector to the prohibition of this form of intervention, notwithstanding the threat thereby posed to international peace and security? It should be recalled that Israel and the United States are not claiming the right to be free of accountability.[43] They are claiming the right to have their conduct judged in relation exclusively to international humanitarian law, which the International Court of Justice has determined to be the *lex specialis*. In the process, they are also claiming the right not to be accountable to human rights monitoring mechanisms, whether the latter are interpreting human rights law in the light of international humanitarian law or not. There are no similar monitoring bodies in the field of international humanitarian law.

Even if it were assumed that there are some fundamental principles, which are nevertheless not norms of *ius cogens*, in relation to which a

---

[41] Both States also argue that human rights law is not applicable outside national territory. This section is not about the scope and content of human rights law but only about the relationship between human rights law and international humanitarian law. The question of the extra-territorial scope of human rights obligations will not be considered further.

[42] It does not constitute an armed attack, giving rise to a right of self-defence: *Military and Paramilitary Activities in and against Nicaragua (Nicaragua v. United States of America)*, Merits, Judgment of 27 June 1986 [1986] *ICJ Rep.* 14.

[43] Except to the extent that the USA seeks to rely on international humanitarian law when it is not in fact applicable, in which case the only accountability would be under human rights law or possibly international criminal law, or where it denies the applicability of both human rights law and international humanitarian law.

State cannot be a persistent objector, it would seem difficult to argue that the non-applicability of human rights law as a result of the applicability of international humanitarian law could be such a principle, at least if humanitarian law were not only applicable but applied.

A bigger difficulty for the two States may be the context in which the principle operates. Persistent objection usually appears to serve the function of a defence, in legal proceedings at least.[44] The claimant State has asserted the existence and applicability of a rule which the respondent State asserts is not opposable to it by the claimant State. Whilst the persistent objection of the respondent is a necessary condition, it seems as though it is not sufficient for the application of the principle. It is necessary, in addition, to establish that the claimant has accepted or acquiesced in the objection. It is not the objection which has any legal effect but the acceptance of or acquiescence in the objection. Viewed in this light, the principle is akin to that of estoppel. Since an exception is being sought to an otherwise applicable rule, acceptance or acquiescence cannot be presumed. At the very least, it must be shown that a party must have known of the objection and did not itself object.[45] The acceptance by State B of State A's persistent objection cannot determine the applicability of the general norm in the relations between State A and State C. This gives rise to particular difficulties in the context of human rights law. Whose acquiescence or acceptance is required? States have created a variety of mechanisms to monitor the implementation of both conventional and non-conventional human rights norms. If those mechanisms are to be treated as having the capacity to acquiesce or accept, by virtue of the functions given to them by States, then their reaction is essential. The acceptance or acquiescence of individual States would not result in the persistent objection being opposable to the monitoring mechanisms, if they did not themselves acquiesce or accept. Each of the monitoring bodies that has been confronted with the objection has made clear their opposition.[46] They have been

---

[44] *Fisheries* case (*United Kingdom v. Norway*), Judgment of 18 December 1951 [1951] *ICJ Rep.* 116. One can imagine circumstances in which an alleged persistent objector would bring a claim based on the effect of their objection on the claim of the defendant State. That serves to reinforce the view that the principle is an essentially bilateral one.

[45] *Ibid.*, pp. 138–9.

[46] For example, the Special Rapporteur on Torture and the Working Group on Arbitrary Detention have continued to assert their authority to examine relevant human rights issues arising out of the armed conflicts in which the USA has been involved since 11 September 2001. It should also be noted that the same is true of human rights treaty bodies, such as the Inter-American Commission on Human Rights, the Human Rights Committee and the Committee on Economic, Social and Cultural Rights.

reaffirmed in their view as to the applicability of human rights law by the recent case law of the International Court of Justice discussed above.[47] It is submitted that whether or not it is possible to be a persistent objector in relation to the applicability of human rights law and whether or not individual States have accepted or acquiesced in the objection, the rejection of the objection by the human rights mechanisms means that it is not opposable to them.

It is not only in this field that international law seems to be taking time to catch up with the implications of the mechanisms it has itself created. Historically, international law was collective in formulating norms but bilateral in enforcing them. So, for example, every State party to a treaty had to accept a reservation before it could be accepted. Similarly, it was not unusual to have a universal applicability clause in a treaty in the field of armed conflicts.[48] If just one party to a conflict was not a party to a particular treaty, the treaty was not applicable to the conflict, even though all the other parties to the conflict were parties to the treaty. That position changed with and subsequent to the Geneva Conventions of 1949. It is now the case that humanitarian law treaties are applicable between those belligerents who are a party to them, even if not all parties to the conflict are parties to the treaty. Similarly, and at about the same time, the reservations regime was made much more flexible. It became easier to obtain rules which were binding on some and not others. In other words, international law moved from a collective system of creating norms to a more fragmented, bilateral system. At the same time, international law relating to the monitoring of compliance and enforcement moved away from exclusive reliance on arbitration and judicial decisions on a bilateral basis. It is not just in the field of human rights law that the past fifty years has seen a proliferation of independent monitoring bodies. Nevertheless, international law does not yet appear to have digested the implications of such developments. That is only too apparent in the field of reservations to human rights treaty provisions.[49] It would appear also to be the case

---

[47] It should, however, be noted that the ICJ did not consider in its Advisory Opinion whether Israel could be said to be a persistent objector to the applicability of human rights law. It simply reaffirmed the general rule regarding simultaneous applicability but it did so in relation to a State that has, as a matter of notoriety, objected to such simultaneous applicability. Furthermore, it expressly endorsed statements made by the Human Rights Committee and the Committee on Economic, Social and Cultural Rights.

[48] For example, Hague Convention IV of 1907 Respecting the Laws and Customs of War on Land, Article 2.

[49] Human Rights Committee, General Comment No.24, CCPR/C/21/Rev.1/Add.6, 4 November 1994, para. 18.

in relation to the opposability of persistent objection to human rights monitoring mechanisms. Very gradually, international law is taking account of the existence and role of such monitoring bodies but it is too soon for it to have provided a coherent and comprehensive set of answers to the questions to which they give rise.

It is submitted that the USA and Israel cannot invoke persistent objection to the applicability of human rights law in situations of conflict vis-à-vis the human rights monitoring mechanisms.

d. The use made of human rights law in the Study

As argued above, the authors had to take account of human rights law since it is expressly designed to apply in situations of conflict. The human rights law which they were required to take into account is customary human rights law. There exists no compilation of that body of rules.[50] This confronted the authors with a problem. If relying on human rights law as a source of direct legal obligation, they would have to be clear that the principle in question had the status of customary law. On the other hand, if they were using human rights law as evidence of state practice and *opinion iuris* merely to provide additional support for a principle established by humanitarian law evidence, then they could afford to be less punctilious about the status of the human rights norm. Such a use of human rights material would be conservative, since it would not be using human rights law as a direct source of legal obligation in situations of conflict, but it would certainly be legitimate. If using material generated from human rights bodies solely as supporting evidence, it is legitimate to use material derived directly or indirectly from human rights treaties, provided that there is evidence that the essence of the treaty norm is to be found in customary human rights law.[51]

This is precisely the use made of human rights law in the Study. It is never used as a direct source of obligation in situations of conflict. It is only used as evidence adding weight to other evidence. It is striking that the main use of such material is in relation to Fundamental Guarantees and related areas.[52] There is scarcely a mention of human rights law in the

---

[50] For an early examination of this issue, see T. Meron, *Human Rights and Humanitarian Norms as Customary Law* (Oxford: Clarendon Press, 1989).

[51] A judgment of a human rights court is treated as indirect reliance on a treaty provision.

[52] See chapter 11. The question of whether what occurs in practice is evidence of violation of a rule or evidence of contrary State practice will be considered in the context of that chapter.

field of the conduct of military operations, even though there exists relevant case law from human rights bodies.[53]

The other use made of human rights materials is to clarify the meaning of a rule or concept established as binding purely on the basis of international humanitarian law. So, for example, the meaning of torture and inhuman treatment is illustrated by reference to human rights case law. The same is true of concepts such as fundamental judicial guarantees and the notion of a court. This is not used as part of the rule itself but only in relation to the discussion of its scope. The human rights material provides specific examples of what a term used in international humanitarian law might mean. Given the claim by certain American authorities that common Article 3 of the Geneva Conventions is too vague to be the basis of criminal proscription, the United States at least ought to be grateful for the guidance provided by the Study.

It is submitted that the way in which human rights law and human rights material is used in the Study is legitimate, necessary and conservative.

---

[53] They thereby avoid the difficult question of whether force can only be used as a last resort in situations of non-international armed conflict or whether any member of an armed opposition group can be killed on sight, irrespective of whether he poses a threat at the time or could have been detained; see generally, CUDIH, Expert Meeting on the Right to Life in Armed Conflicts and Situations of Occupation, www.ucihl.org/research/Right_to_Life_Meeting_Report.pdf. The issue is of considerable concern since the ICRC/TMC Asser Institute meetings on the meaning and implications of the 'direct participation' of civilians in armed conflict appear to be extending the interpretation of situations in which civilians can be regarded as having lost their protection and do not appear to be distinguishing, in this regard, between international and non-international conflicts; ICRC web site, summary reports of meetings in 2003, 2004 and 2005.

PART 2

The status of conflict and combatants:
The ICRC Study

4

Status of armed conflicts

JELENA PEJIĆ*

1. Introduction

Characterising an armed conflict as international or non-international is the first, preliminary step in determining the applicable humanitarian treaty law framework. As is well-known, international armed conflicts are governed by the four Geneva Conventions of 1949 – ratified by 194 States at the time of writing[1] – and by Additional Protocol I if binding on the parties involved.[2] Non-international armed conflicts are regulated by Article 3 common to the Geneva Conventions and by Additional Protocol II if ratified by the State in question.[3] The distinction between international and non-international armed conflicts remains relevant. Not only are the treaty rules applicable to international armed conflicts vastly more developed than those governing non-international armed conflicts, but the status of the parties is also different.

In international armed conflicts members of the armed forces of States are combatants who have the right to take a direct part in hostilities and are entitled to prisoner of war status upon capture. This, among other things, means that they may not be prosecuted by the detaining State for lawful acts of war, but for grave breaches or other serious violations of the

---

* This chapter is written in Ms Pejic's personal capacity and does not necessarily reflect the views of the ICRC.

[1] Geneva Convention for the Amelioration of the Condition of the Wounded and Sick in Armed Forces in the Field, of 12 August 1949; Geneva Convention for the Amelioration of the Condition of Wounded, Sick and Shipwrecked Members of Armed Force at Sea, of 12 August 1949; Geneva Convention relative to the Treatment of Prisoners of War, of 12 August 1949; Geneva Convention relative to the Protection of Civilian Persons in Time of War, of 12 August 1949. For status of ratifications see: www.icrc.org/ Web/Eng/siteeng0.nsf/iwpList103/6C6481C326D8DC31C1256E35004D53AB.

[2] Protocol Additional to the Geneva Conventions of 12 August 1949, and relating to the Protection of Victims of International Armed Conflicts (Protocol I), of 8 June 1977. For status of ratifications (166 States) see: website at note 1 above.

[3] For status of ratifications see website at note 1 above.

laws and customs of war they may have committed. In an internal armed
conflict the only legitimate forces are those of the State. While the parties
are equally bound to respect humanitarian law, members of the non-
State party remain liable to criminal prosecution under domestic law
for all acts committed during the conflict, whether lawful or unlawful
under humanitarian law. There is no entitlement to combatant or
prisoner-of-war status in internal armed conflicts.

The Study assumes a distinction between international and non-
international armed conflicts, but does not examine the differences or the
criteria for determining how to assess whether one or the other exists.
While this may be regretted, it was also inevitable. First, the relevant
treaties, as will be examined below, contain no general definition of what
constitutes an armed conflict, whether international or non-international. While the issue of a definition had occasionally been the subject of
diplomatic discussions, no formula was ever agreed on or included in the
treaties. Attempting to determine a definition of armed conflict or of the
different types of conflicts for the purposes of the Study would therefore
only have regenerated debates that have never been successfully concluded elsewhere.

Second, and more important, State practice did not allow the editors
to put forward definitions that could be said with sufficient certainty to
constitute customary humanitarian law. While States do express positions on whether a situation of violence amounts to an armed conflict –
in the United Nations General Assembly and Security Council, in
regional inter-governmental organisations or through domestic courts –
most of the relevant international resolutions or other instruments refer
only to a 'conflict', leaving open the type involved. Security Council resolutions, for example, 'call on the parties concerned' to undertake or
abstain from certain acts or behaviour. It is frequently unclear who the
parties are, what their status is and what rules the Council regards them
as being governed by. This level of generality may be useful to make a
political point, but is of little value in trying to gauge the opinion of States
as to the legal nature of an armed conflict. Moreover, some States that
have informally commented on the Study have pointed out that their
statements in UN fora and support for the adoption of certain resolutions should not be taken as evidence of practice. With that in mind, it
can almost be said that it is fortuitous that the Study omits a delineation
of armed conflicts under customary humanitarian law.

The Study's main achievement is that it identifies a core set of rules,
147 out of 161 to be precise, which are applicable in *all* situations of

armed conflict. For the remaining rules it will still be necessary to determine the status of an armed conflict. Examining the different types of armed conflicts and who determines that one or the other exists is the subject of this chapter.

2. Determining the status of armed conflicts

There is no body at the international level that can quickly and impartially pronounce on the legal nature of an armed conflict when it commences, or initially classify a situation of violence as armed conflict or not.[4] Needless to say, establishing the facts on the ground has to be undertaken before any legal classification is reached. More often than not, that will be a challenge in and of itself as the facts will be in dispute.

In practice, qualifications are undertaken by States, international organisations,[5] non-governmental organisations, the ICRC, courts, scholars and others. Different conclusions on the status of a situation of armed violence may thus be reached by different authorities or, in some cases, no conclusion is reached at all. Even within a State it is not always clear which body has the authority to make a definitive determination. For example, the Russian Constitutional Court opined in 1995 that Additional Protocol II was applicable to the fighting in Chechnya at that time; when hostilities resumed in 1999 the Executive referred to the situation as a counter-terrorist action.[6]

Moreover, the legal qualification of a situation of violence is almost never free from political considerations. While determining the existence of an international armed conflict is usually not problematic – as such conflicts usually involve States – qualifying a situation as a non-international armed conflict is far more sensitive. More often than not, the State party involved will deny that the level of violence has reached that of an armed conflict and will tend to characterise its actions as 'law enforcement' or 'counter-terrorist' operations. Distinguishing between

---

[4] While the International Court of Justice can, of course, classify armed conflicts and has done so in the past, proceedings before the ICJ are most often initiated after the fact and take years. Security Council determinations that an armed conflict exists usually do not define the nature of the conflict and usually express the international community's political sense.

[5] A recent example of an apparent Security Council determination that an occupation – of Iraq – has ended is provided for in Security Council resolution 1546(2004), 8 June 2004.

[6] For an account of the evolution of legal qualifications of the situation in Chechnya and the corresponding sources, see L. Moir, *The Law of Internal Armed Conflict* (Cambridge University Press, 2002), pp. 127–132.

situations of non-international armed conflict, covered by humanitarian law, and violence clearly falling below the threshold of armed conflict (internal disturbances or tensions) may be said to be an even more difficult task. Although the Study relates only to armed conflict, its section on 'Fundamental Guarantees' (Chapter 32) enunciates many rules that could be said to be obligatory in all situations of violence.

Like the ad hoc Criminal Tribunals for the former Yugoslavia and for Rwanda before it, the International Criminal Court[7] will have to decide on the classification of an armed conflict for the purpose of prosecution and trial of individuals. It would, of course, be preferable if the nature of the conflict was clear before the matter came up for determination before the Court. It is thus likely that the International Criminal Court will have to develop its own jurisprudence on the issue of classification as the two ad hoc Tribunals did. How to reconcile the possibly different legal approaches of these international judicial bodies is a question that has yet to be tackled.

As regards ICRC policy and practice, the classification of armed conflicts is undertaken in order to strengthen the protection of victims of war, to enable transparency in the organisation's work and to provide coherence with legal positions taken in other similar circumstances. While the ICRC qualifies armed conflicts in order to be able to determine the legal regime applicable in a specific context, its decisions are not – and cannot be – binding on the parties. Conversely, the ICRC does not feel that it is obliged to publicly communicate its qualification where this would not be in the interest of the victims or where ICRC operations would be imperilled as a result.

In brief, unless and until the legal regimes of international and non-international armed conflict merge into one, States and others will need to continue determining the status of any conflict in which they or other parties are involved. The Study should prove to be useful in the meantime, because it was found that the great majority of customary law rules apply to both types of armed conflict, thereby rendering the issue of qualification less central.

International armed conflict

Article 2 common to the four Geneva Conventions of 1949 provides that the Conventions 'shall apply to all cases of declared war or of any other

---

[7] Rome Statute of the International Criminal Court (1998).

armed conflict which may arise between two or more of the High Contracting Parties, even if the state of war is not recognised by one of them'.[8] The absence of a definition of either international 'armed conflict' or 'war'[9] in the Conventions, or in any other multilateral treaty, has generated numerous academic, professional and judicial attempts to fill the void. While these formulations do vary in some aspects, there is no question that international armed conflict means inter-State conflict.

An often quoted scholarly definition that preceded the current treaties was provided by Oppenheim: 'War is a contention between two or more States through their armed forces, for the purpose of overpowering each other and imposing such conditions of peace as the victor pleases'.[10] Dinstein has more recently proposed a different definition, based on an analysis of Oppenheim's formulation: 'War is a hostile interaction between two or more States, either in a technical or in a material sense. War in the technical sense is a formal status produced by a declaration of war. War in the material sense is generated by actual use of armed force, which must be comprehensive on the part of at least one party to the conflict'.[11]

According to the International Criminal Tribunal for the former Yugoslavia, whose definition focuses on the concept of armed conflict: 'an armed conflict exists whenever there is resort to armed force between States or protracted armed violence between governmental authorities and organised armed groups or between such groups within a State. International humanitarian law applies from the initiation of such armed conflicts and extends beyond the cessation of hostilities until a general conclusion of peace is reached; or, in the case of internal conflicts, a peaceful settlement is achieved.'[12]

The ICRC commentary to the Geneva Conventions states that: 'Any difference arising between two States and leading to the intervention of members of the armed forces is an armed conflict within the meaning of Article 2, even if one of the Parties denies the existence of a state of war. It

[8] Art. 2 (1) common to the Geneva Conventions.
[9] For the purposes of this chapter, the terms 'international armed conflict' and 'war' are interchangeable. For the legal consequences and the continued relevance of the notion of 'war' see C. Greenwood, 'The Concept of War in Modern International Law' (1987) 36 International and Comparative Law Quarterly 283.
[10] H. Lauterpacht (ed.), Oppenheim's, International Law, Vol. II (London: Longmans, Green & Co. 7th edn, 1952), p. 202.
[11] Y. Dinstein, War, Aggression and Self-Defence (Cambridge University Press, 4th edn, 2005), p. 15.
[12] Prosecutor v. Tadic (ICTY) Decision on the Defense Motion for Interlocutory Appeal on Jurisdiction, Appeals Chamber, 2 October 1995 (1995) Case No. IT-94-1-AR72, at para. 70.

makes no difference how long the conflict lasts, how much slaughter takes place, or how numerous are the participating forces; it suffices for the armed forces of one Power to have captured adversaries falling within the scope of Article 4. Even if there has been no fighting, the fact that persons covered by the Convention are detained is sufficient for its application. The number of persons captured in such circumstances is, of course, immaterial.'[13]

This and other interpretations seem to have been somewhat thrown into doubt by *dicta* of the International Court of Justice in the *Nicaragua* case,[14] in which the Court said that a 'mere frontier incident' should be distinguished from an 'armed attack'.[15] While the discussion focused on aspects of the *ius ad bellum*, the Court's reasoning seems to imply that frontier incidents, never being armed attacks, would also not be subject to the rules of international humanitarian law.[16] In practice, however, States have been reasonable in their assessment of whether a situation involving the use of military force – including a frontier incident – constitutes an armed conflict to which international humanitarian law is applicable or not.[17]

The notion of armed conflict was deliberately included in the Geneva Conventions in order to avoid linking the applicability of humanitarian law to the existence of 'war' in the technical legal sense.[18] While today it is uniformly accepted that the application of humanitarian law is triggered by the facts of a situation and not by declarations, there have recently been attempts to circumvent the Geneva Conventions, either entirely or in the specifics, by means of troubling interpretations.

The first theory posits the non-applicability of the Geneva Conventions to 'failed' States and, stemming from that, the belief that there are international armed conflicts to which their rules do not apply. The 2002 war in Afghanistan[19] has erroneously been mentioned as a case

---

[13] J. Pictet (ed.), *Commentary to the Third Geneva Convention relative to the Treatment of Prisoners of War* (Geneva, ICRC, 1960), p. 23 (hereafter 'GC III Commentary').

[14] *Case Concerning Military and Paramilitary Activities in and against Nicaragua (Nicaragua v. United States of America)*, Merits [1986] *ICJ Reports* 14, (hereafter 'ICJ Nicaragua Judgment').   [15] *Ibid.*, para. 103.

[16] The author is aware that the concepts of 'armed attack' and 'armed conflict' are not synonymous, but that distinction is not relevant for the purposes of this point.

[17] Dinstein, *War, Aggression and Self-Defence*, p. 11.   [18] GC III Commentary, p. 23.

[19] See draft Memorandum for William J. Haynes II, General Counsel, Department of Defense, from John Yoo, Deputy Assistant Attorney General and Robert J. Delahunty, Special Counsel, 'Re: Application of Treaties and Laws to al Qaeda and Taliban Detainees, January 9, 2002' in K.J. Greenberg and J.L. Dratel (eds.), *The Torture Papers: the Road to Abu Ghraib* (Cambridge University Press, 2005), pp. 50–70.

in point. Under international law, the objective criteria for statehood are a permanent population, a defined territory, effective government and the government's capacity to engage in international relations.[20] If one compares the situation in Afghanistan prior to the international armed conflict that began on 7 October 2001 with the requisite conditions, there is little doubt that Afghanistan could not have been deemed a failed State. On the assumption that the fulfilment of the first two criteria (population and territory) was obvious and uncontested, it was also fairly clear that the Taliban exercised effective control over almost the entire territory of Afghanistan and were the *de facto* government.[21] The fact that they had very limited international relations – with only a few States – did not mean that they were incapable of having them, simply that others did not want to enter into relations with that government.

As the case of Afghanistan demonstrates, the designation 'failed State' will often be used in the political and not legal sense and one must be careful to apply it in the latter meaning only when one of the conditions for statehood is really missing. Otherwise, one of the parties to an international armed conflict may be tempted to avoid its obligations under the Geneva Conventions – and probably other bodies of law – in relation to the opposing side simply by declaring its non-existence as a subject of international law.

Another troubling development in terms of the application of humanitarian law in international armed conflicts has been the notion that members of a State's armed forces may be disqualified from combatant, and therefore prisoner-of-war status, based on non-recognition of the government. The conflict in Afghanistan may again be cited as a case in point.[22] While the Taliban were a non-recognised government in terms of general international law, humanitarian law provides for this scenario in order to ensure the continued application of humanitarian norms. The Third Geneva Convention explicitly states that 'members of regular armed forces who profess allegiance to a government or an authority not recognised'[23] by the adversary are entitled to prisoner-of-war status upon

---

[20] J. Crawford, *The Creation of States in International Law* (Oxford: Clarendon Press, 1979).

[21] See C. Greenwood, 'War, Terrorism and International Law' (2003) 56 *Current Legal Problems* 505 at 522.

[22] See Memorandum for Alberto R. Gonzales, Counsel to the President, and William J. Haynes II, General Counsel of the Department of Defense, from Jay S. Bybee, Assistant Attorney General, 'Re: Application of Treaties and Laws to al Qaeda and Taliban Detainees, January 22, 2002' in K.J. Greenberg and J.L. Dratel (eds.), *The Torture Papers: the Road to Abu Ghraib*, pp. 100–102. [23] GC III, Art. 4 (3).

capture. Denying the applicability of the Third Convention to forces that constitute the regular armed forces of a State because the government to which they belong is not recognised may thus be said to contravene the plain language of the treaty.

Apart from regular, inter-state armed conflicts, another category of armed conflicts that may become international are those in which peoples are fighting against colonial domination, alien occupation or racist regimes in the exercise of their right to self-determination (wars of national liberation). While this type of international armed conflict is regulated by the Additional Protocol I to the Geneva Conventions,[24] it is well known that classification of wars of national liberation as inter-national armed conflicts has been one of the reasons for lack of full ratifi-cation of the Additional Protocol I. An additional hurdle consists of the conditions that an authority representing a people fighting a war of national liberation is generally considered to have to fulfil in order to be able to claim applicability of Protocol I.[25] As a result, the practical signifi-cance of the relevant provisions has been fairly small.

Recognition by the State involved of insurgents as a belligerent party was historically also a method by which a civil war could fall under the rules governing international armed conflicts.[26] (Third party recognition of belligerency entailed the application of the laws of neutrality as between the parties to the conflict.[27]) As this practice may probably be said to have fallen into desuetude – according to Gasser the last time bel-ligerency was formally recognised was during the 1902 Boer War[28] – it will not be further mentioned.

The issue of whether a non-international armed conflict in which a third State or a multinational force intervenes (internationalised non-international conflict) is governed by the rules applicable to non-international or international armed conflicts remains subject to debate. As humanitarian law provides no specific guidance in such a case, various opinions have been expressed in the literature. This issue will be addressed in more detail below.

---

[24] Additional Protocol I, Art. 1 (4) and 96 (3).
[25] M. Bothe, K.J. Partsch and W.A. Solf, *New Rules for Victims of Armed Conflicts: Commentary on the Two 1977 Protocols Additional to the Geneva Conventions of 1949,* Article 1: General Principles and Scope of Application (The Hague: Martinus Nijhoff, 1982), pp. 36–52.   [26] Moir, *The Law of Internal Armed Conflict,* pp. 1–21.   [27] *Ibid.*
[28] See Hans-Peter Gasser, 'International Humanitarian Law', in H. Haug (ed.), *Humanity for All: The International Red Cross and Red Crescent Movement* (Berne: Henry Dunant Institute and Paul Haupt Publishers, 1993), p. 559.

Non-international armed conflict

Classifying a situation of violence as a non-international armed conflict rather than as internal disturbances or tensions is the most difficult and yet essential step in determining the relevant legal framework. Roughly speaking, an internal armed conflict signifies that international humanitarian law would be applicable, whereas situations of violence not reaching that threshold would be governed only by human rights and domestic law. The specific interplay between these legal regimes is outside the scope of this text.

The challenge of classification basically lies in determining when common Article 3 can be invoked because the text provides no guidance for ascertaining what 'an armed conflict not of an international character' is. (The situation is easier in respect of Additional Protocol II as it defines, to some extent, the conflicts to which it applies.[29]) What is known is that the omission of a definition in Article 3 was deliberate and that there is a 'no-definition' school of thought which considers this to be a 'blessing in disguise'.[30] Proponents of this view, to which the present author subscribes, believe no definition would be capable of capturing the factual situations that reality throws up and that a definition would thus risk undermining the protective ambit of humanitarian law. The lack of a definition, in any event, means that the facts of a given situation must be analysed based on a series of criteria that have been developed by States in practice and reflected in the legal literature.[31] A crucial criterion is the existence of parties to the conflict.

Common Article 3 expressly refers to 'each Party to the conflict' thereby implying that a precondition for its application is the existence of at least two 'parties'. While, as noted above, it is not so difficult to establish whether a State party exists, determining whether a non-State armed group may be said to constitute a 'party' for the purposes of common Article 3 is far more difficult. It is also a factual issue for which there are no set criteria. Nevertheless, it has been widely recognised that a non-State party to a non-international armed conflict means an armed group with a certain level of organisation and command structure, as well as the

---

[29] Additional Protocol II, Art. 1 (1).   [30] Moir, *The Law of Internal Armed Conflict*, p. 32.
[31] The ICRC Commentaries to common Article 3 contain a summary of the criteria that were put forward by some States at the Diplomatic Conference, but were eventually rejected. (See GC III Commentary, pp. 35–36.) The list, as Moir rightly points out, sets a 'far higher threshold of application than is actually required by the Article itself' (*The Law of Internal Armed Conflict*, p. 35).

ability to implement international humanitarian law.[32] Differently stated, even though the level of violence in a given situation may be very high (The Los Angeles riots of 29 April–1 May 1992 for example), unless there is an organised armed group on the other side, one cannot speak of an internal armed conflict. Humanitarian law may thus be said to regulate an essentially 'horizontal' relationship between the parties to an armed conflict, in contrast to human rights law which, leaving aside possible horizontal effects, mainly governs a 'vertical' relationship between a State and an individual.[33]

Criteria additional to the existence of a 'party' used to determine whether a situation can be classified as a non-international armed conflict are: whether the government is obliged to use military force, the number of victims, the means used to deal with the opposing side, duration and, of course, the level of violence involved.[34] The difficulties in applying the criteria and the unusual results that may be reached were demonstrated in the *Abella* case examined by the Inter-American Commission on Human Rights.[35] In the Commission's view, a confrontation lasting only 30 hours between a group of dissident officers and the Argentine military that occurred at the Tablada military base in 1989 qualified as an armed conflict covered by common Article 3.[36]

[32] See *ibid.*, p. 36.

[33] Moreover, humanitarian law requires identifiable parties because the reality of armed conflict, whatever the type, and the rules governing it are based on an assumption of equality of rights and obligations between them. See C. Greenwood, 'War, Terrorism and International Law', p. 512. The same is not true under domestic law.

[34] Schindler provides a succinct outline of most of the factual criteria: 'Practice has set up the following criteria to delimit non-international armed conflicts from internal disturbances. In the first place, the hostilities have to be conducted by force of arms and exhibit such intensity that, as a rule, the government is compelled to employ its armed forces against the insurgents instead of mere police forces. Secondly, as to the insurgents, the hostilities are meant to be of a collective character, that is, they have to be carried out not only by single groups. In addition, the insurgents have to exhibit a minimum amount of organisation. Their armed forces should be under a responsible command and be capable of meeting minimal humanitarian requirements. Accordingly, the conflict must show certain similarities to a war, without fulfilling all conditions necessary for the recognition of belligerency.' D. Schindler, 'The Different Types of Armed Conflicts According to the Geneva Conventions and Protocols' (1979) 163 *Recueil des cours* 147.

[35] *Abella v. Argentina*, 18 November 1997 OEA/Ser.L/V/II.98, doc. 6 rev, 13 April 1998.

[36] *Ibid.*, para. 156. The Inter-American Commission distinguished the confrontation from internal disturbances based on 'the concerted nature of the hostile acts undertaken by the attackers, the direct involvement of governmental armed forces, and the nature and level of the violence attending the events in question' (*ibid.*, at para. 155.) The Commission further explained: 'More particularly, the attackers involved carefully planned, coordinated and executed an armed attack, i.e. a military operation against a quintessential

A further requirement for the applicability of common Article 3 is that the armed conflict not of an international character takes place 'in the territory of one of the High Contracting Parties'. The International Court of Justice has broadened the scope of application of common Article 3 by stating that its provisions reflect elementary considerations of humanity that must be observed regardless of the type of armed conflict involved.[37] The Court's pronouncement is fortuitous because the strict territorial scope of common Article 3 may not always correspond to protection needs that arise in practice. For example, in a situation where a State's armed forces pursue and continue fighting 'domestic' rebels into the territory of a neighbouring state (e.g. the hostilities between Rwanda and the Interahamwe militia that carried over into the Democratic Republic of the Congo), a strict reading of the territorial scope of common Article 3 would mean that the parties' humanitarian law obligations would stop at the border (of Rwanda). In any 'spillover' scenario like the one just mentioned, the ICRC would consider that both parties continue to be bound by the provisions of common Article 3.

Additional Protocol II to the Geneva Conventions has a higher threshold of applicability than common Article 3 even though the ICRC had initially hoped, before and at the Diplomatic Conference of 1974–1977, that their scope of applicability would be the same.[38] Concerns about the impact of the treaty on State sovereignty resulted in a text that offers more clarity, but is also more restrictive than originally envisaged.

The Protocol's applicability is tied to an armed conflict in which the non-State party must 'exercise such control over a part of' the territory of a State party as to enable it 'to carry out sustained and concerted military operations and to implement this Protocol'.[39] By introducing the element

---

military objective – a military base. The officer in charge of the Tablada base sought, as was his duty, to repulse the attackers, and President Alfonsin, exercising his constitutional authority as Commander-in-Chief of the armed forces, ordered that military action be taken to recapture the base and subdue the attackers . . . despite its brief duration, the violent clash between the attackers and members of the Argentine armed forces triggered application of the provisions of Common Art. 3, as well as other rules relevant to the conduct of internal hostilities.'

[37] 'Art. 3 which is common to all four Geneva Conventions of August 1949 defines certain rules to be applied in the armed conflicts of a non-international character. There is no doubt that, in the event of international armed conflicts, these rules also constitute a minimum yardstick, in addition to the more elaborate rules which are also to apply to international conflicts; and they are rules which, in the Court's opinion, reflect what the Court in 1949 called "elementary considerations of humanity".' ICJ *Nicaragua* Judgment, para. 218.   [38] See Schindler, 'Different Types of Armed Conflicts', p. 148.

[39] Additional Protocol II, Art. 1(1).

of territorial control, the Protocol essentially adopted one of the criteria previously required under international law for recognition of belligerency. Moreover, its applicability was made dependent on the ability of the non-State party to carry out a certain level of military operations and to implement the Protocol, which implies that its application may be called into question depending on the circumstances prevailing at any given time.

Just as importantly, Additional Protocol II expressly applies only to armed conflicts between State armed forces and dissident armed forces or other organised armed groups, and not to conflicts between such groups themselves. Given the number of armed conflicts that have historically involved hostilities between armed groups (Lebanon, Angola) and the ones that continue to occur (Democratic Republic of the Congo), it is clear that a unique opportunity for extending humanitarian law protection to such cases, as a matter of treaty regulation, was missed.

The scope of application of Protocol II is thus narrower than that of common Article 3, with Article 3 maintaining a separate legal significance even when Protocol II is also applicable. The relationship between the respective sets of rules is expressly provided for in Article 1(1) of Protocol II pursuant to which the Protocol 'develops and supplements Article 3 common to the Geneva Conventions of 12 August 1949 without modifying its existing conditions of application'. This clarification is particularly important given that the Protocol makes no mention of the ICRC's right to offer its service to the parties in the type of non-international armed conflict covered. The right therefore exists by virtue of the interface between the two treaty regimes.

In this context, it should be noted that the Study does not distinguish between the different thresholds of non-international armed conflict (under common Article 3 and Additional Protocol II), because it was found that in general States did not make this distinction in practice. By providing a set of rules that are applicable in all circumstances of armed conflict, the result of the Study may be to help overcome the separation between the two types of non-international conflicts that many scholars have considered unsatisfactory[40] (to say the least), and that has been superseded by certain treaties.[41]

---

[40] Schindler, 'Different Types of Armed Conflicts', p. 149.
[41] Protocol on Prohibitions or Restrictions on the Use of Mines, Booby-Traps and Other Devices; amended Protocol II to the 1980 Convention on Prohibitions or Restrictions on the Use of Certain Conventional Weapons (CCW); Protocols I, III, IV and V of the CCW, through paragraph 6 of Art. 1 of the CCW; the Convention for the Protection of Cultural

It has recently been implied that the definition of non-international armed conflict provided in the Statute of the International Criminal Court may constitute a third category of such conflicts. There are writers who argue that the Statute's description of 'armed conflicts that take place in the territory of a State when there is protracted armed conflict between governmental authorities and organised armed groups or between such groups'[42] falls in between the threshold of armed conflict provided for in common Article 3 and in Additional Protocol II.[43] Based on this reading they also believe that the Rome Statute of the International Criminal Court acts as *lex posterior* in relation to the definition in the Additional Protocol.[44]

As already briefly mentioned, it is on the issue of classification of a situation of violence as non-international armed conflict – or not – that political considerations will most particularly come into play. States have traditionally been hesitant to allow the applicability of humanitarian law for fear of acknowledging that internal political instability has reached the level of armed conflict and that their opponents should be treated as a party to the conflict. This is regardless of the fact that the application of humanitarian law, under its express terms, does not affect the parties' legal status.[45]

Political considerations aside, there remains the difficulty of determining and analysing the various factual criteria to which legal conclusions can be pinned. Based on the facts, it can legitimately, if only hypothetically, be asked whether, for example, the situations in Northern Ireland, Turkey and Algeria, constituted internal disturbances or tensions or internal armed conflicts. The general conclusion to be drawn is not that a definition of internal armed conflict would solve the problem – the examples provided above would attest to the contrary – only that knowledge of the facts, careful analysis and a *bona fide* approach to the habitual criteria for assessment are required.

Internationalised non-international armed conflict

In reality, very few non-international armed conflicts are waged without any form of external involvement. This section will attempt to outline the

Property in the Event of Armed Conflict; the Second Protocol to the Hague Convention of 1954 for the Protection of Cultural Property in the Event of Armed Conflict.
[42] Rome Statute of the International Criminal Court, Art. 8(2)(f).
[43] E. David, *Principes de droit des conflits armés* (Bruylant, 3rd edn, 2002), p. 129.
[44] *Ibid.*, p. 119.   [45] Common Art. 3(4).

legal classification of armed conflicts characterised by third State party intervention, having in mind that international humanitarian law provides no answers. It is based on the generally accepted proposition that one criterion for internationalisation is the sending by a State of troops into the territory of another, the other criterion being when domestic rebel forces may be said to be acting on behalf of a third State against their own Government.[46] Examining other situations that some might consider also to constitute internationalisation (e.g. the presence of military advisers, volunteers etc.), is outside the scope of this review.

The ICRC attempted in the early 1970s to propose treaty rules that would govern 'internationalised non-international armed conflicts': it was suggested, depending on the scenario, that either the entirety of humanitarian law or, at a minimum, provisions relating to prisoners of war and civilian internees, should apply.[47] This approach was rejected by States, who feared that it would encourage the parties to an internal armed conflict to invite foreign assistance in order to bring the treaties governing international armed conflict into effect. There have been no serious attempts to revisit the problem since then despite the fact that legal clarity would help address some of the serious humanitarian consequences that arise in practice. As a result, almost every situation of third State intervention in an internal armed conflict elicits a wide range of judicial and scholarly opinions. Two main strands of thought may be discerned.

According to what seems to be a minority view, third State intervention in a non-international armed conflict, provided it reaches a certain level, internationalises the internal conflict as a whole, regardless of the side on which the third party intervenes.[48] If a party to an internal armed conflict could not pursue hostilities against the other without outside help, then the amalgamation between that party and the intervening State justifies qualifying the relations between the two domestic adversaries as international.[49] Any other solution is deemed artificial because it would lead to 'absurd consequences' in practice: a fighter would be granted prisoner-of-war status if captured by the intervening third State, but not if he or she were captured by its national opponent.[50]

While this approach is theoretically simple (i.e. 'objective'[51]), the fact is that States remain reluctant to grant 'domestic' rebels, existing or potential, the status and privileges that humanitarian law reserves for

---

[46] *Prosecutor v. Tadić* (ICTY) Appeals Chamber, Judgment of 15 July 1999, Case IT-94-1-A, 38 Hereafter 'Tadić Appeals Judgment'.

[47] David, *Principes de droit des conflits armés*, pp. 147–148.   [48] *Ibid.*, p. 151.

[49] *Ibid.*   [50] *Ibid.*   [51] *Ibid.*

combatants in international armed conflicts. Moreover, both jurisprudence and the majority of legal scholars have accepted the proposition that a situation of armed conflict may be composed of an international and non-international strand.[52]

It is quite possible to imagine a situation in which a country may be simultaneously involved in a civil and inter-State war, without the two strands being necessarily connected. Some writers cite the situation in Afghanistan in the fall of 2001 as an example: 'The Taliban regime, having fought a long-standing civil war with the Northern Alliance, brought upon itself an inter-State war with an American-led Coalition as a result of providing shelter and support to the Al-Qaeda terrorists who had launched the 9/11 attack against the United States. But, even as the overall character of the armed conflict was transformed from an intra-State to an inter-State war, some specific hostilities continued to be waged exclusively between the domestic foes (namely, the Taliban forces and the Northern Alliance).'[53] It is submitted, as will be explained below, that the two strands of the Afghan conflict continued to be separate until the end of the international armed conflict phase in Afghanistan. Thus, the rules of non-international armed conflict continued to govern not only 'some specific hostilities', but the overall relations between the Taliban and Northern Alliance during that time, including the treatment and rights of captured persons.

Long before the war in Afghanistan, the International Court of Justice had confirmed that the two types of armed conflict, international and non-international, can exist in parallel. As is well-known, one of the issues examined by the Court in the *Nicaragua* case was whether the Contras were acting on behalf of the United States, which the Court answered in the negative. It is in this context that the Court legally distinguished the relationships between the parties involved: 'The conflict between the Contras forces and those of the Government of Nicaragua is an armed conflict which is "not of an international character". The acts of the Contras towards the Nicaraguan Government are therefore governed by the law applicable to conflicts of that character; whereas the actions of the United States in and against Nicaragua fall under the legal rules relating to international conflicts.'[54]

Leaving aside situations of the parallel existence of an internal and international conflict, the majority of cases in which an internal armed

---

[52] See Y. Dinstein, *The Conduct of Hostilities under the Law of International Armed Conflict* (Cambridge University Press, 2004), pp. 14–15. See Tadić Appeals Judgment, para. 84.
[53] Dinstein, *War, Aggression and Self-Defence*, p. 7.   [54] ICJ *Nicaragua* Judgment, para. 219.

conflict is said to be 'internationalised' involve third State interventions on the side of either the government or of the rebels. To refer colloquially to an internal conflict as being 'internationalised' does not, however, always mean that the hostilities will amount to an international armed conflict in the legal sense.

If a third State or States intervene to support the Government of a country against its 'domestic' rebels, it is generally considered that the relationships between all the parties continue to be governed by the rules of non-international armed conflict only (common Article 3 and Additional Protocol II as the case may be, as well as customary law).[55] As the fighting does not oppose the armed forces of two or more States the totality of the Geneva Conventions is not triggered; moreover, as noted, the 'host' country would most probably not countenance their application in relation to the rebels. If it wants to do so, common Article 3 envisages the conclusion of special agreements by means of which a wider range of humanitarian law provisions can be brought into force. In reality, it will sometimes be difficult to determine whether a host Government has freely consented to or called for external assistance in fighting a domestic insurgency. Cases in point are the Soviet intervention in Afghanistan in 1979 and the US intervention in Panama in 1989. Thus, the legal qualification of any situation created by foreign military intervention in response to an invitation from a Government must be carefully analysed.

There is generally no dissent either in jurisprudence or in doctrine that third State intervention in a civil war on the side of the rebels against a government gives rise to an international armed conflict between the States in question (as already mentioned, any distinct fighting between host State and rebels would be a separate non-international armed conflict). 'Internationalisation' of the conflict, this time in the legal sense, will be fairly easy to establish where third State support consists of troops sent to aid the rebels.

It is more challenging to conclude whether another recognised basis for internationalisation exists, namely, whether the rebels are acting on behalf of the intervening State. Somewhat controversially, the legal standard used to evaluate whether the actions of rebels may be attributed to a third

[55] While this author agrees with Dinstein that in the scenario just described the rules of non-international armed conflict govern the relations between all the parties involved (see Dinstein, *War, Aggression and Self-Defence*, p. 7 and pp. 112–114), Moir believes that this situation is 'less clear' as a matter of international law. See Moir, *The Law of Internal Armed Conflict*, pp. 50–51.

State for the purposes of State responsibility has become the standard for qualifying the nature of an armed conflict. Thus, in the *Nicaragua* case, the International Court of Justice held that a third State had to exercise 'effective control' over an insurgent operation for such actions to be attributable to it.[56] The Appeals Chamber of the International Criminal Tribunal for the former Yugoslavia famously rejected the test of 'effective control' and replaced it with the test of 'overall control'[57] when it was called upon to determine whether the armed conflict in Bosnia and Herzegovina remained international after 19 May 1992 or had become internal.[58] The Appeals Chamber explained that 'the legal consequences of the characterization of the conflict as internal or international are extremely important. Should the conflict eventually be classified as international, it would *inter alia* follow that a foreign State may in some circumstances be held responsible for violations of international law perpetrated by the armed groups acting on its behalf.'[59] Based on the opinions of these two international judicial bodies, it is clear that at some point the acts of rebels can be attributed to a third State, thereby triggering the application of the rules of international armed conflict between the involved States. Just when that point is reached remains unclear.

In practice, the internationalisation of an internal armed conflict means that, for example, a member of the armed forces of the intervening State will be entitled to prisoner-of-war status upon capture by the host State, whereas a domestic rebel might not. There is no doubt that this approach is more complicated and leads to the uneven protection of humanitarian law when compared to the 'objective' theory of internationalisation already

---

[56] ICJ *Nicaragua* Judgment, para. 115.

[57] *Ibid.*, para. 131. 'The "effective control" test propounded by the International Court of Justice as an exclusive and all-embracing test is at variance with international judicial and State practice: such practice has envisaged State responsibility in circumstances where a lower degree of control than that demanded by the *Nicaragua* test was exercised. In short, as shall be seen, this practice has upheld the *Nicaragua* test with regard to individuals or unorganized groups of *individuals* acting on behalf of States. By contrast, it has applied a different test with regard to *military or paramilitary* groups'. (*Tadić* Appeals Judgment, para. 124.) The Appeals Chamber clarified that: 'In order to attribute the acts of a military or paramilitary group to a State, it must be proved that the State wields overall control over the group, not only by equipping and financing the group, but also by coordinating or helping in the general planning of its military activity. Only then can the State be held internationally accountable for any misconduct of the group. However, it is not necessary that, in addition, the State should also issue, either to the head or to members of the group, instructions for commission of specific acts contrary to international law.'

[58] See, for example, T. Meron, 'Classification of Armed Conflict in the Former Yugoslavia: Nicaragua's Fallout' (1998) 92 *American Journal of International Law* 236.

[59] *Tadić* Appeals Judgment, para. 97.

mentioned. However, except in rare cases,[60] States are not willing to grant rebels anything like the status and privileges of lawful combatants. Dealing with the variable scope of humanitarian law coverage depending on whether a person falls under the rules of international or non-international armed conflict is thus a constant challenge for humanitarian and other organisations in practice. Whenever possible, the ICRC tries to find pragmatic ways to ensure that the treatment of detainees corresponds to humanitarian standards.

It goes without saying that the same legal issues and challenges, only more complicated, arise in armed conflicts in which a State or group of States intervenes on the side of a Government while another State or group of States supports the rebels. Between the States involved on opposing sides the rules of international armed conflict will apply. The legal relationships between them and the other actors, including the host State, will be determined based on the scenarios outlined above.

The increased use of multinational forces (whether UN or other) has inevitably resulted, on occasion, in their involvement in hostilities in third States. Regardless of the specific missions that have been assigned to such forces, it is submitted that their intervention against a State internationalises an armed conflict in the same way that the intervention of a third State against a host country does. Similarly, where they intervene against non-state actors, the rules of non-international armed conflict would apply.

A separate issue that arises in relation to multinational forces is the source of their obligations under humanitarian law. The consensus is that multinational forces are bound by humanitarian law based on their individual State's adherence to the relevant treaties (or obligations under customary law). The 1999 UN Secretary-General's Bulletin on the observance of humanitarian law by UN forces[61] attempted further to clarify the obligations of UN forces under UN command and control, but remains controversial.

Reclassification of armed conflicts

In practice, cases in which an internal armed conflict becomes partially or wholly internationalised have been fairly common. An example of the

---

[60] See F. Bugnion, 'Jus Ad Bellum, Jus In Bello and Non-International Armed Conflicts' (2003) 6 *Yearbook of International Humanitarian Law* 195.
[61] Secretary-General's Bulletin, Observance by United Nations Forces of International Humanitarian Law, ST/SGB/1999/13, 6 August 1999.

first scenario would be third State intervention on the rebel side against a Government in power, as explained above. Wars of secession, provided the secession is effective, would be an illustration of the second scenario: it can be argued that the armed conflict between the rump Yugoslavia on the one hand and Slovenia and Croatia on the other fell into that category after those countries' declarations of independence in June 1991. The practical consequence of an 'upward' reclassification of armed conflict from internal to international is that the totality of humanitarian law comes into force between the parties.

Less frequent have been cases in which an initially international armed conflict is reclassified 'downward', from international to non-international. Two recent examples are the wars in Afghanistan and Iraq.

In the ICRC's view, the armed conflict in Afghanistan that started in October 2001 ceased to be international upon the convening of the *Loya Jirga* and the establishment of the Karzai Government in June 2002, which was recognised by the entire community of States. After that date, the multinational forces present in Afghanistan have no longer been engaged in hostilities against an opposing State (the legal criterion for international armed conflict), but are fighting remnants of the Taliban and Al-Qaeda with the consent of the new government. Similarly, the international armed conflict phase of the war in Iraq, which began in March 2003, is believed to have ended with the UN Security Council's determination in June 2004 that the continued multinational presence in Iraq is subject to the government's consent.[62] A requalification downward has, among other things, the consequence of excluding from legal analysis controversial issues such as combatant and prisoner-of-war status that are only relevant in international armed conflicts. The treatment and rights of persons detained are governed by common Article 3, Additional Protocol II if applicable, customary international humanitarian law and, to the extent applicable, human rights law.

The 'global war on terrorism'

The 'war on terrorism' has given rise to queries about how situations of violence, perceived as new, may be classified and about the applicable rules of international law.[63] According to one approach, the 'war on terrorism' is

---

[62] Security Council Resolution 1546 (2004), 8 June 2004.
[63] J. Pejic, 'Terrorist Acts and Groups: A Role for International Law?' (2004) 75 *British Year Book of International Law* 71.

an international armed conflict not covered by the Geneva Conventions, but by the principles of the Conventions.[64] It has also been suggested that the new practices being applied in the 'war on terrorism' constitute evidence of the development of customary international law.[65] While it remains unclear who exactly is the other party in that 'global war' (any terrorist group or individual?[66]), more recently it has been suggested that the 'war' is being waged against 'Al-Qaeda, its supporters and affiliates'.[67]

According to a different legal reading espoused, inter alia, by the ICRC, the 'war on terrorism' is a non-legal designation that encompasses the range of steps that States may take – including diplomatic, financial and military – to prevent, stop and punish acts of terrorism. In legal terms, however, each situation of violence arising from the fight against terrorism must be assessed on a case-by-case basis to determine whether it constitutes an international armed conflict, a non-international armed conflict, or whether the situation involved falls outside armed conflict.[68] Thus, when the 'war against terrorism' amounts to an international

[64] See text of 7 February 2002 Order signed by US President Bush: 'However, the war against terrorism ushers in a new paradigm, one in which groups with broad, international reach commit horrific acts against innocent civilians, sometimes with the direct support of states. Our nation recognizes that this new paradigm – ushered in not by us, but by terrorists – requires new thinking in the law of war, but thinking that should nevertheless be consistent with the principles of Geneva.' Available at: http://lawofwar.org/Bush_torture_memo.htm.

[65] W.K. Lietzau, 'Combating Terrorism: Law Enforcement or War?', in M.N. Schmitt and G.L. Beruto (eds.), *Terrorism and International Law, Challenges and Responses* (International Institute of Humanitarian Law and George C. Marshall European Center for Security Studies, 2003), p. 80: 'In making these and related decisions about the treatment accorded our terrorist enemies, we are reminded daily that the current international law templates do not provide guidance clearly applicable to present circumstances. Simply put, we are operating in areas not addressed by applicable treaties and thus are participating in the development of customary international law'. It is submitted that this is a debatable proposition given the fact that the formation of customary law requires the widespread practice of States and a sense that such practice is followed as a matter of legal obligation.

[66] See, for example, the very broad definition of 'enemy combatant' in the US Draft Joint Doctrine for Detainee Operations, Joint Publication 3-63, Final Coordination, 23 March 2005, at http://hrw.org/campaigns/torture/jointdoctrine/jointdoctrine040705.pdf.

[67] As stated by John Bellinger III, US State Department Legal Adviser at a session of the UN Committee against Torture attended by the author on 8 May 2006 at which the Committee reviewed the US's Second Periodic Report to the Committee, see: www.ohchr.org/english/bodies/cat/cats36.htm. More recently, the US Supreme Court seemed to suggest that there was global armed conflict with Al-Qaeda, but not of an international character, to which common Article 3 of the Geneva Conventions applies. See *Hamdan v. Rumsfeld*, United States Supreme Court, 29 June 2006, 548 U.S. [Supreme Court Reports] 196, Section VI-D-ii.

[68] Report prepared by the International Committee of the Red Cross, 'International Humanitarian Law and the Challenges of Contemporary Armed Conflicts', 28th

armed conflict, as was the case initially in Afghanistan, persons captured must be accorded the status and treatment provided for by the Geneva Conventions. Some persons will therefore be entitled to be treated as prisoners of war unless a competent tribunal established under Article 5 of the Third Geneva Convention otherwise determines in case of doubt.

It is the status and treatment of 'unlawful combatants', persons who have taken a direct part in hostilities without being authorised to do so, that has generated the most debate since 11 September 2001.[69] It cannot be emphasised enough that the notion of unlawful belligerency exists only in international armed conflict. There are several consequences of unlawful belligerency under existing law:

First, it is undisputed that a person who takes a direct part in hostilities without being authorised to do so loses protection from direct attack during such participation and may be targeted.

Second, upon capture, such person may be detained until the end of active hostilities, subject to appropriate procedural safeguards. In the ICRC's view, his or her status and rights will depend on whether the criteria for 'protected person' status under the Fourth Geneva Convention are fulfilled or whether the person is covered by the Fundamental Guarantees provisions of Article 75 of Additional Protocol I, either as treaty or customary law. It should be noted that unlawful combatants may, under certain conditions, be deprived of some of the privileges of the Fourth Convention in accordance with Article 5 of that Convention.

Third, as opposed to lawful combatants, 'unlawful belligerents' may be criminally prosecuted and punished for mere participation in hostilities under the domestic law of the detaining State. They do not enjoy 'combatant immunity' from prosecution for such acts.

Lastly, 'unprivileged belligerents', like privileged belligerents, may be tried for any war crimes they may have committed.

Given the measures humanitarian law allows in response to unlawful belligerency, it is unclear what it is that is lacking for the effective prosecution

International Conference of the Red Cross and Red Crescent, 03/IC/09, Geneva, 2003, pp. 17–19.

[69] See K. Doermann, 'The Legal Situation of Unlawful/Unprivileged Combatants' (2003) 85 *International Review of the Red Cross* 46. See also, J. Pejić, 'Unlawful/Enemy Combatants': Interpretations and Consequences', in M.N. Schmitt and J. Pejić (eds.), *International Law and Armed Conflict: Exploring the Faultlines* (Dordrecht: Martinus Nijhoff , 2007) (forthcoming).

of the 'war on terrorism' when it amounts to an international armed conflict. The claim that the current laws of war are too restrictive in terms of
detaining States' ability to interrogate 'unlawful combatants' must be
rejected. The prohibition of torture and other forms of cruel, inhuman or
degrading treatment is a fundamental tenet of humanitarian law applicable to any person detained in relation to an armed conflict. Humanitarian
law does not prohibit interrogation per se; it simply upholds humane
treatment as a time-tested and non-negotiable standard in dealing with all
categories of persons deprived of liberty.

It is believed, under the already mentioned case-by-case approach, that
the 'war on terrorism' may in specific circumstances also amount to a
non-international armed conflict when the fighting does not oppose two
or more States. The current hostilities in Afghanistan – and Iraq – are
cases in point. The applicable legal framework is found in common
Article 3, other rules of customary humanitarian law, human rights law
and domestic law.

With respect to acts of violence committed outside situations of armed
conflict – e.g. the bombings in London, Madrid, Bali, New Delhi, etc. –
the ICRC's view is that these terrorist acts must be dealt with not by application of humanitarian law, but pursuant to other bodies of law such as
international criminal law and human rights law, as well as domestic law.
Importantly, this position is supported by the practice of the affected
countries who responded to those tragic events using the tools of law
enforcement instead of humanitarian law. Persons detained in relation to
the terrorist bombings were deemed criminal suspects, not 'unlawful
combatants'.

The 'war on terrorism' has given rise not only to controversies about the
legal qualification and the status of persons captured, but has also exposed
discrete issues about which international law may be – genuinely –
unclear. One such issue is the legal framework applicable to cross-border
operations undertaken by a State against a terrorist group or individuals
located in another State (sometimes referred to as 'extra-territorial law
enforcement').[70] An example is the US Predator missile strike carried
out in November 2002 that killed six alleged Al-Qaeda members travelling
in a car in the Yemeni desert.[71] While the attack was largely met with
silence on the part of many governments, the late Swedish Foreign

[70] Dinstein, *War, Aggression and Self-Defence*, p. 244.
[71] See B. Whitaker and D. Campbell, 'CIA Missile Kills Al-Qaida Suspects', *The Guardian*,
5 November 2002, at: www.guardian.co.uk/print/0,3858,4539624-111026,00.html.

Minister Anna Lindh publicly – and controversially – called it a 'summary execution'.[72]

Acts of violence carried out by the forces of one State on the territory of another without the latter's consent would usually be regarded as constituting an international armed conflict. Can the same legal assessment be made, however, when the intervening State's aim is not to threaten the host's independence or sovereignty but to neutralise a terrorist group operating from its territory? Leaving aside the *ius ad bellum* aspects of such a scenario (i.e. whether the intervention is justifiable under the right of self-defence), what is the legal regime governing the way in which force is used? For some commentators the Yemen incident was part of the 'war on terrorism' requiring the application of rules of international armed conflict. For others, because the Yemeni government gave its consent at least implicitly, it was governed by the international human rights regime.

Consideration is invited of another, hypothetical, example. If a State is unwilling or unable to deal with a terrorist group in its own territory and another State's military intervenes to remove the organisation resulting in an intense and prolonged campaign, how should such a situation be legally characterised? In the example given, there will be no difficulty in characterising the conflict as international if the 'host' State engages in the hostilities against the intervening State. If it joins the intervening State in battling the armed group the violence will constitute an internationalised non-international armed conflict. But what if the host does nothing at all? Will the intervening State's forces be guided by the rules regulating international or non-international armed conflict or will the rules governing the use of force in law enforcement apply? Alternatively, should each specific operation be legally characterised depending on the facts of the case?

Clearly, the protection of uninvolved civilians in the host State will differ greatly depending on what legal regime controls. Given the likelihood of increased cross-border operations of various kinds, it is submitted that this is an issue on which legal clarification would be both necessary and desirable.

3. Final remarks

Determining the status of an armed conflict, and prior to that whether a situation of violence can be classified as an armed conflict at all, is a

---

[72] Quoted in Howard Witt, 'U.S. Killing of Al Qaeda Suspects Was Lawful', *Chicago Tribune*, 24 November 2002.

preliminary and yet crucial step in establishing the applicable humanitarian law framework. The challenge is first to establish the facts on the ground and then to apply the law to the facts. The absence, in law, of a properly elaborated definition of the possible types of conflicts is an additional hurdle. It is also likely, however, that no definition would be able to encompass the reality of war and could risk creating a legal strait-jacket that would not be more useful than the currently existing criteria. While the Study does not provide a definition of the various types of armed conflicts, it should nevertheless significantly simplify the task of protecting persons affected by such conflicts regardless of the legal classification involved.

5

Combatant status

ANTHONY ROGERS

1. Introduction

The question of combatant status and what this means has been sub-jected to public scrutiny in recent years because of the plight of persons held by the United States under executive authority. While the intern-ment of civilians and prisoners of war in time of armed conflict is not a new phenomenon, the conditions of their internment being laid down in the Geneva Conventions of 1949, some of those at Guantanamo Bay seemed to fall into an intermediate category, being classed neither as pris-oners of war nor civilians and labelled as 'enemy combatants'.[1]

Normally, combatants are entitled to be treated as prisoners of war so, at first sight, this seems a little curious. But, in practice, things are not always as straightforward as they might seem. There is no doubt that an international armed conflict was taking place in Afghanistan in 2001. It was not uncommon for citizens of neutral, or even coalition, States to go to Afghanistan to fight with local militias against the coalition forces. Suppose X is one of these persons and he has joined a militia group and has been issued with an assault rifle. All dressed in the local civilian dress the group take part in an ambush of a coalition military patrol, by firing a rocket-propelled grenade, and destroy a military vehicle. Its occupants are unhurt, having dismounted in time. After a brief exchange of fire, X, who has not fired a single round, is captured. What is his status? Is he a

---

[1] The Court of Appeal (Civil Division) in London passed judgment on 6 November 2002 in the case of *R. (on the application of Abbasi and another) v. Secretary of State for Foreign and Commonwealth Affairs and another* [2002] EWCA Civ 159. Feroz Ali Abbasi, a British national, was captured by United States forces in Afghanistan. In January 2002 he was transported to Guantanamo Bay in Cuba, a naval base on territory held by the United States on a long lease pursuant to a treaty with Cuba. It was under-stood by the Court of Appeal that Mr Abbasi was being held by the United States as an enemy combatant, pursuant to a Military Order issued by the President of the United States.

combatant and a prisoner of war? Is he a civilian? Can he be detained? For
how long? Under what conditions? Can he be prosecuted for taking a
direct part in the hostilities? Under what law?

International lawyers will be familiar with the formulation of combatant status enunciated in Additional Protocol I of 1977.[2] Under the
Protocol, the key elements are that combatants have a right to participate
directly in hostilities and are entitled to prisoner-of-war status on
capture; even violations of the law of war do not deprive them of their
status.[3] It is implicit in this that combatants may not be punished for their
acts of belligerency carried out in accordance with the law of war. The
Protocol's approach to civilians is that they are protected from attack and
entitled to general protection against the dangers of military operations
'unless and for such time as they take a direct part in hostilities'.[4]
Additional Protocol I, of course, applies to international armed conflicts.
Treaties dealing with non-international armed conflicts are silent about
combatant status. It can be inferred from this silence that the status of
persons who participate in non-international armed conflict is governed
by the law of the State where the conflict is taking place.

Additional Protocol I, although ratified by many countries, is by no
means of universal application and several major powers including the
United States and Israel are not parties. The Protocol did not apply as a
matter of law to the hostilities in Afghanistan in 2001. That is one of the
reasons why a study of the customary status of some law of war principles
is necessary and why combatant status is one of the most important
issues addressed in the Study.

The purpose of this chapter is to examine combatant status under customary law and treaty law and to consider whether the relevant Rules of
the Study do indeed reflect the customary law on the matter. This chapter
also discusses current problems relating to combatant status that are not,
or not fully, addressed in the Study and suggests the way forward with
respect to controversial areas.

There are two aspects to the question of combatant status: (a) how is
a combatant defined and (b) what does it mean to be a combatant? In
considering this question, there are four separate, but related and overlapping, legal issues that need to be considered at the same time: the
principle of distinction between combatants and civilians, and the

---

[2] Additional Protocol I, Arts. 43 and 44.
[3] Except the requirement to carry arms openly during deployments and engagements, see
    Additional Protocol I, Art. 44, paras. 3 and 4.   [4] Additional Protocol I, Art. 51.

questions of civilian immunity, combatant status and prisoner-of-war status.

Before turning to the Study, it would be useful to trace the development of combatant status in customary and treaty law.

2. The development of combatant status

The history of the development of combatant status that pre-dates the modern codification of the law of war reveals differences of opinion with respect to the distinction between combatants and civilians, and the rights and duties of each category, that remain to this day. Some have sought the origins of combatant status in the mediaeval law of arms: the idea of an exclusive warrior class with its own rules; woe betide those who violated those rules or who, not belonging to that class, participated in wars.[5] At all events, by the middle of the nineteenth century it was generally accepted that war was a violent contest between States, fought by the armies and navies of those States; commanders being answerable to those States for the actions of those under command but having powers of discipline over their subordinates to ensure, among other things, respect for the laws and customs of war.

Dr Francis Lieber's famous codification in 1863 of those laws and customs, albeit in the context of the American Civil War, did not specifically define combatant status. However, Lieber did make a clear distinction between combatants and civilians: 'All enemies in regular wars are divided into two general classes – that is to say, into combatants and non-combatants, or unarmed citizens of the hostile government'.[6] When referring to what we now know as combatants, he wrote of the 'army', 'the forces', 'hostile army', 'armed enemies' or 'the soldier'; when referring to what we now know as civilians, he used terms such as 'non-combatants', 'unarmed citizen', 'inoffensive citizen'. The nearest the code comes to explaining the meaning of combatant can be found in Article 57: 'So soon as a man is armed by a sovereign government and takes the soldier's oath of fidelity, he is a belligerent.' Lieber considered that prisoner-of-war status was due to 'a public armed enemy' but extended also to 'those attached to a hostile

---

[5] See, e.g., G.I.A.D. Draper, 'The Status of Combatants and the Question of Guerrilla Warfare' (1971) *British Yearbook of International Law* 173. This article, and others by Draper, are conveniently reproduced in M.A. Meyer and H. McCoubrey (eds.), *Reflections on Law and Armed Conflicts* (The Hague: Kluwer, 1998). Future references to Draper in this chapter will, therefore, be to 'Draper, *Reflections*'.

[6] Lieber Code, 1863, Art. 155.

army for active aid', members of a 'rising en masse',[7] and 'citizens who accompany an army', such as 'sutlers, editors, or reporters of journals, or contractors'. Of civilian immunity, Lieber wrote: 'the unarmed citizen is to be spared in person, property, and honor as much as the exigencies of war will admit.'[8]

A number of important points emerge from this early codification. First, the term 'enemy' seems to refer to the enemy State as well as its inhabitants. Secondly, there is a distinction between soldiers, also referred to as belligerents,[9] and unarmed citizens. Soldiers may fight; citizens may not and must be spared. Thirdly, prisoner-of-war status and 'soldier' status are not necessarily synonymous. Fourthly, one finds reference to a category of civilians, members of a 'rising en masse', who are treated as soldiers (or belligerents).

Emphasis was placed, however, at this stage on organisation and authorisation. To be a combatant, one had either to be a soldier or a member of an authorised levy. Members of unauthorised, irregular forces were considered to be war criminals and could be shot when captured. It seems that this was the practice during the Franco-Prussian War of 1870 with regard to the so-called *'francs-tireurs'*.[10] The Institute of International Law's Oxford Manual of 1880 proclaimed that the 'state of war does not admit of acts of violence, save between the armed forces of belligerent States. Persons not forming part of a belligerent armed force should abstain from such acts'.[11] It is to be noted that here the adjective 'belligerent' is used to qualify the noun 'States' and this is, perhaps, the more modern usage.

Although, in the second half of the nineteenth century, the law seemed clear, there was some international sympathy (sympathy that was to re-emerge after the Second World War and again, later, when Additional Protocol I was negotiated) for weak States that felt impelled to resort to unorthodox measures to preserve their territorial sovereignty when confronted by powerful invading forces. The problem was discussed at the

[7] This seems to be qualified in Art. 51 as being limited to those rising under a duly authorised levy 'en masse' to resist an invasion.   [8] *Ibid.*, Art. 22.

[9] This is important when one considers terms used by legal writers such as 'unlawful belligerent'. However, nowadays 'belligerent' is normally used to denote a State participating in an armed conflict.

[10] *Oppenheim's International Law* (ed. H. Lauterpacht), Vol. II (London: Longmans, Green and Co., 7th edn, 1952), p. 256. Dinstein considers *francs-tireurs* to be individuals acting on their own, saying that they 'cannot legitimately conduct a private war against the enemy', see Y. Dinstein, *The Conduct of Hostilities under the Law of International Armed Conflict* (Cambridge University Press, 2004), p. 37.   [11] Oxford Manual, Art. 1.

Brussels Conference of 1874 and Draper referred in this connection to the negotiations between the supporters of the 'military school' and those of the 'patriotic school'.[12] Those in the military school preferred an exclusive definition of combatants, with severe penalties for the excluded if they dared to take part in hostilities. The patriotic school, on the other hand, considered it the duty of every citizen to rise up and repel an invasion.

This philosophical difference continued despite the development in the twentieth century of a treaty regime that tried to address the problems in this area and that also influenced the development of custom.

First in time are the Hague Regulations, 1907, which amounted to a compromise between the patriotic and military schools of thought. The regulations do not explicitly address the question of combatant status. They reflect the earlier drafts produced by the Brussels Conference of 1874 and by the Institute of International Law but tighten the requirements for the *levée en masse*. An important condition for that group is that they form spontaneously in response to an invasion. Article 1 of the Hague Regulations provides that the 'laws, rights, and duties of war' apply to (a) armies, (b) militia and volunteer corps fulfilling certain conditions (see below) and (c) to members of a *levée en masse*[13] carrying their arms openly and respecting the law of war. The word 'combatant' appears only in Article 3, which provides that the armed forces[14] of a belligerent[15] may consist of combatants and non-combatants. The assumption here is that some members of the armed forces will take part in the fighting and some will not.[16]

Being a compromise, the Hague Regulations probably satisfied neither the military nor the patriotic school and merely stored up problems for later. While allowance was made for irregular fighters, the conditions laid down were such as to make it difficult, if not impossible, for them to operate lawfully. During the Second World War, there were many cases of

---

[12] Draper, *Reflections*, pp. 198–199.

[13] General Sir Rupert Smith, uses this term to refer to the general conscription introduced by Napoleon, see *The Utility of Force* (London: Allen Lane, 2005), p. 30. The Hague Regulations refer, however, to inhabitants who spontaneously take up arms to resist an invasion. In this respect, the definition is not as strict as that of the Lieber Code, where authorisation is an important element. It seems that at the Brussels Conference negotiations of 1874, the requirement for authorisation was considered to be unnecessary, see W.E.S. Flory, *Prisoners of War* (Washington, American Council on Public Affairs, 1942), p. 32. [14] The term is not defined but seems to encompass armies, militias and *levées*.

[15] Again, the term 'belligerent' is used to denote a State rather than a person.

[16] It was left to States party to decide which members if its armed forces were non-combatant, so the category was not limited to medical and religious personnel as it is under Additional Protocol I, Art. 43, para. 2.

irregular forces, often supported by the allies, fighting against regular troops in German occupied territory.[17] This sometimes resulted in extreme measures being taken to counter the activities of such irregulars, such as the taking of so-called reprisal hostages, a practice that was condemned by the post-war tribunals.[18]

An opportunity to address the problem arose when the Geneva Conventions of 1949 were negotiated. However, the Geneva Prisoner-of-War Convention, 1949, as its title suggests, dealt with prisoner-of-war status and left untouched the rules on combatant status as set out in the Hague Regulations.[19] So the convention maintains the distinction between combatant status and prisoner-of-war status. There are categories of persons entitled to prisoner-of-war status, such as civilian 'camp followers' or merchant seamen, who are not combatants. Nevertheless, the convention's inclusion of members of organised resistance movements in the list of those entitled to prisoner-of-war status, seems to indicate an acceptance by States parties that combatant status is also due to members of resistance movements. This must be seen as new law that was introduced in the light of experience in the Second World War. Prior to that, resistance to occupation would have been regarded as inadmissible.[20]

By about 1950, therefore, and until the matter of combatant status was dealt with again in Additional Protocol I, one could say that customary law afforded combatant status to combatant members of the armed forces of a State party to the conflict, it being left to the State to decide which members of its armed forces were combatant and which were not. Further, combatant status was due to members of a *levée en masse*, provided the conditions were met of spontaneity, invasion, lack of time, carrying arms openly and respecting the laws and customs or war.[21] Finally, combatant status was also due to members of irregular forces and resistance movements but, in order to qualify as combatants, such persons had to fulfil certain conditions.

---

[17] Draper, *Reflections*, pp. 198–199.

[18] See, e.g., *US v. List et al.* (US Military Tribunal, Germany, 1948) 13 *LRTWC* 62.

[19] See Draper, *Reflections*, p. 199, who refers in this connection to the Geneva Prisoner-of-War Convention, 1949, Art. 135.

[20] See, e.g., Lieber Code, Arts. 52 and 85; Oppenheim, *International Law*, p. 258; Draper, *Reflections*, p. 199 comments: 'the "patriotic" school have won the point they lost in 1907, by the backdoor of POW status into that of privileged belligerency. It is a curious method.'

[21] It appears to this author that a *levée en masse* is unlikely to be able to prevent an invasion by well-trained and equipped opponents, at most slow it down to give the defending forces time to re-group or deploy.

Four conditions for irregular forces were laid down by the Hague Regulations: (1) to be commanded by a person responsible for his subordinates, (2) to have a fixed, distinctive sign recognisable at a distance, (3) to carry arms openly and (4) to conduct their operations in accordance with the laws and customs of war.[22] Draper added two more conditions, which he considered were implicit in the Hague Regulations, namely (5) dependence in some degree upon the government of the belligerent state and (6) a measure of organisation.[23] Dinstein has added a seventh, namely (7) lack of duty of allegiance to the detaining power.[24]

At first sight it seems odd to import conditions that do not appear on the face of the treaty text. But on closer examination of the whole of Chapter I of the Hague Regulations, it does seem that the two additional conditions proposed by Draper can be inferred. Article 2, dealing with the *levée en masse*, for example, talks about such groups not having had time to *organise* themselves in accordance with Article 1, which is the article dealing with militia and volunteer corps, so a measure of organisation was obviously expected of those corps. Article 3, in referring to the armed forces of the *belligerent parties*, seems to relate to any of the armed forces mentioned in the two preceding articles and to have been based on an understanding that they would belong to a belligerent party. Anyway, the point is put beyond doubt by Article 4 of the Geneva Prisoner of War Convention, which may be considered to represent customary international law.[25]

The seventh condition proposed by Dinstein is based on case law, principally the *Koi* case in the United Kingdom Privy Council.[26] In that case, Lord Hodson opined that nationals of the detaining power, as well as other persons owing it a duty of allegiance, were not entitled to prisoner-of-war status. While the opinion of the Privy Council deserves respect, it has always troubled this author, as it seems to undermine the humanitarian objectives of the law of war. There seems to be no reason in principle why a person should not be a prisoner of war and at the same be liable to

---

[22] Hague Regulations IV 1907, Art. 1. Insofar as Art. 4 of the Geneva Convention III can be said to alter the Hague Regulations on combatant status, one finds in Art. 4 another condition: (5) that the armed group concerned belongs to a party to the conflict.

[23] Draper, *Reflections*, p. 217. He goes on to express the view that conditions 1, 5 and 6 apply to the group collectively and that conditions 2, 3 and 4 apply both collectively to the group and to its individual members, see pp. 223–224.

[24] Dinstein, *Conduct of Hostilities*, pp. 36–7.   [25] Being binding on all States.

[26] *Public Prosecutor v. Koi and others*, [1968] AC 829, pp. 856–858.

trial for any offences he may have committed against the domestic law of the State to which he owes allegiance.[27] As this is a matter of international law, the Privy Council decision cannot be conclusive on this issue. Furthermore, it can have no more than persuasive weight in other jurisdictions where a different approach might be adopted.

3. Combatant status in the Study

There is no single Rule in the Study dealing with combatant status, so one has to look at various Rules to try and distil some principles. Rule 1 sets out the principle of distinction between combatants and civilians. Rule 3 defines combatants. Rule 4 defines armed forces. Rule 5 defines civilians. Rule 6 deals with civilian protection. Rule 106 deals with the requirement for combatants to distinguish themselves from civilians. Rules 107 and 108 deal with the special categories of spies and mercenaries.

Putting all these Rules together, one can make up a composite text on combatant status, as follows:

> *Definitions*
> All members of the armed forces of a party to the conflict are combatants, except medical and religious personnel. The armed forces of a party to the conflict consist of all organised armed forces, groups and units, which are under a command responsible to that party for the conduct of its subordinates. Civilians are persons who are not members of the armed forces. The civilian population comprises all persons who are civilians. Mercenaries are as defined in Additional Protocol I.
>
> *Operative rules on combatant status*
> The parties to the conflict must at all times distinguish between civilians and combatants. Attacks may only be directed at combatants.[28] Attacks must not be directed against civilians. Civilians are protected against attack unless and for such time as they take a direct part in hostilities. Combatants must distinguish themselves from the civilian population while they are engaged in an attack or in a military operation preparatory to an attack. If they fail to do so, they do not have the right to prisoner-of-war status. Combatants who are captured while engaged in espionage do not have the right to prisoner-of-war status. They may not be convicted or sentenced without previous trial. Mercenaries do not have the right to combatant or

---

[27] See Geneva Convention III, Arts. 85, 87 and 99. See also, J. Pictet (ed.), *Commentary on III Geneva Convention* (Geneva, International Committee of the Red Cross, 1960), pp. 418–419.
[28] Provided they are not *hors de combat*, see the Study, Vol. I, Rule 47.

prisoner-of-war status. They may not be convicted or sentenced without previous trial.

4. Discussion of the combatant status rules in the Study

The Rules thus define who is a combatant and provide some elements of what it means to enjoy combatant status. Combatants may be attacked. Although not specifically stated, the inference is that they are entitled to prisoner-of-war status on capture. They are required to distinguish themselves from civilians during attacks and preparatory operations. Otherwise they lose prisoner-of-war status, as do mercenaries and spies, but for these categories there are the rights of humane treatment and fair trial set out in Chapter 32 of the Study.

But there are two other important elements of combatant status that are not mentioned in the Rules, namely, the right of combatants in international armed conflicts to participate directly in hostilities and their immunity from trial for acts carried out during those conflicts in accordance with the law of war. Perhaps because the Rules are intended to be applicable in both international and non-international armed conflicts, these points are relegated to the note that precedes Rule 106.

The principle of distinction in Rule 1 is certainly one of customary law and applies equally to cases of non-international armed conflict. That is clear from Common Article 3 to the Geneva Conventions, which makes a distinction between persons taking an active part in hostilities and those not doing so.[29]

In choosing the term 'combatant' for both international and non-international armed conflicts, the authors of the Study explain that to use the term 'fighter' would be no improvement because this would translate as 'combatant' in many languages.[30] Nevertheless, the use of the term 'combatant' in the context of a non-international armed conflict will cause confusion because, as the authors indicate, in those conflicts this designation does not imply a right to combatant status or prisoner-of-war status.[31]

So there is a difference in the Study between 'combatant', which denotes somebody taking an active part in hostilities and 'combatant status', which implies more but does not apply in non-international armed conflicts. The authors state that the term 'combatant' is used in its generic sense to indicate persons who do not enjoy civilian protection.[32]

---

[29] The Lieber Code makes a clear distinction between combatants and non-combatants, see Art. 155.   [30] Study, Vol. I, 13.   [31] Study, Vol. I, 12.   [32] Study, Vol. I, 3.

Rule 1 is aimed at specifying who may legitimately be attacked.[33] It follows that, when dealing with a non-international armed conflict, the term 'combatant' should be understood merely as relating to persons taking an active part in hostilities and the term 'civilian' to persons not so doing.

The definition of combatants in Rule 3 is taken directly from Additional Protocol I[34] and seems, at first sight, not to reflect customary law,[35] under which a belligerent party can decide on the composition of its armed forces. However, it is clear that the authors of the Study accept that there is still latitude on the part of States to decide which parts of its armed forces should be regarded as non-combatant.[36] In practice, unless States widely publicise which members of their armed forces are non-combatant and provide some means of identifying them as such, all members of the armed forces, except medical personnel and chaplains wearing the red cross or red crescent emblem, are likely to be targeted.

Again, the definition of the armed forces in Rule 4 is taken from Additional Protocol I,[37] and so does not include some of the important conditions for combatant status on the part of militias and resistance movements that are laid down by the Hague Regulations. The authors of the Study conclude that the process of assimilation of regular and irregular armed forces, as exemplified by Additional Protocol I, is 'now generally applied',[38] but this author is dubious that this assimilation has reached the level of customary law. In the practice section of the Study, most of the military manuals cited are those of parties to Protocol I. Nevertheless, some of these still contain references to the conditions for militias and resistance movements laid down by the Hague Regulations and Third Geneva Convention. Of the non-parties' manuals cited, only the air force manual of Indonesia and the naval handbook of the United States seem to be based on an assimilated approach.[39]

Although the Rule seems to leave out the *levée en masse* completely, as that by definition is a body that has not had time or organise itself, the

---

[33] Hampson has suggested that a better formulation might have been: 'attacks must not be directed against persons entitled to protection as civilians' and that, in considering combatant status, there are three related questions: who is entitled to take part in hostilities, who can be targeted and what is their treatment? (Meeting on 13 December 2005, see note 95 below.)   [34] Additional Protocol I, Art. 43, para. 2.

[35] As reflected in the Hague Regulations, Art. 3.   [36] Study, Vol. I, 13.

[37] Additional Protocol I, Art. 43, para. 1. However, it leaves out the requirement for an internal disciplinary system, indicating that this is, in effect, part of the requirements of organisation and responsibility, see Study, Vol. I, 16.   [38] Study, Vol. I, 16.

[39] Study, Vol. II, Part 1, 88–97.

commentary makes clear that this group is also included as part of the armed forces,[40] though considered of limited current applicability. It seems to this author that the concept of the *levée en masse* is not yet a dead letter. The circumstances in Afghanistan in 2001, in Iraq in 2003 and Southern Lebanon in 2006 were such that a spontaneous rising to resist invading troops might have qualified as a *levée en masse* if the requirements of Article 2 of the Hague Regulations had been met.

The commentary is right to make the point that the test is whether a person has actually been drafted into the armed forces. Liability for mobilisation because a person is of an age for conscription does not make that person a combatant.[41] Thus it would not be permissible to direct attacks at all men between the ages of 18 and 50 on the basis that they were liable to be called up. The International Criminal Tribunal for the former Yugoslavia takes the view that the law of war provides for a presumption of civilian status,[42] something that this author is happy to accept.

According to Charles Garraway,[43] there are likely to be difficulties in practice, not with the notion of a distinction between combatants and civilians, but in the way they are defined. The authors of the Study have chosen a status-based definition, so that all members of the armed forces (except medical and religious personnel) are regarded as combatants; all others being civilians. That accords with Additional Protocol I. However, the view has been expressed[44] that the term 'combatant' should be defined according to conduct, so that all who take a direct part in hostilities are regarded as combatants. However, a distinction then has to be made between lawful and unlawful combatants[45] and that leads on to a definition based partly on status (members of the armed forces) and partly on conduct (other persons who take an active part in hostilities). Members of the military school generally prefer a status-based definition as this gives rise to fewer practical problems. In that respect, the Study authors' decision to follow the status route may be helpful.

The definition of civilians in Rule 5 again reflects the language of Additional Protocol I,[46] but, as previously mentioned, since customary

---

[40] Study, Vol. I, 386–387.   [41] Study, Vol. I, 14.

[42] *Prosecutor v. Galić*, Judgment of Trial Chamber, 5 December 2003, Case no. IT-98-29, para. 50.   [43] C. Garraway, in discussion with author.

[44] See, e.g., Dinstein, *Conduct of Hostilities*, p. 27.

[45] The debate on this point goes back to the Hague Regulations, where the status term 'belligerent' and the conduct term 'combatant' are used, see the heading of Section 1 and Art. 3.   [46] Additional Protocol I, Art. 50, para. 1.

law makes a clear distinction between the fighting forces and everybody else, this definition seems perfectly permissible.[47]

While the formulation of the principle of civilian immunity in Rule 6 probably reflects current international thinking and has been upheld before the Yugoslav tribunal,[48] it is a comparatively recent arrival to customary law. Practice during World War II seems to have been based more on the Lieber approach, namely that civilians should be spared 'as much as the exigencies of war will admit'.

Although the language of the requirement in Rule 106 for combatants to distinguish themselves from civilians is drawn from Additional Protocol I,[49] the Rule probably reflects customary law in that armed forces traditionally wore uniform and militias and volunteer forces were required at least to wear some fixed distinctive emblem to distinguish themselves from civilians. However, the idea that failure to distinguish leads automatically to loss of prisoner-of-war status does not seem to this author to reflect customary international law, or even Protocol I,[50] because it can be argued that persons entitled to prisoner-of-war status under the Geneva Prisoner of War Convention are always entitled to that protection, with the specific exception of spies and, for parties to Additional Protocol I, mercenaries. Since the law of war is concerned with making room for humanity, there should always be a presumption in favour of protection, either as a civilian or as a prisoner of war, when persons fall within the relevant categories set out in the Geneva Conventions and exceptions should be strictly limited to those cases where an exception is specifically stated in treaty law or is clearly evident in State practice, such as the case of spies.[51]

Rule 107, on espionage, reflects customary law as set out in the Hague Regulations. The language of Rule 108, on mercenaries, comes from Protocol I, part of which is incorporated by reference.

---

[47] Mettraux defines civilians as 'those who are not, or no longer, members of the fighting forces or of an organised military group belonging to a party to the conflict', see G. Mettraux, *International Crimes and the ad hoc Tribunals* (Oxford University Press, 2005), p. 120.

[48] See, e.g., *Prosecutor v. Galić*, para. 62.   [49] Additional Protocol I, Art. 44, para. 3.

[50] See, e.g., Additional Protocol I, Art. 44, para. 6.

[51] Hague Regulations, Arts. 29 to 31, impliedly denies prisoner-of-war status to spies. Additional Protocol I, Arts. 44, para. 4, 46, para. 1, and 47, para. 1 makes specific exceptions in the case of combatants failing to meet the minimum distinction requirements, spies and mercenaries.

5. Practical problems with combatant status and whether they are clarified by the Study

Stating the rules is one thing; applying them in practice is quite another. So long as combatant members of the armed forces do the fighting and everybody else remains peaceful, all is well. However, recent conflicts have shown that the law does not always provide the answers to problems that arise in the actual conduct of military operations. These legal problems tend to arise in two cases.

The first case is where persons who qualify for combatant status fail to distinguish themselves from civilians in order to secure a military advantage.

The second case is where persons who do not qualify for combatant status take part in the fighting.[52] This group can be sub-divided according to whether those persons distinguish themselves from civilians or not. Various terms have been used to describe these persons: unprivileged belligerents, unauthorised combatants, unprivileged combatants, unlawful combatants and even enemy combatants.[53] The trouble with these terms is the inclusion of 'combatant' or 'belligerent'. While this implies that they can be targeted, which is true, it does not mean that they have combatant or prisoner-of-war status. Another approach is to look at these people as civilians who have thrown away their protective shield, which is what they really are. To call them unprotected civilians would not be quite right because that would imply a loss of protected status under the Geneva Civilian Convention, 1949. It is probably better to avoid using the word 'civilian' because this implies, in the first instance, somebody who is entitled to protection from attack. For want of a better expression, this author will call them 'unqualified participants', that is, those who do not belong to the recognised armed forces of a party to the conflict or who fight on behalf of an entity that is not a state.

What are the legal consequences of being in one of these problem categories?

---

[52] The actual term used is to take a direct part in hostilities. Since there is considerable argument about what 'direct' means in this context, this author concentrates here on people who actually take part in the fighting.

[53] See D. Moeckli, 'The US Supreme Court's "Enemy Combatant" Decisions: A "Major Victory for the Rule of Law"?' (2005) 10 *Journal of Conflict & Security Law* 75, at 77.

Do members of the regular armed forces[54] lose combatant status if they fail to comply with the various conditions for combatant status?

On the basis of the Hague Regulations, one would be compelled to answer this question in the negative. The treaty conditions of a responsible command, fixed distinctive sign, carrying arms openly and conducting operations in accordance with the laws and customs of war, were attached only to irregular forces, *levées* and, by virtue of the Geneva Prisoner of War Convention, resistance movements. It was not until the assimilation process in Protocol I that there was any specific attachment of conditions to all members of the armed forces. That meant, for example, that members of the regular armed forces operating in civilian clothes would not forfeit combatant and prisoner-of-war status though, if they carried out offensive operations in civilian clothes, they might commit the war crime of treachery[55] for which they could be tried. If captured in enemy-held territory, they also ran the risk of being denied prisoner-of-war status and charged with spying.

Some consider,[56] however, that the conditions applied to both regular and irregular forces, citing the case law, in particular the *Mohamed Ali*[57] and *Quirin*[58] cases. In both cases the accused were members of the enemy armed forces but they carried out, or deployed for, sabotage attacks on the territory of the capturing State while in civilian clothes. The tribunals held that they were not entitled to prisoner-of-war status and were liable to trial under domestic law. As mentioned above, however, this author considers that the case law is, at best, of persuasive value and not conclusive on the issue.

In dealing with combatant status, Additional Protocol I sensibly concentrates on matters that the force, as a whole, has to comply with in order to qualify as a combatant entity: organisation, responsible command and disciplinary structure.[59] The question of individual failure to comply with the law of war and, in particular, the rule of distinction, is dealt with separately[60] but results in loss of prisoner-of-war status[61] only

---

[54] The term 'regular' is used here to denote persons who are members of the armed forces of a party to an armed conflict. It is not used to distinguish between, for example, full-time soldiers and those whose service is of a part-time, reserve or territorial nature.

[55] Hague Regulations, Art. 23(b).   [56] Dinstein, *Conduct of Hostilities*, p. 36.

[57] *Mohamed Ali v. Public Prosecutor* [1969] AC 430.

[58] *Ex parte Quirin et al.*, 317 US [Supreme Court Reports] 1, pp. 35–36.

[59] Additional Protocol I, Art. 43, para. 1.   [60] Additional Protocol I, Art. 44.

[61] Additional Protocol I, Art. 44, para. 4 refers only to loss of prisoner-of-war status, but para. 5 causes confusion when it proclaims that 'any combatant who falls into the power

in the extreme case of failure to carry arms openly in military deployments prior to attacks and in military engagements. Even then, such persons are entitled to equivalent treatment.[62]

Rule 106 of the Study provides that combatants who fail to distinguish themselves from the civilian population while they are engaged in an attack or in a military operation preparatory to an attack forfeit the right to prisoner-of-war status. However, neither the Rule nor the commentary provides for equivalent treatment.

What is the status of unqualified participants?

Are unqualified participants considered to be members of the armed forces liable to attack, or civilians who lose their protection from attack when directly participating in hostilities, or do they fall in some intermediate category?[63] The point is made in the Study that if they were considered to be civilians, there would be an imbalance if they were allowed to attack members of the armed forces at all times whereas the armed forces could attack them only when they were taking a direct part in hostilities. This imbalance would not exist if they were considered continuously to be taking a direct part in hostilities, or if they were considered not to be civilians.[64] The authors of the Study, reflecting practice, do not reach any conclusion on the status of unqualified participants.[65]

This author considers that there should not be any gaps in the protection afforded by the law of war and that an unqualified participant should be regarded as a civilian, so that, if he attacks members of the armed forces, he forfeits his civilian protection, possibly (see below) commits a war crime, or at least an offence under domestic law, if applicable, for which he can be tried on capture and his treatment should be in accordance with the Geneva Civilian Convention.[66]

of an adverse Party while not engaged in an attack shall not forfeit his rights to be a combatant and a prisoner of war by virtue of his prior activities.'

[62] Additional Protocol I, Art. 44, para. 4.

[63] R. Baxter, 'So-called Unprivileged Belligerency: Spies, Guerrillas and Saboteurs' 1951 *British Yearbook of International and Comparative Law* 322 at 328, considers they are an intermediate category. Dinstein, *Conduct of Hostilities*, p. 29, refers to an unqualified participant as an unlawful combatant, saying that 'he is a combatant in the sense that he can lawfully be targeted by the enemy, but he cannot claim the privileges appertaining to lawful combatancy. Nor does he enjoy the benefits of civilian status.'

[64] Study, Vol. I, 21.   [65] Study, Vol. I, 19, second para.

[66] That is the position adopted by President Barak of the Israeli Supreme Court in his judgment of 13 December 2006 in the case of *The Public Committee against Torture in Israel and another v. The Government of Israel and others*, para. 26.

Is combatant status lost through failure to comply with the rule of distinction?

It has been reported that in the hostilities in Iraq following the coalition invasion in 2003, Iraqi fighters disguised themselves as civilians, faked surrender in order to attack coalition forces and launched suicide attacks against them.[67] At the same time, questions have been asked about the legitimacy of US forces' operating in Afghanistan in civilian clothes.[68]

Additional Protocol I appears[69] to withdraw combatant, as well as prisoner-of-war, status from any combatant who fails, at the very least, to carry arms openly during deployments and engagements. However, the Hague Regulations made combatant status only for militia, volunteer and resistance fighters conditional upon having a fixed distinctive sign, carrying arms openly and complying with the law of war.[70] These conditions did not attach to members of the regular armed forces (armies). If the latter failed to comply with the law of war, they were punishable but did not lose combatant status.

Under customary law, therefore, if a person qualifies as a prisoner of war, he must be accorded prisoner-of-war status even if he has not distinguished himself from the civilian population.[71] So a member of the special forces, operating in civilian clothes behind enemy lines is entitled to prisoner-of-war status. However, he would be criminally responsible for any war crimes he may have committed in the process, such as treachery,[72] and if his mission were to collect intelligence, he would be liable to be treated as a spy, which would entail loss of prisoner-of-war status.[73]

---

[67] R.K. Goldman, The Legal Status of Iraqi and Foreign Combatants Captured by Coalition Armed Forces, on www.crimesofwar.org, accessed on 21 November 2005.

[68] W.H. Parks, ' "Special forces" wear of non-standard uniforms' (2003) 4 *Chicago Journal of International Law* 493.

[69] Additional Protocol I, Art. 44, para. 3, does not specifically say so; it states that a person 'shall retain his status as a combatant, provided. . .'. Nevertheless, para. 4 describes a person who has not complied with those provisos as a combatant and goes on to discuss loss of prisoner-of-war status. Para. 5 talks about loss of combatant and prisoner-of-war status and para. 6 states that the whole article is without prejudice to the right of any person to be a prisoner of war pursuant to Article 4 of Geneva Convention III.

[70] Hague Regulations, Art. 1; Geneva Convention III, Art. 4.

[71] Watkin disagrees, citing Levie and Rosas and the *Koi* case, see K. Watkin, 'Warriors without Rights', Harvard University Programme on Humanitarian Policy and Conflict Research Occasional Paper, Winter 2005, No. 2.   [72] Hague Regulations, Art. 23(b).

[73] Hague Regulations, Art. 29, states that somebody is a spy 'when, acting clandestinely or on false pretences, he obtains or endeavours to obtain information in the zone of operations of a belligerent, with the intention of communicating it to a hostile party'.

The situation is different for irregular armed groups. They have to do more to convince the outside world that they are qualified combatants and not just criminals or thugs. They do so by compliance with the law of war and particularly the requirement to distinguish themselves from civilians. This subtle distinction between regulars and irregulars seems to be maintained by Additional Protocol I. Despite assimilation of regular and irregular forces, and despite the threat of loss of prisoner-of-war (and possibly also combatant)[74] status if a combatant fails, at the very least, to carry arms openly during military deployments and engagements, the provisions are expressed to be without prejudice to a person's right to be a prisoner of war under the Geneva Prisoner of War Convention.[75]

The authors of the Study obviously disagree with what is stated above. Having assimilated regular and irregular armed forces in Rule 4, they provide, in Rule 106, for the loss of prisoner-of-war status where combatants fail to distinguish themselves from the civilian population when engaged in an attack or military operation preparatory to an attack. They comment[76] that:

> Although it is not specifically stated in the Hague Regulations or the Third Geneva Convention, it is clear that regular armed forces have to distinguish themselves from the civilian population during a military operation. Additional Protocol I recognises 'the generally accepted practice of States with respect to the wearing of the uniform by combatants assigned to the regular, uniformed armed units of a Party to the conflict', although the Protocol, like the Hague Regulations and the Third Geneva Convention, does not explicitly make this a condition for prisoner-of-war status.

They cite the *Swarka Case*,[77] where members of the Egyptian armed forces, who had infiltrated Israeli territory and launched an attack in civilian clothes, claimed that they were entitled to prisoner-of-war status because they were regular soldiers in the Egyptian army acting on the orders of their commander. The court, while accepting that neither the Hague Regulations nor the Geneva Prisoner of War Convention provided that the wearing of uniform by members of the regular armed forces at the time of capture was a condition for prisoner-of-war status, considered that it would be illogical to impose that condition on members of

---

[74] As previously noted, there seems to be some inconsistency between paras. 2, 3, 4, 5 and 6 of Art. 44 of Additional Protocol I in this respect.

[75] Additional Protocol I, Art. 44, para. 6.   [76] Study, Vol. I, 385.

[77] Study, Vol. II, Part 2, 2542.

militias and volunteer corps but not on members of the regular forces. The court concluded that the defendants were to be prosecuted as saboteurs. It seems that prosecution and defence may have been under the impression that prisoners of war were not amenable to the jurisdiction of the Israeli courts.

This author considers that the defendants had a good argument on the prisoner-of-war status issue because the treaties did make a distinction between the regular armed forces and other fighting groups and there were logical, historical reasons why that distinction had come about. However, the fact that they were prisoners of war would not have prevented their trial before the Israeli courts for any war crimes that they may have committed, for example, attacking members of the civilian population.[78] The exemption for prisoners of war from trial in respect of acts prior to capture relates to acts carried out in accordance with the law of war.[79]

Do combatants have to wear uniform to distinguish themselves?

It was probably presumed that army personnel would wear uniform because there is no reference to uniform in the Lieber Code, Brussels Project or Hague Regulations. The Oxford Manual required members of a national guard, *Landsturm* or free corps to wear uniform or a fixed distinctive emblem, recognisable at a distance.[80] The Hague Regulations required members of militia and volunteer corps to wear a fixed, distinctive sign recognisable at a distance. Gradually, with the extension of combatant rights to resistance forces and other organised armed groups, the uniform requirement has become diluted, open carrying of arms in engagements and deployments now being the lowest common denominator, though the drafters of Additional Protocol I obviously expected members of regular armed forces to wear uniform.

In practice members of regular armed forces do wear combat gear, a form of uniform that distinguishes them from civilians, when on active military operations. Whether members of irregular forces do so in practice tends to

---

[78] Although not directly in point, since it relates to the wearing of enemy uniform, it is, perhaps, worth mentioning the *Trial of Otto Skorzeny and Others* (US Military Court, Germany, 1947) 11 *LRTWC* 90. The accused were charged with the improper use of American uniforms during the Ardennes offensive in December 1944 by engaging in combat disguised as Americans and treacherously firing upon and killing members of the United States armed forces. The accused were acquitted for lack of evidence. Although one of them admitted firing several shots at an American military police sergeant, there was no evidence that the sergeant had been killed or wounded.

[79] Geneva Convention III, Art. 99.   [80] Oxford Manual, Art. 2.

depend on the circumstances. If they are better organised and control territory, fight alongside the regular forces or appear before a camera, they are
more likely to do so. If they are fighting a guerrilla campaign in enemy-
controlled territory, they are less likely to do so, but then they are at risk on
capture of being considered unqualified participants because of their
failure to meet the conditions laid down in the Hague Regulations. Even if
they do not wear uniform, irregular forces are legally bound when engaged
on military operations[81] to distinguish themselves from civilians in some
way that makes them visibly different from civilians.[82]

The authors of the Study do not express a clear view on the matter of
uniform. They cite various military manuals to the effect that it is 'customary' or 'usual' for members of the regular armed forces to wear
uniform. They consider that State practice indicates that 'combatants are
expected to wear uniform or a distinctive sign and must carry arms
openly'. However, they go on to cite, with apparent approval, the Israeli
military court in the *Kassem* case[83] in 1969. The court held that it was
sufficient for the defendants to wear mottled cap and green clothes since
this was not the usual attire of the local inhabitants.

This author is of the opinion that the Israeli military court adopted the
right test for a tribunal: was the appearance of the accused persons such
that they appeared to be combatants rather than civilians. The only
exception to this general principle relates to members of a *levée en masse*
or organised resistance movement, for whom the minimum distinction
requirement is to carry arms openly. The authors of the Study go further,
at least in the heading on page 387, by including members of liberation
movements among the excepted categories, though their inclusion is not
explained in the commentary. It is doubtful whether this last exception
applies to States that have not ratified Additional Protocol I.[84]

Is unqualified participation by itself a war crime?

The authors of the Study[85] rightly state that the lawfulness of direct participation in hostilities in non-international armed conflict is governed by

---

[81] Dinstein, *Conduct of Hostilities*, p. 37, considers that this means from the beginning of
the deployment to the end of the disengagement.

[82] *Ibid.*, p. 48, considers that in the recent war in Afghanistan 'the Taliban forces did not
wear any uniform in any sense at all, Western or Eastern (nor even any special headgear
that would single them out from civilians).'   [83] Study, Vol. II, Part 2, 2542.

[84] Additional Protocol I, Art. 1, para. 4, applies to a limited range of liberation conflicts and
this author is not aware that the article has been invoked in practice.

[85] Study, Vol. I, 13, 18.

national law. With regard to international armed conflict, however, they state that civilians who participate directly in hostilities may be tried under national law for mere participation in hostilities but do not specify which national law: that of the place of capture or that of the place of detention.

Most writers agree that unqualified participants may be punished. The question is: for what? The old books seem to suggest that unqualified participation is a war crime.[86] That was also the line taken by the US Supreme Court during the Second World War.[87] However, Baxter, writing a very influential article in 1951, took a different view, stating that unprivileged belligerency, a term he used to cover spies, guerrillas and saboteurs, deprived civilians of their protection under international law and put them at the power of the enemy.[88] Baxter concluded that 'only a rigid formalism could lead to the characterisation of the resistance conducted against Germany, Italy, and Japan as a violation of international law'.[89] But this was shortly after the Second World War and smacks of victors' justice. Prior to 1939, resistance to occupation would have been regarded as illegitimate. Baxter seemed to think that all unprivileged belligerents should be treated in the same way as spies. Under customary law, spies have had very little protection, apart from the right to trial before punishment.[90]

It is true that the US military tribunal in *The Hostages Trial*[91] equated actions by guerrillas with those of spies, saying that:

> By the law of war it is lawful to use spies. Nevertheless, a spy, when captured, may be shot because the belligerent has the right, by means of an effective deterrent punishment, to defend against the grave dangers of enemy spying. The principle therein involved applies to guerrillas who are not lawful belligerents.[92]

However, the tribunal went on to say:

> We think the rule is established that a civilian who aids, abets or participates in the fighting is liable to punishment as a war criminal under the

---

[86] E.g., J.E. Edmonds and L. Oppenheim, *The Laws and Usages of War on Land* (London: His Majesty's Stationery Office, 1914), paras. 19, 441, 444; Oppenheim, *International* Law, pp. 256–257; United Kingdom, *The Law of War on Land* (London, Her Majesty's Stationery Office, 1958) (written by H. Lauterpacht and G. Draper) paras. 88, 634. It is not clear if Greenspan subscribes to this view or considers that war criminality arises only if combat is conducted under cover of protected status, see M. Greenspan, *The Modern Law of Land Warfare* (Berkeley, University of California Press, 1959), pp. 53, 57, 61.

[87] *Ex parte Quirin* (note 58 above). See also Watkin, 'Warriors without Rights', p. 47.

[88] Baxter, 'So-called Unprivileged Belligerency', at 343.   [89] *Ibid.*, at 335.

[90] See Hague Regulations, Arts. 29–31. Additional Protocol I treats mercenaries as similar outcasts, see Art. 47, which denies them combatant and prisoner-of-war status.

[91] *US v. List et al.*   [92] *Ibid.*, at p. 58.

laws of war. Fighting is legitimate only for the combatant personnel of a country. It is only this group that is entitled to treatment as prisoners of war and incurs no liability beyond detention after capture or surrender.[93]

The two passages seem contradictory, unless the tribunal was suggesting that a guerrilla was in an intermediate category, neither a combatant nor a civilian.

Draper, writing in 1971, noted that there was some division of opinion among jurists as to the consequences of unqualified participation, but seemed unconvinced by the Baxter argument:

> On balance, the theory that illicit combatants may be killed after capture, as an act of warfare, subject to any restraint imposed by the law of war, is somewhat artificial. There may be some substance to the contention, and it may be more consonant with the war practices of belligerents, the official manuals on the law of war issued by States, and the decisions of national tribunals applying the law of war, that illegal participation in combat is a violation of the law of war exposing the offender to loss of immunity from attack, and, upon capture, to trial and punishment upon conviction. However, the matter is controversial, and there are certain passages in the classical writers on the law of war, such as Grotius, which lend support to the theory of 'unprivileged belligerency'.[94]

Unlike Baxter, Dinstein does not attempt to equate unqualified participation with spying. He explains that the law of war provides a combatant with a legal shield against prosecution in domestic courts for offences such as murder but that an unlawful participant does not have this protective shield. That is a very persuasive argument but it applies only in cases where the accused is subject to the law and jurisdiction of the capturing State,[95] which may not be the case where the accused is operating abroad.

It seems to this author that unqualified participants are not in the same position as spies. Spying is not a contravention of the law of war,

---

[93] Ibid.

[94] Draper, Reflections, p. 209. Grotius distinguishes spies from assassins, as the latter act treacherously, and considers that the sending of spies 'is beyond doubt permitted by the law of nations', see H. Grotius (tr. F. W. Kelsey), De Jure Belli ac Pacis (Oxford: Carnegie, 1925), vol. II, p. 655. However, this author would also distinguish spies from unqualified participants.

[95] Hampson suggests that domestic law could be extended further than is currently the practice. For example it could be made an offence under UK domestic law to attack members of the UK armed forces on duty abroad – F.J. Hampson in an intervention at a meeting on combatant status at the British Institute of International and Comparative Law on 13 December 2005.

but that law does permit the customary trial and punishment of those caught spying and the denial to them of prisoner-of-war status.[96] Unqualified participation is not directly prohibited by the law of war. However, the law of war does provide that only combatants have the right to participate directly in hostilities.[97] The inference is that others do not have the right to participate directly in hostilities and, if they do, they violate the law of war. Unlike the case of spies, there is no treaty provision specifically permitting the trial and punishment of those captured as unqualified participants. Is their violation of the law of war a war crime? Article 6 of the Charter of International Military Tribunal at Nuremberg defined war crimes as 'violations of the laws or customs of war' and then gave a non-exhaustive list of examples of such violations. A similar approach was adopted in the Statute of the International Criminal Tribunal for the former Yugoslavia but the practice has been to qualify 'violations' with the adjective 'serious'. That means that the violation must constitute a breach of a rule protecting important values and the breach must involve grave consequences for the victim.[98]

The International Court of Justice has identified the principle of distinction as one of 'the cardinal principles contained in the texts constituting the fabric of humanitarian law'.[99] So it is a principle that protects important values. Whether the breach would involve grave consequences for the victim would depend on the circumstances, but in the hypothetical case put in the second paragraph of this article, the potential consequences for those under attack are certainly grave.

The negotiators of the Statute of the International Criminal Court did not include unqualified participation as a war crime.[100] In order to secure a conviction under the Statute, it would be necessary to prove that the accused killed or wounded a member of the opposing nation or army and did so treacherously.[101] So the person captured in the hypothetical case put in the second paragraph of this article would not be liable to prosecution for a war crime under the Statute, not even for aiding and abetting, because there had been neither death nor injury.

---

[96] Hague Regulations, Arts. 29–31, as confirmed by Additional Protocol I, Art. 46.
[97] Hague Regulations, Art. 1, as confirmed by Additional Protocol I, Art. 43, para. 2. See also *Prosecutor v. Galić*, para. 48.   [98] See G. Mettraux, *International Crimes*, p. 48.
[99] *Legality of the Threat or Use of Nuclear Weapons*, Advisory Opinion of 8 July 1996 [1996] *ICJ Rep*. 66, 110 *International Law Rep* 163, at 207.
[100] According to one of the negotiators, in an email to this author, 'there was no proposal (including from the UK side) that this should be so and I think any such proposal would have been widely resisted.'   [101] Rome Statute, 1998, Art. 8, para. 2(b)(xi).

While the Statute's omission of unqualified participation is not con-clusive on the matter, this author has yet to meet a law of war expert (apart from the late Gerald Draper) who does not subscribe to the Baxter view. The patriotic school seems to have prevailed. The weight of contemporary legal opinion now seems to be that unlawful participation is not, by itself, an offence under the law of war and that unlawful partic-ipants would have to be tried under that law for any war crimes they may have committed in the course of their activities.

That is, of course, fine where such offences can be established. But if not, as in the example in the second paragraph of this chapter, it would seem to be a choice between domestic law, if applicable, or nothing. That is a pity because it appears to this author preferable to deal with violations of the law of war as matter of international rather than domestic law since there is universal jurisdiction for war crimes. Can the international com-munity really tolerate a regime under which States made it an offence under their domestic law for a foreign national to attack their troops who are fighting in an armed conflict abroad, especially in cases where the legal basis for their presence in those countries may be open to legal debate? The question goes to the root of State sovereignty and is better determined under international law.

Is the nationality of the captured person of significance?

If a captured person who otherwise qualifies as a combatant is a national of a neutral State, his participation in the conflict is not, of itself, an offence against international law.[102] If he is a national of the capturing State, however, he is liable to be prosecuted for offences, such as treason, he may have committed against the domestic law of the cap-turing State and which fall within the jurisdiction of the courts of that State.[103] However, his combatant status would protect him from prose-cution for acts of hostilities that were conducted in accordance with the law of war.

---

[102] Oppenheim, *International Law*, p. 261.

[103] *Public Prosecutor v. Koi.* See also, M. Lachs, *War Crimes* (London: Stevens and Sons, 1945), p. 26; Oppenheim, *International Law*, p. 268, who considers this to be the case whether the person has previously deserted from the armed forces of the capturing state or has never served in those forces. Greenspan, *Modern Law*, p. 62, considers that deserters from, or subjects of, an invading belligerent cannot claim belligerent privileges.

Does it make any difference where the activities occur?

Perhaps the place where a person carries out his hostile acts is of legal significance. If he is operating on the territory of the armed forces to which he belongs, or the territory of an ally, or on the high seas, he could not be subject to the domestic law of the capturing State, except to the extent that such domestic law had extra-territorial effect and he fell within that jurisdiction, perhaps as a national of the capturing power. The situation is different when the combatant acts in the territory of the capturing State, where he would be subject to the domestic law of that State, whatever his nationality.[104]

May an unqualified combatant be detained without trial?

The authors of the Study do not directly address this question, though the note that precedes Rule 118 indicates that in practice persons may be deprived of their liberty during an armed conflict in several cases: combatants who have fallen into the hands of the adverse party, civilian internees and security detainees, as well as those held to face criminal charges.

It seems to this author that, irrespective of whether an unqualified participant is put on trial, customary law does not prevent the capturing State from interning him if, and for so long as,[105] he poses a security threat to that State. Internment is recognised in both Geneva Prisoner of War and Civilian Conventions, which merely impose some standards of treatment during internment.[106] Presumably, the capturing State would pass the necessary domestic laws to enable this to be done.[107] Whether such a law were constitutionally sound or complied with international human rights law would be another question that lies outside the law of war.

Internees who qualify as 'protected persons' under the Geneva Civilian Convention are entitled to special protection under that convention. Protected persons are those who find themselves in the hands of a party

---

[104] That was the situation in the US case of *ex parte Quirin*, which concerned German saboteurs operating on US territory during the Second World War, or in the UK Privy Council case of *Public Prosecutor v. Koi*, which concerned Chinese Malays serving in the Indonesian armed forces, who were wearing civilian clothes when captured.

[105] Geneva Convention IV Art. 43, requires periodic review of the need for continued internment.   [106] See also Dinstein, *Conduct of Hostilities*, pp. 31–32.

[107] Ibid., giving the example of the Israeli Detention of Unlawful Combatants Law of 2002.

to the conflict of which they are not nationals.[108] However, that does not include nationals of neutral or co-belligerent States that maintain normal diplomatic relations with the detaining State, it being presumed that their interests will be protected through diplomatic channels. Those in this excluded category are entitled at the very least to the rights of humane treatment and fair trial.[109] Some elements of protected-person status can be denied in cases of activities hostile to the security of the capturing State; and the right of communication can be regarded as forfeited in such cases in occupied territory, especially those involving spies and saboteurs.[110] However, that does not mean that unqualified participants are generally not entitled to protected-person status.[111]

Does it make a difference if it is a non-international armed conflict?

In the case of non-international armed conflict, no provision is made in treaty law or by customary usage for combatant or prisoner-of-war status to be bestowed unless either belligerency has been recognised or the parties to the conflict have agreed to apply treaty law, for example, the Hague Regulations and Geneva Conventions. In the absence of recognition or agreement, members of armed opposition groups are simply subject to the domestic law of the State concerned and answerable for any violations of that law that they may have committed. Any claim that they are combatants legitimately engaged in an armed conflict will provide no defence unless the domestic law so provides or an amnesty is granted, which may occur if armed opposition groups form the new government at the end of the conflict. Similarly, members of the armed forces of the State have, in the absence recognition of belligerency or agreement, no claim to prisoner-of-war status, their status being governed by domestic law.[112]

---

[108] However, the right of communication may be suspended in the case of spies if it is necessary to do so for security reasons.

[109] This passage is taken from the author's article, 'Combatant Status', in R. Gutman and D. Rieff (eds.), *Crimes of War* (New York: W.W. Norton & Company, 2nd edn, to be published).   [110] See Geneva Convention IV, Art. 5.

[111] See, on this question, Baxter, 'So-called Unprivileged Belligerency', at 328.

[112] Of course, all detainees and captives would also be protected by international human rights law and the law of war would require them to be treated humanely, see, e.g., common Article 3 to the Geneva Conventions of 1949 and, in cases to which the Protocol applies, Additional Protocol II of 1977. An explanation of what humane treatment means in the context of a non-international armed conflict is to be found in M.N. Schmitt, C.H.B. Garraway and Y. Dinstein, *The Manual on the Law of Non-International Armed Conflict* (San Remo: International Institute of Humanitarian Law, 2006), pp. 14–18.

6. Final remarks

The Study provides a convenient digest of customary law on combatant status, with helpful discussion of some of the more controversial areas, but this author has reservations about whether the assimilation of regular and irregular forces has yet reached customary law status. Also he feels that it would be premature to close the door to the argument that members of the regular forces are entitled, as of right, to prisoner-of-war status on capture. In the absence of an 'equivalent treatment' provision for those denied prisoner-of-war status, their position, relying as it does on the fundamental guarantees in chapter 32 of the Study,[113] seems somewhat tenuous. Although this author considers it arguable that unqualified participation in hostilities is, of itself, a war crime, he recognises that this is contrary to current thinking among law of war experts and the Study reflects this.

Returning now to the hypothetical case mentioned in the second paragraph of this chapter, there is little doubt that X was taking a direct part in hostilities. The question of his status would, of course, depend on the precise facts, but, applying Rule 4, one might, depending on those facts, conclude that he was a member of the armed forces and a combatant. In that case Rule 106 would deny him prisoner-of-war status because he had not distinguished himself from the civilian population, unless it was found that he had carried his rifle openly and it was considered that, by so doing, he had met the distinction requirement. If denied prisoner-of-war status, he would not be entitled to protection under the Geneva Civilian Convention, being the citizen of a neutral or co-belligerent State, his only protection being the fundamental guarantees. That, presumably, would not exclude the possibility of internment,[114] nor of trial, if his acts amounted to a war crime under Rule 156. If one applied the Hague Regulations, the result would not be very different. He would probably not be classed as a combatant because of his failure to wear uniform or distinctive sign. He would not be protected by the Civilian Convention. He probably would be interned as a security detainee and, according to the prevailing opinion, liable to trial under the domestic law of the capturing State, with some protection under the law of war because of the fundamental guarantees.

It is evident that there are serious gaps in the protection afforded by the law of war to persons who have taken a direct part in hostilities. That is a

---

[113] Study, Vol. I, 389.
[114] The note preceding Rule 118 of the Study refers to 'security detainees'.

failing of the law, not of the Study, which is a reflection of the law. One would expect the law to provide some level of protection for everybody, yet nationals of neutral and co-belligerent States fall outside the protection of the Civilian Convention; spies and mercenaries seem to be regarded as pariahs, at the mercy of the capturing power save for the right of fair trial; many consider that unqualified participants are in the same position.

It seems to this author, at any rate, that there should be no such gaps and that every person detained in relation to an armed conflict who does not qualify for prisoner-of-war status should be regarded as a civilian and protected by the Civilian Convention.[115] To put the matter beyond doubt one would need a diplomatic conference followed by a further Protocol to the Geneva Conventions to that effect, but in the meantime, States could make unilateral declarations that they would treat persons in that way. To do so would not inhibit military operations and would make room for humanity. It would not preclude internment, within the terms of the Civilian Convention, if necessary, nor trial for war crimes or under domestic legislation, if that applied. But, at least, there would be clarity as to conditions of captivity.

---

[115] Others take a similar view, see, e.g., Watkin, Warriors without Rights'. See also D. Moeckli, 'The US Supreme Court's "enemy combatant" decisions', at 99, who comments, in relation to the US security detainees that it is 'exactly this creation of a special category of detainees, not envisaged by international law, that is at the bottom of the most important controversies surrounding the government's treatment of suspect terrorists'.

PART 3

Commentary on selected Rules from the ICRC Study

6

The law of targeting

MICHAEL N. SCHMITT*

1. Introduction

Targeting law lies at the very core of international humanitarian law. Yet, no treaty with universal participation exists setting out this body of law in any detail, as is the case, for instance, with the treatment of prisoners of war or protection of civilians in occupied territory.[1] The lacuna is unsurprising, for international humanitarian law emerges through a measured balancing of humanitarian objectives with the realities of military necessity. Targeting, the *sine qua non* of warfare, resides at the apogee of military necessity. This being so, States are understandably reluctant to accept constraints on their freedom of action when attacking their enemy.

The 1977 Additional Protocol I to the 1949 Geneva Conventions contains the bulk of generally recognised codified targeting norms.[2] However, standing on its own, the Protocol has seldom formally applied during an armed conflict. First, it binds only parties. Although parties numbered 166 by October 2006, non-parties included, inter alia, India, Indonesia, Israel, Iran, Iraq, Pakistan, Turkey, and the United States. Article 96 of Additional Protocol I provides that Parties are bound when fighting non-parties only in the unlikely event that the latter 'accepts and applies' its provisions. As a result of these two factors, nearly three decades after its adoption, Additional Protocol I has applied in very few major international armed conflicts, two exceptions being that in the Great Lakes region since 1996 (involving Angola, the Democratic Republic of Congo, Rwanda, Uganda, and Zimbabwe) and the 1999 NATO operations (Operation Allied Force) against Yugoslavia (for those

---

* The views expressed herein are those of the author in his personal capacity and should not be construed as the official position of the Government of the United States.
[1] Geneva Convention Relative to the Treatment of Prisoners of War (III), 12 Aug. 1949; Geneva Convention Relative to the Protection of Civilian Persons in Time of War (IV), 12 Aug. 1949. [2] Art. 49.

NATO members party to the Protocol at the time).[3] Instead, it is customary international humanitarian law which typically governs targeting.

This chapter assesses the general targeting Rules set forth in the Study. Rules as to specific types of targets are analysed elsewhere in this volume.[4]

According to the accepted prescription set forth in the Statute of the International Court of Justice (ICJ), customary international law is 'a general practice accepted as law'.[5] Therefore, maturation of a practice into a customary law norm requires (1) general State practice which is (2) engaged in (or refrained from) out of a sense of legal obligation (*opinio iuris*).[6] The practice in question, including that of States that are 'specially affected', must be 'extensive and virtually uniform . . . and should moreover have occurred in such a way as to show a general recognition that a rule of law or legal obligation is involved'.[7] Since targeting law involves prohibitions on conduct (non-action), rather than

---

[3] In fairness, States that are parties (and sometimes States that are not) often apply its provisions as a matter of policy even though they are not applicable as a matter of law. This was the case, for instance, during the 1991 Operation Desert Storm campaign against Iraq. The Eritrea Ethiopia Claims Commission has opined that 'key provisions governing the conduct of attacks' reflect 'customary rules' and that 'most of the provisions of Protocol I were expressions of customary international humanitarian law.' Eritrea Ethiopia Claims Commission, Partial Award, Central Front, Eritrea's Claims, 2, 4, 6, 7, 8 and 22, 28 April 2004, para. 23. This position has been consistently maintained in other Awards by the Commission related to the conduct of hostilities.

[4] See chapter 7, in particular. Similarly this chapter does not address status of participants (Rules 3–5, 9), distinction *vis-à-vis* civilian objects (Rule 7, since relevant issues are encompassed in the discussion on Rule 8), and the specific rules addressing precautions in attack (Rules 16–19, since relevant issues are encompassed in the discussions on Rules 15, 20, and 21). Finally, this Chapter focuses on those norms bearing on the attacker. It must be pointed out that defenders also shoulder obligations designed to safeguard the civilian population from the effects of attacks. Drawn from Additional Protocol I, Art. 58, these are set forth in Rules 22–24. The Study rules are actually less stringent than the Additional Protocol I norms in that the former require taking precautions to the 'maximum extent feasible', whereas the Rules sensibly delete the adjective 'maximum'. Rules 22–24 are accepted by most States and commentators as customary, although there are questions regarding whether a defender who fails to comply with the requirements necessarily accepts the results of an otherwise lawful attack and whether an attacker may 'presume' the defender is taking the requisite precautions when assessing its own duty to take precautions in attack. For a discussion of the attacker's obligation, see discussion of Rule 15 infra.

[5] Statute of the International Court of Justice, Art. 38(1)(b).

[6] See *Continental Shelf (Libyan Arab Jamahiriya v. Malta)*, Judgment, 3 June 1985 [1985] *ICJ Rep.*13, para. 27; *North Sea Continental Shelf* (Federal Republic of Germany/Denmark; Federal Republic of Germany/Netherlands), Judgment, 20 Feb. 1969 [1969] *ICJ Rep.* 3 and generally.   [7] *North Sea Continental Shelf*, para. 74.

courses of action that lead to the emergence of a customary norm, it is necessary to caveat this sweeping proposition. The fact that States occasionally engage in a practice need not preclude a conclusion that it is customarily prohibited. On the contrary, condemnation of the offending actions by other States may strengthen characterisation of the prohibition as customary. So too do attempts by the State actor involved to deny the action took place (or that it has been mischaracterised), claim mistake, or justify their acts on other grounds (e.g., as an exception to the rule).[8]

Both State acts and statements may constitute evidence of an accepted norm.[9] Military manuals are particularly germane when identifying *opinio iuris* regarding international humanitarian law, a point emphasised by the International Criminal Tribunal for the Former Yugoslavia in its deliberations.[10] Also relevant as persuasive (rather than determinative) evidence are judicial decisions of international and domestic tribunals, pronouncements by international organisations such as the United Nations, and the opinions of scholars and specialist entities, such as the ICRC. However, it is essential to keep practice at the forefront of any analysis, as customary law emerges *only* through State practice characterised by *opinio iuris*.

It is not the purpose here to offer an in-depth critique of the Study's methodology; other contributors cover that ground.[11] Suffice it to say

---

[8] As condemnation and denials may be for reasons not directly related to the legality of an act, they do not, standing alone, prove the existence of a customary rule.

[9] See, e.g., *Military and Paramilitary Activities in and Against Nicaragua* (*Nicaragua v. United States*), Merits, Judgment, 27 June 1986 [1986] *ICJ Rep.*, para. 190; *Gabcikovo-Nagymaros Project* (*Hungary v. Slovakia*), Judgment, 25 Sept. 1997 [1997] *ICJ Rep.*, paras. 49–58.

[10] 'When attempting to ascertain State practice . . . it is difficult, if not impossible, to pinpoint the actual behaviour of the troops in the field for the purpose of establishing whether they in fact comply with, or disregard, certain standards of behaviour. This examination is rendered extremely difficult by the fact that not only is access to the theatre of military operations normally refused to independent observers (often even to the ICRC) but information on the actual conduct of hostilities is withheld by the parties to the conflict; what is worse, often recourse is had to misinformation with a view to misleading the enemy as well as public opinion and foreign Governments. In appraising the formation of customary rules or general principles one should therefore be aware that, on account of the inherent nature of this subject-matter, reliance must primarily be placed on such elements as official pronouncements of States, military manuals and judicial decisions.' *Prosecutor v. Tadić*, (ICTY) Decision on the Defence Motion for Interlocutory Appeal on Jurisdiction, Appeals Chamber, 2 October 1995 (1995) Case No. IT-94-1-AR72, at para. 99.

[11] See, esp., chapter 1, Bethlehem, and chapter 2, Scobbie.

that the project captured little actual recent targeting practice, thereby necessitating substantial reliance on military manuals.[12] This is regrettable, for the authority of a purported customary law norm depends directly on demonstrated State practice.

True, military manuals often provide a useful indication of whether the issuing State believes a practice to be obligatory (or prohibited) as a matter of law. Yet, manuals also reflect policy and operational concerns. One must, therefore, be cautious not to infuse them with a normative character that may have been unintended by the promulgating States. Unfortunately, the Study seldom explicitly takes on the admittedly challenging task of distinguishing legal from policy or operational mandates.

Methodological issues aside, the Study does accurately and comprehensively 'codify' the 'received' textual content of the broad customary targeting principles. States are apt to accept most targeting rules as set forth. Some commentators have criticised the heavy mirroring of the Additional Protocol I text as a not-so-subtle ICRC effort to impose the Protocol on recalcitrant non-Party States.[13] Such criticism should not bear on the targeting rules, for most policy makers, commentators, practitioners, and academics recognise the Protocol targeting provisions as in great part reflecting customary law, often including them in national articulations of targeting norms. This is true even of fervent Protocol opponents like the United States.[14] Thus, the Protocol text constitutes a useful 'straw man' in the search for customary targeting law.

---

[12] Some practice from conflicts such as the Korean War, Vietnam War and first Gulf War is included. Moreover, it must be noted that the editors were constrained by the comprehensiveness (or lack thereof) of State practice reports provided by the national research teams.

[13] See, e.g., Y. Dinstein, 'The ICRC Customary International Humanitarian Law Study' (2006) 36 *Israel Yearbook on Human Rights* 1, at 14.

[14] For instance, the United States adopts in their entirety the Additional Protocol I textual definition of military objectives and the rule on proportionality. US Navy/Marine Corps/Coast Guard, *The Commander's Handbook on the Law of Naval Operations*, NWP 1-14M, MCWP 5-2.1, COMDTPUB P5800.7, paras. 8.1.1 (1995), reprinted in its annotated version as vol. 73 of the US Naval War College International Law Studies (1999) [hereinafter *Commander's Handbook*]. The US position on API is authoritatively set out in Memorandum for Assistant General Counsel (International), Office of the Secretary of Defense, 1977 Protocols Additional to the Geneva Conventions: Customary International Law Implications, 8 May 1986 (on-file with author) [hereinafter OSD Memo]. For an unofficial, but fairly authoritative, delineation of the US position, see M.J. Matheson, 'The United States Position on the Relation of Customary International Law to the 1977 Protocols Additional to the 1949 Geneva Conventions' (1987) 2 *American University Journal of International Law and Policy* 419.

This being so, if the Study's objective was to produce *textual* expressions of customary targeting law acceptable to States, it is a noteworthy success. In a sense, the Study represents the customary equivalent of a treaty in which imprecision is required to secure acceptance by States responsive to differing national interests.

But, if the objective was to accurately and precisely identify targeting *practices* reflecting *opinio iuris*, the Study has fallen somewhat short. It leaves much of the vagueness in the law of targeting intact by adopting the very text from which the uncertainty in question springs. Equally disappointing is the failure of the commentary to identify various unresolved issues with a clarity and depth that would sensitise practitioners to grey areas of the law. Although the editors were constrained by the extent and detail of the practice which was reported to them while conducting the project, these shortcomings are nevertheless problematic for practitioners charged with operationalising the Study's Rules.

Finally, the Study ambitiously purports to capture both international and non-international armed conflict norms, a requirement imposed on the ICRC by States when mandating the Study. With regard to non-international armed conflict, the task shouldered by the ICRC was especially daunting. It is in such conflicts that States are least likely to be forthcoming about their conduct (and most likely to distort their opponent's), least likely to acknowledge *opinio iuris* status, least likely to style any military guidance (such as manuals) as driven by legal rather than policy or operational concerns, and most likely to resist the characterisation of norms as customary. After all, since rebel forces are treasonous criminals from their perspective, States are understandably loath to constrain their own discretion over how to handle them. In light of the inherent uncertainty in any such endeavour, this chapter does not evaluate, critically or approvingly, the Study's claims that all of the targeting Rules analysed in the chapter (except, perhaps, Rule 21) apply in non-international armed conflict.[15]

---

[15] That said, in 2006, the International Institute of Humanitarian Law released the *Manual on the Law of Non-international Armed Conflict*. M.N. Schmitt, C.H.B. Garraway and Y. Dinstein, *The Manual on the Law of Non-International Armed Conflict: With Commentary* (San Remo, International Institute of Humanitarian Law, 2006), reprinted in (2006) 36 *Israel Yearbook on Human Rights* (Special Supplement) [hereinafter *NIAC Manual*]. Although not the product of an exhaustive study of State practice, it represents the sense of those scholars and practitioners participating in the drafting process as to the rules governing internal conflicts. Thus, the comparable *Manual* provisions have been provided in this survey's footnotes as an indication of the extent to which consensus on certain basic principles may be emerging.

2. The Rules

Rule 1

The parties to the conflict must at all times distinguish between civilians and combatants. Attacks may only be directed against combatants. Attacks must not be directed against civilians.

Additional Protocol I, Article 48: In order to ensure respect for and protection of the civilian population and civilian objects, the Parties to the conflict shall at all times distinguish between the civilian population and combatants and between civilian objects and military objectives and accordingly shall direct their operations only against military objectives.

Additional Protocol I, Article 51.2: The civilian population as such, as well as individual civilians, shall not be the object of attack.[16]

This Rule unquestionably represents accepted customary law. Indeed, the ICJ labelled distinction a 'cardinal principle' of international law in its *Nuclear Weapons* Advisory Opinion.[17]

Rule 1 distinguishes between combatants and civilians.[18] There is an ongoing debate over whether civilians who directly participate in hostilities retain their 'civilian' qualification or become combatants,

---

[16] For non-international conflict, see also *NIAC Manual*, para. 1.2.2: 'A distinction must always be made in the conduct of military operations between fighters and civilians.' *NIAC Manual*, para. 2.1.1: 'Attacks must be directed only against fighters or military objectives.' *NIAC Manual*, para. 2.1.1.1: 'Attacking the civilian population as such, as well as individual civilians, is forbidden.' See also Additional Protocol (II) to the Geneva Conventions; Convention on Prohibitions or Restrictions on the Use of Certain Conventional Weapons Which May be Deemed to be Excessively Injurious or to have Indiscriminate Effects, Protocol on Prohibitions or Restrictions on the Use of Mines, Booby Traps and Other Devices (Protocol II), as amended, Art. 3.7; CCW, Protocol on Prohibitions or Restrictions on the Use of Incendiary Weapons (Protocol III), Art. 2.1; Rome Statute, Art. 8.2(e)(i). In addition to Additional Protocol I, Arts. 48 and 51(2), for international armed conflict see also Hague Convention (IV) respecting the Laws and Customs of War on Land, Annexed Regulations, Art. 25; CCW, Protocol on Prohibitions or Restrictions on the Use of Mines, Booby Traps and Other Devices (Protocol II), Art. 3.2, and amended Protocol II, Art. 3.7; CCW, Protocol III, Art. 2.1(incendiary weapons); Rome Statute, Art. 8.2(b)(i).

[17] *Legality of the Threat or Use of Nuclear Weapons*, Advisory Opinion, 8 July 1996 [1996] *ICJ Rep.* 66 at para. 78. The other principle is 'unnecessary suffering'.

[18] Curiously, the dichotomy in Rule 5 is between civilians and members of the armed forces. This is a less exacting standard than civilians–combatants. For instance, medical and religious personnel serving in the armed forces are not combatants. There are also individuals who are combatants without being members of the armed forces. In particu-

albeit unlawful ones. The debate, which is the subject of a separate contribution to this volume,[19] need not detain us because both the commentary to Rule 1 and Rule 6 itself make the targetability of those who 'directly participate' manifest.

Of greater interest is the term 'attack'. Inclusion in Rule 1 marks improvement over Article 48's prohibition on directing 'operations', language which has sowed confusion. The Rule implicitly recognises that the principle of distinction applies only to attacks, i.e., that military operations not qualifying as an 'attack' are permissible unless they violate a specific prohibition found elsewhere in international humanitarian law. For instance, the principle of distinction does not ban psychological operations directed against the civilian population, such as transmitting broadcasts or dropping leaflets, that cause no physical harm.[20] Since Article 48 was nearly alone among targeting norms in its failure to reference 'attack', incorporation of the term into the foundational rule of distinction produces consistency.[21] Thus, Rule 1 is a useful refinement of Article 48's sometimes confusing reference to 'operations'.

Of particular relevance in this regard is the advent of technologies that allow offensive operations to be conducted against the civilian population without necessarily causing them corporeal harm. For instance, a belligerent could target the enemy's civilian population through computer network attacks designed to interrupt television transmissions, alter commercial e-transactions, disrupt air traffic control, or shut off

---

lar, 'members of militias and other volunteer corps' under Article 4A(2) are distinct from members of the armed forces under 4A(1) of Geneva Convention III.

[19] See Rogers chapter 5.

[20] That said, if the operation is intended to terrorise the civilian population, it is unlawful even though it does not rise to the level of an 'attack'. Additional Protocol I, Art. 51.2, and Study, Rule 2. An example would be a psychological campaign designed to convince the enemy civilian population that it had been infected with a deadly disease.

[21] Note that although Article 57.1 speaks of 'military operations' rather than 'attacks', subsequent sub-paragraphs specifically refer to 'attacks'. Additional Protocol I prohibit attacking medical units, combatants who are *hors de combat*, those parachuting from disabled aircraft, the civilian population and individual civilians, civilian objects, works or installations containing dangerous forces, objects indispensable to the civilian population, and non-defended localities: Arts. 12, 41, 42, 51.2, 52.1, 56.1, 54.2, and 59.1. Indiscriminate attacks and attacks against other than military objectives are forbidden, as are reprisals, including reprisal attacks against the environment; Arts. 51.4, 52.2, 51.6, and 55.1. Attackers are required to take 'precautions in attack' that might minimise harm to civilians and civilian objects, and defenders are required to adopt measures safeguarding them against the effects of attacks: Arts. 57 and 58. Finally, the rule of proportionality is framed in terms of attacks: Arts. 51.5(b) and 57.2(b).

vital nuclear reactor functions. The question is whether the principle of distinction bars such non-kinetic activities.

One school of thought argues that since Article 48 is not framed in terms of 'attacks', and because the operations are 'directed against' other than a military objective, they fall within the four corners of the Article's express prohibition.[22] It further notes that Article 52.2, which defines 'military objectives', speaks in terms of entities 'whose total or partial destruction, capture or neutralisation, in the circumstances ruling at the time, offers a definite military advantage'. Capture and neutralisation need not involve kinetic actions.

The opposing school notes that while Article 48 refers to military operations, all other targeting prohibitions are framed in terms of 'attack', a term expressly defined in Article 49 as 'acts of violence against the adversary, whether in offence or in defence'.[23] Even the ICRC Commentary to Article 48 explains that the term 'operations' 'refers to military operations during which violence is used', in other words, an 'attack'.[24]

It would be incongruent to suggest that a kinetic (violent) attack causing death (e.g., by gunshot) falls within the prohibition, but not a deadly non-kinetic operation (e.g., by causing subway crashes through manipulation of computerised switching systems). Therefore, the school's advocates claim, the reference to violence in Additional Protocol I and the Commentary can logically only be interpreted in terms of consequences. 'Attack' is merely shorthand for the types of consequences caused by violence, specifically death of, or injury to, civilians and damage to, or destruction of, civilian objects.[25]

Although it would seem that adoption of 'attack' in Rule 1 strengthens the hand of the latter school, it does not settle matters. Therein lies the weakness – or, more accurately, 'opportunity lost' – of the Rule, and of the Study generally. Although most commentators would agree Rule 1

---

[22] See, e.g., K. Dörmann, 'Applicability of the Additional Protocols to Computer Network Attacks' on-line article at 4, www.icrc.org/Web/eng/siteeng0.nsf/htmlall/68LG92/$File/ApplicabilityofIHLtoCNA.pdf.

[23] See, e.g., M.N. Schmitt, 'Wired Warfare: Computer Network Attack and International Law' (2002) 84 (No. 846) International Review of the Red Cross 365, reprinted in M.N. Schmitt and B. O'Donnel (eds.), Computer Network Attack and International Law (Newport: Naval War College, 2002), at 187.

[24] Y. Sandoz, C. Swinarki and B. Zimmerman (eds.), Commentary on the Additional Protocols of 8 June 1977 to the Geneva Conventions of 12 Aug 1949 (Geneva, ICRC, 1987), para. 1875 (hereafter Commentary).

[25] Injury would logically include severe mental suffering.

contains acceptable 'text,' it leaves unaddressed an issue of growing importance in twenty-first century warfare, the use of non-kinetic means of warfare against a civilian population.

In this regard, two approaches could have been adopted. First, the drafters might have crafted a rule setting forth the unambiguous, universally agreed to, prohibited practice. Since there is collective agreement that any operation directed at civilians which causes death, injury, damage, or destruction is prohibited, the Study Rule could have been crafted in such terms. Alternatively, had there been hesitancy to deviate from existing *lex scripta*, the commentary could have highlighted the ambiguity and indicated the points on which all parties concurred. Doing so would have provided some granularity to those tasked with operationalising the rule for the battlefield.

Rule 2

Acts or threats of violence the primary purpose of which is to spread terror among the civilian population are prohibited.

Additional Protocol I, Article 51.2: Acts or threats of violence the primary purpose of which is to spread terror among the civilian population are prohibited.[26]

There is little doubt that the text of this Rule is generally accepted as customary. However, it might be suggested that the Rule is slightly overbroad in terms of application because neither it, nor its commentary, answers the question of 'attacks against what (or whom)?'

The issue surfaced prominently, albeit indirectly, during Operation Allied Force, the 1999 NATO air campaign against the Federal Republic of Yugoslavia. During the conflict, NATO's air commander, Lieutenant General Michael Short, proclaimed: 'I felt that on the first night the power should have gone off, and major bridges around Belgrade should have gone into the Danube, and the water should be cut off so the next morning the leading citizens of Belgrade would have got up and asked 'Why are we doing this?' and asked Milosevic the same question.'[27]

---

[26] See also *NIAC Manual*, para. 2.3.9: 'Acts or threats of violence intended primarily to spread terror among civilians are forbidden, even if this is done for military purposes.' For non-international armed conflict, see also Additional Protocol II, Arts. 13.2 and 4.2(d) (collective punishment).

[27] C.R. Whitney, 'The Commander: Air Wars Won't Stay Risk-Free, General Says', *New York Times*, 18 June 1999, at A1.

Short's comments appeared to suggest that NATO should have struck targets that 'terrorised' the civilian population in order to weaken Milosevic's support base.

Although Short was advocating the targeting of civilian morale, the appropriate legal question was arguably whether the targets he cited were military objectives and, therefore, lawful to bomb. Short later made exactly this point at a 2001 Naval War College conference:

> I am not going to think that you are so naive that I do not say to myself and to my planners that this will also make the Serb population unhappy with their senior leadership because they allowed this to happen. But that is a spin off – a peripheral result – of me targeting a valid military objective.[28]

Short's refinement is partially reflected in the UK *Manual of the Law of Armed Conflict*. In commentary accompanying a provision identical to the Study Rule, the *Manual* notes: 'It does not apply to terror caused as a by-product of attacks on military objectives or as a result of genuine warnings of impending attacks on such objects.'[29] As the *Manual* drafters realised, civilians are often terrified by lawful military operations. To prohibit attacks having such effects would completely destroy the balance between humanitarian concerns and military necessity that underpins international humanitarian law. It is regrettable that the Rule 2 commentary failed to make this essential point.

It might even be claimed that inclusion of the term 'primary' is a red herring. For instance, consider strikes in the first days of a war. Can it be customary law that an attacker may not strike legitimate military targets in the capital's centre if it harbours the primary objective of shocking the civilian population into opposition to the conflict?

Focusing on the subjective intent of the attacker (why is the attacker striking), rather than applying an objective standard (does the target qualify as a military objective), imposes a standard difficult to apply in practice. In fact, an unlawful target tends to be a condition precedent to allegations of terrorising the civilian population. Consider ICTY case law. In *Dukić*, the accused was charged with having 'deliberately or indiscriminately fired on civilian targets that were of no military significance in order to kill, injure, terrorise and demoralise the civilian population of

---

[28] M. Short, 'Operation Allied Force from the Perspective of the NATO Air Commander,' in A.E. Wall, *Legal and Ethical Lessons of NATO's Kosovo Campaign* (Newport: Naval War College, 2002), at 19, 29.

[29] UK Ministry of Defence, *The Manual of the Law of Armed Conflict* (Oxford University Press: 2004), at para. 5.21.1.

Sarajevo'.[30] Similarly, in *Martić*, the offences involved rocket attacks against the civilian population in order to terrorise it.[31] In *Karadžić and Mladić*, the indictment alleges the accused fired on civilian gatherings, including sniping on civilians,[32] to terrorise the population, and in *Galić*, the accused was charged with, and convicted of, inflicting terror and mental suffering on the civilian population by shelling and sniping civilians.[33] These cases and the other 'practice' cited in the CILHS Practice Volume (II) indicate that the attacks contemplated by States *vis-à-vis* the prohibition on terrorising civilians are those directed against *unlawful targets*. Evidence of any customary prohibition on terrorising the civilian population through attacks on military objectives is markedly absent in the Study. Unfortunately, the matter was not analysed in the Study.

Rule 6

Civilians are protected against attack, unless and for such time as they take a direct part in hostilities.

Additional Protocol I, Article 51.3: Civilians shall enjoy the protection afforded by this section, unless and for such time as they take a direct part in hostilities.[34]

The issue of direct participation is of such importance that it is dealt with in a separate contribution to this volume. Therefore, this chapter addresses it in brief.

The commentary to Rule 6 deals with the issue of what conduct amounts to direct participation head on, concluding that 'a clear and uniform definition of direct participation in hostilities has not been developed in State practice'. Whatever standard is ultimately adopted,[35] it is in the area of leadership strikes that the issue typically surfaces in the

---

[30] Prosecutor *v. Djukić* IT-96-20, Initial Indictment, 29 Feb. 1966, para. 7.

[31] Prosecutor *v. Martić*, IT-95-11, Initial Indictment, 25 July 1995, paras. 16 and 18.

[32] Prosecutor *v. Karadžić and Mladić*, IT-95-5/18, First Indictment, 24 July 1995, paras. 26 and 44.

[33] Prosecutor *v. Galić*, IT-98-29, Initial Indictment, 24 April 1998, count 1; Judgement of Appeals Chamber, 30 November 2006, Judgment of Trial Chamber, 5 December 2003.

[34] See also *NIAC Manual*, para. 2.1.1.2: 'Civilians lose their protection from attack if they take an active (direct) part in hostilities.' For non-international armed conflict, see also Additional Protocol II, Art. 13.3.

[35] An ICRC/Asser Institute sponsored group of experts is grappling with the topic. See 'Experts Meetings Reports' at www.icrc.org/web/eng/siteeng0.nsf/html/participation-hostilities-ihl-311205.

public domain. Unfortunately, neither the Rule 6 commentary nor the Practice Volume (II) mention leadership strikes.

Operation Iraqi Freedom demonstrated their centrality in modern warfare.[36] Indeed, the first air sortie was an attack on Saddam Hussein. Over the course of the conflict, the Coalition conducted some 50 decapitation missions, all unsuccessful. Not every targeted individual was a combatant, and there is some question whether all of the rest were directly participating in hostilities.[37]

Lawful targeting requires that the leaders in question either qualify as combatants[38] or as civilians directly participating in hostilities. The distinction is one of status versus activity. The former may be lawfully targeted simply by virtue of the fact that they meet the requirements of combatancy, for instance by being members of the armed forces (other than religious and medical personnel). Whether they actually engage in any combat-related activity is irrelevant.

Sometimes, the status determination for leaders is complicated. For instance, is the US President, who constitutionally serves as 'Commander-in-Chief', a combatant? What about a royal family, members of which occupy purely ceremonial positions in the nation's military? The Study nowhere addresses leadership qualification as combatants.

But even more complex is the issue of direct participation by civilian leadership. Do parliamentarians directly participate through control over the military budget or approval of senior officer promotions? Are civilian leaders who direct the production of war materiel direct participants? To what extent does involvement in the acquisition, production, and

---

[36] Although, OIF post-dated the practice survey underpinning the Study, decapitation operations were certainly not a new phenomenon. In Afghanistan, Coalition forces in Operation Enduring Freedom actively sought to kill the Taliban leader, Mullah Omar. Earlier, during Operation Allied Force, NATO bombed Milošević's residence, as well as government ministries other than the Ministry of Defence. Perhaps most famously, the US Air Force Chief of Staff, General Michael Dugan, was unceremoniously fired after he correctly suggested that killing Saddam Hussein was an objective of the Operation Desert Storm air campaign.

[37] Targeting individuals during an armed conflict must be distinguished from assassination. In international humanitarian law terms, assassination is the 'treacherous' killing or wounding the enemy, as in feigning protected status to attack a specific individual: Hague Regulations IV, Art. 23(b). As a method of warfare, it was forbidden as early as 1863. War Department, Adjutant General's Office, Instructions for the Government of Armies of the United States in the Field, General Orders No. 100 (Lieber Code), Art. 148, 24 April 1863. On assassination in armed conflict, see M.N. Schmitt, 'State Sponsored Assassination in International and Domestic Law' (1992) 17 Yale Journal of International Law 609; and W. Hays Parks, 'Memorandum of Law: Executive Order 1233 and Assassination' (1989) The Army Lawyer 4.   [38] Study, Rules 3 and 4.

dissemination of intelligence render them targetable? Does the senior leadership of a political party exercising influence over national strategy and policy, as the Iraqi Baath Party did, qualify? Does it matter whether the activities in question affect the strategic, operational or tactical levels of the conflict?

This is not the place to resolve these and the myriad other scenarios involving possible direct participation by leaders.[39] However, neither Rule 6 nor the accompanying commentary set forth any constructive standard of general *practice* accepted as customary that might speak to such matters.[40]

Also problematic is retention of the 'for such time' phrase from Additional Protocol I. The commentary fails to fully address a long-standing and critical debate over its scope. In the *Commentary* to Article 51.3, the ICRC notes that several delegations expressed their view that direct participation includes 'preparations for combat and the return from combat', but that '[o]nce he ceases to participate, the civilian regains his right to the protection'.[41] The United States does not accept Article 51.3 as customary, in great part due to the 'for such time' clause.[42] Indeed, the clause is absent in the direct participation provision of the US *Commander's Handbook on the Law of Naval Operations*, the most current of the US international humanitarian law manuals.[43]

The 'revolving door' debate, as it has become known, is usually illustrated by the notional civilian who is a guerrilla by night and a farmer by day. Can it be that the opposing side must wait until the guerrilla leaves his home to attack him before mounting a strike to kill him? Does he really reacquire immunity from attack upon reaching home? Although such contentions fly in the face of common sense grounded in the realities of armed conflict, many in the international legal community embrace this interpretation of direct participation's temporal component. Others argue, in contrast, that a civilian who directly participates in hostilities remains a valid military objective until unambiguously opting out of hostilities through extended non-participation or an affirmative

---

[39] On the subject see, M.N. Schmitt, 'Humanitarian Law and Direct Participation in Hostilities by Private Contractors or Civilian Employees' (2005) 5 *Chicago Journal of International Law* 511, in which it is suggested that to constitute direct participation, the leaders in question must engage in decision-making regarding military operations at the tactical or operational level.

[40] The commentary does note that there is consensus over the use of weapons or other means to commit acts of violence, but it goes no further and is, therefore, of little use in analysing leadership strikes.   [41] *Commentary*, paras. 1943 and 1944.

[42] OSD Memo.   [43] *Commander's Handbook*, para. 11.3.

act of withdrawal. They point out that guerrillas are often most vulnerable to attack when distant from the battlefield.[44] To allow the 'for such time' proviso to immunise them during this time would be absurd, so the argument goes.

On a more positive note, the Study has not adopted the requirement in Additional Protocol I, Article 50.1 that '[i]n case of doubt whether a person is a civilian, that person shall be considered to be a civilian'. Its discussion of the matter in the Rule 6 commentary may appear unusual because the status of an individual as a civilian is governed by Rule 5. However, the real issue is one of force protection, i.e., when can an individual possibly posing a threat be considered either a combatant or direct participant and be attacked to defend oneself or one's forces? The United Kingdom, for instance, attached a statement to its ratification of the Protocol in 1998 to the effect that the presumption does not 'overrid[e] a commander's duty to protect the safety of troops under his command or to preserve his military situation'.[45] Of course, there is a point at which so much doubt exists that it is unreasonable to act, but the bald statement 'in case of doubt' contained in Article 50.1, in the absence of any qualification, does not reflect customary law. Its omission in the Study demonstrates that the ICRC has not blindly followed the language of Protocol I, but rather has at times taken appropriate account of disagreement over certain of its provisions.

Rule 8

In so far as objects are concerned, military objectives are limited to those objects which by their nature, location, purpose or use make an effective contribution to military action and whose partial or total destruction, capture or neutralisation, in the circumstances ruling at the time, offers a definite military advantage.

Additional Protocol I, Article 52.2: In so far as objects are concerned, military objectives are limited to those objects which by their nature, location, purpose or use make an effective contribution to military action and whose

---

[44] Since they are usually out-gunned, guerrilla forces often use stealth to conduct their attacks (e.g., ambushes) and quickly retreat from the fray. In fact, as demonstrated by the use of improvised explosive devices (IEDs) to conduct roadside bombings in Iraq, guerrillas may be all but invisible at the time of attack.

[45] UK Statement on Ratification of Additional Protocol I, 28 Jan. 1998, para. (h), reprinted in A. Roberts and R. Guelff (eds.), *Documents on the Laws of War* (Oxford University Press, 3rd edn, 2000), pp. 510–512.

total or partial destruction, capture or neutralisation, in the circumstances ruling at the time, offers a definite military advantage.[46]

Rule 7 provides that '[t]he parties to the conflict must at all times distinguish between civilian objects and military objectives. Attacks may only be directed against military objectives. Attacks must not be directed against civilian objects.' It is a 'cardinal principle' of international humanitarian law according to the ICJ and its characterisation as customary cannot be seriously doubted.[47]

But Rule 8 holds the key to the prohibition. As noted in Article 52.1 of Additional Protocol I, '[c]ivilian objects are all objects which are not military objectives'. Since the identification of civilian objects occurs through exclusion as a military objective, it is the definition of military objectives that proves determinative. The formula set forth in Rule 8 is universally accepted, a fact aptly demonstrated in the Rule's commentary and the Practice Volume (II).

The commentary usefully discusses a number of relevant definitional concerns. For instance, it notes that many States take the position that the military advantage to be anticipated from an attack is that of the attack as a whole, not any particular component thereof. The United Kingdom did so both when ratifying Additional Protocol I[48] and in its *Manual*.[49]

---

[46] For non-international conflict, see also *NIAC Manual*, 1.1.4: 'Military objectives are objects which by their nature, location, purpose, or use make an effective contribution to military action and whose total or partial destruction, capture, or neutralisation, in the circumstances at the time, offers a definite military advantage.' See also CCW, amended Protocol II, Art. 2.6 (mines, booby traps, and other devices); CCW, Protocol III, Art. 1.3 (mines, booby traps, and other devices); Second Protocol to the Hague Convention of 1954 for Protection of Cultural Property in Event of Armed Conflict, 26 March 1999, Art. 1(f) (for cultural property).

For international armed conflict, see also CCW, Protocol II, Art. 2.4 (mines, booby traps, and other devices); CCW, amended Protocol II, Art. 2.6 (mines, booby traps, and other devices); CCW, Protocol III, Art. 1.3 (incendiary weapons); Second Protocol to the Hague Convention of 1954, Art. 1(f) (for cultural property).

[47] *Nuclear Weapons* (note 17 above), para. 78. For international armed conflict, see also Additional Protocol I, Arts. 48 and 52.2; CCW, amended Protocol II, Art. 2.6 (mines, booby traps, and other devices); CCW, Protocol III, Art. 2.1 (incendiary weapons); Rome Statute, Art. 8(2)(b)(ii). For non-international armed conflict, see *NIAC Manual*, 1.2.2; CCW, amended Protocol II, Art. 3.7 (mines, booby traps, and other devices); CCW, Protocol III, Art. 2.1 (incendiary weapons).

[48] 'In the view of the United Kingdom, the military advantage anticipated from an attack is intended to refer to the advantage anticipated from the attack considered as a whole and not only from isolated or particular parts of the attack.' UK Statement on Ratification, para. (i). Note that the statement referred to Articles 51 and 57 (which address proportionality).

[49] *UK Manual*, para. 5.4.4j.

Although the matter usually arises in the context of proportionality (discussed below), it does bear on the status of objects as military objectives. Consider, for example, a bridge or other line of communication. Even though it may lie far from the intended location of a general attack, the attacker might still strike it as a ruse designed to deceive the enemy into believing the attack will fall in that area. In such a case, the attack results in definite military advantage in the context of the overall operation, which it might (arguably) not do if the bridge strike was assessed in isolation. Highlighting this position correctly precludes any assertion that a narrower interpretation is customary.

Also useful is the acknowledgement that for some States, including the United States,[50] anticipated military advantage can include increased security (force protection) for the attacking or other friendly forces. Again, while primarily bearing on proportionality, the clarification can also relate to military objective status. For instance, the destruction of residential buildings next to an encampment might offer a definite military advantage if they would otherwise be likely to be used for sniping positions. That certain States embrace this position bars any argument that force protection relevance does not affect an object's status as a military objective.

A third positive aspect of the commentary deals with risk to civilians. There is an increasing tendency to argue that certain targets are off-limits because of proximity to civilians. Typically, such claims are made in the context of urban warfare. The commentary correctly points out that various States expressly note that the presence of civilians in or near a military objective does not render it immune from attack. Both the US and UK manuals make this point.[51] It cannot be otherwise. The very existence of a proportionality rule eviscerates claims to the contrary; after all, there would be no need for such a rule if the presence of civilians blocked characterisation of an object as a military objective.[52]

Surprisingly, the Study devotes only slight attention to the four criteria of nature, location, purpose, or use – despite the existence of numerous debates surrounding their application (although Volume II does catalogue practice according to the categories). As an example, disagreement

---

50 *Commander's Handbook*, para. 8.1.1.
51 *Commander's Handbook*, paras. 11.2 and 11.3; *UK Manual*, para. 5.4.4b.
52 The Study cites workers in a munitions factory to illustrate the point. Unfortunately, some disagreement still persists within the international humanitarian law community over whether munitions workers fully qualify as civilians or have some lesser status (e.g., quasi combatants).

exists over whether lines of communication such as highways and rail lines are military objectives by nature or only through use or purpose. One distinguished commentator has suggested that '[a]rteries of transportation of strategic importance, principally mainline railroads and rail marshalling yards, major motorways (like the interstate roads in the USA, and the Autobahnen in Germany and the autostradas in Italy), [and] navigable rivers and canals (including the tunnels and bridges of railways and truck roads)' qualify as military objectives by nature.[53] Others assert that they only become military objectives through use (by military forces), purpose (future use), or location (relevant to military operations), i.e., on a case-by-case basis.[54] Objects evoking the same sort of disagreement might include, inter alia, civilian airfields capable of handling military aircraft, railway rolling stock, electrical grids, and port facilities.

The debate is not academic. During Operation Allied Force, NATO conducted air strikes against bridges and lines of communication that were distant from the hostilities in Kosovo and which arguably had little connection to either the hostilities there or to Yugoslav air defences. If such facilities are military objectives by nature, they were per se legitimate targets for attack. However, if not, they could not qualify as military objectives absent some specific nexus to the hostilities.[55]

Another issue left unaddressed is the degree of certainty necessary with regard to an object's purpose. The ICRC Commentary to Article 52 notes that purpose 'is concerned with the intended future use of an object'.[56] But how certain must be an attacker of the intended future military use of an object that was not designed for military purposes? In some cases, future use is self-evident: consider a public decision to employ the national airlines to transport troops. But in many others, the enemy's future plans may be less evident. It has been suggested that '[p]urpose is predicated on intentions known to guide the adversary, and not on those figured out hypothetically in contingency plans based on a "worst-case scenario"'.[57] But others would contest a requirement of actual knowledge, urging instead a standard of reasonable reaction to reasonably reliable

[53] Y. Dinstein, *The Conduct of Hostilities Under the Law of International Armed Conflict* (Cambridge University Press, 2004), pp. 89 and 92.
[54] For instance, they would contest a claim that British military operations in southern Iraq rendered all Scottish motorways legitimate targets.
[55] For an argument that the latter position is accurate, see M. Bothe, 'The Protection of the Civilian Population and NATO Bombing on Yugoslavia: Comments on a Report to the Prosecutor of the ICTY' (2001) 2 *European Journal of International Law* 531, at 534.
[56] *Commentary*, para. 2022.   [57] Dinstein, *The Conduct of Hostilities*, p. 90.

evidence of enemy intentions.[58] This might sometimes require worst-case planning because opportunities to preclude worst-case scenarios can be fleeting. Indeed, it could be argued that the purpose criterion is met even in the absence of evidence of enemy intent if the assumed enemy course of action is that which any reasonable war fighter would take.

The dominant controversy surrounding qualification as a military objective is the US notion of 'war-sustaining'.[59] In the *Commander's Handbook*, the United States defines military objectives as 'combatants and those objects which, by their nature, location, purpose, or use, effectively contribute to the enemy's war-fighting or war-sustaining capability and whose total or partial destruction, capture, or neutralisation would constitute a definite military advantage to the attacker under the circumstances at the time of the attack'.[60] It notes that '[e]conomic targets of the enemy that indirectly but effectively support and sustain the enemy's war-fighting capability may also be attacked'.[61] Footnotes characterise this as 'a statement of customary law', using the example of cotton export revenues funding the Confederate war effort during the US Civil War.[62] The contemporary illustration would be reliance on a single export, such as oil.

The commentary creates the impression that only the US takes this position, even though the Practice Volume (II) indicates that other countries, such as Ecuador (which adopts the US manual *in toto*) and New Zealand, employ analogous language in their manuals.[63] Moreover, there is ample practice of striking economic targets in past conflicts, some of which is cited in the Practice Volume (II), which devotes a section to 'economic installations'. In contemporary practice, for instance, oil refineries were targeted during both Operations Desert Storm in 1991 and Allied Force in 1999.

---

[58] M.N. Schmitt, 'Fault Lines in the Law of Attack,' in S. Breau and A. Jachec-Neale (eds.), *Testing the Boundaries of International Humanitarian Law* (London: British Institute of International and Comparative Law, 2006), at 277, 280.

[59] For an influential early criticism of the narrow approach, see W. Hays Parks, 'Air War and the Law of War' (1990) 32 *Air Force Law Review* 1, at 135–145.

[60] *Commander's Handbook*, para. 8.1.1.   [61] *Commander's Handbook*, para. 8.1.1.

[62] *Commander's Handbook*, para. 8.1.1, notes 10 and 11, citing General Counsel, Department of Defense, letter of 22 Sept. 1972, reprinted in (1973) 67 *American Journal of International Law* 123–124. US joint doctrine reinforces this approach by providing that '[c]ivilian objects consist of all civilian property and activities other than those used to support or sustain the adversary's warfighting capability.' Joint Chiefs of Staff, Joint Doctrine for Targeting, Joint Publication 3-60, 17 Jan. 2002, at A-2. The term 'war sustaining' also appears in the Instructions for the US Military Commission at Guantanamo. Department of Defense, Military Commission Instruction No. 2, Crimes and Elements for Trials by Military Commission (30 Apr. 2003), para. 5D.

[63] Study, Vol. 2, Part 1, 279, paras. 218 and 219.

This is particularly regrettable because economic warfare is increasingly relevant in contemporary warfare strategy and doctrine. For instance, in compellance (coercive) campaigns such as Operation Allied Force, which seek to compel an opponent into a particular course of action (or desist from one), economic targets prove particularly attractive because they may shape an opponent's cost-benefit analysis more effectively than strikes against the military. Similarly, effects-based operations doctrine, which advocates identifying targets likely to generate specific effects rather than simply serially destroying the enemy's military, may contain a logic which leads military planners away from traditional target sets towards sustainability targets.[64] For instance, consider the effect of computer network attacks against a banking system or stock market on a nation's ability to fund its war effort.

Finally, the absence of commentary discussion regarding the interpretation of either 'effective contribution to military action' or 'definite military advantage' is surprising. It would have been useful to explore how States relate the two criteria to each other and, as they are subjective, how they apply (or even explain) them in practice. Illustrating the importance of these issues, the UK *Manual* (which was not issued when the Practice Volumes were compiled) specifically notes that '[t]he second part of the definition limits the first' and that both must be met for an object to qualify as a military objective.[65] It also explains the terms 'military action',[66] 'definite',[67] and 'military advantage'.[68] Other States have also addressed these issues in their guidance to the military. Although some of these, like the UK *Manual*, post-date the Study's research phase, the issue was certainly present in informed discourse at that time.

Rule 9

Civilian objects are all objects that are not military objectives.

---

[64] See generally, Joint Publication 3-60, at I-1. See also, M.N. Schmitt, 'Effects Based Operations and the Law of Aerial Warfare' (2007) 6 *Washington University Global Studies Law Review* (forthcoming).   [65] *UK Manual*, para. 5.4.4a.

[66] 'Military action generally, not a limited or specific military operation'. *UK Manual*, para. 5.4.4g.

[67] 'A concrete and perceptible military advantage rather than a hypothetical and speculative one'. *UK Manual*, para. 5.4.4i.

[68] 'The advantage anticipated from the attack considered as a whole and not only from isolated or particular pats of the attack. The advantage need not be immediate'. *UK Manual*, para. 5.4.4j.

Rule 10

Civilian objects are protected against attack, unless and for such time as they are military objectives.

Additional Protocol I, Article 52:

1. Civilian objects shall not be the object of attack or of reprisals. Civilian objects are all objects which are not military objectives as defined in paragraph 2.

3. In case of doubt whether an object which is normally dedicated to civilian purposes, such as a place of worship, a house or other dwelling or a school, is being used to make an effective contribution to military action, it shall be presumed not to be so used.[69]

Rule 10 is the functional equivalent of the direct participation principle for civilians; it confirms that civilian objects can become military objectives through use, purpose, or location. In this regard, it adds little to the general prohibition against striking military objectives contained in Rule 7 and the definition of military objectives found in Rule 8.

However, Rule 10's significance lies in its omission of the Article 52.3 presumption of civilian object status. The commentary's explanation is on point. It accurately points to the US Department of Defense's Report to Congress on the First Gulf War. That report noted that the doubt provision was 'not a codification of customary practice,' and that '[i]t shifts the burden for determining the precise use of an object from the party controlling that object (and therefore in possession of the facts as to its use) to the party lacking such control and facts, i.e., from defender to attacker. This imbalance ignores the realities of war in demanding a degree of certainty of an attacker that seldom exists in combat. It also encourages a defender to ignore its obligation to separate the civilian population, individual civilians and civilian objects from military objectives.'[70]

In all likelihood, the prime concern is the quantum of doubt. It would certainly seem logical and reasonable for an attacker to shoulder a substantial degree of responsibility for determining the use of an object it desires to attack. A better question, however, is: can it attack when a

[69] See also *NIAC Manual*, para. 2.1.1.1: 'It is also forbidden to attack civilian objects, unless they become military objectives.'
[70] Department of Defense, *Conduct of the Persian Gulf War*, Final Report to Congress, April 1992, at 616.

degree of doubt exists, as is often the case?[71] The *de facto* benchmark may well be that of 'the reasonable warfighter in same or similar circumstances', who must consider all relevant factors, including the degree of doubt, importance of the target, ability to strike at a later time, alternatives to achieving the same objective through other means, and so forth. Whatever the standard, the Study is to be applauded for excluding this particular Additional Protocol I provision.

Rule 11

Indiscriminate attacks are prohibited.

Rule 12

Indiscriminate attacks are those:

(a) **which are not directed at a specific military objective;**
(b) **which employ a method or means of combat which cannot be directed at a specific military objective; or**
(c) **which employ a method or means of combat the effects of which cannot be limited as required by international humanitarian law; and consequently, in each such case, are of a nature to strike military objectives and civilians or civilian objects without distinction.**

Additional Protocol I, Article 51.4: Indiscriminate attacks are prohibited. Indiscriminate attacks are:

(a) those which are not directed at a specific military objective;
(b) those which employ a method or means of combat which cannot be directed at a specific military objective; or
(c) those which employ a method or means of combat the effects of which cannot be limited as required by this Protocol;

and consequently, in each such case, are of a nature to strike military objectives and civilians or civilian objects without distinction.[72]

---

[71] In addressing this issue, Israel has adopted a standard of 'significant doubt', such that a commander 'has to determine whether the possibility of mistake is significant enough to warrant not launching the attack'. Report on Practice of Israel, 1997, ch. 1.3, cited in Study, Vol. II, Part 1, 244.

[72] For international armed conflict, see also CCW, Protocol II, Art. 3.3 (mines, booby traps, and other devices); CCW, amended Protocol II, Art. 3.8 (mines, booby traps, and other devices). For non-international conflict see *NIAC Manual*, para. 2.1.1.3: 'Indiscriminate attacks are forbidden. Indiscriminate attacks are those that are not specifically directed against fighters or military objectives.' And, CCW, amended Protocol II, Art. 3.8 (mines, booby traps, and other devices).

As noted, the ICJ has styled the prohibition on indiscriminate attacks as 'cardinal'. There can be no doubt that Rules 11 and 12 reflect the customary textual expressions of that norm. But with Rule 12, the challenge of operationalising an accepted textual formula surfaces yet again. Unfortunately, the commentary and Practice Volume offer little assistance, for they fail to survey actual State practice in applying the proscription.

Consider the phrase 'a means or method that cannot be directed'. During World War II, it took nine thousand 2,000-pound bombs to achieve a 90 per cent 'probability of kill' (PK) on a single target. This is because the 'circular error probable' (CEP) of the weapon was roughly 3,300 feet.[73] By 1972, the same PK could be achieved by dropping 176 2,000-pound bombs, each with a CEP of 400 feet. In the First Gulf War, similar results were achievable with a single bomb having a CEP of 10 feet.[74]

It is inconceivable today that a weapon with a 3,300 feet CEP would be considered 'directable'. Rather, the requisite directability of the indiscriminate attack norm is technologically dependent, shifting over time. But the Study explores no State practice that might provide an indication of the criteria for fixing the norm's parameters at any one time. As a result, the Rule lacks practical effectiveness except at the extremes, where all would agree the weapon can or cannot be sufficiently aimed.

Equally undeveloped is the notion of 'uncontrollable effects'. The commentary tenders the standard of 'weapons whose effects are uncontrollable in time and space and are likely to strike military objectives and civilians or civilian objects without distinction', offering the paradigmatic example of biological weapons. But how uncontrollable must effects be? Must they be uncontrollable in both time and space? Biological weapons, for example, can be limited in time and space by using perishable toxins in an area where only combatants are present.

In twenty-first-century warfare, the paramount issue in this regard is information warfare, particularly computer network attack.[75] CNA attacks against military nets can easily generate consequences for civilian systems. Under what circumstances might such attacks be indiscriminate? To what extent do defensive systems, such as firewalls and anti-virus software, affect the determination? How are time and space to be understood in virtual warfare? For instance, are shared networks

---

[73] In other words, 50 per cent of such bombs would fall within a circle with a radius of 3,300 feet.   [74] United States Air Force Transformation Flight Plan (2004), at 61.
[75] See M.N. Schmitt, 'Wired Warfare.' See also M.N. Schmitt, 'Computer Network Attack: The Normative Software' (2001) 4 *Yearbook of International Humanitarian Law* 53.

limited in space? That the Study did not address these specific issues is understandable, for they only began to surface as the project was winding down. However, the relative paucity of general guidelines as to how States have interpreted and applied the norm precludes confident application to new methods and means of warfare.

Rule 13

Attacks by bombardment by any method or means which treats as a single military objective a number of clearly separated and distinct military objectives located in a city, town, village or other area containing a similar concentration of civilians or civilian objects are prohibited.

Additional Protocol I, Article 51.5: Among others, the following types of attacks are to be considered as indiscriminate:

(a) *an attack by bombardment by any methods or means which treats as a single military objective a number of clearly separated and distinct military objectives located in a city, town, village or other area containing a similar concentration of civilians or civilian objects;*

(b) *...*[76]

Rule 13, replicating the Additional Protocol I formula, sets forth the accepted textual articulation of the customary norm. However, the commentary devotes little attention to practice or understandings regarding the meaning of 'clearly separated and distinct', the fulcrum on which the norm rests. The sole exception is its mention of the US position. At the Diplomatic Conference leading to adoption of the Protocol, the US asserted that 'clearly separated' implies a distance 'at least sufficiently large to permit individual military objectives to be attacked separately'.[77]

---

[76] For non-international conflict, see also *NIAC Manual,* para. 2.1.1.3: 'Indiscriminate attacks are forbidden. Indiscriminate attacks are those that are not specifically directed against fighters or military objectives.' The Rule itself is described in the commentary: 'The second method is an attack that treats a number of clearly separate and distinct military objectives collocated with civilians or civilian objects as a single entity, such as carpet-bombing an entire urban area containing dispersed legitimate targets. This prohibition only applies where it is militarily feasible to conduct separate attacks on each of the objectives. If it is not, then the issue is proportionality, not discrimination.' For international and non-international armed conflict, see also CCW, amended Protocol II, Art. 3.9 (mines, booby traps, and other devices).

[77] US, Statement at the CDDH, Official Records, vol. XIV, CDDH/III/SR.31, 14 March 1975, at 307.

A passing remark in the commentary that '[t]his view was supported by some other States' does not do justice to the importance of the point.

It is an issue central to the Rule's application. The US position implicitly ties the requisite separation to the *attacker's* capabilities through use of the words: 'to permit . . . to be attacked'. In other words, it is not so much the actual separation of the targets that matters, but rather the accuracy and reliability of the attacker's weapon systems, the availability of particular weapons systems, the nature of enemy defences, the time of attack and the weather in which it is conducted, and so on. The standard is subjective, despite the fact that Rule 13 appears to impose an objective one.

The distinction merited further State practice analysis because it was on this point that the Conference negotiations temporarily foundered. On the one hand, only a subjective test makes sense, for whether or not two or more targets can be struck separately is case-specific.[78] But on the other, as noted by the Additional Protocol I *Commentary*, the objective test was favoured out of 'fear of encouraging area bombardment, for in such a case the attacking forces could use their own judgement, taking into account the weapons available and the circumstances, as to whether the individual objectives were too close together to be attacked separately'.[79]

Furthermore, the subjective approach implies normative relativity in that not all attackers are equally equipped; whether an attacker can strike targets separately depends on factors like those delineated above. Poorly equipped States may arguably, by this standard, lawfully conduct area bombardment that would be forbidden to well-equipped States. Not all States would welcome this result as appropriate (or fair).

A second uncertainty surrounding the Rule is how to handle a military area in which civilians or civilian objects are located.[80] For instance, military family housing, stores, and family recreation facilities reside within many modern military installations. Moreover, military downsizing, privatising, and other factors have led to dramatic increases in the number of civilian workers on military installations. While they may not be targeted unless directly participating in hostilities, does their presence bring Rule 13 into play? It has been suggested, on the one hand, that civilian

---

[78] Art. 24(3) of the 1923 Hague Rules of Air Warfare, which never came into effect, took this approach by focusing on whether it was possible to bombard the targets discriminately, i.e. they focused on the capabilities of the attacker.   [79] *Commentary*, para. 1971.

[80] See, e.g., discussion in Dinstein, *The Conduct of Hostilities Under the Law of International Armed Conflict*, p. 121.

employees on a military installation should perhaps be excluded alto-gether from targeting equations.[81] Others argue that the presence of civilians and civilian objects on military installations does not alter appli-cation of the basic targeting rules.[82] They are civilians to be treated as such. A refinement of the latter position urges that, where it is impossible to verify that individual facilities on an installation are military objectives (e.g., it is uncertain what a warehouse contains), a presumption that they are military attaches.[83] Whatever the correct solution, the debate goes unmentioned in the Study despite the growing phenomenon of civilians and civilian objects on military installations.

Rule 14

Launching an attack which may be expected to cause incidental loss of civilian life, injury to civilians, damage to civilian objects, or a combi-nation thereof, which would be excessive in relation to the concrete and direct military advantage anticipated, is prohibited.

Additional Protocol I, Article 51.5: Among others, the following types of attacks are to be considered as indiscriminate:
. . . (b) an attack which may be expected to cause incidental loss of civil-ian life, injury to civilians, damage to civilian objects, or a combination thereof, which would be excessive in relation to the concrete and direct military advantage anticipated.

Additional Protocol I, Article 57.2: With respect to attacks, the following pre-cautions shall be taken:
(a) those who plan or decide upon an attack shall:
. . . (iii) refrain from deciding to launch any attack which may be expected to cause incidental loss of civilian life, injury to civilians, damage to civilian objects, or a combination thereof, which would be excessive in relation to the concrete and direct military advantage anticipated.[84]

---

[81] W. Hays Parks, 'Air War and the Law of War' (1990) 32 *Air Force Law Review* 1 at 174.
[82] See discussion at M.N. Schmitt, 'Targeting and Humanitarian Law: Current Issues' (2004) 34 *Israel Yearbook on Human Rights* at 59 and 97–98.
[83] *Ibid.*, at 100. This is because the rebuttable presumption in Additional Protocol I, Art. 52.3 that a prospective target is not making an effective contribution to military action, and therefore not targetable, applies only to objects 'normally dedicated to civilian pur-poses, such as a place of worship, a house or other dwelling, or a school'.
[84] For non-international conflict, see also *NIAC Manual*, para. 2.1.1: 'An attack is forbidden if it may be expected to cause incidental loss to civilian life, injury to civilians, damage to

The text of Rule 14 is fundamental. It is also the rule which warfighters find most difficult to apply in practice because it involves the consideration of dissimilar values in relation to each other through application of a highly subjective standard, excessiveness. How many civilians can be killed 'incidentally' before the number is excessive relative to the value of a tank? A command and control centre? An enemy soldier?

Interpretive obstacles prove even more daunting as analysis probes deeper. For example, the value of military objectives shifts over time depending on the course of battle. Further, value assessments of civilians and civilian objects can be affected by factors like the well-being of a population (value of food when starvation is rampant versus plentiful), past experiences (relative sensitivity to death and suffering), or evolving awareness of a civilian object's value (such as the environment). The Study failed to examine such realities, although, in fairness, they are not particularly susceptible to resolution through State practice surveys.

The proportionality commentary does make several key points. First, it notes that a number of States emphasise that it is the overall military advantage which must be considered when making proportionality assessments, not just that directly resulting from an attack. Cited above in the military objectives discussion, this approach has greater relevance to proportionality. In fact, the UK statement on point was specifically as to Articles 51 and 57. Note also that Article 8(2)(b)(iv) of the International Criminal Court Statute, which sets out proportionality in the criminal context, adds 'overall' to a textual formula otherwise identical to that of Additional Protocol I. During the Rome Conference, the ICRC acknowledged that inclusion of the word implied no change in the Protocol's standard.[85] Indeed, the Practice Volume documents so much agreement that it might well have been appropriate and useful to include 'overall' in Rule 14. Its absence

---

Footnote 84 (*cont.*)
  civilian objects, or a combination thereof, which would be excessive in relation to the concrete and direct military advantage anticipated. It is recognised that incidental injury to civilians and collateral damage to civilian objects may occur as a result of a lawful attack against fighters or military objectives.' For international and non-international armed conflict, see also CCW, amended Protocol II, Art. 3.8(c) (mines, booby traps, and other devices). For international armed conflict, see also CCW, Protocol II, Art. 3.3(c) (mines, booby traps, and other devices).

[85] K. Dörmann, *Elements of War Crimes under the Rome Statute of the International Criminal Court: Sources and Commentary* (Cambridge University Press, 2002), pp. 169–170.

demonstrates the importance placed in the Study on maintaining fidelity to received textual formulae.[86]

The commentary also helpfully notes that numerous States have adopted the position that commanders must make proportionality estimates based on the information available to them at the time. The UK statement upon ratification is illustrative: 'Military commanders and others responsible for planning, deciding upon, or executing attacks necessarily have to reach decisions on the basis of their assessment of the information from all sources which is reasonably available to them at the relevant time.'[87] Although seemingly self-evident, the fact that many States felt compelled to reiterate the principle demonstrates their disquiet over the possibility of hindsight judgements.

Finally, the Study briefly spotlights an issue drawing increasing attention in proportionality discussions – how to treat force protection. In other words, does the survival of an attacking force constitute military advantage that may be considered when determining whether collateral damage to civilian objects and incidental injury to civilians is excessive?

The question engaged public debate during Operation Allied Force when NATO aircraft operated above the threat envelope of Yugoslav defences. Criticism ensued. Human Rights Watch, for example, claimed 'if precision would have been greater (and civilian casualties lessened) had NATO pilots flown lower, it could be argued that NATO was "obligated" to have its pilots fly lower'.[88] The ICRC's Additional Protocol I Commentary, which refers to 'ground gained' and 'annihilating or weakening the enemy armed forces' when discussing military advantage, is supportive.[89] For those taking this position, risk to the attacker is relevant to 'precautions in attack' (discussed below), not to proportionality.

The alternative is to treat survival of the combatant and the weapon system as an element of the military advantage to be factored into the proportionality calculation. This makes practical sense, for survival permits the launch of later attacks, a measurable advantage to a commander. In fact, the cumulative military value of future attacks may outweigh

---

[86] To some extent, according to an exchange between the author and one of the editors, this was done at the behest of some governmental experts who expressed concern over differentiations in formulations.   [87] UK Statement on Ratification, para. (c).

[88] Human Rights Watch, Civilian Deaths in the NATO Air Campaign, Feb. 2000, www.hrw.org/reports/2000/nato/index.htm. The organization analysed the Djakovica Road incident, during which Albanian refugees were mistaken for a convoy of Serbian military forces. It opined that because 'higher altitude seems to have impeded a pilot from adequately identifying a target . . . inadequate precautions were taken to avoid civilian casualties'.   [89] Commentary, para. 2218.

that of the strike in question. And, to be fair, loss of the attacking combatant and weapon system would unquestionably be considered a 'military *dis*advantage'.

Finally, advocates of this approach caution against exaggerating its *de facto* impact. Only when collateral damage and incidental injury is otherwise excessive, a subjective assessment by any measure, must the military advantage inherent in combatant and weapon system survival be considered. Regardless of relative merits of the opposing methods, the Study's acknowledgement that some States consider security of the attacking force when making proportionality determinations is constructive.

On the other hand, the Study fails to address a number of noteworthy topics. First, the Rule states that violation requires 'excessive' collateral damage to civilian objects and/or incidental injury to civilians. Regrettably, the ICRC's *Commentary* to Article 51 avers that '[t]he Protocol does not provide any justification for attacks which cause extensive civilian losses and damages. Incidental losses and damages should never be extensive'.[90]

This would appear a demonstrable misstatement of law. To begin with, it runs counter to the premise that '[t]he entire law of armed conflict is, of course, the result of an equitable balance between the necessities of war and humanitarian requirements'.[91] If international humanitarian law is ultimately a balancing act, presumably there must be military advantages so great that extensive collateral damage and incidental injury could be lawfully caused to achieve them. This appears to be what the ICJ suggested in the *Nuclear Weapons* case when it refused to exclude the possibility that use of nuclear weapons might comply with international humanitarian law where the survival of the State was at stake.[92]

That no degree of civilian injury or damage to civilian objects negates the need to consider military advantage is also suggested by the ICC Statute's modification of 'excessive' with the adjective 'clearly' in Article 8.2(b)(iv). The ICRC's *Elements of War Crimes* confirms that addition of the term was not meant to change existing law.[93] It should be clear that

---

[90] *Commentary*, para. 1980.

[91] *Commentary*, para. 2206, which discusses proportionality in the context of Additional Protocol I, Art. 57.

[92] The Court could not 'conclude definitively whether the threat or use of nuclear weapons would be lawful or unlawful in an extreme circumstance of self-defence, in which the very survival of a State would be at stake': *Nuclear Weapons* case (note 17 above), para. 105E.

[93] Dörmann, *Elements of War Crimes*, pp. 169–170.

the *Commentary* reference to 'extensive' is not the law. Regrettably, the Rule 14 commentary neglected the opportunity to remedy the confusion triggered by the *Commentary*.[94]

The Study commentary further fails to discuss reverberating effects, also known as secondary effects, knock-on effects, or indirect effects. The issue first arose with the Coalition attack on Baghdad's electrical grid during Operation Desert Storm. It was claimed that the attacks against this military objective spawned deadly secondary effects, illustrated most emotively by allegations that they caused hospital incubators to shut off. Similar allegations arose publicly when NATO attacked Belgrade during Operation Allied Force.

Reverberating effects raise three questions, two of which remain unsettled. The first is whether the attacker must include reverberating effects in its proportionality analysis. It appears to have been resolved in the affirmative. In particular, US targeting doctrine validates the obligation to do so.[95]

The second and third are more problematic. Can reverberating effects become so remote that they do not count (and if so when) and to what degree does the opposing side have to explore the possibility of reverberating effects before authorising attack? As to the former, while there must logically be a point at which the chain of causation is broken through attenuation, no consensus exists as to when. For example, need there be an independent intervening cause? Does an unforeseeable contributing cause suffice? Is there a point when the reverberating effect is so remote in time and space that it need not be considered by the attacker?

Finally, must an attacker call on experts capable of identifying potential reverberating effects or train mission planners to make such assessments? Or is it sufficient that those otherwise involved in the process simply do their best to anticipate reverberating effects? To a great extent, the issue is one of 'precautions in attack', codified in Additional Protocol I, Article 57, and set out in Rule 15 of the Study (discussed below). The Article and Rule impose the requirement of taking 'feasible' precautions to comply with international humanitarian law attack requirements such as proportionality. But what is 'feasible' in estimating reverberating effects?

Reverberating effects are becoming central in assessing contemporary combat operations. Of particular importance is the network-centric

[94] Although updating, correcting, or clarifying the *Commentary* was not a purpose of the Study.   [95] Joint Publication 3-60, at I-6.

warfare practised by first-tier militaries. Some military networks, especially intelligence communications systems, are closed.[96] In the absence of an entry or exit point, the potential for causing reverberating effects in civilian systems is slim (although increasingly possible in light of wireless technology). On the other hand, attacks against systems with connectivity to civilian networks pose a considerable risk of reverberating effects. Because most military networks fall into this category, and as practice and analysis on this issue advances, it is suggested that the next edition of the Study might usefully address reverberating effects.

Finally, in international humanitarian law working groups on various topics over the past few years, the subject of human shields has surfaced. As noted in Rule 97, the use of human shields, known as counter-targeting, violates customary international law. However, the Study does not address the effect of human shields upon proportionality calculations. This is unfortunate, for differences in opinion exist in both academic circles and among practitioners that could have usefully been noted.

To begin, one must distinguish between voluntary and involuntary shields. With regard to the former, there are two schools of thought. The first asserts that because voluntary shields are civilians, their death or injury during an attack against the object they are shielding must be factored into the proportionality analysis.[97] This position rejects characterisation of their activities as direct participation in hostilities.

The countervailing position is that they qualify as direct participants.[98] In shielding a military objective, they are mounting a highly effective defence because the attacker will hesitate to cause civilian casualties, images of which the media may instantly beam around the world. As direct participants in hostilities, the shields become lawfully targetable, and thus it would be contradictory to factor them into a proportionality calculation.[99]

Disagreement over involuntary shields is even more nuanced. Three approaches exist. The first holds that involuntary shields are civilians; they do not lose this status by virtue of the enemy's unlawful actions. Thus, they fully count when assessing proportionality. Additional Protocol I, Article 51.8, supports this position in providing: '[a]ny

[96] I.e., there is no interface between the military and civilian systems.
[97] See, e.g., Human Rights Watch, International Humanitarian Law Issues in a Potential War in Iraq, 20 Feb. 2002, www.hrw.org/backgrounder/arms/iraq0202003.htm#1.
[98] Maintained by the United States. See, e.g., Department of Defense, Background Briefing on Targeting, 5 March 2003, www. defenselink.mil/news/Mar2003/t03052003_ t305targ. html.   [99] Study, Rule 6; Additional Protocol I, Art. 51.3.

violation of these prohibitions [includes the prohibition on shielding] shall not release the Parties to the conflict from their legal obligations with respect to the civilian population and civilians'.

At the other extreme are those who urge that involuntary shields do not count because if they did the enemy would reap the benefits of its unlawful actions. Advocates argue that Article 51.8 is not customary law (it is not addressed in the Study Rules) and that there is precedent for disallowing a party the benefits of its international humanitarian law violations, as in the (disputed) law of reprisals. As one commentator has noted, under customary international law, '[a] belligerent State is not vested . . . with the power to block an otherwise legitimate attack against combatants (or military objectives) by deliberately placing civilians in harm's way'.[100]

The third approach amounts to a middle ground (and could arguably also apply to voluntary shields). It suggests that even if the principle articulated in Article 51.8 applies, 'the actual test of excessive injury to civilians must be relaxed'.[101] Proponents point out that enemy misconduct does sometimes weaken the safeguards to which protected objects are entitled. As an example, a hospital from which combatants are operating may be attacked once a warning to desist has been ignored.[102]

Rule 15

In the conduct of military operations, constant care must be taken to spare the civilian population, civilians and civilian objects. All feasible precautions must be taken to avoid, and in any event to minimise, incidental loss of civilian life, injury to civilians and damage to civilian objects.

Additional Protocol I, Article 57.1: In the conduct of military operations, constant care shall be taken to spare the civilian population, civilians and civilian objects.

2. With respect to attacks, the following precautions shall be taken:
(a) those who plan or decide upon an attack shall:

---

[100] Dinstein, *The Conduct of Hostilities*, p. 131. The author cites in support Parks, at 162–163.

[101] *Ibid.* p. 131. The author does not find this to be a customary law principle.

[102] See, e.g., Additional Protocol I, Art. 13.

(i)   *do everything feasible to verify that the objectives to be attacked are neither civilians nor civilian objects and are not subject to special protection but are military objectives within the meaning of paragraph 2 of Article 52 and that it is not prohibited by the provisions of this Protocol to attack them;*

(ii)   *take all feasible precautions in the choice of means and methods of attack with a view to avoiding, and in any event to minimising, incidental loss or civilian life, injury to civilians and damage to civilian objects;*

(iii) *refrain from deciding to launch any attack which may be expected to cause incidental loss of civilian life, injury to civilians, damage to civilian objects, or a combination thereof, which would be excessive in relation to the concrete and direct military advantage anticipated;*

(b) an attack shall be cancelled or suspended if it becomes apparent that the objective is not a military one or is subject to special protection or that the attack may be expected to cause incidental loss of civilian life, injury to civilians, damage to civilian objects, or a combination thereof, which would be excessive in relation to the concrete and direct military advantage anticipated.

(c) . . .[103]

Rule 15 sets forth the basic premise that an attacker must take precautions designed to minimise collateral damage to civilian objects and incidental injury to civilians. For the first time in the Study targeting Rules, the format differs significantly from that of Additional Protocol I. Following Rule 15, which is the combination of the introductory provision of Article 57.1 and the feasibility notion permeating the remainder of the Article, are individual Rules governing target verification (16), choice of methods and means of warfare (17), and proportionality (18 and 19). This format constitutes a marked improvement over the unwieldy Article 57.

The commentary to Rule 15 (and the respective entries in the Practice Volume) perceptively point to the three core issues posed by the precautions in attack norms: (1) What does 'feasible' mean?; (2) What information is used to decide on precautions?; and (3) Who decides what is feasible? These are exactly the right questions.

---

[103] For international armed conflict, see also CCW, amended Protocol II, Art. 3.10 (mines, booby traps, and other devices); Second Protocol to the Hague Convention of 1954, Art. 7 (for cultural property). For non-international conflict see *NIAC Manual*, para. 2.1.2a: 'All feasible precautions must be taken by all parties to minimise both injuries to civilians and damage to civilian objects.' See also CCW, amended Protocol II, Art. 3.10 (mines, booby traps, and other devices); Second Protocol to the Hague Convention of 1954, Art. 7 (for cultural property).

As to feasibility, the commentary wisely highlights a standard which appears to have achieved consensus – practicality. The UK Statement on ratification is reflective: 'The United Kingdom understands the term "feasible" as used in the Protocol to mean that which is practicable or practically possible, taking into account all circumstances ruling at the time, including humanitarian and military considerations'.[104]

The practicality standard essentially mandates a 'reasonable warfighter' inquiry. Feasibility determinations would consequently consider, for example, the nature and availability of weapons systems; survival of attacking forces; intelligence, surveillance, and reconnaissance (ISR) asset capabilities and availability; and competing demands for the systems in question. Reference to the standard in the commentary will assist those applying the Rule to address such issues as whether precision guided munitions must be used whenever available or whether they may be withheld for employment later in the conflict (and if so, under what circumstances).

Regarding the information on which the feasibility assessment is to be made, the commentary points out that numerous States have stressed that the standard is situational. The UK Statement upon ratification is archetypal, with one exception: 'Military commanders and others responsible for planning, deciding upon, or executing attacks necessarily have to reach decisions on the basis of their assessment of the information from all sources which is reasonably available to them at the relevant time.'[105]

The exception is the qualifier 'reasonably' in the UK Statement, which is omitted in the formula propounded by the commentary. Its omission potentially obfuscates matters. In the absence of this term, commanders and others might be judged in light of information available to them only through great effort. This is certainly not a customary law norm, for military decision-makers typically act in fast-paced combat situations on the information at hand or that which can easily be obtained within the practical time constraints of mission execution. In other words, the criterion applied is that of reasonableness.

---

[104] UK Statement on Ratification, para. (b). Protocols II and III of the Conventional Weapons Convention and the Second Protocol to the Cultural Property Convention, as well as many military manuals and training material, repeat this formula. CCW, amended Protocol II, Art. 2.6 (mines, booby traps, and other devices); PIII, Art. 1.3 (incendiary weapons); Second Protocol to the Hague Convention of 1954, Art. 1(f) (for cultural property); *Commander's Handbook*, para. 8.1.1.

[105] UK Statement on Ratification, para. (c).

Finally, the commentary usefully highlights the question of to whom the requirements apply. Article 57.2 refers to 'those who plan or decide upon an attack'. By contrast, Rule 15 makes no reference to any particular individual, while the subsequent Rules on precautions in attack impose obligations on 'each party'. The Rules thus beg the question of 'who' it is on each side that makes the determination as to the feasibility of the available precautions and who bears legal responsibility for making the choice.

As the commentary notes, some States expressed apprehension regarding the words: 'those who plan and decide', issuing statements as to their understanding of the norm's reach. Among these was the United Kingdom, which in its Statement upon ratification noted: 'The United Kingdom understands that the obligation to comply with paragraph 2(b) only extends to those who have the authority and practical possibility to cancel or suspend the attack.'[106] Although the UK statement related only to the specific obligation of suspending or cancelling an attack, it is apparent that the United Kingdom was concerned lest legal responsibility for evaluating options in combat drop too low. Other countries were more direct. For instance, as noted in the commentary, Switzerland insisted that the obligations only apply to commanding officers at the battalion or group level and higher.

On the other hand, many in the international humanitarian law community maintain that the obligation should logically flow down to any combatant with the ability to comply. The paradigmatic example is the pilot with orders to bomb a particular point. If questions regarding the nature of the target arise during execution of the mission, why should the pilot not employ other feasible means of verification? Similarly, if the pilot has reason to believe the mission should be aborted for a legal reason, why would the law relieve him or her of the obligation to do so? Indeed, this is the standard to which most mature militaries train.

In its *Manual*, the United Kingdom takes the position that the level of responsibility is situational. 'Whether a person will have this responsibility will depend on whether he has any discretion in the way the attack is carried out and so the responsibility will range from the commanders-in-chief and their planning staff to single soldiers opening fire on their own initiative. Those who do not have this discretion but merely carry out orders for an attack also have a responsibility: to cancel or suspend the attack if it turns out that the object to be attacked is going to be such that the proportionality rule would be breached.'[107]

---

[106] UK Statement on Ratification, para. (o).   [107] *UK Manual*, para. 5.32.9.

The point to be made is that agreement is lacking. All would agree that commanders and others 'with authority' shoulder the obligation. In the absence of consensus beyond that point, skirting of the matter in the text would appear appropriate, although it might have been helpful to provide fuller treatment of the issue in the commentary.

Rule 20

Each party to the conflict must give effective advance warning of attacks which may affect the civilian population, unless circumstances do not permit.

Additional Protocol I, Article 57.2 (c): [E]ffective advance warning shall be given of attacks which may affect the civilian population, unless circumstances do not permit.[108]

This Rule derives not only from Additional Protocol I, but also from Article 26 of the 1907 Hague Regulations: 'The officer in command of an attacking force must, before commencing a bombardment, except in cases of assault, do all in his power to warn the authorities.'[109] The distinction between assault and bombardment is important. In 1907, warnings did not place the attacker at risk because bombardment was typically conducted by distant artillery. Warning of an assault, by contrast, would not only place the attacker in danger, but also likely result in defeat by permitting the enemy to focus its defences.

As bombardment moved to the air, warnings became tactically imprudent in many scenarios. Enemy ground-based air defences could be positioned in the target area and along the ingress and egress routes or enemy interceptors could lie in wait for the attackers. Although warnings by radio or leaflet dropping occasionally occurred during World War II, in most cases attacks were without warning.[110] Since then, the practice (to the extent there is any) has been to issue general warnings

---

[108] For international armed conflict, see Hague Regulations IV, Art. 26; CCW, amended Protocol II, Art. 3.11 (for mines, booby traps and other devices); Second Protocol to the Hague Convention of 1954, Arts. 6(d) and 13.2(c)(ii) (for cultural property). For non-international conflict, no warning requirement appears in the *NIAC Manual*. But see CCW, amended Protocol II, Art. 3.11 (for mines, booby traps and other devices); Second Protocol to the Hague Convention of 1954, Arts. 6(d) and 13.2(c)(ii) (for cultural property).   [109] Hague Convention (IV), Annexed Regulations, Art. 1.

[110] *Commentary*, para. 2224.

that certain types of targets will be attacked or, more generally, that attack is imminent.[111]

In contemporary conflicts, there has been a resurgence of pre-attack warnings, even involving assaults. During Operation Iraqi Freedom, for instance, it was standard practice for Marines attacking urban areas such as Fallujah to warn the civilian population to depart prior to launch of the operation.[112] But the general practice remains to warn only to the extent that it does not forfeit the attacker's advantage.

The ICJ styled the Hague Regulations 'customary' in both the *Wall* and *Nuclear Weapons* Advisory Opinions.[113] Further, the International Military Tribunal at Nuremberg held that the 'rules laid down in the [Hague] Convention were recognised by all civilised nations, and were regarded as being declaratory of the laws and customs of war'.[114] Despite these characterisations, the absence of a textual reference to prevailing circumstances in the Hague formula can no longer be deemed as imposing an absolute warning requirement. Moreover, the repeated (perhaps predominant) practice of not warning would preclude characterising such an interpretation as customary. Article 57 wisely recognised this reality through inclusion of the 'unless circumstances do not permit' caveat.

Rule 20 sensibly adopts the Additional Protocol I format rather than that of the Hague Regulations. In support, the commentary highlights State interpretations of the norm as taking account of the need for surprise, speed of response, operational security, lack of specificity in warnings, etc.

It might even be suggested that the Rule itself is not customary, despite the 'circumstances permit' caveat. In this regard, the Practice Volume (II) devotes little attention to actual State practice, or lack thereof. Therefore, while it cannot be definitively asserted that *lack* of practice rules out the

---

[111] In Vietnam, for instance, over a billion leaflets were dropped in conjunction with radio broadcasts warning civilians to stay away from military objectives during air campaigns such as Operation Rolling Thunder in 1968. J.D. Reynolds, 'Collateral Damage on the 21st Century Battlefield: Enemy Exploitation of the Law of Armed Conflict, and the Struggle for a Moral High Ground' (2005) 56 *Air Force Law Review* 1, at 18.

[112] This was accomplished through use of both leaflets and loudspeakers. Author interview with senior US Marine Corps officer, 10 Oct. 2006.

[113] *Legal Consequences of the Construction of a Wall in the Occupied Palestinian Territory*, ICJ Advisory Opinion of 9 July 2004 (2004), para. 89; *Nuclear Weapons* case (note 17 above), para. 79.

[114] International Military Tribunal (Nuremberg) Judgment and Sentences, reprinted in (1947) 41 *American Journal of International Law* 172, p. 65.

customary character of the warning requirement, nor can it be demonstrated that the practice was so definitive that challenges to its customary character are baseless.

Rule 21

When a choice is possible between several military objectives for obtaining a similar military advantage, the objective to be selected must be that the attack on which may be expected to cause the least danger to civilian lives and to civilian objects.

Additional Protocol I, Article 57.3: When a choice is possible between several military objectives for obtaining a similar military advantage, the objective to be selected shall be that the attack on which may be expected to cause the least danger to civilian lives and to civilian objects.[115]

The commentary to Rule 21 correctly notes that the United States has emphasised that the obligation to select among military objectives is 'not absolute'. However, the commentary softens the US position. In fact, the full text of the US stance, as extracted in the Practice Volume (II), reads:

> The language of Article 57(3) of Protocol I . . . *is not part of customary law.* The provision applies 'when a choice is possible . . .'; it is not mandatory. An attacker may comply with it if it is possible to do so, subject to mission accomplishment and allowable risk, or he may determine that it is impossible to make such a determination.[116]

Textually, Article 57.3 is nearly identical to Rule 21. This being so, it is difficult to imagine how the Rule could constitute customary international law unless the US position has changed . . . and there is no persuasive evidence it has done so. After all, the United States is the world's dominant military power. Moreover, as noted by the ICJ in the *North Sea Continental Shelf* cases, the subsequent practice of *non-party* States is of particular relevance in determining whether a treaty norm has matured into customary international law. Only from non-party practice can an

---

[115] For non-international conflict see also *NIAC Manual*, para. 2.1.2(d): 'When a reasonable choice is available between several military objectives for obtaining a similar military advantage, the objective expected to minimise the danger to civilians and civilian objects must be selected.' For international and non-international armed conflict, see also Second Protocol to the Hague Convention of 1954, Art. 6 (cultural property).

[116] Study, Vol. II, 416, citing US, Message from the Department of the Army to the legal adviser of the US Army forces deployed in the Gulf, 11 Jan. 1991, para. 8(H), Report on US Practice, 1997, ch. 1.6.

'inference . . . justifiably be drawn that they believed themselves to be applying a mandatory rule of customary international law'.[117]

It is unfortunate the Rule 21 was not drafted with more care, especially in light of the general congruity of the US position. The qualification 'subject to mission accomplishment and allowable risk' hints at the notion of feasibility found elsewhere in Article 57. And US targeting procedure includes a search for targets that achieve the objective while causing the least collateral damage and incidental injury. Doing so lies at the heart of the US effects-based targeting doctrine. This is one case where slight departure from the precise text of Additional Protocol I would have been well-advised.

3. Final remarks

Reviews all too often take on a condemnatory feel. It is to be hoped that that has not been the case here. In great part, the Rules accurately set forth customary international humanitarian law as reflected in State practice. Moreover, in nearly every case, the Rules are likely to be accepted by States as a correct enunciation of the targeting norm in question. In both regards, then, the Study, at least with regard to targeting, is a great success.

However, while the Study's textual fidelity to the received *lex scripta* is laudable, one is left with the sense of missed opportunity. In particular, the Rules retain numerous ambiguities found in Additional Protocol I which could have been clarified through textual modification based on the extent and nature of State practice. Compounding matters, the commentary occasionally brushes over, or neglects altogether, discussion of those matters about which uncertainty or disagreement exists. By this more demanding standard, the Study remains a success, albeit a qualified one.

---

[117] *North Sea Continental Shelf (Federal Republic of Germany v. Denmark; Federal Republic of Germany v. Netherlands)* ICJ Rep. 3, para. 76. See discussion of this point in chapter 2 above (at p. 29).

7

Protected persons and objects

SUSAN C. BREAU

1. Introduction

The principle of distinction between civilians and combatants is one of the most fundamental in international humanitarian law. The Rules proposed for the elaboration of this principle are discussed in chapter 6 above. But over and above the protections afforded to all civilians and civilian objects, the law singles out certain categories of civilians for special protection. Special protection includes two elements – respect and protection. It provides not only for the negative prohibition of sparing an object or person from attack but includes a positive obligation on belligerents to adhere to special measures of respect.[1] Rules 25–42 of the Study propose statements of customary law with regard to certain categories deserving of special protection. This chapter discusses those Rules and the treaty law which lies behind them. Additionally this chapter discusses the broader focus of protection of women, children, and the elderly, disabled and infirm which extends from combat to occupation and which is addressed in Rules 134–138.

The listing of specifically protected persons and objects dates from the earliest humanitarian law instrument. Although the Study deals with rules of customary international law, there has been extensive and long-standing development of treaty rules in this area which either reflect existing custom or lead to a codification of custom.[2] Although the Study claims to take a cautious approach to treaties,[3] Ian Scobbie asserts in chapter 2 of this book that 'the Study took into account the practice of States parties to conclude that "the great majority" of the provisions of

---

[1] Geneva Convention I, Arts. 12, 19, 24, and 25, and Geneva Convention IV, Arts. 16, 18, 20, and 21 use the term respect and protect.

[2] For discussion of the Study's approach to the International Court of Justice case law on the relationship between custom and treaty see Scobbie, chapter 2, pp. 23–31.

[3] Chapter 2, p. 26 and Study, Vol. I, xliv.

the Geneva Conventions and Hague Regulations have customary status'.[4]
This may cause difficulty in certain areas of the Study but in the case of
special protection in international armed conflict, there may be more
reason to rely on treaty provisions than in some of the areas to be discussed. The treaty provisions cited in support of these customary rules
have long historical antecedents prior to Additional Protocol I and
arguably have universal application. However, this does not mean, as
Scobbie persuasively argues in chapter 2, that all provisions of the universally ratified Geneva Conventions are automatically customary.[5]

Before discussing the Rules in detail, it is useful to examine the
humanitarian law Codes and Conventions that considered issues of
special protection prior to the adoption of the Additional Protocols. The
provisions of the Additional Protocols and the 1954 Hague Convention
for the Protection of Cultural Property will be referred to in the discussion of specific Rules. These treaties have not been universally ratified
and there are significant non-party States such as the United States and
Israel.

Lieber code

The 1863 Lieber Code included a rule for the protection of hospitals and
cultural property. Although it was not an international treaty, this Code
has been used as the example of one of the first national military manuals
delineating the laws of war. It influenced many other military manuals.
Domestic discussion of the law of armed conflict prepared the way for the
two Hague Peace Conferences.[6]

Article 35 of the Code listed specially protected locations and objects.
It did not include personnel although their protection may have been
implicit in the text. The rule read as follows:

> Classical works of art, libraries, scientific collections, or precious instru-
> ments, such as astronomical telescopes, as well as hospitals, must be
> secured against all avoidable injury, even when they are contained in forti-
> fied places whilst besieged or bombarded.[7]

---

[4] Chapter 2, p. 29.   [5] Chapter 2, p. 32.

[6] A. Roberts and R. Guelff, *Documents on the Laws of War* (Oxford University Press, 3rd
edn, 2000), pp. 12–13.

[7] General Orders No. 100: Instructions for the Government of Armies of the United States
in the Field, Prepared by Francis Lieber, promulgated as General Orders No. 100 by
President Lincoln, 24 April 1863.

Article 37 contained a provision of special protection for 'the persons of the inhabitants, especially those of women: and the sacredness of domestic relations'. Article 44 of the Lieber Code contained a specific prohibition against rape.

1864 Geneva convention

The first Geneva Convention of 1864 contained rules requiring respect for, and marking of, medical personnel, transports and equipment. The marking was by using an emblem: at the time a red cross on a white background. Articles 1, 2 and 7 included protection for ambulances, military hospitals, hospital and ambulance personnel and provision that the Red Cross emblem was to be adopted for hospitals, ambulances and evacuation parties.[8]

The first Geneva Convention, unlike the Lieber Code, did not contain any provision for the protection of cultural property. This is due to the fact that the International Committee of the Red Cross had been founded by Henri Dunant out of concern for the wounded and sick on the battlefield.[9] Therefore, hospitals, medical and ambulance personnel and chaplains were specifically protected. These provisions were improved and supplemented by the Geneva Conventions of 1906 and 1929.[10]

1899 and 1907 Hague regulations

The 1899 and 1907 Hague Conferences led to the development of rules for the conduct of armed conflict that are still in existence to this day. The 1899 and 1907 Hague Conventions included a series of regulations respecting the laws and customs of war on land. The regulations contained specific rules on targeting of objects including undefended locations and cultural property. Articles 25 and 27 prohibited attacks or bombardment of towns, villages, habitations or buildings which were undefended and provided that all necessary steps were to be taken to spare 'as far as possible' edifices devoted to religion, art, science, and charity and hospitals and places where the sick and wounded were collected. These buildings should be protected by a particular and visible sign, continuing the regime of marking protected locations established in

[8] Geneva Convention 1864.

[9] H. Dunant, *A Memory of Solferino* (ICRC, Geneva, 1986).

[10] Geneva Convention 1906 (this Convention was solely devoted to the amelioration of the wounded and sick on the battlefield), and Geneva Convention 1929, Arts. 9 and 10.

the 1864 Geneva Convention. However, the Regulations indicated that it was the duty of the besieged to notify the enemy beforehand of the presence of these buildings.[11]

The 1907 Hague Convention IV Regulations expanded the protection from bombardment by any means and added historic monuments which expanded the cultural property protection. In Article 5 of Hague Convention IX of 1907 there was a protection for the same edifices from bombardment of naval forces.[12] In these provisions the qualification 'as far as possible' was included which signified that the protection was not absolute. These prohibitions from attack did not include movable property.[13]

These two Hague Conventions included protection for journalists but not from targeting. Article 13 of the Hague Regulations of 1907 stated:

> Individuals who follow an army without directly belonging to it, such as newspaper correspondents and reporters, sutlers and contractors, who fall into the enemy's hands and whom the latter thinks expedient to detain, are entitled to be treated as prisoners of war, provided they are in possession of a certificate from the military authorities of the army which they were accompanying.[14]

1949 Geneva conventions

The 1949 Geneva Conventions reflect the determination of the post-war world further to codify rules of international humanitarian law. Recently these Conventions have achieved universal ratification and accession. The 1949 Geneva Conventions contain many provisions relating to exemption from targeting for specially protected persons and objects. None of the Conventions include protection for cultural objects. Nor do they have specific rules for aerial bombardment which has become the principal method of targeted combat. World War II had been noted for carpet bombing of cities including medical, educational, religious and cultural objects.

Geneva Convention I for the Amelioration of the Condition of the Wounded and Sick in Armed Forces in the Field contains several clauses on the protection of hospitals, hospital ships and medical personnel. An

---

[11] 1899 Hague Regulations, Arts. 25 and 27.
[12] 1907 Hague Regulations, Arts. 25 and 27.
[13] Y. Dinstein, *The Conduct of Hostilities under the Law of International Armed Conflict* (Cambridge University Press, 2004), pp. 153–154.
[14] 1907 Hague Regulations, Arts. 13.

innovation in these articles includes a provision that medical units should be situated in such a manner that attacks against military objectives could not imperil their safety.[15] Article 24 extends the protection to medical personnel 'exclusively engaged in the search for, or the collection, transport or treatment of the wounded and sick, or in the prevention of disease' or in the administration of medical units or establishments. It also provides that chaplains should be respected and protected in all circumstances.[16]

Article 21 of Geneva Convention I contains an important provision with respect to cessation of protection which is repeated in the Additional Protocols. Protection ceases if medical units, after warning, committed outside their humanitarian duties 'acts harmful to the enemy'. Yves Sandoz in the Commentary to the Additional Protocols states:

> the definition of *harmful* is very broad. It refers not only to direct harm inflicted on the enemy, for example, by firing at him, but also to any attempts at deliberately hindering his military operations in any way whatsoever.[17]

Article 22 of Geneva Convention I outlines acts that are not harmful including possession of light weapons for defence and specifies that these units could be guarded by sentries. Dinstein comments on the difficulty in determining hostile acts and points out that 'the exact permutation of the impermissible conduct depends on the circumstances and the nature of the group benefiting from protection'.[18]

Geneva Convention IV includes detailed provisions concerning hospital zones and safety zones and protection of the civilian population not yet occupied from the effects of war. Article 14 states:

> In time of peace, the High Contracting Parties and, after the outbreak of hostilities, the Parties thereto, may establish in their own territory, and if the need arises, in occupied areas, hospital and safety zones and localities so organized as to protect from the effects of war, wounded, sick and aged persons, children under fifteen, expectant mothers and mothers of children under seven.[19]

The Article also provides that agreements can be concluded on mutual recognition of these zones and localities, facilitated by the protecting

---

[15] Geneva Convention I, Arts. 19 and 20.   [16] Ibid., Art. 24.
[17] Y. Sandoz, 'Article 13', in ICRC, *Commentary on the Additional Protocols of 8 June 1977 to the Geneva Conventions of 12 August 1949* (Dordrecht: Martinus Nijhoff, 1987), 173, at 175.   [18] Dinstein, *The Conduct of Hostilities*, p. 151.
[19] Geneva Convention IV, Art. 14.

powers or the International Committee of the Red Cross. A draft agreement is provided in the Annex to Geneva Convention IV. The Convention also includes protection for neutralised zones in Article 15 which are zones intended to shelter from the effects of war wounded and sick combatants and non-combatants and civilian persons taking no part in hostilities. These zones can only be established with the express written agreement by the parties to the conflict. Special protection is also given to persons engaged in the operation and administration of civilian hospitals (Article 20), convoys of vehicles or hospital trains for the transport of sick and wounded, (Article 21) and medical aircraft (Article 22).

Once again this Convention specifies how this protection might be lost. Article 19 states:

> The protection to which civilian hospitals are entitled shall not cease unless they are used to commit, outside their humanitarian duties acts harmful to the enemy. Protection may, however, cease only after due warning has been given, naming, in all appropriate cases, a reasonable time limit, and after such warning has remained unheeded.[20]

Geneva Convention I contains a provision on respect and protection for staff of National Red Cross Societies and other Voluntary Aid Societies. There is a specific condition that each party shall notify the other', in times of peace or at the commencement of or during hostilities, the names of the societies which it has authorised to render assistance to the regular medical service of the armed forces.[21] This provision is repeated in Geneva Convention II for hospital ships of the National Red Cross Societies or officially recognised relief societies on the condition that they placed themselves under the control of one of the parties to the conflict and had previous consent of their own governments and of the party to the conflict concerned.[22]

The four Geneva Conventions do not contain any special protection for journalists from targeting. The category of journalists known as war correspondents are dealt with in the Third Convention concerning the treatment of prisoners of war with the statement that a war correspondent who has fallen into the power of the enemy has the status of a prisoner of war. This does not include any protection from targeting.[23]

Geneva Convention IV regarding Civilians contains a measure of special protection for women that they should be 'specially protected

---

[20] Ibid., Art.19.   [21] Geneva Convention I, Art. 26.   [22] Geneva Convention II, Art. 25.
[23] Geneva Convention III, Art. 4, A (4).

against any attack on their honour, in particular against rape, enforced prostitution, or any form of indecent assault'.[24] There are no specific provisions for children, the elderly or the disabled.

2. The Rules

The Rules contained in Part II of the Study reflect, for the most part, the regime established in the Geneva Conventions; and in the case of special protection, the practice volume of the Study relies on these earlier treaty provisions.[25]

A general comment concerning these Rules is that the persons or objects they cover are generally civilians, who are also protected by the general rules of distinction in Part I.[26] However, Part II of these Rules continues the tradition of giving greater specificity to the respect and protection of certain civilians and civilian objects. The personnel and objects identified in the Study as warranting measures of special protection are: medical and religious personnel and objects; humanitarian relief personnel and objects; personnel and objects involved in peacekeeping missions; journalists; protected zones; and cultural property. As seen above, hospitals, religious personnel and protected zones have a long history of treaty rules granting special protection but the other personnel and objects may have a more recent pedigree of protection in treaty provisions so that the question to be resolved is whether these newer personnel and objects receive special protection in customary international law. This is particularly the case for the Rules with respect to peacekeeping personnel and journalists. Another area needing close review is the specific protection for cultural objects which are not included in the Geneva Conventions of 1949.

Medical and religious personnel and objects

Rules 25, and Rules 27–29[27]

These Rules, which specify that medical personnel, medical transports. medical units and religious personnel are to be respected and protected, are taken almost verbatim from Geneva Conventions I and II of 1949.

---

[24] Geneva Convention IV, Art 27.
[25] Practice for these Rules is included in the Study, Vol. II Part 1, 453–813.
[26] Medical and religious personnel can be members of the military.
[27] These Rules are not set out as they are non-controversial.

There is no doubt that the general Rules prohibiting the targeting of medical and religious personnel and objects unless they commit acts harmful to the enemy constitute customary international law as similar provisions date from the 1864 and 1906 Geneva Conventions.[28]

Although the Rules themselves are general, the Commentary following each Rule seeks to include the additional special protection provisions contained in Additional Protocol I to both international and non-international armed conflict. Additional Protocol I contains several Articles concerning protection of the wounded, sick and shipwrecked.[29] The first alteration from the Geneva Conventions in Additional Protocol I is the expansion of protection to civilian medical personnel and units and civilian religious personnel. The Rules themselves do not specify whether the personnel or objects warranting special protection are civilian or military. It is left to the Commentary for the authors to argue that the extension to civilian medical or religious personnel in Additional Protocol I is 'widely supported in State practice' which refers to personnel without distinguishing their civilian or military status.[30]

The other significant change in Additional Protocol I is the expansion of categories of medical personnel and facilities under special protection to such facilities as blood transfusion centres, preventive medical centres and pharmaceutical stores.[31] This is argued in the Commentary to the Study to represent customary international law as the expansion is widely accepted in State practice.[32]

In both of these situations it cannot be argued that the clarification in the Commentary to support the provisions in Additional Protocol I is part and parcel of the Rules but in this case the Rules are general enough that they could include civilians and a wide variety of medical establishments. It should also be noted that Geneva Convention IV included special protection from attack for civilian hospitals and their personnel and civilian medical transportation units.[33]

There is however, difficulty with the evidence used in the Study to establish these Rules as customary international law. The Study primarily relies on treaty provisions and recent military manuals and national legislation in support of these Rules. It is certain that these general Rules are historically customary, dating from the earliest military manuals and Geneva Conventions. To further support their customary status, the State practice in the Study could have been traced back to the late 1860s

---

[28] 1864 Geneva Convention, Art. 21.   [29] Additional Protocol I, Arts. 8–32.
[30] Study, Vol. I, 79, 88–89.   [31] Additional Protocol I Arts. 21–31.
[32] Study, Vol. I, 82.   [33] Geneva Convention IV, Arts. 18–22.

and did not need to rely solely on more recent material. The national practice in the Study relies on reports of rapporteurs on recent practice but the evidence of special treatment of medical personnel must be far more extensive than these rapporteurs have outlined, particularly practice that took place during the two World Wars.[34]

Nevertheless, the national practice that is set out in Volume II is well worth examining. It contains several instances of violation of these Rules, including the Vietnam War, the Iraq/Kuwait conflict and the war in Yugoslavia. What is significant about the negative practice is the condemnation by other States of the violation of these Rules. However, according to the report on US Practice 'customary practice has proceeded little beyond the specific rules of the Geneva Convention, with a few exceptions'.[35]

The five Rules of special protection for medical personnel and objects and religious personnel can be confirmed to be customary in State practice. This would include the additional protections provided in Additional Protocol I for civilian religious and medical personnel and objects and the expansion of types of facilities. The customary status is established in the Study not only in examples of compliance but in the many instances documented of condemnation for non-compliance. As further substantiation, most military manuals contain language similar to these Rules and do not specify military personnel or objects or the types of facilities.

In the case of medical, religious personnel and objects there is no difficulty in asserting that these Rules also apply in non-international armed conflict. Additional Protocol II includes, in Article 9, protection of medical and religious personnel; it indicates that they should be 'respected and protected and shall be granted all available help for the performance of their duties'. This is extended in Article 10 to medical units and transportation. The Article also provides that protection for these units will cease if they are used to commit hostile acts but only after a warning has been given and the warning remains unheeded. In Article 12 the distinctive emblems of the Red Cross, Red Crescent or Red Lion and Sun are to be displayed by medical and religious personnel and on medical units and medical transports. These Articles do not specify

---

[34] As Scobbie asserts in chapter 2, the ICRC has acknowledged that the practice is incomplete but the reader does not have the resources available to make an independent evaluation of the practice, Scobbie chapter 2, p. 20. There is an example of World War I practice with respect to condemnation of attacks on hospital ships, Study, Vol. II, Part 1, 548.   [35] Study, Vol. II, Part 1, 472.

whether the personnel or objects are civilian or military but the practice outlined in the Study supports the applicability of the Rules to both civilian and military personnel. For example the report on the practice of Algeria notes that in Algeria's war of independence there were no instances of attacks against medical personnel or objects.[36]

Rule 26

Punishing a person for performing medical duties compatible with medical ethics or compelling persons engaged in medical activities to perform acts contrary to medical ethics is prohibited.

This Rule departs from the main focus of special protection, the principle of distinction between civilians and combatants. In this Rule the application is towards the duties of medical personnel. The first part of the Rule is reflected in Article 18(3) of Geneva Convention I which states that 'no one may ever be molested or convicted for having nursed the wounded or sick'. This provision was in the Hague Convention of 1907. It is the second part of the Rule that does not have any treaty antecedents other than Article 16 of Additional Protocol I and Article 10(2) of Additional Protocol II.

The practice is not very extensive in discussion of this second part of the Rule, although it cites several military manuals including those of Argentina, Australia, Canada, Netherlands, New Zealand, Senegal and Spain, which include the provision that medical personnel must not be compelled to perform acts contrary to medical ethics.[37] Further the Doctors Trial[38] at Nuremberg dealt with medical experimentation, not with the issue of being forced to perform duties contrary to medical ethics.

The Study contains examples of contrary practice from the United States, a non-party to Additional Protocols I and II. In 1968 the United States Army Board of Review in the *Levy* case held that medical ethics could not excuse disobedience to the orders of a superior. In 1987 in submitting Additional Protocol II to the US Senate for advice and consent the US President recommended a reservation to Article 10 to preclude the possibility that it might affect the administration of discipline. However, in juxtaposition to this practice the volume also cites in the 1996 State Department Country Reports on Turkey a commentary that medical

---

[36] *Ibid.*, 469.   [37] *Ibid.*, 487–489.
[38] *US v. Brandt et al. (Doctors' trial)* US Military Tribunal, Judgment 19 August 1947 in 2 TWC, 171.

personnel should not be punished for treating the wounded. This does not resolve the difficulty about the issue of compulsion.[39]

It is difficult to argue that the first part of Rule 26 is not customary due to long-standing treaty antecedents; however, that is not the case with the second part. The Study does not contain the scope of practice needed and therefore, this part of the Rule cannot be said to be unequivocally customary.

Rule 30

Attacks directed against medical and religious personnel and objects displaying the distinctive emblems of the Geneva Conventions in conformity with international law are prohibited.

This Rule prohibits the targeting of the specially protected personnel and objects displaying the distinctive emblem. The Rome Statute specifies that such attacks are war crimes in both international and non-international armed conflict.[40] The Study establishes that this Rule is customary for both international and non-international armed conflict with inclusion of a significant amount of practice. This includes a quotation from the 1919 Report on responsibility for outrages in World War I which cited a breach of rules relating to the Red Cross.[41] The practice is probably not as extensive as it should be in respect of non-international armed conflict but the practice of the International Red Cross and Red Crescent Movement in these types of conflict is persuasive.[42]

Humanitarian relief personnel and objects

Rule 31

Humanitarian relief personnel must be respected and protected.

Rule 32

Objects used for humanitarian relief operations must be respected.

Humanitarian relief personnel and objects were included in the Geneva Convention of 1906 which set out that the personnel of volunteer aid societies duly recognised and authorised by their own governments and assimilated into 'sanitary formations' (these were the medical units)

---

[39] Study, Vol. II, Part 1, 489–490. [40] Rome Statute, Art. 8(2)(b) (xxiv) and (e)(ii).
[41] Study, Vol. II Practice, Part 1, 574. [42] *Ibid.*, 587.

were to receive respect and protection.[43] There are provisions in Geneva
Conventions I and II for special protection of aid societies provided
they have the consent of the belligerent party in whose territory they are
operating.[44] Articles 70 and 71 of Additional Protocol I greatly expands
the relief activities from medical activities to delivery of relief consignments. The Articles adhere to the formula that the belligerent party in
whose territory the relief activity is to be conducted has to give
consent.[45] The provision for relief action in not as extensive in Protocol
II but again the provision includes the requirement of consent of the
party concerned.[46]

On the other hand, the two Rules do not mention this aspect of
consent and contain mandatory language of respect and protection. One
of the difficulties involved in analysing these Rules is the paucity of practice to support the formulation contained in the Rules which permit
humanitarian relief activities without the necessity of obtaining permission. The practice included in the Study seems to be relatively recent and
does not reflect a crystallisation of custom. It should be emphasised that
relief personnel are civilians and are entitled to the general protection
from targeting afforded to civilians but the issue here is whether there is
customary international law supporting special protection.

The majority of practice cited in the Study derives from the United
Nations Security Council in the 1990s. The question arises if this indeed
reflects the consensus of the international community as a whole. The
supporting material, particularly with regard to attacks on the safety of
humanitarian relief personnel, contains an interesting collection of
domestic criminal legislation which illustrates a clear trend towards particular protection from attack of these personnel. The national practice
outlined contains answers to the practice questionnaire; there was consensus from Egypt, India, Iraq, Jordan, Kuwait, the Netherlands, Rwanda,
Nigeria, the United Kingdom and Zimbabwe that humanitarian personnel should be protected according to customary international law.[47]
There is no contrary practice cited. The United Kingdom *Manual on the
Law of Armed Conflict* (hereafter *UK Manual*) does not include a section
on humanitarian relief personnel.

Stoffels argues that the duty to protect relief consignments and relief
personnel is only established in Additional Protocol I for international

---

[43] Geneva Convention 1906, Art. 10.
[44] Geneva Convention I, Art. 26, Geneva Convention II, Art. 25.
[45] Additional Protocol I, Arts. 70 and 71.   [46] Additional Protocol II, Art. 18.
[47] Study, Volume II, Part 1, 591–593.

armed conflicts.[48] In non-international armed conflict the right to humanitarian aid could be deduced from common article 3 (prohibition on violence to life and person) of the four Geneva Conventions.[49] She asserts that recent international practice, essentially from declarations and resolutions of international bodies (Commission on Human Rights, United Nations Security Council and General Assembly, European Union and others) showed a 'general acceptance that these obligations apply to all States and to all types of conflict'.[50] This assertion may indeed be correct, but there needs to be an analysis of the practice of those States that supported these resolutions and statements in the United Nations. A Statement by the President of the Security Council, for example, may only reflect the consensus of the Security Council not the community of States.

In terms of other international practice, the two Statutes of the International Criminal Tribunals in Yugoslavia and Rwanda contain no provision for violations relating to humanitarian assistance.[51] The Rome Statute includes in the section on war crimes that directing an attack against personnel, installations, material, units or vehicles involved in a humanitarian assistance mission is a serious violation of the laws and customs of war.[52]

As with the Rules respecting medical personnel and objects, it seems that there could have been a longer historical record discussed, particularly of the operation of the International Committee of the Red Cross in armed conflicts since the Geneva Convention of 1906. However, that practice would probably have revealed the necessity of securing consent to operate in the territory of a belligerent party.

The logical reason for the necessity of consent has to be the difficulty of protecting these personnel in the middle of an armed conflict, as they are often within areas of combat activity. There are many Security Council resolutions cited in the Study calling for protection of humanitarian personnel in these situations, including with regard to Somalia, Rwanda, Kosovo and Sudan.[53] Even though the Additional Protocol I articles provide that these relief operations should not be impeded, realistically this must be only if the party in control of the territory permits such activities to be conducted. An illustration of the difficulties that still remain is the 2006 conflict in Lebanon when Israel refused to agree that

---

[48] R.A. Stoffels, 'Legal Regulation of Humanitarian Assistance in Armed Conflicts: Achievements and Gaps' (2004) 86 *International Review of the Red Cross* 515.
[49] Study, Vol. II, Part I, 519.   [50] *Ibid.*, 521–522.   [51] *Ibid.*, 531.
[52] Rome Statute, Art. 8(2)(b)(iii) and 8(2)(e)(iii)
[53] Study, Vol. II, Part 1, 593–602 and 613–625.

such personnel would be exempt from attack. Note that Article 71 states that 'Only in case of imperative military necessity may the activities of the relief personnel be limited or their movements temporarily restricted.'

Given the lack of practice and the necessity for permission to operate in an area of conflict, the logical conclusion would be that these Rules are customary provided there is a clause inserted in each Rule about the necessity of obtaining permission of the party in whose territory the relief action will be conducted.

Personnel and objects involved in peacekeeping missions

Rule 33

Directing an attack against personnel and objects involved in a peace-keeping mission in accordance with the Charter of the United Nations as long as they are entitled to the protection given to civilians and civilian objects under international humanitarian law, is prohibited.

This first specific mention of protection for United Nations personnel is included in Protocol II to the Certain Conventional Weapons Convention of 1980. Article 8 specifies that a United Nations force or mission should be notified about the location of mines by the belligerent party or the mines or booby-traps should be removed. This protection is repeated in the 1996 Amended Protocol II.[54] The 1994 Convention on the Safety of United Nations mandates that 'United Nations and associated personnel, their equipment and premises shall not be made the object of attack'.[55] The United Nations Convention excludes certain actions from the scope of the Convention, specifically Chapter VII enforcement actions. The Rome Statute of the International Criminal Court includes a prohibition of attacks against peacekeepers which is included in the same section as the criminalisation of attacks on humanitarian relief.[56] Neither Additional Protocol I nor Additional Protocol II includes provisions on special protection for peacekeeping personnel.

The *UK Manual* contains a chapter on the Application of the Law of Armed Conflict during Peace Support Operations. Section 14.15 states:

---

[54] UN Convention on Conventional Weapons, Protocol II, Art. 8 and Amended Protocol II, Art. 12 (hereafter CCW Convention).

[55] Convention on the Safety of United Nations and Associated Personnel, Art. 7.

[56] Rome Statute, Art. 8(2)(b)(iii).

More generally, where a United Nations force or other PSO (Peace support operations) force is not engaged as a party to an armed conflict, its personnel and equipment would not constitute a military objective and attacks on them will therefore be unlawful.[57]

The evidence cited in the Study in support of this Rule is the existence of the United Nations Convention on the Safety of United Nations and Associated Personnel of 1994 and Protocols to the CCW Convention: Protocol II, Article 8 and Amended Protocol II, Article 12(2). However, it has to be pointed out that these treaties have not been widely ratified. The other evidence cited is Article 8(2)(b)(iii), and (e)(iii) of the Rome Statute and the case of *Prosecutor v. Karadžić and Mladić* in the International Criminal Tribunal for Yugoslavia.[58] There are criminal provisions in national law prohibiting attacks on peacekeepers and some case law is cited, but the majority of practice is based on statements made in the United Nations in the 1990s.

There is very little State practice outlined in the Study. As with the Rules respecting humanitarian personnel, the practice emphasised is United Nations practice, rather than the actual State practice necessary for the formation of customary international law. There are very few military manuals cited, only those of Cameroon, Germany, New Zealand, Nigeria and Spain. There is also evidence of national legislation but it is not widespread. The other national practice is sparse indeed with only the report of Malaysia specifically mentioning that Malaysian armed forces are trained to respect peacekeeping forces.[59] Therefore, this rule may be reflective of developing customary practice. It should be noted that this Rule is not essential because any attack against civilians is prohibited and personnel in peacekeeping missions are civilians.

Journalists

Rule 34

Civilian journalists engaged in professional missions in areas of armed conflict must be respected and protected as long as they are not taking a direct part in hostilities.

[57] UK Military Manual, s. 14.15, p. 379.
[58] *Prosecutor v. Karadžić and Mladić*, Review of the indictments pursuant to Rule 61 of the Rules of Procedure and Evidence, 16 July 1996. Case no. IT-95-5-R61 and Case no. l IT-95-18-R61.   [59] Study, Vol. II, Part 1, 646.

The section on journalists has incorporated a distinction between war correspondents and civilian journalists. This chapter deals with civilian journalists; war correspondents are dealt with only incidentally.[60] However, with the rise of the CNN factor, the distinction between journalists and war correspondents has become muddy. Journalists embedded with a unit are still civilians if they comply with the criteria in Rule 34 of 'civilian journalists engaged in professional missions . . . as long as they are not taking a direct part in hostilities'. The practice is not very extensive and this may well be because war correspondents were the model in previous conflicts and civilian journalists are more common in recent armed conflicts. The Rule is very similar to Article 79 of Additional Protocol I and does not have previous treaty antecedents.

It should be noted that the *UK Manual* includes journalists in the section on prisoners of war and not on conduct of hostilities. However, the provision is in general terms:

> Apart from war correspondents accredited to the armed forces, who have prisoner of war status on capture, journalists engaged in professional missions in areas of armed conflict are entitled to the protection afforded to a civilian.[61]

This means being exempt from being a military target.

It seems clear that the treaty law until the 1977 Additional Protocol I was that protection for journalists was limited to periods of detention and to journalists accredited to armed forces.[62] There has been a proposal for a United Nations Convention to protect journalists but that work was suspended when a decision was made to draft Article 79 of the Additional Protocol I.[63] Again this provision was only applicable to international armed conflict. Additional Protocol II for non-international armed conflict does not contain any specific protection for journalists but the argument can be made that as they have been customarily treated as civilians upon capture, they should be exempt from attack in accordance with Article 13.[64]

The question is whether the Rule reflecting Article 79 of Additional Protocol I is customary international law in either international or non-international armed conflict. The State practice cited is limited with use of military manuals of some countries, responses to questionnaires,

---

[60] Study, Vol. I, 115–118.   [61] *UK Manual*, section 8.18, p. 149.
[62] Hans-Peter Gasser, 'The Protection of Journalists Engaged in Dangerous Professional Missions' (1983) 232 *International Review of the Red Cross* 3.
[63] *Ibid.*, Grasser is critical of the lack of a specific convention.   [64] *Ibid.*

national legislation, case law and practice of the United Nations. However, in examining the practice of the United Nations, this Rule, at least with respect to international armed conflict, can be seen to reflect current customary law as there is practice of condemnation of attacks on civilian journalists and a long standing tradition of viewing these persons as civilians and exempt from targeting.[65]

It is more difficult to make this same determination with respect to non-international armed conflict. The Study cites the many instances of journalists being murdered in non-international armed conflict. During 1999 more than 80 journalists were killed or murdered.[66] However, if journalists are considered civilians then they must also be protected by the general prohibition in non-international armed conflict on killing civilians. The issue of whether special protection is part of customary international humanitarian law is not resolved.

Another factor that concerns the military is the necessity to defend these journalists when they are embedded with the forces. We have seen in the more recent conflicts that journalists have been specifically targeted. However, it is clearly customary law that as civilians they are not to be the object of military attacks even when embedded.

Protected zones

Rule 35

Directing an attack against a zone established to shelter the wounded, the sick and civilians from the effects of hostilities is prohibited.

Hospital and civilian safety zones are granted special protection in Geneva Convention I and Geneva Convention IV.[67] The Rule does not include the Geneva Convention condition that medical establishments and units should be situated in such a manner that attacks against military objective cannot imperil their safety.[68] The Rule also does not include the condition in Geneva Conventions I and IV that the Parties conclude agreements on the mutual recognition of these zones and localities.[69]

---

[65] Study, Vol. II, Part 1, 664–666.   [66] *Ibid.*, 667.
[67] Geneva Convention I, Art. 19, Geneva Convention IV, Art. 18.
[68] Study, Vol. II, Part 1, 673
[69] Geneva Convention I, Art. 23., Geneva Convention IV, Art. 14, see G. Aldrich, 'Customary International Humanitarian Law – an Interpretation on behalf of the International Committee of the Red Cross' (2006) 76 *British Yearbook of International Law* 503 at 511–512.

This Rule is established in the Study to be customary international law due to the extensive volume of practice included. However, the Rule should include the two conditions that exist in the Convention as acknowledgement in the Commentary that these conditions exist does not make them part of the Rule. The Practice establishes that these zones have been located as far from hostilities as possible and that agreements have been concluded between belligerent parties.[70]

Rule 36

Directing an attack against a demilitarised zone agreed upon between the parties to the conflict is prohibited.

Additional Protocol I is the only treaty that introduces the concept of a demilitarised zone. However, there are conditions for the establishment of such a zone in addition to an agreement between the parties. Article 60 sets out the conditions for the creation of such a zone:

(a) all combatants, as well as mobile weapons and mobile military equipment must have been evacuated;
(b) no hostile use shall be made of fixed military installations or establishments;
(c) no acts of hostility shall be committed by the authorities or by the population; and
(d) no activities in support of military operations shall be undertaken.[71]

As the ICRC commentary to Additional Protocol I revealed, demilitarised zones could mean different things. A first example could be a zone created subsequent to an armed conflict. The Versailles Treaty of 1919 dictated that Germany could have no fortification or military establishment on the left bank of the Rhine or in an area 50 kilometres east of that river. A second example could be where two or more countries have agreed that certain areas are to be demilitarised such as Antarctica. A third was is that there could be a buffer zone between two parties such as established in Security Council resolution 1701 (2006) on Lebanon. However, these are not the type of zones envisaged in Article 60 of Additional Protocol I as these are zones specifically created to protect civilians from attack during an armed conflict. However, it is also possible that politically created zones are demilitarised for the purposes of Article

---

[70] Study, Vol. I, 120.   [71] *Ibid.*, Art. 59.

60. The problem is that the Rule continues the confusion with respect to this category of protection.[72]

The summary of the Rule defines demilitarised zone as 'an area agreed upon between the parties to the conflict, which cannot be occupied or used for military purposes by any party to the conflict'.[73] This would not seem to include the three types of zones discussed above.

The Rule, once again, omits the conditions for the establishment of these zones. These conditions are mentioned in the commentary but should be part and parcel of the Rule itself.

Rule 37

Directing an attack against a non-defended locality is prohibited.

Article 59 of Additional Protocol 1 deals with attacks on non-defended localities but goes further than the Geneva Conventions and specifies the conditions for a non-defended locality including that:

(a) all combatants, as well as mobile weapons and mobile military equipment must have been evacuated;
(b) no hostile use shall be made of fixed military installations or establishments;
(c) no acts of hostility shall be committed by the authorities or by the population; and
(d) no activities in support of military operations shall be undertaken.[74]

Aldrich has serious concerns about the lack of inclusion of these conditions in the Rule:

> Clearly these conditions which were essential for the acceptance of the concept of non-defended localities, will normally be difficult to secure, and the adverse Party is obligated to respect such a locality only if it, in fact, meets those conditions.[75]

According to Gasser, this last condition means that undefended zones must be handed over to the enemy without fighting or they will lose their special protection.[76]

---

[72] ICRC, *Commentary on Additional Protocol I*, www.icrc.org.   [73] *Ibid.*, pp. 120–121.
[74] *Ibid.*, Art. 59.   [75] Aldrich, 'Customary International Humanitarian Law'.
[76] Hans-Peter Gasser, 'Protection of the Civilian Population' in D. Fleck (ed.), *The Handbook of Humanitarian Law in Armed Conflicts* (Oxford University Press, 1999), p. 513.

The Commentary to this Rule states that 'the concept of non-defended localities is rooted in the traditional concept of an "open town" '.[77] Open towns are not mentioned in treaties but could be covered by Article 59(2) Additional Protocol I. Open towns or cities seem to have a long historical tradition in conflict; when a town declared itself to be open it would not be subject to attack. Again the practice is not fully developed, although Rome in 1944 is given as an example of a city that was not open due to lack of declaration or voluntary behaviour. The question is whether these zones are relevant in today's conflicts?

The *UK Military Manual* contains two sections on these zones that are remarkably similar to these rules. The first section sets out the types of localities and zones under special protection including:

(a) undefended towns, villages, dwellings, or buildings;
(b) hospital zones and localities for the protection of the wounded and sick of the armed forces and medical personnel;
(c) safety zones for wounded and sick civilians, old people, expectant mothers, and mothers of small children;
(d) neutralised zones for protection of the wounded and sick, both combatants and civilians, and also civilians taking no part in hostilities;
(e) non-defended localities;
(f) demilitarised zones.[78]

As the second section in the *UK Manual* argues, it is important to point out that these rules specify agreement between the parties as to the location of these zones which can be difficult in non-international armed conflict and terrorism. The failure of the zones of protection in Srebrenica and Zepa pointed to the difficulty of actually securing protection in armed conflict. The *Manual* states:

> The question of what measures of force may be necessary to defend UN-established safe areas have proved difficult in practice. Following the fall of the 'safe area' of Srebrenica to Bosnian Serb forces in July 1995 and the killing of large numbers of inhabitants, a UN report urged the need for a clearer commitment to the use of forces in the defence of such areas.[79]

Given that the whole premise of these areas is that they are supposed to be undefended, using force to protect them seems to be contrary to the historical bases for the development of these rules.

---

[77] Study, Vol. I, 122.   [78] *UK Manual*, s. 5.31, p. 80.
[79] *Ibid.*, p. 80 quoting *Report of the Secretary-General pursuant to General Assembly Resolution 53/35: The Fall of Srebrenica*, UN Doc. A/54/549, New York, 15 November 1999.

The practice manual contains extensive State practice on all three types of zones.[80] Given that these zones are included in Hague and Geneva law prior to the Protocols, the conclusion is that these Rules clearly reflect long-standing customary international law but should also include the preconditions for the establishment of these zones.

Cultural property

Rule 38

Each party to the conflict must respect cultural property:

A. **Special care must be taken in military operations to avoid damage to buildings dedicated to religion, art, science, education or charitable purposes and historic monuments unless they are military objectives.**

B. **Property of great importance to the cultural heritage of every people must not be the object of attack unless imperatively required by military necessity.**

Rule 39

The use of property of great importance to the cultural heritage of every people for purposes which are likely to expose it to destruction or damage is prohibited, unless imperatively required by military necessity.

As the Geneva Conventions do not deal with cultural property, the most important treaty in this area is the 1954 Hague Convention for the Protection of Cultural Property in the Event of Armed Conflict.[81] The inspiration for this treaty was stated to be that World War II 'wreaked havoc on the cultural heritage of Europe'.[82] The first innovation from earlier treaties is the definition of cultural property:

(a) movable or immovable property of great importance to the cultural heritage of every people, such as monuments of architecture, art or history, whether religious or secular; archaeological sites; groups of

---

[80] Study, Vol. II, Part 1, 671–722.
[81] There was a previous instrument, the 1935 Roerich Pact which protected cultural property but it was a regional instrument, and space does not permit its discussion.
[82] H. Abtahi, 'The Protection of Cultural Property in Times of Armed Conflict: The Practice of the International Criminal Tribunal for the Former Yugoslavia' (2001) 14 *Harvard Human Rights Journal* 1, at 7.

buildings which, as a whole, are of historical or artistic interest; works of art; manuscripts, books and other objects of artistic, historical or archaeological interest; as well as scientific collections and important collections of books or archives or of reproductions of the property defined above;

(b) buildings whose main and effective purpose is to preserve or exhibit the movable cultural property defined in sub-paragraph (a) such as museums, large libraries and depositories of archives, and refuges intended to shelter, in the event of armed conflict, the movable cultural property defined in subparagraph (a);

(c) centres containing a large amount of cultural property as defined in subparagraphs (a) and (b), to be known as 'centres containing monuments'.[83]

This definition of cultural property is all-inclusive and includes, for the first time, movable property. The protection includes refraining from any act of hostility against the property including any act directed by way of reprisals or acts of theft, pillage, vandalism, misappropriation or requisition. The parties also agree to refrain from any use of the property or its immediate surroundings which might expose it to destruction. Presumably this means use for military purposes.[84]

One important innovation of the Hague Convention is the introduction of a new emblem to enhance visibility and, hence, protection: the blue and white shield. The Hague Convention also eliminates reciprocity in Article 5 by stating that no party can evade its obligations simply because another party has not applied the measures of safeguard delineated in Article 3.

The protection for cultural property in this Convention is not absolute and although the 'as far as possible' wording of the Hague Regulations is eliminated, Article 4 (2) states that the obligations can be waived 'only in cases where military necessity imperatively requires such a waiver'.[85] Therefore, parties could decide to attack when 'imperative military necessity' demands. Dinstein states:

> If imperative requirements of military necessity can trump the protection of cultural property, no real progress has been achieved since the days of the 'as far as possible' exhortation, since the attacking force is prone to regard almost any military necessity as 'imperative'.[86]

---

[83] 1954 Hague Convention for the Protection of Cultural Property in the event of Armed Conflict, Art. 1.   [84] *Ibid.*, Art. 4.   [85] *Ibid.*, Art. 4 (2).
[86] Dinstein, *The Conduct of Hostilities*, p. 158.

Article 8 of the Convention introduces special protection for cultural property of 'very great importance' provided it is situated at an adequate distance from any large industrial centre or important military objective and it is not used for military purposes.[87] This protection is extended to sites near to military objectives provided these sites are entered into the 'International Register of Cultural Property under Special Protection' and that no use is made of the military objective near by. Even this protection can be withdrawn 'in exceptional cases of unavoidable military necessity, and only for such time as that necessity continues'.[88] This necessity can only be established by an officer commanding a force the equivalent of a division in size or larger. The opposing party should be notified, a reasonable time in advance, of the decision to withdraw immunity.[89] Although this withdrawal is only for 'unavoidable military necessity' it signifies that cultural property is never under absolute protection.

In 1999 the Second Protocol to the Hague Convention of 1954 specified in Article 6 that attacks cannot be launched against cultural property unless the specific object has been converted into a military object and clarified the meaning of the waiver contained in Article 4 of the 1954 Convention:

(a) a waiver on the basis of imperative military necessity pursuant to Article 4 paragraph 2 of the Convention may only be invoked to direct an act of hostility against cultural property when and for so long as:
  (i) that cultural property has, by its function, been made into a military objective; and
  (ii) there is no feasible alternative available to obtain a similar military advantage to that offered by directing an act of hostility against that objective;
(b) a waiver on the basis of imperative military necessity pursuant to Article 4 paragraph 2 of the Convention may only be invoked to use cultural property for purposes which are likely to expose it to destruction or damage when and for as long as no choice is possible between such use of the cultural property and another feasible method for obtaining a similar military advantage.

The decision to invoke imperative military necessity can only be taken by an officer commanding a force the equivalent of a battalion in size or larger, or a force smaller in size where circumstances do not permit

---

[87] 1954 Hague Convention for the Protection of Cultural Property in the event of Armed Conflict, Art. 8.   [88] *Ibid.*, Art. 11.   [89] *Ibid.*, Art. 11.

otherwise and an effective advance warning is to be given whenever circumstances permit.[90]

The 1999 Protocol expands the precautions necessary in attack which
includes that each party to the conflict is to do 'everything feasible' to
verify that the objectives to be attacked are not cultural property, to take
'all feasible precautions' in the choice of means and methods of attack to
minimise incidental damage to cultural property and to refrain from
launching any attack that could cause incidental damage to cultural
property which would be excessive in relation to the concrete and direct
military advantage. Parties to this Protocol would be expected to cancel
or suspend an attack if it became apparent that either the objective was
cultural property or the attack could be expected to cause incidental
damage to cultural property.[91]

Chapter 3 of the Protocol enunciates measures of enhanced protection
for cultural heritage of the greatest importance for humanity. Under
Article 13 this type of cultural property can only lose its protection 'if,
and for as long as, the property has, by its use, become a military objective'. Any attack has to be authorised at the highest operational level of
command with effective advance warning and when it is 'the only feasible
means of terminating the use of the property'.[92]

It is important to note that this Convention is not universally ratified;
there are 116 States parties, and 93 parties to the Additional Protocol to
this Convention. Not all of the Convention and its Protocols can be said
to codify customary international law.

Additional Protocol I also confirms protection of cultural property in
conflict. Article 53 lists prohibited acts including acts of hostility, and
reprisals against cultural objects and places of worship, prefaced by the
words: 'Without prejudice to the provisions of the Hague Convention for
the Protection of Cultural Property in the Event of Armed Conflict of 14
May 1954, and of other relevant international instruments'. The regime
of the Hague Convention thus continues, including the military necessity
waivers in Articles 4 and 11. Dinstein argues that the waiver is 'irreconcil-
able with the protection guaranteed in Protocol I to all civilian objects'.[93]
A difference between this provision and Article 1 of the 1954 Hague
Convention is that Article 1 of that Convention refers to property that is
'of great importance to the cultural heritage' whereas Protocol I refers to

---

[90] 1999 Second Protocol to the Hague Convention, Art. 6.   [91] *Ibid.*, Art. 7.
[92] 1999 Second Protocol to the Hague Convention, Art. 13.
[93] Dinstein, *The Conduct of Hostilities*, p. 160.

objects that constitute 'the cultural or spiritual heritage of peoples'. The Commentary to the Additional Protocols argues that the basic idea of the two provisions is the same.[94]

The Rules in the Study concerning cultural property are far more general than the extensive provisions of the Hague Convention of 1954, discussed above. The first general Rule, in fact, is very similar to the provisions contained in the Hague Regulations of 1899 and 1907.

There is no specification in either Rule 38 or 39 of the meaning of military necessity. The Hague Convention contained in Article 4 a waiver of protection in the event of military necessity. The conditions for waiver were specified in the Hague Convention 2nd Protocol of 1999. The Commentary on these Rules argues that the waiver included in the 1999 Protocol should be applied as follows:

(1) the cultural property in question has, by its function, been made into a military objective; and (cumulative)
(2) there is no feasible alternative to obtain a similar military advantage to that offered by attacking that objective.[95]

The Protocol has been ratified by only 42 States. It is also very restrictive as to how protection can be waived. It has been argued by several countries that the first part of the test should be sufficient. They would question the utility of the second part when the customary rule would seem to be that a cultural object could be attacked if it has been made into a military objective and imperative military necessity required it.[96] However, the formula in the 1999 Protocol is repeated for both Rules 38 and 39.

The United Kingdom and the United States are not parties to the 1954 Hague Convention or its Protocols. However, the UK Manual contains a detailed section on the Convention recognising its importance as many NATO European States are parties. The rules as outlined in this Manual contain much of the specificity that is contained in the Convention.[97] As with the Rule 38, the Manual requires that it is prohibited to commit any act of hostility directed against the historic monuments, works of art, or place of worship which constitute the cultural or spiritual heritage of peoples (5.25 (a)). The Manual states that Protocol I:

> needs to be read in conjunction with the Cultural Property Convention, even for states not party to the latter, because an attack on cultural

---

[94] Abtahi, 'The Protection of Cultural Property' at 8.   [95] *Ibid.*, p. 130.
[96] Study, Vol. II, Part 1, 725–726 and p. 745.
[97] *UK Manual*, Sections 5.25–5.26.8, pp. 70–74.

property is regarded as an aggravated form of attack on a civilian object, necessitating special care in operational planning.[98]

The *Manual* also quotes in detail the only circumstances when the protection of cultural property may be waived in the case when the property has become a military objective and there is no feasible alternative for dealing with the situation and a prior warning is given except for immediate self-defence. The waiver of protection must be given by the appropriate commander at the various three levels of protection: basic, special and enhanced.[99] The Rules in the Study are far more general and this explanatory section cannot be said to be part of the customary rules.

It can be concluded that Rules 38 and 39, containing similar language to treaty provisions dating back to the Hague Regulations, are indeed customary international law. The Commentary argues that the application of the 1954 Hague Convention, ratified by 111 States is part of customary law extending to non-international armed conflict as recognised by the *Tadic* decision in the ICTY.[100] The Study not only traces the treaty provisions back to the Hague Regulations but also includes the 1863 Lieber Code and the 1874 Brussels Declaration, the 1880 Oxford Manual and the 1923 Hague Rules on Aerial Warfare. It also includes numerous entries in military manuals, national criminal codes and several pages of national practice. This section contains the detail necessary to justify the argument that these two rules are customary in both international and non-international armed conflict.

Rule 40

The use of property of great importance to the cultural heritage of every people for purposes which are likely to expose it to destruction or damage is prohibited, unless imperatively required by military necessity.

Rule 41

Each party to the conflict must protect cultural property:

A. **All seizure or destruction or wilful damage done to institutions dedicated to religion, charity, education, the arts and sciences, historic monuments and works of art and science is prohibited.**

---

[98] *Ibid.*, p. 71.
[99] *Ibid.*, p. 73 – basic: battalion commander; special: divisional commander; enhanced: higest operational level of command.   [100] Study, Vol. I, 129.

B. Any form of theft, pillage or misappropriation of, and any acts of vandalism directed against, property of great importance to the cultural heritage of every people is prohibited.

Rule 41

The occupying power must prevent the illicit export of cultural property from occupied territory and must return illicitly exported property to the competent authorities of the occupied territories.

Rule 40 prohibits seizure and destruction of cultural property and Rule 41 states that the occupying power must prevent the illegal export of cultural property. These Rules do not involve the targeting of these sites but seem to reflect established custom dating back to World War II; there were war crimes trials on the destruction and removal of cultural property after World War II.[101] Rule 41 is one of the very few Rules in the Study on occupation law.

Works and installations containing dangerous forces

Rule 42

Particular care must be taken if works and installations containing dangerous forces, namely dams, dykes and nuclear electrical generating stations, and other installations located at or in their vicinity are attacked, in order to avoid the release of dangerous forces and consequent severe losses among the civilian population.

Of all the Rules analysed in this chapter, this one is probably the most controversial. The Rule does not repeat the extensive provision in Article 56 of Additional Protocol I which prohibits attacks against these facilities and contains provisions for the cessation of protection. The Rule specifies only that particular care must be taken if works and installations containing dangerous forces are attacked. Article 85(3)(c) of Additional Protocol I provided that launching an attack against these objects in the knowledge that it would cause excessive loss of life would be a grave breach of the Protocol.

---

[101] Study, Vol. II, Part 1, 133 citing for example, *Von Leeb (The High Command Trial)* and *Weizsäcker (Ministries case)* cases which convicted the accused of seizure and destruction of cultural property: *US v. Wilhelm von Leeb et al.* (US Military Tribunal, Germany, 1948) 12 *Law Reports of Trials of War Criminals* 1 and *US v. Weizsäcker (Ministries case).* (US Military Tribunal, Nuremberg, 1948) 14 *Trials of War Criminals* 308.

A critical piece of evidence against Article 56 having customary status is provided both in the practice manual and in the Commentary to the Rule; that is, the reservations by both the United Kingdom and France with respect to Article 56. Their reservations stated that they could not grant absolute protection to works and installations containing dangerous forces which were military objectives but would take precautions to avoid severe collateral losses.[102] These reservations seem to form the basis of Rule 42 although neither reservation stated that they would take precautions specifically to avoid the release of dangerous forces.

The volume on practice gives extensive citations. The authors of the Study are to be commended for the thorough research contained within this section. There are numerous citations from military manuals; the quotations from the military manuals of Israel and of the United States are particularly informative. First of all, Israel's manual states that although Article 56 is not binding it is 'nevertheless widely accepted as a binding provision' and attacks would lead to the unleashing of destructive forces 'resulting in tens of thousands of civilian victims, and therefore it is forbidden'.[103] The *US Air Force Pamphlet*, *Air Force Commander's Handbook*, and the *US Naval Handbook* and *Supplement* all contain language confirming the restraint doctrine and the avoidance of excessive civilian casualties in adherence to the principle of proportionality.

There is also extensive citation of national legislation penalising in national criminal law attacks on these types of installations. It has to be noted that most of the States concerned are parties to Additional Protocols I and II. However, there is support for the customary status of this Rule in the section of other national practice. First of all the report on the practice of China recalled that in 1938 the Nationalist government decided to bomb a dam on the Yellow River to use the water to halt the Japanese offensive. The floods caused many casualties and the Communist government later condemned this method of warfare.[104] The practice of Colombia which is not a party to Additional Protocol II consisted of a statement of the Presidency of the Colombian Republic in 1994 that it would not occur to any sensible military officer to bomb a dam in order to dislodge guerrillas and thus cause a deluge that would sweep away the inhabitants.[105] Indonesia is not a party to either Additional Protocol I or II and yet the report on the practice of Indonesia states that

---

[102] Study, Vol. I, 140 and Vol. II, Part 1, 815.   [103] Study, Vol. II, Part 1, 820–821.
[104] *Ibid.*, 830.   [105] *Ibid.*, 830–831.

installations containing dangerous forces could not be attacked as long as they were not used for military purposes.[106]

Further support for this Rule's customary status can be found in the practice materials on Iran and Iraq in relation to their armed conflict from 1980 to 1988. During this conflict Iran denied that it had attacked a power station at Ducan dam and stated that it considered the protection of nuclear plants to be part of customary international law. Iraq, according to Iran, had attacked one of their nuclear plants at Bushehr. Iraq's practice cited a letter to the UN Secretary-General complaining of US attacks in the Saddam Dam area and a letter from the President of Iraq to the World Association for Peace and Life against Nuclear War in 1983 condemning attacks on peaceful nuclear installation as tantamount to an attack by nuclear weapons.[107]

The practice of Pakistan, another State not a party to Additional Protocol I is very informative. During the wars of 1965 and 1971 Pakistan refrained from striking against installations that contained dangerous forces. In response to rumours that India was planning to attack Pakistan's nuclear facilities, Pakistan took a very stern position. This is significant practice from a State that had been involved in international armed conflict. It would have been interesting to see practice from India as well, the other party to the conflict.

Finally, there is extensive analysis of the practice of the United States. First of all it was reported that during the Korean War, the US air force regularly targeted dams. However, there is a significant piece of practice during the Vietnam War. In 1972 the US planned to attack a hydroelectric plant which included a dam; if the dam had been breached as many as 23,000 civilians could have died. The plant was authorised to be attacked by President Nixon but using laser guided bombs because that gave a 90 per cent chance that the dam would not be breached. This is an example of the proportionality principle being utilised with respect to dangerous forces. The statements of the US officials cited from 1987 through 1997 clearly state that they do not consider that there are any restrictions on attack against works and installations containing dangerous forces but their actual practice and military manuals reveal a use of proportionality particularly directed at these targets.[108]

The extensive and thorough analysis of State practice conducted by the ICRC leads this author to the conclusion that the Study has established that Rule 42 is customary in internal and international armed conflict.

---

[106] *Ibid.*, 832.   [107] *Ibid.*, 832.   [108] *Ibid.*, 834–836.

Significantly, it is the practice of non-States parties to Additional Protocol I that supports, at the very least, precautions in attacking installations containing dangerous forces. The Rule does not attempt to reflect the absolute prohibition in Article 56 of Additional Protocol I but supports an analysis which is based on the customary rule of proportionality. This Rule then is merely a part of the proportionality test that must be used when any military objective is considered. As Aldrich, the principle drafter, of Article 56 states:

> This standard is reasonable and is a formulation I would have been satisfied to use in Protocol I, but it would have been unacceptable then at the conference to a group of States led by Switzerland and the Netherlands.[109]

Other persons afforded specific protection

The rules of special protection for women, children, the elderly and disabled intersect situations of combat and the laws of occupation. As the introduction of this section states, international humanitarian law provides the same protection for women as men whether they be civilians, combatants or persons *hors de combat*. However, these are further rights and protections given 'their specific needs and vulnerabilities'. It is a tragedy of all combat that sexual assault is often used as a weapon of war and, therefore, these rules are a necessity.

Rule 134

The specific protection, health and assistance needs of women affected by armed conflict must be protected.

The specific protection of women and children although implicit in earlier Conventions was not finally adopted until Article 76 and 77 of Additional Protocol I. This Rule does not provide the detail of these Articles: specifically the Rule does not mention protection for women against rape, forced prostitution and any form of sexual assault, and protection for children against indecent assault. It also does not include the prohibition against the pronouncement of the death penalty against pregnant women or women having dependent infants. In this case the Rule could have been more extensive although the commentary refers back to the fundamental guarantee in Rule 93 which states that rape and other forms of sexual violence are prohibited. It also details the particular

---

[109] Aldrich, 'Customary International Humanitarian Law' at 513.

care for pregnant women and mothers of young children including the death penalty. However, these obligations are not specified in the Rule itself.[110]

The general statement of special protection of women in Rule 134 reflects customary law with long historical antecedents going back to Articles 19 and 37 of the Lieber Code. Article 12(4) of both Geneva Conventions I and II specified that 'women shall be treated with all consideration due to their sex' and Article 14 of Geneva Convention III had a similar provision'. The most extensive provisions were in Geneva Convention IV: Article 27(2) provided that 'women shall be specially protected against any attack on their honour' and Article 119(2) provided that in relation to disciplinary punishments 'account shall be taken of the internee's age, sex and state of health'.[111]

The discussion of State practice in the Study is disappointing. Given the long history of special protection of women there could have been discussion of prohibitions of sexual assault dating back to World War I. The international outcry from the so-called Rape of the Belgians during that conflict is well known.[112] The reaction to the 'comfort women' used by the Japanese Army in World War II continues to this day.[113] These could have been utilised as examples of State practice especially in statements of condemnation by national governments.

The Study relates extensive and persuasive practice from the 1990s which, if it were combined with earlier practice, would support this Rule's customary status and provide a specific addition to the Rule for protection from sexual assault. Rape is still used commonly as a weapon of conflict but the condemnation of the practice by many governments would support customary status. The vast number of military manuals which include the prohibition of sexual assault would also support the rule that women are entitled to special respect and protection.[114]

Specific protection for pregnant women and women with young children was also specified in the 1949 Geneva Convention IV and has customary status. The issue of custom however, arises with respect to the

---

[110] Study, Vol. I, 477.   [111] Study, Vol. II, Part 2, 3059.

[112] The events that took place in the German occupation of Belgium are disputed but international condemnation of sexual assault of women during combat or occupation has long historical antecedents.

[113] C. Sarah Soh, *Japan's Responsibility Toward Comfort Women Survivors*, Japan Policy Research Institute Working Paper No. 77, May 2001, although Japan would not acknowledge responsibility and no one was tried at the IMT for Japan, governments such as the Republic of Korea have demanded compensation for victims.

[114] Study, Vol. II, Part 2, 3060–3062.

death penalty and pregnant women. The prohibition against executing
pregnant women and women with young children was not specified in
the Geneva Conventions until 1977. Article 6(5) of the International
Covenant on Civil and Political Rights of 1966 set out that sentences of
death should not be carried out on pregnant women but there was no
mention of women with young children. Once again the tendency would
be to argue that this is customary but the research is lacking in the volume
on practice.

Rule 135

**Children affected by armed conflict are entitled to special respect and
protection.**

The rights of children are specified in more detail in the Commentary to
the Rule which outlines the meaning of special protection for children as
including:

- Protection against all forms of sexual violence;
- Separation from adults when deprived of liberty unless they are
  members of the same family;
- Access to education, food and health care;
- Evacuation from areas of combat for safety reason;
- Reunification of unaccompanied children with their families.[115]

Once again there is no doubt that the general statement is customary,
dating back to Geneva Convention IV although the reference in the
Geneva Articles was to children under 15. The 1989 Convention on the
Rights of the Child also has achieved almost universal ratification and
specifies in Article 38(4):

> In accordance with their obligation under international humanitarian law
> to protect the civilian population in armed conflicts, States Parties shall
> take all feasible measures to ensure protection and care of children who are
> affected by armed conflict.

The State practice reported is extensive and supports the specific obligations outlined in the Commentary, as quoted above, in both international
and non-international armed conflict.

The definition of child in the Convention on the Rights of the Child
comprises every person under 18 years of age so that the age of special

---

[115] Study, Vol. I, 481.

protection would arguably be 18.[116] Many of the military manuals cited in the Study specify the age for protection as being under 15 years old, [117] but ratification of the Convention on the Rights of the Child by almost every State, together with State practice, supports special protection for children under 18.

Rule 136
Children must not be recruited into armed forces or armed groups.

Rule 137
Children must not be allowed to take part in hostilities.

The issue of child soldiers has come to the forefront in recent years with the extensive use of child soldiers in such conflicts as those in Sierra Leone, the Democratic Republic of Congo and Uganda. The prohibition against recruitment of children dates back to Article 50(2) of Geneva Convention (IV) which states that the occupying power may not enlist children 'in formations or organisations subordinate to it'.[118] The 1989 Convention on the Rights of the Child also included a prohibition against recruiting persons who have not yet attained the age of 15 years into their armed forces.[119] The *Norman* case in the Sierra Leone Special Court found that customary law had criminalised this prohibition.[120] It is interesting that the first indictee to be detained by the International Criminal Court is Thomas Lubanga Dyilo from the Democratic Republic of Congo on charges of conscription and enlisting children under 15 in armed conflict.[121]

In this case there is extensive practice cited which supports the existence of the Rule. Although many States argue that the age limit should be increased to under 18 years old, the age for a ban on military recruitment is under 15 years of age.[122] The Commentary to the Rules reveals the vigorous debate on the age issue which is not resolved. The Optional Protocol to the Convention on the Rights of the Child on the Involvement

[116] Convention on the Rights of the Child, 1989, Art. 1.
[117] Study, Vol, II, Part 2, 3078–3083.   [118] Geneva Convention IV, Art.50 (2).
[119] Convention on the Rights of the Child, 1989, Art. 38 (3).
[120] *Prosecutor v. Norman*, (Special Court for Sierra Leone) Decision on Preliminary Motion based on lack of Jurisdiction, 31 May 2004, Case No.SCSL-2004–14-AR72(E) with Judge Robertson dissenting.
[121] International Criminal Court, indictment of Thomas Lubanga Dyilo, www.icc-cpi.int/library/cases/ICC-01-04-01-06-356-Anx2_English.pdf, accessed on 31 January 2006.
[122] Study, Vol. II, Part 1, 4010–4042.

of Children in Armed Conflict calls for States to take all feasible measures
to ensure that members of the armed forces under the age of 18 do not
take direct part in hostilities.[123]

Rule 138

**The elderly, disabled and infirm affected by armed conflict are entitled
to special respect and protection.**

There are no specific treaty provisions for the protection of the elderly
save removal from besieged areas of aged persons in Article 17 of Geneva
Convention IV and some provisions in relation to the treatment of
detained persons that the age of the person should be taken into
account.[124] However, there are extensive provisions in the 1949 Geneva
Conventions on special care and protection for disabled civilians and
combatants.[125] Although in each category the reporting of State practice
is limited, special protection for infirm and disabled is established as customary, while this may not yet be the case for the elderly.

3. Final remarks

In this chapter it is concluded that the Rules in this part of the Study
either reflect current customary law or, in respect of peacekeepers and
humanitarian personnel, developing custom. The paucity and reliance
on recent practice is a continuing problem with the Study and this is certainly evident in parts of this section of the Rules. It can be accepted,
however, that it is difficult to establish practice of compliance. However,
the long-standing history of treaty provisions for medical and religious
personnel and undefended localities substantiate the customary practice,
since the fact of almost universally ratified treaties can codify or result in
customary law.

One of the unique aspects of this part of the Study is that the Rules
require expansion with the inclusion of essential conditions within the
Rules. This is particularly the case for consent of the belligerent parties to
the operation of humanitarian relief efforts and the establishment of

---

[123] Study, Vol. I, 488 and Optional Protocol to the Convention on the Rights of the Child on
the Involvement of Children in Armed Conflict, Arts. 1 and 4.
[124] Geneva Convention III, Arts. 16, 44, 45 and 49 Geneva Convention IV, Arts. 27, 85
and 199.
[125] Geneva Convention III, Arts. 30 and 110 Geneva Convention IV, Arts. 16,17, 21, 22,
and 127.

protected zones. The Rules should have included the essential part of long-standing rules of conduct in the law of armed conflict. The Study in its extensive analysis of practice in the area of special protection has confirmed the obligation to respect and protect medical establishments and their personnel, religious personnel, humanitarian personnel and ensure special status for women and children.

8

Natural environment

KAREN HULME

1. Introduction

In 1977 two provisions were adopted in Additional Protocol I[1] that had as their focus the protection of the natural environment. Recognised as having no basis in existing customary law,[2] the two provisions were viewed as new additions to the law governing international armed conflict. While similar provisions were discussed for Additional Protocol II,[3] these did not appear in the final adopted text. The objective of the two new provisions in Additional Protocol I was the absolute prohibition of environmental damage beyond a specific threshold. Consequently, Article 35(3) prohibits the use of methods or means of warfare intended or expected to cause widespread, long-term and severe damage to the natural environment, whether the harm is direct or collateral. Positioned in the 'Basic Rules' of Part III of Additional Protocol I, concerning 'Means and Methods of Warfare', the environmental protection provisions are located alongside the established customary principle of unnecessary suffering. Cementing the prima facie civilian status of the natural environment, a further three aspects of environmental protection are provided in Article 55:

(1) a general obligation of environmental awareness in the conduct of warfare,
(2) a specific prohibition on means and methods of warfare causing widespread, long-term and severe environmental damage and thereby prejudicing the health or survival of a population, and

---

[1] Additional Protocol I, Arts. 35(3) and 55.
[2] Comments of Federal Republic of Germany that the provisions were an 'important new contribution' to the protection of the natural environment in times of international armed conflict, Official Records of the Diplomatic Conference on the Reaffirmation and Development of International Humanitarian Law Applicable in Armed Conflicts, Geneva (1974–1977), Vol. VI, CDDH/SR.39, O.R., 25 May 1977, 115.
[3] Additional Protocol I.

(3) a prohibition on environmental reprisals.[4]

While these provisions of Additional Protocol I were the first to recognise the specific need for environmental protection in armed conflict, the environment has benefited from ancillary protections for centuries. Hague law,[5] for example, prohibits the wanton destruction of property during military operations[6] and promotes the concept of usufruct in occupied territories.[7] Similarly, although not specifically environmental in scope, other provisions within Additional Protocol I provide ancillary protection, such as Article 54, which prohibits the destruction of objects indispensable to the civilian population and Article 56, which prohibits certain attacks on works and installations containing dangerous forces.[8] So, while the two environmental provisions in Additional Protocol I were important, indeed landmark, developments in 1977, they should not be viewed as existing in a legal vacuum of wartime environmental protection. Further, as a consequence of a deepening global environmental awareness since the 1970s, means and methods of warfare have increasingly been scrutinised on environmental grounds. An early example is demonstrated in the condemnation of US ground clearance methods used during the Vietnam Conflict. It was the environmental destruction caused by the use of chemical defoliants, in particular, in addition to more general fears of environmental manipulation as a weapon of war, which led to the adoption of further rules on environmental protection in the form of the 1977 United Nations ENMOD Convention.[9]

Although considered a legal development in 1977, the concept of environmental protection in wartime had gained sufficiently in importance by the late 1990s that the inclusion within the 1998 Rome Statute of the International Criminal Court[10] of an environmental war crime was not contentious.[11] While the environmentally destructive tactics of the Vietnam conflict provided the initial impetus for regulation, it was the 1991 Persian Gulf conflict that first put this to the test. Yet this was not as a result of binding treaty obligations, since the provisions of Additional Protocol I were not binding on any of the principal parties to the conflict.

[4] Environmental reprisals will not be analysed in this chapter; see chapter 14, see pp. 367–368   [5] Hague Regulations 1907.
[6] Hague Regulations 1907, Art. 23(g).   [7] Hague Regulations 1907, Art. 55.
[8] See chapter 7, pp. 192–193.
[9] United Nations Convention on the Prohibition of Military or Any Other Hostile Use of Environmental Modification Technique (hereafter ENMOD).
[10] Rome Statute of the International Criminal Court.
[11] Rome Statute, Art. 8(2)(b)(iv).

Further environmental concerns arose from tactics and weapons used in the Yugoslav and Kosovan conflicts. These conflicts highlighted environmental concerns regarding particular weapons, such as depleted uranium ammunition, and targets, such as chemical and pharmaceutical factories. Recent conflicts in Vietnam, the Persian Gulf and Yugoslavia, therefore, have all contributed evidence of State practice as to the customary, or non-customary, status of humanitarian law obligations of environmental protection.

The scope of customary law obligations to protect the natural environment is the concern of Chapter 14 of the Study. Positioned within Part II, concerning 'Specifically Protected Persons and Objects', the Study identifies three rules of customary law relating to the natural environment: Rules 43, 44 and 45. Rule 43 appears to gather together three established rules of humanitarian law and to extend the protections therein to the environment, including the principles of distinction and proportionality and the prohibition on the destruction of property except in the case of imperative military necessity. Rule 44 contains a general obligation of due regard for the natural environment in the choice of means and methods of warfare, and requires precautions in the conduct of military operations. Rule 45 prohibits the use of means and methods of warfare causing widespread, long-term and severe damage to the natural environment, as well as the destruction of the natural environment as a weapon in itself.

This chapter will proceed chronologically with the analysis of the evidentiary basis, formulation and substance of the three Rules. Given the relatively short space of time since adoption of Additional Protocol I, and the scarcity of circumstances in which the provisions gave rise to discussion, it is no surprise that the authors' evidence is largely drawn from official statements, particularly those submitted to the International Court of Justice for the *Advisory Opinion on Nuclear Weapons*[12] and in the 1974 and 1995 *Nuclear Tests* cases,[13] military manuals and other military training aids and General Assembly resolutions. As regards actual State practice, the environment is an inevitable casualty of war. Even if destruction were centred on cities and had minimal impact on 'green' spaces, chemical and explosive pollutants would have some negative impact in

---

[12] *Legality of the Threat or Use of Nuclear Weapons*, Advisory Opinion of 8 July 1996 [1996] *ICJ Rep.* 66.

[13] *Request for an Examination of the Situation in Accordance with Paragraph 63 of the Court's Judgment of 20 December 1974 in the Nuclear Tests case (New Zealand v. France)*, Order 22 September 1995 [1995] *ICJ Rep.* 283.

the atmosphere, the water table and the soil. Actual instances of State practice, therefore, occur with every bomb dropped or missile launched. However, when it comes to direct targeting of the environment, or the causation of very substantial environmental damage, there appears to be an overwhelming absence of breach. Two particularly important examples, however, can be drawn from the destruction of oil installations during the 1991 Gulf conflict[14] and chemical facilities during the 1999 Kosovo conflict,[15] in addition, of course, to the use of chemical defoliants and other methods of vegetation clearance during the Vietnam conflict.[16]

2. The Rules

Rule 43

The general principles on the conduct of hostilities apply to the natural environment:

A. No part of the natural environment may be attacked, unless it is a military objective.
B. Destruction of any part of the natural environment is prohibited, unless required by imperative military necessity.
C. Launching an attack against a military objective which may be expected to cause incidental damage to the environment which would be excessive in relation to the concrete and direct military advantage anticipated is prohibited.

Rule 43 has two aspects: (1) the umbrella notion that the natural environment is included within the rules and principles governing the conduct of hostilities, and (2) sub-rules A–C which extend the remit of three established rules and principles of humanitarian law to include the natural environment. The Commentary to this section refers to the principles of distinction and proportionality and to the rule prohibiting the destruction of property not justified by military necessity. The

---

[14] See *Conduct of the Persian Gulf War, Final Report to Congress Pursuant to Title V of the Persian Gulf Conflict Supplemental Authorization and Personnel Benefits Act of 1991* (Public Law 102–25), April 1992, Appendix O (1992) 31 *ILM* 615, p. 624.

[15] See *The Kosovo Conflict: Consequences for the Environment and Human Settlements* (Switzerland, United Nations Environment Programme and United Nations Centre for Human Settlements (Habitats), 1999); and Tom Walker, 'Poison Cloud Engulfs Belgrade', *The Times*, 19 April 1999, p. 1.

[16] A.H. Westing, *Ecological Consequences of the Second Indochina War* (Stockholm: Almqvist and Wiskell International, 1976).

Commentary asserts that Rule 43 is customary in both international and non-international armed conflicts.

Although the language of Rule 43 refers to 'general principles' on the conduct of hostilities, the titular reference in Volume II is to 'general rules'.[17] While distinction (in A) and proportionality (in C) are certainly viewed as principles of humanitarian law, destruction of property (in B) is not. This was clearly a simple textual error but merely for the sake of accuracy, therefore, Rule 43 and Volume II should refer to both terms, hence 'the general principles and rules'. A further slip can be found in references to the very subject matter of the provisions: the *natural* environment. While references to the 'natural environment' can be found within Rule 43A and B, only the 'environment' is mentioned in 43C. Similarly, the wording of Rule 44 refers to both formulations. This was clearly an unintentional slip, but does raise an interesting debate. While the term 'natural environment' was widely used at the negotiation stage of the Protocols, and became the adopted text, its use has subsequently declined, partly because society no longer makes a distinction between natural and man-made parts of the environment. Certainly States do not appear to have made such a distinction on the battlefield. In military manuals, treaties and statements, however, practice is not consistent. The majority of references appear to be to the established language of the Protocol, the 'natural environment', particularly in treaty law such as the 1998 Statute of the International Criminal Court and the 1980 UN Conventional Weapons Convention,[18] and in military manuals of State parties to Protocol I.[19] Interestingly, Volume II of the Study shows that non-party States have adopted either term,[20] while the 1992 and 1994 General Assembly resolutions,[21] the ICRC's 1994 Guidelines on the

---

[17] Study, Vol. II, Part I, 844 and 844–859.
[18] 1980 United Nations Convention on Prohibitions or Restrictions on the Use of Certain Conventional Weapons which may be deemed to be Excessively Injurious or to have Indiscriminate Effects.
[19] For example see Study, Vol. II, Part I, Chapter 14, for the military manuals of Australia (§ 79), South Korea (§ 80), Argentina (§ 163), Canada (§ 168), Germany (§§ 172–3), Spain (§ 180); but see Russia (§ 189) and Switzerland (§ 182).
[20] Those adopting *natural environment* include non-party States such as the United States, see Study, Vol. II, chapter 14, (§§ 185–6 and 266) and Israel (§ 241); and pre-ratification States include the United Kingdom (§ 184) and Belgium (§ 166); non-party States adopting the term *environment* include the Philippines (§ 101) and the United States (§ 263); and pre-ratification states include France (§ 89).
[21] UN GA res. 47/37, *Protection of the Environment in Times of Armed Conflict*, A/RES/47/37, 25 November 1992, 73rd plenary meeting; UN GA Res. 49/50, *United Nations Decade of International Law*, A/RES/49/50, 9 December 1994.

Protection of the Environment in Times of Armed Conflict[22] and States proposing a customary obligation of wartime environmental protection have opted for the term 'environment' alone.[23] For the sake of clarity, this chapter will adopt the term 'environment'.

Rule 43A

No part of the natural environment may be attacked, unless it is a military objective.

Rule 43A restates the customary principle of distinction (Rule 7) as it applies to the environment. It is universally accepted that the environment is prima facie a civilian object, although terming the environment an *object* has always appeared to be a little clumsy. In removing that terminology, the Study's approach is to be welcomed. Reference is rightly made in the Commentary to declarations made by a number of States upon signature of Additional Protocol I to the effect that 'a specific area of land' may also constitute a military objective if it fulfils all of the criteria for Article 52(2) of the Protocol,[24] most notably due to its location. A further example is provided of how the environment can fulfil the definition of a military objective, in the form of a quote from Protocol III (relating to the use of incendiary weapons) to the 1980 Conventional Weapons Convention,[25] notably when the environment provides cover, or is used to conceal or camouflage military objectives, or is itself a military objective.[26] Clearly, the Protocol III provision, concerning the use of incendiary weapons, is rooted in US tactics of chemical defoliation during the Vietnam conflict, as, of course, are the environmental provisions contained within Additional Protocol I. Further support for the Rule, which the authors may care to add to a revised version of the Study, is provided in the 2006 Manual on the Law of Non-International Armed Conflict, published by the International Institute of Humanitarian Law, which states that, 'the natural environment is a civilian object'.[27]

---

[22] Study, Vol. II, Part I, 845.

[23] See the statements in the Study, Vol. II, Part I, Chapter 14, of Nauru (§ 249) and the Solomon Islands (§ 257).   [24] Study, Vol. I, 143.

[25] Protocol III on Prohibitions or Restrictions on the Use of Mines, Booby-Traps and Other Devices to the 1980 United Nations Convention on Prohibitions or Restrictions on the Use of Certain Conventional Weapons which may be deemed to be Excessively Injurious or to have Indiscriminate Effects.   [26] *Ibid.*, Art. 2(4).

[27] M.N. Schmitt, C.H.B. Garraway and Y. Dinstein, *The Manual on the Law of Non-International Armed Conflict* (San Remo: International Institute of Humanitarian Law, March 2006), para. 4.2.4, (hereafter *2006 IIHL Manual*).

Two comments may be made as to the formulation of the Rule. The first comment concerns the term 'attacked', which as noted by Schmitt appears to narrow down the scope of 'direct operations against' as used in Article 48 of Additional Protocol I.[28] Schmitt's argument is that new technologies of computer network attack, electronic warfare, and so forth have made it possible to direct operations against the civilian population and civilian objects without causing them physical harm. Consequently, these are not 'attacks', defined in Article 49 as 'acts of violence', because they do not cause injury, death, damage or destruction. Unlike the example given of electronic warfare, however, it is difficult to imagine 'operations', as opposed to 'attacks', that would not cause some physical or actual damage to the environment. As a result, Rule 43A probably leaves little, if anything, outside the Rule by adopting the terminology of attack.

The second comment concerns the word 'part'. Reference to 'no part of the environment' appears to be new phraseology in this area of law; it is certainly not reflected in the language used by States. While the objective in using this new term is clearly to demonstrate that the environment is not just one entity, but includes smaller entities, for example a forest, lake or desert which might be subject to attack, it reflects neither the language used by States in humanitarian law nor in environmental law. Certainly, within the body of international environmental law, smaller environmental 'components', for want of a better term, are recognised, such as the air, marine resources, forests and flora and fauna.[29] Reference to 'part' of the environment is, therefore, not a completely dissimilar approach to that taken in environmental law. The introduction of new, undefined terminology in humanitarian law may, however, create unnecessary confusion. For example, how small is a part? While very small parts, such as individual animals, will rarely qualify as military objectives for consideration within Rule 43A, the point is not without significance when considering Rule 43B and the question of the destruction of environmental parts. Secondly, one interpretation might require the attack of larger targets, for example a forest providing cover to troops, to be divided into their parts, with the result that the attack is limited only to those parts of

---

[28] See chapter 6, p. 138.
[29] Environmental law also generally reflects an ecosystem approach, which directs that harm cannot be assessed narrowly, but that the effect on the ecosystem as a whole should be a factor. For the ecosystem approach, see Principles 2 and 6 of the 1972 Declaration of the United Nations Conference on the Human Environment, Stockholm (1972) 26 *YUN* 319.

the forest qualifying as military objectives. Hence, if the term 'part' is to be interpreted so as to limit the attack against the environment only to the extent that it qualifies as a military objective, this simply reflects the principles of distinction and proportionality. If this was the aim of the authors, it might more easily have been achieved by the following phraseology which is a truer reflection of humanitarian law: 'The natural environment may not be attacked, unless it is a military objective and only to the extent that it is a military objective.'[30]

Since Rule 43A is based on the customary principle of distinction, the authors are correct to state that it is equally applicable to international and non-international armed conflict.

Rule 43B

Destruction of any part of the natural environment is prohibited, unless required by imperative military necessity.

Rule 43B prohibits the destruction of the environment during hostilities, when not being used for military purposes or when there is no military necessity for its destruction.[31] The context, within which this provision is placed, sandwiched between the principles of distinction and proportionality, does not make immediate sense except that it gathers together *other* rules of hostilities affecting the environment. It would arguably have made for a better structure if the positions of sub-rules B and C were reversed; hence, the rule on destruction would follow the rules of attack.

A purely literal reading of Rule 43B in isolation would appear to suggest that while part of the environment can be attacked (when it is a military objective) or caused collateral damage, it is nevertheless prohibited to cause the 'destruction' of that part without the additional test of imperative military necessity.[32] If this were truly the law, it is being ignored on a daily basis. Take the example of a tree blocking the line of sight to a tank:

---

[30] An alternative formulation was suggested by Françoise Hampson during the meeting at the British Institute of International and Comparative Law which discussed the environmental provisions, as follows: '. . . and only in relation to that which is a military objective'.

[31] See *Conduct of the Persian Gulf Conflict*, Appendix O, at 621; and 2004 *Operational Law Handbook*, Judge Advocate General's School, United States, available online at www.jagcnet.army.mil/, p. 13.

[32] Interestingly only one military manual evidenced actually adopts the adjective *imperative*, see Study, Vol. II, Chapter 14, for the military manual of Iran (§ 41), which appears in the form of a direct quotation of Article 23(g). All of the other manuals refer simply to *military necessity* in the context of the environment.

in addition to being militarily advantageous, is its destruction imperative? The bombing of a chemical factory: is the collateral destruction caused to trees and species in the surrounding area imperative? While the customary principle of military necessity is at the core of humanitarian law, it is reflected in the laws governing attacks through the concept of military advantage. The test for launching an attack is governed by military advantage, as required by Article 52(2) of Additional Protocol I, and not by necessity. A plain reading of Rule 43B, however, appears to require the additional element of imperative military necessity when destruction of the environment, or part of it, may result from military actions such as attacks. On this basis, the Rule is clearly not an accurate statement of the law. Of course, this is not the intended interpretation; the intended interpretation is the prohibition of the (wanton) destruction of civilian property (as in Rule 50[33]). This interpretation is not apparent from the language of the Rule or its wider context, but is only to be gauged from the Commentary. An ordinary reading of the Rules in isolation, therefore, would not necessarily provide a full and accurate statement of the law. This may highlight one of the dangers inherent in the Study's approach, should the Rules emerge with a stand-alone character, without the guidance of the Commentary.

The origin of Rule 43B is, in fact, the customary prohibition on 'destruction or seizure of the enemy's property unless imperatively demanded by the necessities of war', stated in Article 23(g) of the 1907 Hague Convention IV.[34] In essence, the prohibition in Article 23(g) is one of intentional destruction caused without military purpose (necessity): irrelevant or wanton destruction of property that does not fulfil the criteria for classification as a military objective. Again, the term *wanton* is not referred to in the Rule, or indeed in the original Hague provision, but is generally included in the elucidation of the prohibition as a grave breach of the Geneva Conventions.[35] Of the suggested State practice for Rule 43B, admittedly only one statement of the United States refers to the element of 'wanton' destruction.[36] However, as Schmitt recognises, although laws of war manuals often fail explicitly to include an element of intent, there should nevertheless be read into the provision the absence of

---

[33] See chapter 9 for Rule 50, see p. 244.
[34] Note that the original Hague provision as well as Rules 50 and 43B do not apply to occupied territory.
[35] Geneva Convention IV, Art. 147, and Rome Statute, Art. 8(2)(a)(iv), both also require the level of *extensive* destruction of property.
[36] Study, Vol. II, Part I, Chapter 14, 853.

intent to secure a military purpose – akin to 'wanton'.[37] This approach is reflected in the *Hostages* case, where the Tribunal stated, 'Destruction as an end in itself is a violation of international law. There must be some reasonable connection between the destruction of property and the overcoming of the enemy forces.'[38]

The original applicability of Article 23(g) to property is maintained in Rule 50 of the Study, leaving Rule 43B specifically applicable to the environment. Where the two Rules differ, however, is in relation to seizure and ownership. Seizure is the temporary[39] taking of some thing (property) by the military forces, such as radios, communications equipment and vehicles, for use by them. Practical scenarios involving the seizure of a part of the environment are, admittedly, scarce. This scarcity of practical application is reflected in the evidence supplied in Volume II, which at no point relates the term *seizure* to the environment. However, certain species of animal, for example, horses, camels, even elephants, can be seized in the same way as other property of the adversary, as means of transportation. Such species would qualify also as property of the adversary (publicly or privately owned)[40] and would be governed by Rule 50. The inconsistency between Rules 43B and 50 raises the question whether the authors of the Study considered the environment to be covered by both Rules or by Rule 43B only. The Study does not give an answer. This approach requires the military to view the environment as two different concepts – as an entity in itself and as property. This issue is not new and results from the bolt-on effect of a later inclusion of the environment as an object of protection within a more traditional property-based legal system. In that sense, such problems are inescapable without the negotiation of a new, holistic environmental instrument. If, on the other hand, seizure was specifically not included in Rule 43B due to lack of State practice, then it would have been helpful if this observation had been provided in the Commentary.

As regards ownership of property, Rule 50 adopts the focus of the Hague provision albeit adapting the language from that of 'enemy' to

---

[37] See M.N. Schmitt, 'Green War: An Assessment of the Environmental Law of International Armed Conflict' (1997) 22 *Yale Journal of International Law and Policy* 1, at 53. See also *Conduct of the Persian Gulf Conflict*, Appendix O, p. 611.

[38] *US v. List et al.* (US Military Tribunal, Germany, 1948) 13 *LRTWC* 62 at 66. See also D. Bodansky, *Legal Regulation of the Effects of Military Activity on the Environment* (Berlin: Erich Schmidt Verlag, 2003), pp. 31–32.

[39] *US Operational Law Handbook*, p. 250.

[40] Although the Hague provision specifically refers to the 'enemy's property', it is accepted that this includes all property and not merely that of the State. See M.N. Schmitt, 'Green War', at 63.

'adversary' in order to allow applicability to non-international armed conflict. What remains under Rule 50 is a prohibition during hostilities as regards the property of the other party to the conflict. In reformulating the customary provision in relation to the environment, however, no reference is made to the owner of the environment concerned. Indeed, the provision refers to the 'destruction of any part' of the environment, apparently, therefore, including the environment owned or controlled by the party to the conflict. This is clearly not simply an adaptation of the Hague provision to the specific circumstance of the environment, but an extension of it, requiring that a party cannot, even in defence, destroy part of its own environment (other than those constituting objects indispensable to the survival of the civilian population) without imperative military necessity.[41]

While the authors have adopted the language of environmental 'destruction', several of the statements provided in Volume II also refer to the term 'damage'.[42] Indeed, the notion of environmental destruction raises some theoretical difficulties, not least due to the environment's regenerative character (meaning that a destroyed forest, for example, may regenerate) but particularly regarding the *threshold* for 'destruction'. A prohibition on the destruction of the environment, as a whole, is clearly too high a threshold and, therefore, worthless. On the other hand, prohibiting the destruction of a 'part' of the environment may establish too low a threshold of harm. The same questions are again raised: what constitutes a *part* of the environment? How small is a 'part'? Finally, certain environmental components are not capable of destruction, in the ordinary sense of that term, one example being the air. Thus, the Study might have prohibited both 'destruction' and 'damage' in Rule 43B. This dual formulation is also used in the *San Remo Manual* governing armed conflict at sea,[43] possibly due to the recognition that destruction of the seas is a very high threshold indeed.[44] Again, however, the Commentary is silent as to the specific formulation of the rule, particularly as to what has been omitted and why.

---

[41] Since the scope of Arts. 35(3) and 55 applies to the territory of the parties to the conflict, any such destruction would need to remain within the limits of widespread, long-term and severe damage to the environment for treaty parties.

[42] The concept of damage is recognised in the statements in Study, Vol. II, Part I, Chapter 14, of the United States (§ 11), Nicaragua (§ 22), Spain (§ 25), Canada (§ 36) and Iran (§ 42).

[43] L. Doswald-Beck (ed.), *San Remo Manual on International Law Applicable to Armed Conflicts at Sea*, International Institute of Humanitarian Law (Grotius Publications, Cambridge University Press, 1995).   [44] *Ibid.*, para. 44.

There is no doubt that the rule as accurately restated in Rule 50 reflects customary law in both international and non-international armed conflict.[45] There are doubts that the same can be said for Rule 43B in its present form. Rule 43B may perhaps be superfluous.

Rule 43C

Launching an attack against a military objective which may be expected to cause incidental damage to the environment which would be excessive in relation to the concrete and direct military advantage anticipated is prohibited.

Rule 43C largely restates the customary principle of proportionality (Rule 14) as it applies to the environment. It is universally accepted that the principle of proportionality applies equally to the environment as it does to other civilian objects. This recognition is clearly evidenced in State practice and largely follows from the classification of the environment as a prima facie civilian object under the principle of distinction. It might have been more logical if the principle of proportionality had followed directly after that of distinction, hence as Rule 43B.

While the environment is undoubtedly included within the customary proportionality principle, its inclusion raises the difficulty of calculation and evaluation of excessive environmental damage. This difficulty is inherent in the proportionality equation, even when applied to collateral human harm, but is exacerbated when applied to the environment. The Study helpfully refers to the comments made by the Committee Established to Review the NATO Bombing Campaign against the Federal Republic of Yugoslavia[46] to the effect that substantial military advantage would probably need to be shown for attacks causing 'grave environmental harm'.[47] This appears to be the only official pronouncement on the matter, and the lack of discussion in the Study largely reflects practice. It is arguable that when applied to the environment the proportionality principle would prohibit very little. Indeed, since the principles of military necessity and proportionality afford a large measure of discretion to

---

[45] The Fourth Hague Convention (1907) on Land Warfare and the Regulations annexed thereto, was considered by the 1945 Nuremberg Tribunal to represent customary law; International Military Tribunal (Nuremberg) Judgment and Sentences, reprinted in (1947) 41 *American Journal of International Law* 172.

[46] International Criminal Tribunal for the Former Yugoslavia (ICTY): *Final Report to the Prosecutor by the Committee Established to Review the NATO Bombing Campaign against the Federal Republic of Yugoslavia*, 8 June 2000, (2000) 39 *ILM* 1257. See Study, Vol. I, 146.

[47] *ICTY Review Committee, ibid.*, at para. 22. See Study, Vol. II, Part I, 856–857.

the military, a considerably important military advantage might legitimately outweigh very serious collateral damage to the environment. This
point is clearly evidenced in the *Nuclear Weapons* case.[48] The conclusion
of the Court on this occasion, that nuclear weapons might be lawful,
rested on the notion of extreme cases of self-defence. Hence, if the use of
nuclear weapons might be lawful in such circumstances, the very severe
collateral damage caused to the environment would also be legitimate.

In its formulation of the precautionary principle, Rule 43C raises a
problem in focusing too narrowly – and to the detriment of the environment and civilian persons and objects – on collateral effects solely to the
environment. While it is possible to envisage situations resulting 'only' in
collateral damage to the environment, for example the marine environmental damage caused in the striking of an oil tanker at sea, such examples will be rare. The more likely scenario is that civilian persons and/or
property will also be harmed. It is the totality of civilian persons or objects
(including the environment), therefore, that is reflective of the customary
principle.[49] While the same result can be achieved by reading together
Rules 14 and 43C, it would have been clearer to include the complete formulation in Rule 43C – particularly once the decision was taken to isolate
the environmentally protective rules in one section. It is suggested that
the provision should read: 'Launching an attack against a military objective which may be expected to cause incidental damage to the *environment, civilians and civilian objects, or a combination thereof*, which would
be excessive in relation to the concrete and direct military advantage
anticipated is prohibited' (emphasis added). It is damage to the combination of objects which may pass the excessive threshold, and not environmental damage alone. It is noted that the reference to 'parts' of the
environment found in Rules 43A and B is not included within Rule 43C.

The approach of the authors in restating the applicability of the proportionality principle to the environment is to be welcomed. The singling
out of certain protections, however, raises the question of the applicability to the environment of those Rules not included within Chapter 14. For
example, while the principle of proportionality has been stated to apply to
the environment as a civilian object, there is no similar environmentally
specific provision concerning precautionary measures in attack (Rule 19,
reflecting Article 57(2)(b) of Additional Protocol I) which refers to the

---

[48] *Nuclear Weapons* case, paragraphs 97 and 105(2)(E).
[49] Interestingly, the *2006 IIHL Manual* also isolates the environmental effects as regards the
principle of proportionality, see paragraph 4.2.4.

suspension or cancellation of such an attack. Rule 44 on precautions does not specifically cover the same issues as Article 57(2)(b), and no mention is made of the environment in the Commentary to Rule 19. There is no doubt that Rule 19 applies to the environment as a civilian object, but this approach of singling out certain rules will inevitably lead to the question being raised. A simple answer may be to add the word 'including' to the formulation of the umbrella notion: 'The general principles on the conduct of hostilities apply to the natural environment: *including . . .*' (emphasis added).

Since Rule 43C is based on the customary principle of proportionality, the authors are correct to state that it is equally applicable to international and non-international armed conflict.

Rule 44

Although not separated into specific sub-rules, as in Rule 43, the three sentences of Rule 44 will be analysed individually, since each appears to raise slightly different issues. The Commentary asserts that this Rule is customary in international, and arguably also in non-international, armed conflicts.

Rule 44, One

Methods and means of warfare must be employed with due regard to the protection and preservation of the natural environment.

The opening statement of the Commentary to Rule 44 is that State practice demonstrates that the environment is protected in wartime for its own sake. While this was not the view of the United Kingdom,[50] for example, during the negotiations in 1977, it probably does now represent the opinion of most, if not all, States. The current *UK Military Manual*[51] reflects this recognition and refers to Article 35(3) as providing direct protection to the environment.[52] More recently, the customary status of the general rule was denied as late as 1995, in the case of France,[53] and 1997, the Philippines.[54] However, Volume II does provide much practice

---

[50] Note the opinion of Mr Eaton, the UK delegate, at Official Records, Vol.XIV, *CDDH/III/SR.38*, 10 April 1975, para. 46. The United Kingdom appeared to interpret Article 35(3) as a duplication of Art. 55, and argued that Art. 35(3) should be envisaged only in the context of the health and survival of the civilian population.
[51] United Kingdom Ministry of Defence, *Manual of the Law of Armed Conflict* (Oxford University Press, 2004).   [52] *Ibid.*, para. 5.29.
[53] Study, Vol. II, Part I, 862–863.   [54] *Ibid.*, 865.

in favour of the customary nature of such a general rule today. This was particularly highlighted by State condemnations of the Iraqi oil pollution incidents during the 1991 Persian Gulf conflict.[55] Consequently, there is little that is controversial in the substance of this part of the Rule; its formulation, however, merits discussion.

The obligation of due regard is modelled on a number of instruments. Primarily, Article 55(1) of Additional Protocol I stipulates that, '[c]are shall be taken in warfare to protect the natural environment against widespread, long-term and severe damage.' Is there a difference, therefore, between an obligation of care and one of due regard? There is probably little that separates the two terms; they both appear to entail an obligation akin to due diligence – the obligation to take reasonable steps to protect the environment in warfare. There is, however, no commentary as to the chosen formulation in the Rule; nor is it explained by the evidence provided in Volume II, which largely reflects the treaty language of Article 55(1) binding on the 166 States parties. On the contrary, there is no evidence of State practice as to the use of the term 'due regard' outside the confines of the law governing naval warfare.[56] From the overwhelming evidence of State practice, and from the point of view of the ordinary meaning of words (taking *care* may be more understandable to the common soldier), there appears to be no reason to depart from the Protocol's terminology.

While the core of the obligation in both the Rule and Article 55(1) is probably the same, they differ as to the threshold of prohibited harm. Unlike Rule 44, Additional Protocol I established an obligation of environmental care only when the resulting harm was likely to pass the high threshold of widespread, long-term and severe environmental damage. Correctly, the Study identifies that State practice over the past thirty years has dropped the threshold requirement for environmental due diligence.[57]

A further difference between the Rule and Article 55(1) is the notion of 'preservation', which appears as an additional term within Rule 44's

---

[55] See the comments in Study, Vol. II, Part I, Chapter 14, of Germany (§ 91), Iran (§ 94), Holland (§ 99) and the United Kingdom (§ 105).

[56] The authors quote the *US Naval Handbook* (Study, Vol. II, Part I, 861) and the *1994 San Remo Manual* applicable to armed conflicts at sea, (Study, Vol. II, Part I, 845). The formulation as adopted is very similar to that of paragraph 44 of the *San Remo Manual*.

[57] In line with environmental law, generally a *de minimis* level of environmental harm would nevertheless be required. See the comments in Study, Vol. II, Chapter 14, of Australia (§ 79), South Korea (§ 80), United States (§ 81) and Yemen (§ 109).

obligation of environmental due regard. The term appears to be drawn from the maritime context, but no explanation is provided for its inclusion within a land-based obligation. Furthermore, the term 'preservation' is not reflective of State practice either in peacetime or armed conflict, so far as conflict on land is concerned. In the context of peacetime use of the marine environment, the 1982 Law of the Sea Convention[58] imposes an obligation of protection and preservation.[59] That obligation is also reflected in the naval war context and the *San Remo Manual*[60] requires States to take into account the 'relevant rules of international law'[61] when performing their obligation of environmental due regard in utilising means and methods of warfare. While the *San Remo Manual* does not specifically link the due regard obligation with environmental 'preservation',[62] this can be read into it.[63] Indeed, the only State practice evidenced in Volume II that specifically makes this connection is the *US Naval Handbook*.[64] In the domestic context, the US has also recognised an obligation to *preserve* the land environment in its 1969 National Environmental Policy Act (NEPA).[65] Yet this acceptance of terminology by the US is not generally reflective of State practice in peacetime.[66] It would appear, therefore, that this is a misapplication of the rules in the *San Remo Manual*, which are not applicable beyond naval warfare.[67] There is, in fact, no evidence to support the inclusion of the term 'preservation' within the Rule as it relates to land warfare.

The concept of preservation raises a further difficulty. It is rarely used in environmental law, and even more rarely defined. On one interpretation, 'preservation' denotes a heightened standard of conservation – the notion of maintaining a viable level of species stocks for future

---

[58] Part XII, United Nations Convention on the Law of the Sea (hereafter UNCLOS).
[59] UNCLOS, Article 192.   [60] Para. 44, *San Remo Manual*.   [61] *Ibid.*
[62] The term preservation was adopted in paras. 34 and 35 of the *San Remo Manual*, governing hostile actions undertaken in the exclusive economic zone or continental shelf of a neutral state.   [63] See also the *UK Manual*, at para. 13.30.
[64] Study, Vol. II, Part 1, 861.
[65] Sec. 101(c), NEPA as amended is available online at http://ceq.eh.doe.gov/nepa/regs/nepa/nepaeqia.htm.
[66] Cf. the statement by Qatar (Study, Vol. II, Chapter 14, at § 102) to the ICJ in the *Nuclear Weapons* case, to the effect that there is an emergence within the international community 'of an *opinio juris* concerning the *preservation* of the environment' (emphasis added). See also the Preamble of the 1994 Agreement Establishing the World Trade Organization, Marrakesh, 15 April 1994, in force 1 January 1995, (1994) 33 *ILM* 1125, which refers to the objective of sustainable development and the *preservation* of the environment (emphasis added).
[67] See Study, Vol. I, Introduction, xxx for the use to be made of the *San Remo Manual*.

exploitation, such as fish stocks.[68] 'Preservation', therefore, denotes a more restrictive approach to species exploitation, for example, an absolute prohibition on the taking of a particularly endangered species, such as the moratorium on the taking of certain whale species.[69] Preservation measures, therefore, have generally been reserved for particularly endangered species and delicate ecosystems, including the marine environment.[70] Despite the definitional difficulties, it would appear that the concept of preservation only applies after a certain point of species exploitation or environmental damage has occurred. As such, the concept appears to include a threshold of harm. The inclusion of the term 'preservation' in the Rule may well have resulted in an unintentional reintroduction of a threshold requirement.

Rule 44 falls into a small sub-group of Rules, which the authors assert are 'arguably' customary international law in non-international armed conflict. While this conclusion was undoubtedly an unsatisfactory one for the authors, it is difficult to disagree with it in relation to Rule 44. While the proposal to include an environmental protection provision within Additional Protocol II ultimately proved fruitless, the initial vote (forty-nine in favour, four against and seven abstentions) suggests a high measure of support. The original measure was, however, not one of due regard or care but of a prohibition of widespread, long-term and severe environmental damage, akin to Article 35(3) of Additional Protocol I. The authors of the Study assert that there are 'indications' and a 'certain amount of State practice' that provide evidence for a rule in non-international armed conflict.[71] The value of the evidence provided, however, is rather dubious. While the evidence for an obligation of due regard is based on peacetime international environmental law,[72] not one piece of State practice directly supports an obligation of due regard in respect of non-State actors in non-international armed conflict. The Colombian

---

[68] See the 1923 Convention for the Preservation of the Halibut Fishery of the North Pacific Ocean.

[69] Note the 1946 International Convention for the Regulation of Whaling, imposed conservation measures only. The Moratorium was imposed by States party to the International Whaling Commission in 1982 (commencing 1986).

[70] See for example UNCLOS, Art. 194(5), 'The measures . . . include those necessary to protect and *preserve* rare or fragile ecosystems as well as the habitat of depleted, threatened or endangered species and other forms of marine life'; in addition to Articles 192 and 193. Although 'preservation' is used, the obligations are closer to conservation.

[71] Study, Vol. I, 149.

[72] See the statements in Study, Vol. II, Part 1, Chapter 14, by Egypt (at § 88), Iran (at § 93) to the ICJ in the *Nuclear Weapons* case refers to the Stockholm Principle 21 as regards State responsibility in peacetime for transboundary environmental damage.

statement from the Office of the Ombudsman, for example, does indeed refer to the environmental effects of guerrilla activities.[73] However, such attacks are criticised for their effects on water sources and the productivity of the land. Hence, this statement is hardly a ringing endorsement of the protection of the environment per se, or of a due regard obligation. Similarly, a number of statements submitted to the ICJ in the *Nuclear Weapons* case are mentioned.[74] It is difficult, however, to gauge just how far such statements are relevant in the context of non-international armed conflict. In addition, the authors note that a number of States emphasised to the ICJ that the environment be protected for the benefit of all.[75] Does this notion, however, necessarily evidence a due regard obligation in non-international armed conflict?

More recent State practice may be of value. In the *UK Manual*, the United Kingdom has recognised an obligation during non-international armed conflict that 'regard must be had to the natural environment in the conduct of all military operations'.[76] This is clearly not a treaty require-ment. Other, more recent, practice by the International Institute of Humanitarian Law, in its attempt to compose a manual on the law of non-international armed conflict, purposely does not list a general oblig-ation of environmental protection as a customary rule.[77] Battlefield examples would have been useful.[78] One example may be taken from the 1992 Yugoslav conflict, in which the local UNPROFOR commander ordered the capture of the Peruč hydroelectric dam, specifically in order to prevent flooding of the Cetina valley.[79] As it stands, however, there is

---

[73] Study, Vol. II, Part 1, 862.

[74] See the statements in Study, Vol. II, Part 1, Chapter 14, of Egypt (§ 88), Iran (§ 93), Malaysia (§ 97), Qatar (§102), Solomon Islands (§103), Costa Rica (§87), Mexico (§ 98), Rwanda (§253), Sri Lanka (§104) and Ukraine (§261).

[75] It is interesting to note that none of the States listed in footnote 38 (Study, Vol. I, 149) use this term; some mention non-international armed conflict, see for example in Study, Vol. II, Part 1, Chapter 14, the statements of Argentina (§ 29), Ukraine (§ 261) and Sri Lanka (§ 104); however, some refer to environmental protections in peacetime, Iran (§ 93), the Solomon Islands (§ 103) and Egypt (§ 88); others statements are simply vague, such as Rwanda (§ 253), Qatar (§ 102), Italy (§ 10), South Korea (§ 80), Malaysia (§ 97).

[76] Para. 12.20, *UK Manual.*

[77] See the *2006 IIHL Manual* para. 4.2.4, which simply refers to the obligation of propor-tionality.

[78] For a recent report of the protection of rhinos in the Democratic Republic of the Congo, see David Adam, 'Wildlife Expert Persuades Notorious Rebel Army to Join Fight to Save Rare White Rhino', *The Guardian*, 13 September 2006.

[79] See the 1993 Human Rights Report by the USA, available online at http://dosfan.lib.uic.edu/ERC/democracy/1993_hrp_report/93hrp_report_eur/Croatia.html, and Security Council resolution 779 (1992), 6 October 1992.

probably insufficient State practice to evidence this obligation as customary law.

Rule 44, Two

In the conduct of military operations, all feasible precautions must be taken to avoid, and in any event to minimise, incidental damage to the environment.

The second sentence of Rule 44 applies to the environment the same provisions as are found in Rules 15 and 17. Since the environment has been viewed as a prima facie civilian object since the 1970s, there is no controversy with the substance or customary nature of this sentence. Since the authors conclude that Rules 15 and 17 are customary for non-international armed conflict,[80] by extension this sentence of Rule 44 would also be customary. However, there is an issue of evidential adequacy. The one piece of evidence provided to support this conclusion refers only to 'water sources',[81] and was adopted in the context of the protection of the civilian population, not the environment specifically.

Rule 44, Three

Lack of scientific certainty as to the effects on the environment of certain military operations does not absolve a party to the conflict from taking such precautions.

This sentence may appear to flow naturally from the previous one, that the military must take precautions as regards environmental damage in attack even in those cases where it is not absolutely certain what level or type of environmental damage might be caused. Scientific certainty is a rarity on the battlefield. Interpreted in this sense, the provision would then appear to be stating the obvious and the commander would work on the basis of the information available to him at the time.

On the other hand, it might be queried how the commander is to know what precautions to take if there is no scientific certainty as to the effects on the environment. A more theoretical issue is raised by the apparent assumption in the Rule, that effects on (or indeed *in*) the environment are only ever negative or detrimental. One example of the positive benefits accruing to the environment from warfare can, rather surprisingly, be seen in the use of landmines. If properly marked and fenced off, such

---

[80] Study, Vol. I, 51 and 57.   [81] Study, Vol. I, 150 and Vol. II, Part 1, 875.

area-denial tactics can allow regeneration of damaged and over-exploited environments by keeping people away. As regards the effects of 'certain military operations', this appears to be a further unintentional slip.

There is little controversy in the formulation of the Rule itself. Controversy is raised, however, by the Commentary, more specifically in the adoption of the so-called precautionary principle. While not addressed directly in the wording of the Rule, the principle is used as the title to both the Commentary and Volume II. It is this apparent endorsement in times of armed conflict of an international environmental law concept that is surprising. Furthermore, the titles and Commentary appear to endorse the precautionary principle in a way that is not necessarily true of the actual formulation of the Rule. On this occasion, therefore, it may be wise to break with previous advice and advocate the separation of Rule 44, Three from its Commentary.

While the Study does not state outright that the precautionary principle is a customary obligation even in peacetime, the authors do state that the principle 'has been gaining increasing recognition',[82] which is true. However, the authors continue that, 'there is, furthermore, practice to the effect that this environmental law principle applies in armed conflict'.[83] Of note at this point is the use of the term 'practice' as opposed to 'State practice'. Indeed, no practice of any endorsement of the precautionary principle in an armed conflict context appears to have been found amongst all of the military manuals available to the authors. The practice that is relied upon in the Commentary is threefold: environmental law treaties and non-binding environmental law declarations; State comments submitted to the ICJ (both the 1995 *Nuclear Tests* case and in the 1996 *Nuclear Weapons* case); and a comment in the ICRC's own report in 1993 submitted to the General Assembly on the protection of the environment during armed conflict.[84]

While New Zealand submitted arguments in the *Nuclear Tests* case based on the precautionary principle[85] and clearly asserted that principle to be customary, this was contested by the respondent State, France.[86] In the *Nuclear Weapons* case, the ICJ made the following comment, which is

---

[82] Study, Vol. I, 150.   [83] *Ibid.*

[84] Paragraphs of the Report are reprinted in Study, Vol. II, Part 1, 876.

[85] A number of States intervened on the side of the applicant, New Zealand, and also invoked the precautionary principle, including Australia, Samoa, the Solomon Islands, the Marshall Islands and Micronesia.

[86] France argued that the status of the principle was still uncertain, but that she had complied with it in any event; Oral Hearings, Tuesday 12 September 1995, at 10 a.m., CR/95/20, available online at www.icj-cij.org/icjwww/icases/inzfr/inzfr_cr/iNZFR_iCR9520_19950912.PDF p. 60.

referred to by the authors to evidence the customary status of the precautionary principle, 'in [the *Nuclear Tests* case] the Court stated that its conclusion was "without prejudice to the obligations of States to respect and
protect the natural environment". Although that statement was made in
the context of nuclear testing, it naturally also applies to the actual use of
nuclear weapons in armed conflict.'[87] However, it is not at all clear what
the ICJ was referring to in the *Nuclear Tests* case; it is highly unlikely that
the Court would suggest in such a vague way that the precautionary principle had evolved into a customary norm. This, however, appears to be
the interpretation offered by the authors when they state, 'this would
include, inter alia, the precautionary principle which was central to the
arguments in the latter [*Nuclear Tests*] case'.[88] The precautionary principle may have been central to the arguments advanced by New Zealand,
but the quoted passage does not declare that States are bound by the principle; the Court refers only to the obligations of States to 'respect and
protect'. Moreover, in his dissenting opinion, Judge Weeramantry suggested only that the precautionary principle is 'gaining increasing
support as part of the international law of the environment'.[89] The
authors may have overstated the evidential value of the Court's rulings.

As regards the evidence of the ICRC Report in 1993, it was there suggested by the ICRC that the precautionary principle was at that time an
'emerging' principle of international law.[90] Whether the principle is one of
international law or only one of environmental law will be addressed
shortly, but the authors in the Commentary make the point that this assertion was not contested by any State.[91] It is not clear whether the authors
are asserting that no State contested the statement which was included in
the ICRC Report, or that no State contested this issue during the General
Assembly debate. It is difficult to attach great weight to a statement that
many States may simply not have bothered to contest in a situation where
no binding rules were to be created.[92] Too much weight should not be
attached to State inaction, or lack of adverse comment, on such occasions.

As regards the use of environmental law instruments as evidence of the
precautionary principle, the first point to note is that the continuing
applicability of environmental law treaties during armed conflict is not
the subject of consensus. The authors do address this point in a separate

[87] *Nuclear Weapons* case, para. 32, and Study, Vol. II, Part 1, 875. The statement is mentioned in Study, Vol. I, 150.   [88] *Ibid.*
[89] *Nuclear Weapons* case, Dissenting Opinion, Judge Weeramantry, p. 58, see also Study,
Vol. II, Part 1, 876.   [90] Study, Vol. II, Part 1, 876.   [91] Study, Vol. I, 150.
[92] See Scobbie, chapter 2, see p. 45.

section of the Commentary, which is well written.[93] The authors also clearly make the point that a binding obligation in peacetime does not necessarily bind in times of armed conflict.[94] However, it is clear that peacetime environmental law is the original source for the precautionary principle and it is here that the Commentary rightly begins. What the commentary fails to emphasise, however, is the controversial nature of the precautionary principle even in peacetime.

The precautionary principle is stated in Principle 15 of the 1992 Rio Declaration[95] as follows: 'Where there are threats of serious or irreversible damage, lack of full scientific certainty shall not be used as a reason for post-poning cost-effective measures to prevent environmental degradation.' The earliest environmental protection measures were put into place following scientific assessments which demonstrated that a particular species or natural resource had already been significantly damaged.[96] This 'wait and see' approach to environmental damage, however, proved problematic. First, if conservation measures are desirable, waiting for damage to be scientifically proven inevitably leads to a worsening of the damage and, hence, greater costs of remediation or conservation. Secondly, there emerged in the 1970s the realisation that proof of damage may never reach the point of certainty, particularly in a few select cases where the possibility was of very severe, if not apocalyptic, environmental damage, notably that of climate change. The precautionary principle, therefore, first developed due to the increasingly uncertain nature and extent of environmental damage. The 1985 Vienna Convention for the Protection of the Ozone Layer,[97] for example, was the first treaty to recognise the need for precautionary measures to control substances deemed harmful to the ozone.[98] Since then, the principle has been specifically adopted in a number of instruments[99] and

---

[93] Study, Vol. I, 151. Instances of observance, include river management treaties during the 1990–91 Gulf conflict despite suggestions that halting the river's flow would aid military operations; and NATO efforts during the Kosovo conflict to remove a brown bear out of the conflict zone to safety – crossing an international border – in line with the 1973 Convention on International Trade in Endangered Species of Wild Fauna and Flora (hereinafter CITES).   [94] Study, Vol. I, 150.

[95] 1992 Declaration on Environment and Development, Rio de Janeiro, 31 *ILM* 874.

[96] See for example the 1946 International Whaling Convention.

[97] Vienna, 22 March 1985, in force 22 September 1988.   [98] Preamble, *ibid.*

[99] Article 3(3) of the 1992 United Nations Framework Convention on Climate Change, Article 2(2)(a) of the 1992 Convention for the Protection of the Marine Environment of the North-East Atlantic. See also the following treaties which do not specifically refer to the precautionary principle but do adopt a precautionary *approach*, Preamble to the 1992 Convention on Biological Diversity, Rio de Janeiro, and Article 10(6) of the 2000 Cartegena Protocol on Biosafety to the Convention on Biological Diversity.

also forms part of the notion of sustainable development.[100] An example of widespread adoption of the principle is that of the European Community, which since 1992 has based its environment policy on the precautionary principle.[101]

One controversial aspect of the principle is that of the (reversed) burden of proof. What the reverse onus would mean is that instead of the complainant proving that the activity causes harm, the burden would shift to the polluter/State to prove that the activity does not cause significant harm. Thus a reverse onus would cause a shift not only in expense, but if the potential polluter (or polluting State) could not prove that his activity did not cause such harm, it would be a breach of international law to carry out the proposed activity.[102] The reverse onus was argued in the claim of New Zealand, in the context of the 1995 *Nuclear Tests Case*, such that the precautionary principle would 'place the onus of proof on France to offer satisfactory evidence that this [nuclear] testing is safe'.[103] As previously indicated, the Court, however, did not specifically rule on the status or nature of the principle. It might be suggested that the reverse onus issue has been one reason for the failure of the specialist Tribunals specifically to recognise and enforce the principle. The Tribunals of the World Trade Organisation and the Law of the Sea Convention, for example, have approached the principle with caution; largely refraining from applying the principle directly even in environmental cases. In the *Southern Bluefin Tuna*,[104] *MOX Plant*[105] and *Beef Hormones*[106] cases the International Tribunal for the Law of the Sea[107] and the Appellate Body of the World Trade Organisation although clearly applying a precautionary approach ruled only in terms of *caution* and *prudence*. In the latter case,

---

[100] See P. Sands, *Principles of International Environmental Law* (Cambridge University Press, 2nd edn, 2003), pp. 266–279.   [101]   Art. 174 (2), 2002 Treaty on European Union.

[102] See P. Sands , *Principles of International Environmental Law*, p. 273.

[103] See Oral Hearings, Monday 11 September 1995, at 3.30 p.m., CR/95/19, p. 31, available online at www.icj-cij.org/icjwww/icases/inzfr/inzfr_cr/iNZFR_iCR9519_19950911.PDF.

[104] *Southern Bluefin Tuna Cases (Australia v. Japan, New Zealand v. Japan)* (Provisional Measures) (1999) 38 *ILM* 1624, at para. 77. Ultimately, Japan's claim that the tribunal did not have jurisdiction in the case was upheld, and so the merits of the case were not heard.

[105] *MOX Plant (Ireland v. the United Kingdom)*, ITLOS Order of 3 December, 2001, (2002) 41 *ILM* 405. MOX is an abbreviation of mixed oxide fuel which was to be manufactured at the plant.

[106] EC, Measures Concerning Meat and Meat Products (Hormones), WT/DS48/AB/R, 16 January 1998; *WT/DS26/R/USA* and *WT/DS48/CAN*, 18 August 1997. The issue essentially was whether the European Union was entitled to invoke the precautionary principle to justify its ban on the import of US beef derived from growth hormone-treated cattle.

[107] ITLOS is the specialist tribunal established under UNCLOS.

this was despite specific mention of the precautionary principle in the Preamble to the WTO Agreement. Here the two parties defending the claim, the United States and Canada, denied that the principle had attained customary status at that point (1997/8), although Canada was prepared to say it may have been an emerging principle of international law. Indeed, the United States prefers to recognise not a precautionary principle, but a precautionary 'approach', which may be viewed as a lesser obligation, particularly with respect to the reverse onus.[108] Furthermore, in failing specifically to recognise the precautionary principle and apply it, the Tribunals have also failed to recognise it as a principle (potentially) binding beyond the sphere of environmental law.

Despite its broad acceptance within environmental law, due to the questions that surround its very nature it is at present seriously debatable whether the precautionary principle is recognised as a customary obligation in peacetime. For example, there is no clear authority as to how exactly the precautionary principle would apply to a particular situation. In particular, there are issues surrounding the threshold of applicability which the Commentary does not address. At its most basic, the principle can be said to represent a common-sense view that States need to act with care and caution when engaging in activities that may have an adverse effect on the environment.[109] According to a different interpretation of the principle, however, it relates only to 'serious or irreversible'[110] threats to the environment, such as climate change and ozone depletion. While some treaties have adopted lower thresholds,[111] it is still not clear what threshold would prevail if the precautionary principle were to form part of customary law. In drafting Rule 44, the authors appear to have adopted a very low threshold entailing avoiding and minimising incidental environmental damage. For this reason alone, while Rule 44 may be reflective of the general notion of precautions in warfare, it may not be reflective of the precautionary principle. It is also difficult to maintain that such an ambiguous principle in peacetime is already binding in times of armed conflict. Such difficulties would have been avoided, if the Commentary had maintained the obligation as one requiring feasible precautions regardless of any scientific uncertainties that remain. This position would be suitable for use in armed conflict, when of course States are under a

---

[108] P. Sands, *Principles of International Environmental Law*, p. 277.   [109] *Ibid.*, p. 272.

[110] See, for example, Article 3(3), 1992 Climate Change Convention.

[111] See Article 4(3)(f) of the 1991 Convention on the Ban of Import into Africa and the Control of Transboundary Movement and Management of Hazardous Wastes within Africa, where no threshold of harm is included.

pre-existing obligation of general precautionary measures. One common-sense approach would be for States to undertake assessments of potential outcomes and effects of any military operations on the environment, and to base their feasible precautions on the results.

A final point relates to the use made by the authors of environmental law treaties. In the introductory section of the Study, the authors declare that their usage of international human rights instruments is to 'support, strengthen and clarify analogous principles of international humanitarian law'.[112] In Rule 44, however, it appears that the authors are adopting a principle from environmental law; the status of the principle in general international law being somewhat questionable. In addition to adopting principles from environmental law, the authors appear to come very close to using environmental law instruments as evidence of customary law during armed conflict. Indeed, reliance is placed on both environmental treaties and non-binding environmental declarations as evidence for the Rules. One example is the statement regarding the 'need to protect the environment during armed conflict' being 'set forth in several international instruments'.[113] In the footnote to that statement the authors quote four instruments, three of which are soft-law environmental declarations.[114] There appears to be a degree of inconsistency in approach between that stated for human rights instruments and for environmental treaties.

Rule 45, One

The use of methods or means of warfare that are intended, or may be expected, to cause widespread, long-term and severe damage to the natural environment is prohibited.

The first sentence of Rule 45 is a restatement of Article 35(3) of Additional Protocol I, which was adopted, together with Article 55(1), in reaction to, and in condemnation of, US military tactics during the Vietnam conflict. The consensus that emerged from the Geneva drafting committee was that the prohibition contained in those two provisions

---

[112] Study, Vol. I, Introduction, xxxi. See also Hampson, chapter 3.

[113] Study, Vol. I, 148.

[114] *Ibid.*, footnote 29 refers to Principle 20 of the 1972 Stockholm Declaration, Principle 24 of the 1992 Rio Declaration, and Principle 5 of the 1982 World Charter for Nature, annexed to General Assembly Resolution 37/7, 28 October 1982, (A.RES/37/7)(1983) 22 *ILM* 456. The footnote also refers to two instruments with more applicability to armed conflict; the *San Remo Manual*, and the 1994 ICRC Guidelines.

would be absolute beyond a particular threshold: a very high threshold incorporating the three criteria of widespread, long-term and severe environmental damage. The Commentary recognises this same high threshold as custom,[115] and it has been retained in its original form in Rule 45. In adopting a shortened title, however, which was designed to describe the entirety of the Rule, the authors refer only to 'Causing *serious* damage to the natural environment' (emphasis added).[116] Difficult though it may have been, it would perhaps have been better to organise the rules differently rather than risk lowering the prohibited threshold of harm. Certainly in most areas of law, including environmental law, the concept of 'serious' damage is a lower level of damage than that of 'severe' damage, and certainly lower than the specific threefold threshold adopted in Article 35(3), and Rule 45.

Throughout the Commentary, the authors refer to 'this prohibition' to denote those contained in both Articles 35(3) and 55(1).[117] Yet these two prohibitions are not exactly the same; a point that was made clear at the time of adoption in that Article 55(1) has an additional element of consequent human harm. Since many States do appear to refer to both formulations,[118] the Commentary could have addressed this point. The commentary is very useful, however, on the interpretation of the threshold criteria. While it was the rather vague and undefined character of the three terms, inter alia, which originally caused the United States to refuse to ratify Additional Protocol I,[119] that stance may have recently relaxed. In its 2004 Operational Law Handbook for Judge Advocate Generals, the US advances 'credible' interpretations, which are akin to those found in ENMOD.[120] Further editions of the Study may wish to include this State practice as evidence for Rule 45. Furthermore, continuing US objections to Articles 35(3) and 55(1) are more strongly based on the notion of absolute thresholds. Alien to humanitarian law in general, the environmental

---

[115] Study, Vol. I, 157.   [116] Study, Vol. II, Part 1, 845 and 877–911.

[117] Study, Vol. I, 152–155.

[118] See Study, Vol. II, Chapter 14, for the military manuals of Australia (§§ 164–5), Belgium (§ 166), Canada (§ 168), Colombia (§ 169), the Netherlands (§ 176) and New Zealand (§ 178); all are quoted in footnote 52, Commentary to Chapter 14, p. 152.

[119] See M. Matheson, Deputy Legal Adviser, US State Department, (1987) *ASIL Proceedings* 28. See also A. Roberts, 'Failures in Protecting the Environment in the 1990–91 Gulf War', in P. Rowe (ed.), *The Gulf War in English and International Law* (London, Routledge, 1993), p. 126.

[120] *US Operational Law Handbook*, p. 195. This is, of course, not to suggest that the terms of Article 35(3) are binding as custom or that this represents an adoption of the provision by the United States. The *US Operational Law Handbook* is not to be equated with the Military Field Manuals that the US issues to its armed forces.

prohibition is an absolute threshold of harm which does not allow for considerations of military necessity. While the Commentary clearly recognises this issue,[121] emphasising it as the main US objection to the environmental provisions would have provided a very useful explanation as to the conclusion of the authors that the United States constitutes a persistent objector to the first part of Rule 45.

While the authors clearly conclude this part of the Rule to be a customary obligation in international armed conflict, the evidence provided for this conclusion is not entirely convincing. While the authors do not declare that Article 35(3) has evolved into customary law, since this was not the stated approach of the Study,[122] this in essence is what is presented in this part of the Rule. Article 35(3) was new law in 1977, but the authors suggest that 'significant practice has emerged' since adoption 'to the effect that this prohibition has become customary'.[123] Primary emphasis is then placed on the military manuals of twenty States.[124] Two of those sources, quoted as the US and UK military manuals, are in fact only training manuals and do not necessarily reflect binding legal obligations on those States.[125] Of the remaining eighteen military manuals referenced, only one State (Kenya) was not party to Additional Protocol I at the date the manual was written, and so was not bound by Article 35(3) as treaty law.[126] Kenya ratified Additional Protocol I only two years later, and, therefore, may arguably have drafted its military manual prospectively. Similarly, the authors evidence the criminalisation of the prohibition in the domestic laws of twenty-one States.[127] Again, of those twenty-one States, two constitute draft legislation only, while only one State (Azerbaijan) was neither party to Additional Protocol I nor to the Statute of the International Criminal Court at the date of the enactment of the domestic law concerned.[128] Clearly, States parties to either instrument would be treaty bound to apply the relevant environmental provisions.[129] Finally, the

---

[121] Study, Vol. I, 157.   [122] Volume I, Introduction, xxx.   [123] Study, Vol. I, 152.
[124] Ibid., footnote 52.
[125] Study, Vol. II, Part 1, 882–883. See Scobbie, chapter 2, pp. 38–39.
[126] Although not specifically referenced by the authors, the Belgian acceptance of these provisions is evidenced in Study, Vol. II, Part 1, Chapter 14, § 166. Belgium's military manual is dated 1983, but Belgium did not ratify Additional Protocol I until 1986.
[127] Study, Vol. I, 152, footnote 53.
[128] Azerbaijan was however part of the Soviet Union until 1991, which had ratified Additional Protocol I. In addition, Ireland was not at the time of enactment a party to these instruments, but ratified within one year.
[129] Rome Statute, Art. 8(2)(b)(iv).

Study refers to practice of five 'States not, or not at the time, party to Additional Protocol I'.[130] The five States listed are the UK, US, Vietnam, Belgium and Azerbaijan. While the same criticism may be made of the use of the UK and US (non-binding) training guides,[131] Vietnam did in fact ratify Additional Protocol I in 1981, and so was a treaty party when its 1990 penal code was enacted.[132] In addition, the practice of Vietnam does not support the language adopted by the authors. The practice of Vietnam, and indeed many of the communist States at that time, makes no reference to the widespread, long-term and severe formulation for environmental damage, but prefers that of 'ecocide'.[133] Finally, this leaves Belgium,[134] which ratified within three years of the enactment of its penal code, and Azerbaijan,[135] which did not ratify either treaty instrument.

According to the authors, further evidence of the customary nature of this first Rule is found in the submissions of States to the ICJ for the *Nuclear Weapons* case.[136] The Commentary quotes nine States which 'indicated in their submissions . . . that they considered the rule [in articles 35(3) and 55(1)] to be customary',[137] and seven 'other States appeared to be of the view that these rules are customary'.[138] On closer inspection of the evidence, however, three States appear to fall within both categories,[139] suggesting an actual total, not of sixteen but, of thirteen States. On further inspection, it is suggested that only the comments of four States are unequivocal in their perception of the environmental prohibition as customary law.[140] The remainder of the statements refer either in very vague language to an environmental principle or environmental obligations under international humanitarian law, or to treaty obligations. The Commentary does, of course, recognise that the ICJ did not find that the Article 35(3) prohibition was reflected in customary law.[141] Certainly, practice does not need to refer to a rule as customary law for it to contribute

---

[130] Study, Vol. I, 152, and footnote 54.   [131] Study, Vol. II, Part 1, 882–883.

[132] *Ibid.*, § 219. The Code was first adopted in 1985.

[133] This is how Vietnam perceived the damage caused to its country during the conflict. Note the negotiations for Additional Protocol I, Official Records, Vol.XIV, *CDDH/III/SR.26*, 27 February 1975, paras. 9–17. See also Study, Vol. II, Part 1 for the state practice of Belarus (§ 192), Kazakhstan (§ 204), Kyrgyzstan (§ 205), Moldova (§ 207), Russia (§ 212), Tajikistan (§ 215) and Ukraine (§ 217).   [134] Study, Vol. II, Part 1, 880.

[135] *Ibid.*, p. 883.   [136] Study, Vol. I, 152, and footnote 55.   [137] *Ibid.*

[138] *Ibid.*, p. 152, footnote 56.   [139] Namely New Zealand, Sweden and Zimbabwe.

[140] Study, Vol. II, Part 1, for the statements of Solomon Islands (§ 257), Zimbabwe (§ 272), India (§ 232) and Nauru (§ 249).

[141] This recognition can be found a further two paragraphs along, Study, Vol. I, 153.

to the formation of customary law, but here the authors specify these States as having done just that; it is suggested that this may not be the case.

While the evidence in Volume II demonstrates wide acceptance of the prohibition, there is little evidence that States view this obligation as one of customary law. The majority of States have ratified Additional Protocol I, with no significant reservations to the environmental provisions. This is valuable evidence in itself.[142] While the stated approach of the authors was not to analyse the status of individual treaty provisions, but to assess a customary law basis inductively from State practice, the overwhelming majority of evidence for this Rule emanates from treaty parties, and the practice is of a kind that does not address the specific issue of customary status.[143] While it may be true that there are few, if any, examples of this kind of damage being caused, of itself this does not prove the Rule to be customary. The lack of violation may more easily be explained by the excessively high threshold criteria. While the environmental pollution caused by Iraqi actions during the Gulf conflict and NATO bombing during the Kosovo conflict was the subject of widespread condemnation, State opinion was not absolutely clear that the damage caused in either incident breached the threshold imposed by Article 35(3).[144] Consequently, there may be explanations, other than the customary status of Article 35(3), as to why this type of damage has not regularly been caused during armed conflict.

On the other hand, there is sufficient evidence to suggest that the Article 35(3) prohibition is at least an emerging customary norm; this was indeed the view of the Review Committee established to investigate the NATO bombings in Kosovo in 2000.[145] While in 1994, even in the immediate aftermath of the Gulf conflict, the ICRC could not secure a binding instrument on environmental damage, by 2000, at least, one international body was asserting the prohibition to be emerging as custom.[146] The task of proving custom in this case is easier once the US is granted persistent objector status, but it is still not entirely clear that States generally view this Rule as one of customary law. As a consequence, this Rule may have been more appropriately worded as 'arguably' custom even for international armed conflict.

---

[142] As admitted in the Study's Introduction, but not specifically referred to for Article 35(3). See Study, Vol. I, Introduction, xlii–xliii.

[143] See the *2006 IIHL Manual*, which does not find that the Article 35(3) and 55 prohibition has been accepted as customary law in either international or non-international armed conflict.

[144] See the opinion of the US in *Conduct of the Persian Gulf War*, p. 625; and *ICTY Review Committee*, paras. 15–17.   [145] *ICTY Review Committee*, para. 15.   [146] *Ibid.*

With regard to non-international armed conflict, the authors are correct to assert that, at most, this Rule is 'arguably' custom. On this point, the Commentary is very useful. Recent practice that may be added is that of the United Kingdom. Here, however, the *UK Manual* recognises only an obligation of 'regard [for] the natural environment in the conduct of all military operations'.[147] Essentially, therefore, the UK recognises the first obligation within Rule 44, not the prohibition contained in Article 35(3) nor Rule 45.

Finally, the controversial aspect of Protocol I's applicability to nuclear weapons must be addressed. It was this issue which originally provoked US objections to the environmental provisions within Protocol I. Furthermore, as is recognised in the Commentary, a number of States specifically entered reservations to the Protocol to the effect that the new rules contained within it would not apply to the use of nuclear weapons.[148] Among those States were the United Kingdom and France, and the new rules in this case were those in Articles 35(3) and 55(1). These points are addressed in the Commentary, and are generally very well made.[149] The Commentary recognises the three States (United States, United Kingdom and France) as specially affected States for their role in possessing nuclear weapons.[150] It also identifies them as persistent objectors.[151] However, it is respectfully submitted that this conclusion is flawed. Having found the three States to be specially affected States, the only conclusion open to the authors was that these States have prevented this Rule from maturing into custom with respect to the use of nuclear weapons.[152] Consequently, no State would be bound, as a result of customary law, by this Rule when using nuclear weapons; it is not only, as the authors suggest, the three mentioned States which are excluded from an otherwise functioning customary rule.

Rule 45, Two

Destruction of the natural environment may not be used as a weapon.

US cloud-seeding experiments in the Vietnam conflict demonstrated the environment's potential for abuse.[153] Iraqi actions during the 1991 Gulf

---

[147] *UK Manual*, para. 15.20.   [148] *Ibid.*, p. 154.   [149] *Ibid.*   [150] *Ibid.*, pp. 154–155.
[151] *Ibid.*, p. 155, and in the Summary, p. 151.
[152] For the rules on persistent objectors, see Study, Vol. I, Introduction, xxxviii–xxxix and Scobbie, chapter 2, see pp. 33–36.
[153] A.H. Westing, *Ecological Consequences of the Second Indochina War* (Stockholm: Almqvist and Wiskell International, 1976).

conflict led to the notion of environmental damage being used as a weapon
or tactic of warfare. It was the deliberate nature of the Iraqi environmental
destruction (marine and atmospheric pollution) which seemed novel.
While the ENMOD Convention[154] had been designed to deal with US
environmental manipulation tactics, it appeared ill-equipped to tackle
what was widely labelled as environmental terrorism or environmental
warfare.[155] The label of terrorism might at the simplest level denote actions
designed to induce fear, shock or revulsion, as well as lacking military
advantage. In wasting Kuwaiti oil, Iraq was depleting Kuwaiti oil reserves
and causing environmental damage: two issues that appeared to be important to the Coalition. Consequently, the Iraqi actions were met with widespread condemnation.[156] In this sense, there would appear to be some
evidence to suggest that States may view as custom a duty not to use environmental destruction as a tactic or instrument of war. It is difficult to see,
however, what is gained by the existence of this provision that is not already
achieved by the principles of distinction and proportionality, rules governing attacks, and the prohibition on wanton destruction.

As to the formulation of the Rule, it is to be noted that the aspect of
destruction does not relate to only a *part* of the environment as is the case
for Rules 43A and B. Such, possibly minor, inconsistencies will inevitably
invite speculation, and it would have been useful for the authors to have
explained their reasoning. Two further comments may be made about the
formulation of this part of the Rule. First, while some of the evidence presented in Volume II refers to 'destruction' of the environment, others refer
to 'exploitation' of the environment.[157] With so few examples provided it
would appear difficult to choose between the two formulations for the
purposes of customary law. Indeed, the Commentary adds another possibility: 'a deliberate attack on the environment as a *method* of warfare'
(emphasis added).[158] What may have influenced the terminology are the
references to 'ecocide' by former Soviet Union countries and its definition

[154] *Ibid.*
[155] References to terrorism can be found in the Study, Vol. II, Part 1, in the comments of
Kuwait at § 245. It was the opinion of the Ottawa Conference of Experts in 1992 that the
Iraqi actions would not have fallen within the remit of ENMOD, see *Conduct of the
Persian Gulf War*, Appendix O, p. 625.
[156] See the comments in Vol. II, Part 1, Chapter 14, of Germany (§ 91), Iran (§ 94), Holland
(§ 99) and the United Kingdom (§ 105).
[157] For references to *destruction*, see the comments in Study, Vol. II, Part 1, Chapter 14, of
Sweden (§ 48); and for *exploitation*, see Jordan (§ 301), Kuwait (§ 245) and Iraq (§ 237).
[158] Emphasis added, Study, Vol. I, 155. Note the opening line of the Commentary refers to
destruction of the environment as a form of weapon.

as 'mass destruction' of the flora and fauna.[159] Secondly, the notion of environmental damage as a 'weapon' may not be apposite, particularly if the Iraqi actions can be said to form the basis of the customary rule. While States may have used the word 'weapon' in letters to the UN Secretary-General's Office,[160] the meaning of the term here is akin to a tactic, policy or method of warfare. The term weapon, as used in humanitarian law more generally, refers to small or mobile armaments,[161] as used in the first part of Rule 45. Furthermore, as it stands, the Rule appears to introduce a new prohibition on defensive measures of scorched earth tactics, which were specifically preserved in Additional Protocol I.[162] As a consequence, the meaning of the Rule is unclear.

While the heart of this Rule seems to be a prohibition on the deliberate destruction of the environment as a weapon, the Commentary commences with discussion of the 1977 ENMOD Convention. The ENMOD Convention prohibits use of environmental modification techniques, effectively prohibiting the manipulation of the environment and the consequent use of the forces created as a means of inflicting harm on the enemy. Examples of ENMOD techniques include cloud-seeding to produce rainfall and floods, as attempted by US forces in Vietnam, and exploding a nuclear device in the oceans to direct a tsunami at the enemy.[163] The environment would not necessarily be harmed, or destroyed, by the use of such techniques. The ENMOD Convention was, therefore, more a means of halting at its infancy the creation of a new and very dangerous weapon – the creation of catastrophic environmental forces as a means of warfare. Although the Commentary is relatively clear on this issue of environmental modification within ENMOD, the authors invite confusion simply by using ENMOD as evidence for a rule on environmental destruction, or at least referring to ENMOD within this section. The Rule appears to concern the deliberate destruction of the environment as a tactic or policy; the

---

[159] Study, Vol. II, Part 1, Chapter 14, comments of Armenia (§ 189), Belarus (§ 192), Kazakhstan (§ 204), Kyrgyzstan (§ 205), Moldova (§ 207), Russia (§ 212), Tajikistan (§ 215), and Ukraine (§ 217).

[160] See the letters in Study, Vol. II, Part 1, Chapter 14, by Iraq (§ 237), Jordan (§ 309) and Kuwait (§ 245).

[161] See for example Additional Protocol I, Arts. 13(2)(a), 25, 35(2), 36, 56, 59, 60, and 65; 1907 Hague Convention IV, Art. 23(a).

[162] Art. 54(5), Additional Protocol I. It must be remembered that for States parties to Additional Protocol I, the absolute threshold of environmental harm in Arts. 35(3) and 55(1) applies to the causation of environmental damage in whatever territory caused.

[163] For further examples, see Westing, *Ecological Consequences of the Second Indochina War*.

Convention concerns the use of the environment as a *means* of destruction. It is to the latter aspect, therefore, that States' references to 'an instrument of war' and 'exploitation of the environment' appear to be aimed.[164] As a result, it is not clear how the ENMOD Convention is being used by the authors. They conclude: 'Therefore, irrespective of whether the provisions of the ENMOD Convention are themselves customary, there is sufficiently widespread, representative and uniform practice to conclude that the destruction of the natural environment may not be used as a weapon.'[165] The conclusion of the authors clearly links the two concepts: that of environmental modification from ENMOD and destruction as portrayed in the Rule.

Doubts must be raised as to the necessity for Rule 45, Two. Since the authors conclude Rule 43 to be custom, it follows that the environment is protected both as a civilian object by the principles of distinction and proportionality, and as a military objective by the principle of proportionality in attack, precautionary measures and the prohibition against destruction of property. In either case, according to the authors, customary law imposes a ceiling of widespread, long-term and severe environmental damage. Accordingly, either the prohibition in Rule 45, Two was designed to outlaw incidents of destruction, such as those perpetrated by the Iraqi forces, or the use or manipulation of the environment as a weapon to attack the enemy. The existing law would appear to be sufficient to outlaw the former,[166] leading to the conclusion that this provision might be superfluous, while the latter would require the prohibition contained in the ENMOD Convention to have achieved customary status, which the authors admit is not proven. In conclusion, State condemnations of the Iraqi actions may perhaps be better viewed as political statements only, rather than as evidence of a separate legal obligation.

The Commentary states that this is 'arguably' a customary rule in non-international armed conflicts, and admits the lack of evidence for this conclusion.

3. Final remarks

There is no doubt that the Study represents a very valuable attempt to restate humanitarian law as applicable to the environment. The Study is a

---

[164] Comments in Study, Vol. II, Part 1, Chapter 14, of the United States (§ 316) and Jordan (§ 309) respectively.   [165] Study, Vol. I, 156.
[166] Note the US comments in *Conduct of the Persian Gulf War*, Appendix O, p. 621.

helpful first step in opening a dialogue between States, which it is hoped will eventually lead to consensus on this vital issue.

Rules 43A and C will be relatively uncontroversial, with Rules 43B and 44 likely to meet with some discussion, albeit probably fairly muted. It is suggested that, as was found in State condemnations of Iraqi pollution incidents during the Gulf conflict, it is possible to protect the environment quite reasonably during armed conflict on the basis of the Hague and Geneva Conventions and basic principles of humanitarian law. On the other hand, it will be interesting to see State reactions to the Study's finding that Rule 45 forms part of customary law, essentially placing Article 35(3) of Additional Protocol I on a customary basis.[167]

Some criticism may be made of the terminological inconsistencies in Rules 43–45, but this should not overshadow the successes of the Study. More specific observations are the lack of explanation in the *Study* as to the chosen formulations for rules and particular terms, and its adoption of environmental law principles and concepts. It is hoped that a future edition will be able to include such explanations. While many of the authors' conclusions will be welcomed by those familiar with environmental law, particularly as regards recognition of the precautionary principle, it is suggested that they are not yet all a true reflection of the status of customary law.

---

[167] See, however, the comments of G. Aldrich, which support the customary status of Rule 45: 'Customary International Humanitarian Law – an Interpretation on behalf of the International Committee of the Red Cross' (2005) 76 *British Yearbook of International Law* 503 at 514–6.

9

Specific methods of warfare

WILLIAM FENRICK

1. Introduction

Part III of the Study, although entitled 'Specific Methods of Warfare', embraces a miscellaneous range of topics: denial of quarter (Rules 46–48), destruction and seizure of property (Rules 49–52), starvation and access to humanitarian relief (Rules 53–56), deception (Rules 57–65), and communication with the enemy (Rules 66–69).

Treaty-based roots for the laws concerning specific methods of warfare are, for the most part, found in Hague Law provisions. The Lieber Code of 1863, which was adopted by Federal forces in the American Civil War of 1861–65 (a non-international armed conflict but one on a massive scale), prohibits the denial of quarter (Articles 60–62, 66), limits the right of one side to exercise control over the property of the other or of its nationals (Articles 31, 34–38, 44–45, 72–73), prohibits assassination (Article 148), prohibits acting in bad faith (Article 11), explicitly permits starvation as a method of war (Articles 17–18), addresses espionage and sabotage (Articles 83–84, 88, 98–100, 102, 104), permits ruses and prohibits perfidy (Article 101), and addresses modalities of communication (Articles 111–114).

The Regulations annexed to Hague Convention IV of 1907 Respecting the Laws and Customs of War on Land, which updated a similar convention adopted as Hague Convention II in 1899, also address specific methods of warfare. In particular: Article 23 addresses denial of quarter, treacherous killing or wounding, improper use of flags of truce and enemy uniforms, and destruction or seizure of enemy property; Article 24 addresses ruses of war; Articles 28 and 47 prohibit pillage; Articles 29–31 address spies; Articles 32–34 address modalities of communication; and Articles 46 and 49–54 address treatment of property in occupied territory.

The 1949 Geneva Conventions, insofar as they regulate international conflict, do not address denial of quarter, deception, communication with the enemy or starvation as a method of warfare. The Fourth (Civilians) Convention supplements the 1907 Hague Regulations and repeats the prohibition of pillage (Article 33); addresses treatment of property in occupied territory (Article 53) and addresses provision of relief supplies in occupied territory (Articles 59–63). Articles 33 and 35 of the First Convention contain specific rules applicable to military medical units. Article 18 of the Third (Prisoners of War) Convention indicates what items found with prisoners of war are not to be considered booty. Further, the First (Article 50), Second (Article 51), and Fourth (Article 147) Conventions list 'extensive destruction and appropriation of (protected) property, not justified by military necessity and carried out unlawfully and wantonly' as grave breaches. Common Article 3 of the 1949 Conventions implicitly prohibits denial of quarter in non-international armed conflicts.

Additional Protocol I of 1977 addresses what have traditionally been regarded as both Hague Law and Geneva Law issues, in fact effecting a merger of the two branches of the law of armed conflict. Articles 40–42 and 85 address denial of quarter. Articles 22, 23, 30 and 67 address military property assigned to civil defence purposes. Article 54, for the first time in a treaty, prohibits starvation of civilians as a method of warfare and Articles 68–71 address relief in favour of the civilian population in areas under enemy control. Article 37 defines and prohibits perfidy while clearly indicating that ruses of war are permissible. Articles 38 and 39 prohibit improper use of certain distinctive emblems, including, in certain circumstances, enemy uniforms.

Additional Protocol II of 1977, which applies to non-international armed conflicts, prohibits denial of quarter (Article 4), prohibits starvation of civilians as a method of warfare (Article 14), and prohibits misuse of the distinctive emblem of the red cross (Article 12).

Most recently, the Rome Statute of the International Criminal Court 1998 which is, of course, prospective, indicates that grave breaches of the Geneva Conventions are war crimes (Article 8(2)(a)), and goes on to prohibit for international armed conflicts: making improper use of flags of truce, distinctive emblems, and enemy uniforms (Article 8(2)(b)(vii)); treacherous killing or wounding (Article 8(2)(b)(xi)); denial of quarter (Article 8(2)(b)(xii)); destroying or seizing enemy property without military necessity (Article 8(2)(b)(xiii)); pillage (Article 8(2)(b)(xvi)), and starvation of civilians as a method of warfare (Article 8(2)(b)(xxv)). For non-international armed conflicts, prohibited acts include: pillage (Article 8(2)(e)(v)); treacherous killing or wounding (Article 8(2)(e)(ix)); denial of quarter (Article 8(2)(e)(x)); and destroying or seizing the adversary's property without military necessity (Article 8(2)(e)(xii)).

As one might expect with any attempt to state customary law related to a particular area of law, the Rules in this Part of the Study do not provide a comprehensive code related to specific methods of warfare and, inevitably, in some cases lack the degree of precision one might prefer. Further, quite frequently, one must refer to the Commentary to the Rules in order to have an adequate understanding of their intended meaning. Unfortunately, treaty rules developed through multilateral negotiation tend to lack precision because of the need to obtain consensus and customary rules tend to lack precision because they are the product of an accretion of state practice.

As has been observed, however, the treaty-based rules of law concerning specific methods of warfare are found in what has been referred to traditionally as Hague Law, not Geneva Law. Hague Law has been concerned with what States or their armed forces may do as well as what they may not do. It may be that identification of the customary law in this area requires some extra emphasis on the range of potentially permissible military activities. For example, the Study does not contain specific rules relating to activities such as sabotage, espionage, siege warfare, ambush or assassination although one might argue that there is an adequate basis for deriving customary rules setting acceptable parameters for at least some of these activities. Siege warfare, ambush and assassination are addressed in the Commentary related to some of the Rules in Part III although one might query whether the treatment is sufficient. These references will be discussed below. Rule 107,[1] which is contained in Part V (Treatment of Civilians and Persons *Hors de Combat*) addresses the treatment of spies after capture but there is no other treatment of espionage in the Study.

2. The Rules

Denial of Quarter

Rule 46

Ordering that no quarter will be given, threatening an adversary therewith or conducting hostilities on this basis is prohibited.

---

[1] Rule 107: 'Combatants who are captured while engaged in espionage do not have the right to prisoner-of-war status. They may not be convicted or sentenced without previous trial.'

This is a basic and longstanding rule of customary international humanitarian law and it is most unlikely that anyone would challenge its existence or content. It is also contained in Article 40 of Additional Protocol I (adopted by consensus) and in Article 4 of Additional Protocol II (also adopted by consensus). It is of particular importance to military commanders.

Rule 47

Attacking persons who are recognized as *hors de combat* is prohibited. A person *hors de combat* is:

(a) **anyone who is in the power of an adverse party;**
(b) **anyone who is defenceless because of unconsciousness, shipwreck, wounds or sickness; or**
(c) **anyone who clearly expresses an intention to surrender; provided he or she abstains from any hostile act and does not attempt to escape.**

This, too, is a longstanding rule of customary international humanitarian law. It is also contained in Articles 41(1) and 85(3)(e) of Additional Protocol I (both adopted by consensus), and, implicitly, in common Article 3 of the Geneva Conventions and in Article 4 of Additional Protocol II (adopted by consensus). Persons who are *hors de combat* under Rule 47(a) and (b) do not pose a threat to an attacker and compliance with these parts of the Rule should not be difficult under normal circumstances. It must, however, be emphasised that once a person is in the power of an adverse party, as the result of a surrender or otherwise, that person may not be attacked even if it is extremely difficult to keep or evacuate prisoners. For example, if a reconnaissance patrol captures a combatant then it may not kill the prisoner even if his or her presence makes mission accomplishment difficult or impossible.

The only real issue is the interpretation and application of Rule 47(c). In particular, how is it to be determined that the person purportedly attempting to surrender has the intent and capacity to do so and that he or she has demonstrated that intent in a timely fashion? It is clear that the simple fact that troops are retreating does not demonstrate an intent to surrender. The Report on United Kingdom Practice cited a former British Director of Army Legal Services who, adverting to an incident in the 1982 Falklands Conflict, stated that UK soldiers were not required to risk their own lives in granting quarter. He added that capture was to take place when circumstances permitted and that, as an example, it might not be practicable to accept surrender of one group of enemy soldiers while under fire from another group.[2] Somewhat similarly, the Report on US Practice referred to an incident in the 1990–91 Gulf War in which tanks equipped with earthmoving plough blades breached trench lines, then turned and filled in the trenches entombing Iraqi defenders.[3] The US defended this practice and asserted 'a soldier who fights to the very last possible minute assumes certain risks. His opponent either may not see his surrender, may not recognize his actions as an attempt to surrender in the heat and confusion of battle, or may find it difficult (if not impossible) to halt an onrushing assault to accept a soldier's last minute effort at surrender.'[4] As a hypothetical example, one might also envisage a situation in which troops behind their own lines are overflown by aircraft of an attacking force. Such troops may purport to indicate an intent to surrender by downing arms or putting their hands up, for example. If, however, these troops are not in a position where, because of their location and the resources available to the attacking side, they have the physical capacity to surrender, one might query whether they remain potentially subject to legitimate attack. Persons purporting to surrender must possess both the intent and the capacity to surrender. If an offer to surrender is impossible of acceptance attack is permissible.[5]

Rule 48

Making persons parachuting from an aircraft in distress the object of attack during their descent is prohibited.

This Rule was first codified in Article 42 of Additional Protocol I and, at that time it was not adopted by consensus because some States were of the view that persons landing in their own territory could not be regarded as *hors de combat*. At the present time, there appears to be a general consensus that all persons parachuting from aircraft in distress should be regarded as *hors de combat* and therefore immune from attack. Once parachutists have landed they would normally be regarded as ceasing to be *hors de combat* and therefore subject to the normal attack rules. The Commentary to the Rule suggests that such parachutists landing in territory under the control of the adverse party should be given an opportunity to surrender unless it is apparent they are engaging in a hostile act.[6]

---

[2] Study, Vol. II, Part 1, 975.   [3] *Ibid.*, Vol. II, Part 1, 962–963.
[4] *Ibid.*, Vol. II, Part 1, 963.   [5] *Ibid.*, Vol. I, 172.   [6] *Ibid.*, Vol. I, 172.

Rule 48 does not apply to troops who are airborne as part of a military operation and are not bailing out in distress.

Destruction and Seizure of Property

Rule 49

The parties to the conflict may seize military equipment belonging to an adverse party as war booty.

Although one may query the precise parameters of war booty, there is no question that this Rule is well embedded in customary law related to international armed conflict. The compilers and authors of the Study were, however, unable to identify a rule of customary law which would either permit or prohibit such seizures in non-international armed conflicts. One might debate this conclusion as, presumably, whether formally labelled war booty or not, the parties to non-international armed conflicts seize and use military equipment belonging to the adverse party whenever possible. It is suggested that a more rigorous approach, perhaps an unnecessarily rigorous approach, has been adopted concerning the identification of rules related to permissible activities as regards property than that concerning the identification of other rules related to non-international armed conflict. That being said, it must be noted that, if one assumes seizure or destruction of military equipment belonging to an adverse party is always required by imperative military necessity, Rule 49 is subsumed under Rule 50 and Rule 50 does apply to all conflicts.

Rule 49 indicates seizure must be by an adverse party and for an adverse party. It does not legitimise seizure for private purposes, such as war trophies. It also limits the scope of such seizures. There are special rules applicable to military medical units set forth in the First Geneva Convention (Articles 33 and 35), and to medical ships and aircraft and to material and buildings of military units permanently assigned to civil defence organisations set forth in Additional Protocol I (Articles 22, 23, 30, and 67 respectively). War booty includes all enemy military equipment or property captured or found on the battlefield except for the personal belongings and protective gear of prisoners of war. If private property found on the battlefield includes arms, ammunition, military equipment or military papers it may also be seized as booty. Booty may be used without restriction and need not be returned to an adversary on the cessation of hostilities.

Rule 50

The destruction or seizure of the property of an adversary is prohibited, unless required by imperative military necessity.

For international armed conflicts this is a long-standing part of customary law codified in Article 23(g) of the Hague Regulations among other places. More recently, for non-international conflicts, it is prohibited by Article 8(2)(e)(xii) of the Statute of the International Criminal Court. Leaving aside the Statute provision, which is prospective, one might query whether the evidentiary basis for the application of this Rule to non-international conflicts is substantially stronger than the evidentiary basis for Rule 49; the Study could not conclude whether or not Rule 49 applied to non-international conflicts. Perhaps it is considered more appropriate to apply Rule 50 to such conflicts because of its more general nature.

As worded, Rule 50 might be regarded as applicable both to destruction of property in territory under the control of an adversary by means of an attack and to destruction of property belonging to an adversary in territory under the control of the party by other means. If it does, then 'imperative military necessity' must be equated with the 'definite military advantage' derived from an attack on a military objective (Rule 8). One might query whether this is practicable or desirable. For all practical purposes, Rule 50 has been applied in such a way by a Trial Chamber of the International Criminal Tribunal for the former Yugoslavia.[7] In that case, in substance, the court held that an attack which resulted in damage to a civilian object and which was directed at the civilian object was not required by imperative military necessity. Presumably the court would also have decided that an attack which was directed at a military objective but which resulted in excessive/disproportionate damage to civilian objects could not be justified by imperative military necessity. Whether

---

[7] *Prosecutor v. Pavle Strugar* Judgment of Trial Chamber, 31 January 2005, Case No. IT-01-42-T. Strugar was convicted for the shelling of the Old Town of Dubrovnik for a violation of Article 3(d) of the ICTY Statute which, among other things, penalised destruction or wilful damage done to institutions dedicated to religion and to historic monuments but the analysis of culpability involved essentially similar legal issues. The Old Town of Dubrovnik is generally regarded as constituting, in entirety, a cultural or historic monument. The Trial Chamber was satisfied that the elements of related charges for attacking civilian objects and for causing devastation not justified by military necessity were established but held that the Article 3(d) charge most effectively encapsulated the prohibited conduct.

the approach adopted by the ICTY will be followed in future remains to be seen.[8]

Rule 51

In occupied territory:

(a) **movable public property that can be used for military operations may be confiscated;**

(b) **immovable public property must be administered according to the rule of usufruct; and**

(c) **private property must be respected and may not be confiscated; except where destruction or seizure of such property is required by imperative military necessity.**

Quite clearly this is a longstanding rule of customary law for international armed conflicts, which is codified in the Hague Regulations (Articles 46, 53–56). The question is whether it can or should be applied in non-international armed conflicts. A substantial reason for not doing so is that the concept of occupied territory is one which is usually regarded as applying only to international armed conflicts. Further, one might query what constitutes the public property of the side which is not represented by the 'official' government in a non-international armed conflict. That being said, perhaps a *mutatis mutandis* application of the rule to non-international armed conflicts might be useful if Rule 50 is regarded as having some deficiencies.

Rule 52

Pillage is prohibited.

This Rule is a longstanding part of customary law and is, in substance, a specific application of the general principle of law prohibiting theft. It is also codified in Article 33 of the Fourth Geneva Convention and in Article 4 of Additional Protocol II. Pillage and plunder are synonyms. In brief, pillage involves the forcible taking of property for private purposes from the adverse party or from persons linked to the adverse party.

---

[8] As a former staff member of the ICTY Office of the Prosecutor, the author must observe that prosecutors will tend to adopt a defensible practice of multiple charging unless there is substantial jurisprudence indicating only one charge is appropriate, in order to ensure that the prohibited conduct is accurately identified to the satisfaction of the Trial Chamber.

Starvation and Access to Humanitarian Relief

Rule 53

The use of starvation of the civilian population as a method of warfare is prohibited.

Starvation of civilians as a method of warfare was first prohibited by treaty in Article 54 of Additional Protocol I and Article 14 of Additional Protocol II. Prior to the adoption of the Additional Protocols in 1977, starvation of civilians was regarded as an acceptable method of warfare. Since then it would appear from the Study to have developed into a rule of customary law applicable to all conflicts. One might query the extent to which this development applies to long-established methods of warfare such as siege and blockade. One might also query how the Rule would apply if a 'Hunger Blockade' similar to that imposed on Germany by the Allies in World War I was imposed today. If the authorities in an encircled area make a conscious decision to choose guns over butter with the result that civilians in the encircled area are deprived of essential foodstuffs, presumably it would be inappropriate to accuse the commander of the encircling forces of using starvation as a method of warfare. The Study itself states: 'The prohibition of starvation as a method of warfare does not prohibit siege warfare as long as the purpose is to achieve a military objective and not to starve a civilian population.'[9] It also states: 'Likewise, the prohibition of starvation as a method of warfare does not prohibit the imposition of a naval blockade as long as the purpose is to achieve a military objective and not to starve a civilian population.'[10] One might query whether these rather modest qualifiers are sufficient. One highly respected but relatively conservative legal writer, Yoram Dinstein, has subjected Article 54 of Additional Protocol I (and, by implication, Article 14 of Additional Protocol II) to ferocious criticism where siege warfare is concerned as, in his view, there is no alternative means, other than assault which is almost always extremely costly to all, for bringing about the capture of defended towns,[11] concluding: 'It stands to reason that the practice of States will not confirm the sweeping abolition of siege warfare affecting civilians. Possibly, a construction of the language of Article 54 will be arrived at, whereby siege warfare will continue to be

---

[9] Study, Vol. I, 188.   [10] *Ibid.*, Vol. I, 189.
[11] Y. Dinstein, *The Conduct of Hostilities Under the Law of International Armed Conflict* (Cambridge University Press, 2004), pp. 133–137.

acquiesced with – notwithstanding civilian deprivations – at least in those circumstances when the besieging force is willing to assure civilians a safe passage out.'[12]

A.P.V. Rogers, another highly respected writer but one who normally tends to adopt a more liberal or progressive position than that of Professor Dinstein, has also expressed concerns about the viability of a strict application of Article 54 to a siege situation.[13] Considering the importance of the issue, it might well have been appropriate for the authors of the Study to have included more extensive rules, similar to those in the recent UK *Manual of the Law of Armed Conflict* related to blockade and siege, which are specific methods of warfare and also highly relevant to the starvation issue.[14] In particular, one should note para. 5.34.3 of the UK *Manual* which states:

> The military authorities of the besieged area might decide not to permit the evacuation of civilians or the civilians themselves might decide to stay where they are. In those circumstances, so long as the besieging commander left open his offer to allow civilians and the wounded and sick to leave the besieged area, he would be justified in preventing any supplies from reaching that area.

Rule 54

Attacking, destroying, removing or rendering useless objects indispensable to the survival of the civilian population is prohibited.

The Study regards this Rule as a corollary to Rule 53 above. As with Rule 53, the first treaty law prohibitions of such attacks are contained in Article 54 of Additional Protocol I and Article 14 of Additional Protocol II. Both Articles list examples of such objects including foodstuffs, agricultural areas for the production of foodstuffs, crops, livestock, drinking water installations and supplies and irrigation works. The lists are not intended to be exhaustive and the Commentary to Rule 54 suggests other items might well be included such as medical supplies and means of shelter.[15] The Commentary also adverts to two exceptions to the rule referred to in Additional Protocol I: (i) objects may be attacked if they are

---

[12] *Ibid.*, p. 137.

[13] A.P.V. Rogers, *Law on the Battlefield*, (Manchester University Press, 2nd edn, 2004), pp. 101–103.

[14] UK Ministry of Defence, *The Manual of the Law of Armed Conflict* (Oxford University Press, 2004), para. 5.34 for sieges and paras. 13.65–76 for blockades.

[15] Study, Vol. I, 193.

used as sustenance solely for combatants or otherwise in direct support of
military action provided, in the latter case, that such action does not
starve the civilian population or force its movement (Article 54(3)), and
(ii) when a State, on the basis of imperative military necessity, uses a
'scorched earth policy' on and in defence of national territory against
invasion. The Commentary suggests, however, that neither exception
applies to non-international armed conflict because they are not referred
to in Additional Protocol II.[16]

The Rule has been criticised as overly broad in a recent decision of the
Eritrea/Ethiopia Claims Commission.[17] In that decision, the Commission, which is evaluating claims in an international armed conflict, was
required to determine customary law relating to attacks on a water reservoir. It held that 'the provisions of Article 54 (of Additional Protocol I)
that prohibit attacks against drinking water installations and supplies
that are indispensable to the survival of the civilian population for the
specific purpose of denying them for their sustenance value to the adverse
Party had become part of customary international humanitarian law by
1999'.[18] The same decision concluded, in footnote 23, that the ICRC
Study 'concludes that a broader prohibition than the one stated in Article
54(2) has become customary law. The Commission need not, and does
not, endorse the study's broader conclusion.' It would appear, however,
that the scope of Rule 54 standing alone is narrowed by the Study
Commentary.

Rule 55

**The parties to the conflict must allow and facilitate rapid and unim-
peded passage of humanitarian relief for civilians in need, which is
impartial in character and conducted without any adverse distinction,
subject to their right of control.**

This Rule is an abbreviated version of Article 23 of Geneva Convention
IV and of Article 70 of Additional Protocol I. There is no analogous provision in Additional Protocol II. It would appear to balance the requirements of the parties to the conflict to exercise control over activities in
areas within their power with the need for passage of humanitarian relief
to civilians. Optics notwithstanding, the parties do retain a substantial

[16] *Ibid.*, Vol. I, 192–193.
[17] Eritrea–Ethiopia Claims Commission, Partial Award Western Front, Aerial Bombardment
and Related Claims, Eritrea's Claims 1, 3 , 5, 9–13, 14, 21, 25 and 26, 19 December 2005.
[18] *Ibid.*, pp. 28–30.

right of control over the process. Because of this factor, it should be acceptable as a customary law rule for all conflicts.

Rule 56

The parties to the conflict must ensure the freedom of movement of authorised humanitarian relief personnel essential to the exercise of their functions. Only in case of imperative military necessity may their movements be temporarily restricted.

This Rule is a slightly modified version of Article 71(3) of Additional Protocol I. There is no analogous provision in Additional Protocol II. As with Rule 55 above, the parties do retain a degree of control over the process and, because of this, it should be an acceptable customary rule for all conflicts. Although Article 71(4) of Additional Protocol I is not referred to in the Rule or the related commentary, perhaps it is included by implication. It states:

> Under no circumstances may relief personnel exceed the terms of their mission under this Protocol. In particular, they shall take account of the security concerns of the Party in whose territory they are carrying out their duties. The mission of any of the personnel who do not respect these conditions may be terminated.

Deception

Rule 57

Ruses of war are not prohibited as long as they do not infringe a rule of international humanitarian law.

This Rule is an extremely useful statement of the obvious. No military commander views combat as a fair fight. If the odds are even, something is wrong. Most recently, Article 37(2) of Additional Protocol I codified this area of the law as follows:

> Ruses of war are not prohibited. Such ruses are acts which are intended to mislead an adversary or to induce him to act recklessly but which infringe no rule of international law applicable in armed conflict and which are not perfidious because they do not invite the confidence of an adversary with respect to protection under the law.

There is no similar provision in the final version of Additional Protocol II but the applicability of the Rule to non-international armed conflict is unlikely to be questioned. Belligerent forces are expected to be on guard against legitimate ruses but they are entitled to expect their opponents to comply with applicable international humanitarian law. The list of permissible ruses is never closed. The current UK *Manual* gives several examples, including surprises and ambushes, at para. 5.17.2.

Rule 58

The improper use of the white flag of truce is prohibited.

This Rule of customary law predates the 1907 Hague Regulations and is codified in Article 37 of Additional Protocol I. There is no similar provision in the final version of Additional Protocol II but the applicability of the rule to non-international armed conflict is unlikely to be questioned. The purpose of the white flag is to indicate a request to communicate, in order to negotiate a surrender or cease-fire. Any use of the flag to gain a military advantage would be improper.

Rule 59

The improper use of the distinctive emblems of the Geneva Conventions is prohibited.

This Rule was codified as early as the 1899 Hague Regulations and is now referred to in a range of international instruments, including both Additional Protocols (Article 38(1) Additional Protocol I and Article 12 Additional Protocol II). The only proper use of the distinctive emblems is to identify medical and religious personnel, medical units and medical transports, and also personnel and property of the components of the International Movement of the Red Cross and Red Crescent. It is unlikely to be challenged as a rule of customary law for all conflicts.

Rule 60

The use of the United Nations emblem and uniform is prohibited, except as authorised by the organisation.

This Rule is contained in Article 38(2) of Additional Protocol I. There is no similar provision in the final version of Additional Protocol II but the applicability of the Rule to non-international conflict is unlikely to be questioned.

Rule 61

The improper use of other internationally recognised emblems is prohibited.

Various treaties provide for a range of internationally recognised emblems, including emblems to identify cultural property, civil defence, and works and installations containing dangerous forces. It would appear that the authors of the Study considered the absence of contrary practice, of assertions by parties to conflicts that it would be lawful to use improperly internationally recognised emblems, to be of particular weight in establishing the Rule.[19] This approach is not unreasonable.

Rule 62

Improper use of the flags or military emblems, insignia or uniforms of the adversary is prohibited.

The Commentary concludes this Rule is customary for international armed conflicts and should also apply in non-international armed conflicts when the parties to the conflict do in fact wear uniforms. This conclusion is quite reasonable. The question, however, is: what is improper use? There has been a longstanding debate on this issue in which, generally speaking, representatives of major military powers argue that enemy military uniforms could be worn except in combat while representatives of smaller military powers argue that use of enemy uniforms is prohibited in a much wider range of circumstances. Prior to the development of Additional Protocol I, the applicable rule would appear to have been the so-called Skorzeny Rule. In the Trial of Otto Skorzeny following World War II, all of the accused were acquitted by an American court because the prosecution did not establish that the accused, German soldiers, had actually worn American uniforms in combat during the Ardennes Offensive in December 1944 although it had established they wore such uniforms in the operational area.[20] Although an American court acquitted Skorzeny and his co-accused in their trial in 1947, 18 members of Skorzeny's unit who were captured in US uniforms during the Ardennes Offensive were executed as spies shortly thereafter.[21]

---

[19] Study, Vol. 1, 213.   [20] *US v. Skorzey et al.*, 9 *LRTWC* 90, pp. 90–93.

[21] James J. Weingartner, 'Otto Skorzeny and the Laws of War' (1991) 55 *The Journal of Military History* 207 at 217–218 referred to in W. Hays Parks, 'Special Forces Wear of Non-Standard Uniforms' (2003) 4 *Chicago Journal of International Law* 493 at 545.

Article 39(2) of Additional Protocol I states:

> It is prohibited to make use of the flags or military emblems, insignia or
> uniforms of adverse Parties while engaging in attacks or in order to shield,
> favour, protect or impede military operations.

Quite obviously, this rule imposes much greater restrictions on the use of
enemy uniforms than the Skorzeny Rule. The only Party to Additional
Protocol I which has reserved on Article 39(2) is Canada, for reasons
probably impossible to decipher at the present time. Before and since the
adoption of Additional Protocol I, many States have continued to have
some of their forces make use of enemy uniforms in a variety of circumstances. The respected American author, W. Hays Parks, has compiled a
substantial but not exhaustive list of examples of use of enemy uniforms
in a variety of circumstances by several countries.[22] Although this list is
extremely impressive, it is by no means clear what legal weight should be
assigned to it as one cannot determine whether States authorised these
acts on the assumption they were legally permissible or as a calculated
risk taken in defiance of the applicable legal norms.

The Commentary tends to beg the question of the parameters of permissible use of enemy uniforms by stating: 'It cannot be concluded that
the wearing of enemy uniforms outside of combat would be improper.'[23]
It is submitted that, bearing in mind present State practice, the following
less anaemic formulation must be preferred: 'the wearing of enemy uniforms outside of combat is permitted.' This approach is not applicable to
military aircraft. As the insignia on military aircraft cannot be changed in
mid-flight, any use of enemy insignia on military aircraft in areas where
they might be engaged in operations is prohibited.

Rule 63

**Use of the flags or military emblems, insignia or uniforms of neutral or
other States not party to the conflict is prohibited.**

This Rule is contained in Article 39(1) of Additional Protocol I. There is
no equivalent provision in Additional Protocol II. The authors of the
Study found no evidence supporting or opposing the practice in non-
international armed conflict. They concluded the Rule was arguably
applicable in non-international armed conflict by reason of a general
principle of sorts: 'It is very likely that the fact of implying involvement of

---

[22] *Ibid.*, Annex, at 545–560.   [23] Study, Vol. I, 216.

a third state in a non-international armed conflict by wearing its uniform, for example, would be denounced by that State, as well as by the adverse party, as unlawful conduct.'[24] This is a reasonable approach.

Rule 64

Concluding an agreement to suspend combat with the intention of attacking by surprise the enemy relying on that agreement is prohibited.

This is a long-standing rule of customary international law and is based on the principle of good faith. For non-international armed conflict, there is no specific relevant treaty provision although an early draft of Additional Protocol II contained the rule. It is a defensible rule of customary law for all conflicts.

Rule 65

Killing, injuring or capturing an adversary by resort to perfidy is prohibited.

This is a long-standing rule of customary international law. The final version of Additional Protocol II does not contain a perfidy provision. It is codified and defined in Article 37(1) of Additional Protocol I which states in part:

> It is prohibited to kill, injure or capture an adversary by resort to perfidy. Acts inviting the confidence of an adversary to lead him to believe that he is entitled to, or is obliged to accord, protection under the rules of international law applicable in armed conflict, with intent to betray that confidence, shall constitute perfidy.

The same provision goes on to give the following examples of perfidy:

> (a) the feigning of an intent to negotiate under a flag of truce or of a surrender;
> (b) the feigning of an incapacitation by wounds or sickness;
> (c) the feigning of civilian, non-combatant status; and
> (d) the feigning of protected status by the use of signs, emblems or uniforms of the United Nations or of neutral or other States not Parties to the conflict.

These examples are just that, examples. They are prohibited in all conflicts, not merely international conflicts. It should be noted that

---

[24] *Ibid.*, Vol. 1, 219.

improper wearing of enemy uniforms as referred to in Rule 62 above is not perfidious because international law does not require a party to a conflict to accord protection to soldiers wearing its own uniforms.

The Commentary notes that the Hague Regulations prohibit 'to kill or wound treacherously' while Additional Protocol I prohibits 'to kill, injure or capture an adversary by resort to perfidy' and asserts, quite reasonably, that killing, injuring or capturing by resort to perfidy are all prohibited under customary law.[25] Although the Rome Statute (Article 8(2)(b)(xi) and (e)(ix)) uses the Hague Regulation formulation in listing war crimes, the risk of killing or injuring is so high in attempting to capture by means of perfidy that excluding capture from Rule 65 is nonsensical.

The Commentary to this Rule discusses what it refers to as 'treacherous attempt upon the life of the enemy' and what might also be referred to as 'assassination'.[26] It appears to regard assassination as being embraced in entirety by either or both of treacherous killing or attacking civilian(s). One might question whether a separate rule is needed for this particular topic. Bearing in mind the range of State practice as referred to in the Study, the potential significance of the topic, even in wartime, and the desirability of addressing closely related issues such as outlawry and offering rewards, it is submitted that inclusion of a rule essentially similar to the rules in paras 5.13 and 5.14 of the current UK *Manual* addressing both assassination and outlawry would be desirable and justifiable.

Communication with the Enemy

Rule 66

Commanders may enter into non-hostile contact through any means of communication. Such contact must be based on good faith.

This is a generalised version of a longstanding rule of customary international law and is, as stated, premised on good faith. It is also a rule of common sense and its applicability to all conflicts is appropriate. Traditionally, and as set out in Hague Rule Article 32, communication was carried out by means of a *parlementaire*, a person authorised by one side to enter into communication with the other who advanced bearing a white flag and accompanied by a trumpeter, bugler or drummer. Modern means of communication, such as telephone and radio, have obviated the

[25] *Ibid.*, Vol. I, 225.   [26] *Ibid.*, Vol. I, 225–226.

need for musical accompaniment. Contact should be initiated by a commander. Individual combatants do not have the right under their national laws to initiate such contact. Such contact may be sought for a variety of reasons, including to search for the wounded, sick, and dead; to exchange prisoners, and to evacuate persons from a besieged area. The opposing commander is not obligated to respond favourably to requests to initiate communication although he or she is prohibited from declaring in advance that such requests will be rejected.

Rule 67

Parlementaires are inviolable.

This is a long-standing rule of customary international law. If *parlementaires* are used, they and the persons accompanying them are inviolable and this inviolability applies until they are returned to friendly territory. The *parlementaire*, with his white flag and accompanying party must advance towards the other party. In these days such an advance might take place in an armoured vehicle flying a white flag, accompanied by a driver, radio and loudspeaker operator, and an interpreter. A party advancing with a white flag may not be fired upon but there need not be a complete cease-fire in the sector through which the *parlementaire* is seeking to advance.

Rule 68

Commanders may take the necessary precautions to prevent the presence of a *parlementaire* from being prejudicial.

This is a long-standing rule of customary international law. Measures may be taken to prevent the *parlementaire* from gaining useful current intelligence. If such intelligence is disclosed to the *parlementaire* inadvertently, he or she may be detained temporarily until the disclosure of the intelligence will not be advantageous to the other party.

Rule 69

***Parlementaires* taking advantage of their privileged position to commit an act contrary to international law and detrimental to the adversary lose their inviolability.**

This is a long-standing rule of customary international law. Such acts might include deliberately collecting useful intelligence (spying), carrying out acts of sabotage or encouraging soldiers to desert. If a *parlementaire* abuses his or her position, the *parlementaire* may be detained and tried in accordance with national legislation subject to the fair trial guarantees which apply as a matter of international law.

3. Final remarks

The degree of objectivity involved in determining which acts constitute State practice and what customary law rules can be derived from that body of practice can easily be exaggerated. The body of State practice accumulated by those involved in preparing the Study is truly impressive, although some might suggest that a greater degree of attention should have been devoted to battlefield behaviour.[27] It is unlikely, however, that a greater emphasis on battlefield behaviour in the compilation of State practice for Part III of the Study would have resulted in a substantial difference in the derived Rules, as most of these Rules have been firmly embedded in customary law, at least for international armed conflicts, for a very long time. Further, when relatively furtive activities such as those involving the use of enemy uniforms are at issue, one may well query whether States are applying or ignoring the applicable law. On the other hand, it is much more difficult to ignore actual battlefield behaviour when one is attempting to derive rules related to target selection or the principle of proportionality.

Bearing in mind how many of the topics addressed, or not addressed, in Part III have their roots in well-established Hague Law and also that the rules of land warfare annexed to Hague Convention IV of 1907 were considered to be customary law as early as the decision of the International Military Tribunal at Nuremberg,[28] it is surprising to see some topics omitted from the Rules, even if they are occasionally referred to in the commentary. As one example, Articles 29–31 (concerning spies) of the Land Warfare Rules Annexed to Hague Convention IV of 1907 are probably customary law yet the only reference to spies in the Study is Rule 107 which is merely an adaptation of Article 30. It is suggested that a revised addition of Part III of the Rules could and should include rules related to the following specific methods of warfare:

---

[27] W. Hays Parks is a particularly strong supporter of the need to emphasise actual battlefield behaviour as exemplified in 'Special Forces Wear of Non-Standard Uniforms' (note 21 above).

[28] International Military Tribunal (Nuremberg) Judgment and Sentences, reprinted in (1947) 41 *American Journal of International Law* 172.

siege, blockade, sabotage, espionage, rewards/outlawry, and assassination. In particular, specific rules related to siege and blockade might
constitute a constructive refinement for the Rule prohibiting the use of
starvation (Rule 53).

10

Weapons, means and methods of warfare

STEVEN HAINES

1. Introduction

The law relating to weapons was one of the most controversial issues to emerge during and after the operation in the city of Fallujah in Iraq in November 2004. US military forces engaged insurgents in intense urban combat some months after the period of belligerent occupation had come to an end, when Iraq was no longer 'ruled' by the coalition; it was in theory governed by an Iraqi authority, with coalition forces deployed within the State to assist with security. The military situation in Fallujah was, however, one that, in purely military terms, demanded the application of force at a level consistent with combat during an armed conflict. Military commanders contemplating deploying units into the city were, very understandably, anxious to provide them with the ability to respond with lethal force in combat, as they believed the situation demanded, rather than to constrain them within minimum force limits appropriate to a domestic law enforcement or internal security situation. The decision was made to regard the operation as one in which international humanitarian law should be applied, 'for policy, humanitarian and legal reasons'.[1] The situation described is of a nature that modern conflict is increasingly creating – the so-called 'three block war' described by former US Marine Corp Commandant, General Charles Krulak.[2]

---

[1] E-mail exchanges between the author and a US Government legal adviser about the application of international humanitarian law in Fallujah (11–15 November 2004).

[2] General Charles C. Krulak, 'The Strategic Corporal: Leadership in the Three Block War' in *Marines: Official Magazine of the Marine Corps*, January 1999. A 'three block war' is one in which several different types of operation are ongoing simultaneously in the same theatre, with different intensities of conflict being experienced by the same force. In one part of the operational theatre troops may be providing humanitarian aid in relatively benign circumstances, while other units are engaged elsewhere but in close proximity in riot control, at the same time that yet other units from the same force are engaged in high intensity urban warfare against insurgents. There is no common situation throughout the operational theatre and troops on the ground will need to shift from one to another as required.

At the time, allegations were made about the United States deploying chemical weapons against the insurgents. The State Department responded by making reference to white phosphorous munitions and stressing that their use had been confined to the illumination of enemy positions at night.[3] At first, the State Department's response seemed to put an end to the emerging controversy. However, in the March/April 2005 edition of the journal *Field Artillery*, there appeared an article by three US soldiers, who claimed that white phosphorous (WP):

> proved to be an effective and versatile munition. We used it for screening missions at two breaches and, later in the fight, as a potent psychological weapon against the insurgents in trench lines and spider holes when we could not get effects on them with HE (high explosive munitions). We fired 'shake and bake' missions at the insurgents, using WP to flush them out and HE to take them out.[4]

This article in what was an official US military publication did not have a major immediate effect. But, on 8 November 2005, Italian public television broadcast a documentary claiming that US forces had deployed white phosphorous directly against insurgents in the city.[5] Once this was aired, the controversy became intense. The United States was being accused of both using banned weapons and then attempting to cover up their use.

During the debate that followed, reference was made to three treaties in particular: the 1925 Geneva Gas Protocol; the 1993 Chemical Weapons Convention; and the 1980 Protocol III to the 1980 Conventional Weapons Convention (dealing with Incendiary Weapons). The official US position was that white phosphorous was not covered by any of the aforementioned treaties because its characteristics fall outwith the definitions of both chemical weapons and incendiary weapons. So, the weapon was not itself banned.

However, it is interesting to take the analysis on a little further to consider the use of white phosphorous. The UK position, for example, is covered in its new official manual on international humanitarian law, published five months before the operation in Fallujah. It states as follows:

---

[3] See D.P. Fidler, 'Insight: The Use of White Phosphorous Munitions by US Forces in Iraq' *American Society of International Law*, 6 December 2005.

[4] Captain James T. Cobb, First Lieutenant Christopher A. LaCour, and Sergeant First Class William H. Hight, 'TF2-2 in FSE AAR: Indirect Fires in the Battle of Fallujah', in *Field Artillery*, March–April 2005, at p. 26.

[5] Fidler, 'Insight: The Use of White Phosphorous Munitions by US Forces in Iraq'.

Use of weapons such as napalm and flamethrowers against combatant personnel is not dealt with specifically in the Conventional Weapons Convention or any other treaty. Such uses are governed by the unnecessary suffering principle so that they should not be used directly against personnel but against armoured vehicles, bunkers and built up emplacements, even though personnel inside may be burnt. *The same applies to white phosphorous, which is designed to set fire to targets such as fuel and ammunition dumps or for use to create smoke, and which should not be used directly against personnel.*[6]

It is not sufficient merely to establish the position in treaty law when assessing the lawfulness or otherwise of a particular weapon, means or method of warfare. While a weapon may well not be banned by specific treaty law, there may be a customary rule that covers both its inherent legality and the separate issue of the legality of its use. The use of white phosphorous in Fallujah demonstrates quite clearly that reliance on treaty law alone can provide a less than satisfactory analysis of the legitimacy of a weapon or a means and method of warfare. The Study into customary international humanitarian law is clearly, therefore, potentially of some considerable importance.

Part IV of the Study deals with the law relating to weapons and means or methods of warfare in twelve chapters, covering a total of seventeen identified rules of customary law (Rules 70–86). The first of these chapters covers the Rules dealing with general principles governing the use of weapons (Chapter 20; Rules 70 and 71). With one notable exception (Chapter 22 dealing very briefly with nuclear weapons, for which no rules are posited[7]), each of the chapters that follows (Chapters 23 to 31) identifies Rules relating to various categories and types of weapons.

Each of these proposed rules of customary law has the effect of either banning the weapon to which it refers, or restricting its use. The authors' introduction to the Study makes the point that the Rules it contains are not exhaustive and that there could be customary rules not included

---

[6] UK Ministry of Defence, *The Manual of the Law of Armed Conflict* (hereafter *UK Manual*) (Oxford University Press, 2004), at para. 6.12.6, p. 112 (emphasis added).

[7] This chapter does not consider the law relating to nuclear weapons. The Study did not cover nuclear weapons because, at the time the study team commenced its work, the International Court of Justice (ICJ) was dealing with the UN General Assembly request for an Advisory Opinion on the legality of the threat or use of nuclear weapons. The Advisory Opinion that emerged was unsatisfactory (amongst other shortcomings it did not, for example, address customary law and nuclear deterrence) and the authors of the Study, perhaps wisely, decided not to visit the questions left open by the ICJ. See Study Vol. I, 255.

within the Study. Given the thoroughness and attention to detail of the Study's authors, however, it is most unlikely that any customary rules relating to weapons will have 'slipped through the net' so that they are not included in the Study.

There are ten weapons, means or methods of warfare that the authors of the Study chose to include. They are as follows:

- Poison (Rule 72);
- Biological weapons (Rule 73);
- Chemical weapons (Rules 74 to 76);
- Expanding bullets (Rule 77);
- Exploding bullets (Rule 78);
- Weapons primarily injuring by non-detectable fragments (Rule 79);
- Booby-traps (Rule 80);
- Landmines (Rules 81 to 83);
- Incendiary weapons (Rules 84 and 85);
- Blinding laser weapons (Rule 86).

This is an area of international humanitarian law largely covered by treaties. Those covering the weapons dealt with in the Study are as follows:

- **Poison:** Article 23(a) of the 1907 Hague Regulations;
- **Biological weapons:** 1972 Biological Weapons Convention;
- **Chemical weapons:** 1899 Hague Declaration II concerning Asphyxiating Gases, the 1925 Geneva Gas Protocol and the 1993 Chemical Weapons Convention;
- **Expanding bullets:** 1899 Hague Declaration III Concerning Expanding Bullets;
- **Weapons primarily injuring by non-detectable fragments:** 1980 Protocol I to the 1980 Conventional Weapons Convention;
- **Booby-traps:** 1980 Protocol II and 1996 Amended Protocol II to the 1980 Conventional Weapons Convention;
- **Landmines:** 1997 Ottawa Convention, 1980 Protocol II and 1996 Amended Protocol II to the 1980 Conventional Weapons Convention;
- **Incendiary weapons:** 1980 Protocol III to the Conventional Weapons Convention 1980;
- **Blinding laser weapons:** 1995 Protocol IV to the Conventional Weapons Convention 1980;

The main purpose of most weapons treaties has been to establish new rules about specific weapons at the point of agreement, rather than to codify pre-existing customary norms. So, it should not be assumed that the emergence of a treaty rule will necessarily reflect already established customary law in this area. Customary law will, however, be important for two reasons:

- For establishing the general legality or illegality of a weapon, means or method of warfare that is covered by a treaty not widely adopted.
- For establishing the legality or illegality of a new weapon, means or method of warfare not covered by any specific treaty law.

Methodology used in the Study to identify customary law on weapons

The authors of the Study have used the various weapons treaties as a first point of reference when setting about identifying customary rules. Many of the relevant weapons conventions are relatively recent instruments. Indeed, in the case of the Conventional Weapons Convention, the treaty is very much 'live', with additional protocols under constant consideration. This raises questions about the extent to which customary rules based on recent treaty provisions could have developed within such a short space of time. In relation to each proposed Rule, it is necessary to assess whether relevant practice is sufficient to warrant the acceptance of a customary norm.

The number of treaty rules that are considered in the Study to have already achieved customary status is perhaps surprising. Indeed, one is inclined to wonder if the authors of the Study found it instinctively difficult to accept that some of the Rules suggested may not have developed beyond *de lege ferenda*. There is one exception in this regard. Antipersonnel landmines are considered in the context of the Ottawa Convention, as follows: 'About a dozen non-party States have used antipersonnel mines in recent conflicts . . . This practice means that it cannot be said at this stage that the use of anti-personnel landmines is prohibited under customary international law.'[8]

One issue that also deserves some treatment here is the distinction between international and non-international armed conflict. The Study tends towards the assumption that weapons prohibitions applicable in international armed conflicts will also be applicable in non-international armed conflicts. In support of this view it quotes the International Criminal Tribunal for the Former Yugoslavia in the *Tadić Case*, as follows:

---

[8] Study Vol. I, 282.

elementary considerations of humanity and common sense make it preposterous that the use by States of weapons prohibited in armed conflicts between themselves be allowed when states try to put down rebellion by their own nationals on their own territory. What is inhumane and consequently proscribed in international wars cannot but be inhumane and inadmissible in civil strife.[9]

Nevertheless, the Study proceeds to include separate consideration of the application to non-international conflicts under each of the proposed Rules on weapons law. In none of these sections does it conclude that the prohibitions applied in international armed conflicts are inapplicable in non-international conflicts – or, indeed, that there are any restrictions to be applied in non-international armed conflict that would not also apply in international conflict. With no evidence to suggest that there is any difference in applicability, it is tempting to conclude that there is none. However, it is by no means satisfactory to reach such a conclusion, not least because it is less than clear that evidence of State practice is of either sufficient quantity or quality to dispense with the distinction.

What follows is commentary on each of the weapons law Rules proposed in the Study. Where comment on the distinction between international and non-international armed conflict is relevant, it is included.

2. The Rules

General principles on the use of weapons

There are two Rules posited in the Study that cover the general principles underpinning weapons law: Rule 70 and Rule 71. It is important to stress the importance of the principles these two Rules incorporate. Weapons are invariably judged against their likelihood of resulting in superfluous injury and unnecessary suffering and their ability to distinguish between either civilians and combatants or civilian objects and military objectives. These two Rules are, therefore, of profound importance.

Rule 70

The use of means and methods of warfare which are of a nature to cause superfluous injury or unnecessary suffering is prohibited

On first appearance, Rule 70 seems an entirely acceptable rule of customary law because it quite obviously reflects the long and very well

---

[9] Study, Vol. I, 240.

established humanitarian principle dealing with superfluous injury and unnecessary suffering. As the Study points out, the principle relating to superfluous injury and unnecessary suffering is included in various treaties, including the St Petersburg Declaration and the early Hague declarations and regulations.[10] To refer to the St Petersburg Declaration in particular, the 'only legitimate object . . . during war is to weaken the military forces of the enemy' and 'for this purpose it is sufficient to disable the greatest possible number of men' and 'this object would be exceeded by the employment of arms which uselessly aggravate the sufferings of disabled men, or render their death inevitable'.[11] To quote a more recent example, the wording of Rule 70 is very close to that of Article 35(2) of the 1977 Additional Protocol I, which refers to 'methods of warfare of a nature to cause superfluous injury and unnecessary suffering'.

These principles date back to the middle of the nineteenth century and beyond, and while it is always possible to argue that a customary norm has not yet been established, some are so recognisable to those most familiar with the law that they attract virtually no informed opposition. The principles covered by Rule 70 certainly fall into this category. Nevertheless, the wording of Rule 70, in common with that of Article 35(2) of Additional Protocol I, is arguably inadequate in a small yet significant way which renders it worth examining afresh.

There are many weapons that are lawful in relation to their normal anticipated use but which are open to alternative uses that are capable of producing superfluous injury and unnecessary suffering. It is possible, for example, to imagine even a simple firearm being used in such a way. While an instance of use may be unlawful, a weapon itself may not be. It would clearly be wholly inappropriate to ban a weapon for fear that someone using it may abuse the law by using it inappropriately to cause superfluous injury or unnecessary suffering. This would result in the 'banning' of all available weapons – and have the inevitable consequence of bringing the law into disrepute.

While previous frequent use of Rule 70 in treaty law – or a variation of it – means that its wording is well established, in actual practice it is inadequate because it fails to take account of the two quite distinct means by which superfluous injury or unnecessary suffering can be caused. The

---

[10] Study Vol. I, 237.
[11] 1868 St Petersburg Declaration Renouncing the Use in Time of War of Explosive Projectiles Under 400 Grammes Weight.

Rule could easily be redrawn effectively to reflect practice by dividing it into two separate Rules that have different emphasis:

• The use of means or methods of warfare, the very nature of which will inevitably cause superfluous injury or unnecessary suffering, is prohibited; and
• The use of means or methods of warfare in a manner that is likely to cause superfluous injury or unnecessary suffering, is prohibited.

In effect, the two Rules proposed above express the proper interpretation of the wording of Rule 70. If, by using a weapon in a particular way, one knows that superfluous injury or unnecessary suffering will result, that use would breach the norm. This applies even if there appears no other way for a military force to prevail. It is, of course, a fundamental principle of international humanitarian law that military necessity cannot excuse a departure from the law.[12]

The Study might have taken account of this important distinction between the inherent nature of weapons and the consequences of their use in inappropriate ways leading to superfluous injury and unnecessary suffering. The Study authors' reasons for not doing so relate to their interpretation of the meaning of the word 'method'. It is their contention that 'method' refers to how the 'means' (the weapon) is actually used. Clearly, given this interpretation, the proposed additional rule above would be superfluous. It is by no means generally obvious that the word 'method' should be interpreted in this way, however. Even if that was at some point the intention, it is by no means now unambiguous in that respect. Indeed, this interpretation is not mentioned in a good cross-section of the leading texts dealing with the subject.[13] Nor is it stated in Article 35 of Additional Protocol I, which by its wording seems not to support the Study authors' interpretation. Regardless, therefore, of the apparent strict accuracy of that interpretation, the general ambiguity seems sufficient to justify the degree of clarification proposed above.

---

[12] *UK Manual*, para. 2.2.1, p. 22.
[13] Those consulted include: the *UK Manual*; D. Fleck (ed.), *The Handbook of Humanitarian Law in Armed Conflicts* (Oxford University Press, 1995); L.C. Green, *The Contemporary Law of Armed Conflict* (Manchester University Press, 2nd edn, 2000); A.P.V. Rogers, *Law on the Battlefield* (Manchester University Press, 2nd edn, 2004); Y. Dinstein, *The Conduct of Hostilities under the Law of International Armed Conflict* (Cambridge University Press, 2004).

Rule 71

The use of weapons which are by nature indiscriminate is prohibited.

This Rule is at first sight both adequate and uncontroversial. Indeed, as the Study notes, the need for distinction has been recognised as one of the 'cardinal principles' of international humanitarian law by the International Court of Justice (ICJ) in its advisory opinion in the *Nuclear Weapons* case.[14] In a similar vein to the observation relating to Rule 70 above, however, there is a possible shortcoming with the Rule's wording that is worth briefly considering. This issue is raised because of a statement attributed to Judge Higgins that is quoted in the discussion about Rule 71.

In the *Nuclear Weapons* case, Judge Higgins declared in her dissenting opinion that a weapon is indiscriminate in nature if it is incapable of being targeted at a military objective. The Study quotes this and it is certainly a useful criterion consistent with the need to relate discrimination to the nature of the target. Nevertheless, this almost certainly means that in some circumstances some weapons may be indiscriminate while in others they will not be. An air to surface missile may be capable of being fired with pin-point accuracy at a military installation (e.g. an aircraft hangar or an armoured formation) but it may be potentially indiscriminate if it were used to single out enemy combatants amongst a civilian population during urban warfare. There is clearly a vital relationship between the weapon and the type or nature of military target for which it is ordinarily intended. And, of course, one needs also to reflect on this in the light of Rules 12 and 14 dealing with discrimination and proportionality. The United Kingdom has invariably adopted the position that a judgment as to the discriminatory ability of a weapon should be made in relation to its designed purpose rather than to its possible effects in all circumstances and against all possible military objectives.[15]

This approach obviates the need to consider inappropriate uses of weapons (and their effects when used inappropriately) when considering their general legal status in accordance with Article 36 of the Additional Protocol I. This is eminently sensible. Indeed, the issue raised here about the inappropriate use of weapon systems is perhaps best covered by reference to Rules 1 and 7 in the Study. These deal with the principles of distinction between civilians and combatants (Rule 1) and between civilian objects and military objectives (Rule 7). Given these points, the only sensible conclusion that one can reach about Rule 71 is that it is about weapons

[14] Study Vol. I, 246.   [15] A point confirmed to the author by Group Captain Bill Boothby.

that are manifestly indiscriminate in all circumstances because they are incapable of being directed at a specific military objective. Very few weapons will fall into this category. Examples include biological weapons and those poisons and chemical weapons for which it is impossible to either predict or control adequately the spread of the agent deployed. The Study itself lists various weapons that are considered to have indiscriminate characteristics in certain or all contexts. It additionally lists, for example, anti-personnel landmines, cluster bombs, booby traps, Katyusha rockets, SCUD missiles and incendiary weapons, while noting that there is insufficient evidence to support the existence of a customary rule prohibiting their use.[16] Indeed, the suggestion that they are all manifestly indiscriminate in all circumstances would be particularly controversial and the authors of the Study were wise to resist declaring them as such.

Specific weapons, means and methods of warfare: Poison

Rule 72

The use of poison or poisoned weapons is prohibited.

The text directly supporting the Rule[17] mentions the Lieber Code and the Hague Regulations, as well as the Japanese *Shimoda* case dating from 1963.[18] While a single case in a single State may be regarded as 'weak' supportive case law, the advisory opinion of the ICJ in the *Nuclear Weapons* case (also quoted) is very much more compelling.[19]

What is notable about the supporting evidence contained in Volume II of the Study is the paucity of evidence of actual physical practice compared with the lengthy account of evidence of verbal practice in the form of manuals, legislation, positions in debates, official statements, etc. This is, of course, understandable as the physical practice is clearly negative and, therefore, compliant with the Rule. The simple fact is that States have rarely resorted to poison or poisoned weapons in modern times and the verbal practice quoted demonstrates the extent to which States believe themselves to be under a legal obligation to refrain from the use of poison. The combination of a paucity of examples of physical use combined with the large number of statements supportive of the view that such weapons would be unlawful provides us with a compelling combination of practice

---

[16] Study Vol. I, 249–250.   [17] Study Vol. I, 251–254.
[18] See also Study Vol. II, Part 1, 1597 at para. 75.
[19] See Study Vol. II, Part 1, 1602–1603, para. 111.

and *opinio juris*. We can safely conclude that the ban is an established rule of customary law on this alone.

Poison and poisoned weapons could also breach Rules 70 and 71 in some respect. A general deployment of poison (say, by poisoning the water in a well) would very likely breach Rule 71 on discrimination. The use of a poisoned weapon (e.g. the smearing of poison on a bullet to compound the injury caused by the bullet entering the body) would be in breach of Rule 70 on superfluous injury and unnecessary suffering. So, while the Rule is in general uncontroversial, it is notable that even without it one might very easily conclude that poison and poisoned weapons would, in any case, be in breach of the general customary rules underpinning weapons law.

Specific weapons, means and methods of warfare: Biological weapons

Rule 73

The use of biological weapons is prohibited.

The evidence included in the Study to support this Rule is profoundly compelling and the Rule itself is uncontroversial.[20] Indeed, it is so compelling that one is prompted to ask why the authors of the Study did not choose to go one step further by acknowledging a customary ban on the possession of the weapons as well as on their use. The Study did not venture into the question of possession, however, presumably on the basis that possession is not, strictly, a matter exclusively for international humanitarian law (it also being to do with arms control law). Nevertheless, while one is reluctant to claim that a work already extending to over 5,000 pages is somehow lacking substance, some of the value of the Study is lost by the absence of any specific comment about the possession of biological weapons. The relevant chapter certainly mentions State practice in relation to possession in support of the contention that use is customarily forbidden.

Specific weapons, means and methods of warfare: Chemical weapons

There are three Rules included in the chapter dealing with chemical weapons. As well as one dealing with generic 'chemical weapons', there are also Rules dealing with both riot control agents and herbicides. The first of the Rules deals merely with the use of chemical agents and avoids

---

[20] Study Vol. I, 256–258.

mention of possession. The second, while dealing with the use of riot control agents in warfare, implicitly accepts the legality of possession for their use in other circumstances. The third acknowledges that not all uses of herbicides would be a breach of customary law.

Rule 74

The use of chemical weapons is prohibited.

The evidence deployed in the Study to support this Rule is generally compelling and it is not intended to rehearse that evidence here. In general terms we can accept that the use of chemical weapons is prohibited. Unlike the case with biological weapons, however, there is also very good reason for not including a ban on possession. Both these last two statements are related to Rule 75 below and are more appropriately discussed in more detail under that heading.

Rule 75

The use of riot-control agents as a method of warfare is prohibited.

This Rule is generally acceptable. One point should be discussed, however. It is important to recognise the possible utility of 'non-lethal' riot control agents in essentially law enforcement or 'internal security' style operations mounted in close proximity to war-fighting or combat operations. While evidence of actual State practice in this respect is almost certainly very limited, the Study might usefully have at least mentioned this possibility, given the fact that this is the principal point of contention in relation to riot control agents viewed in the light of the general ban on the use of chemical weapons during armed conflict.

The difficulty arises as a result of the nature of situations in which combat operations are beginning to give way to something of a lower intensity, more akin to internal security or law enforcement. This happens as the combat phase of an operation ends and as a situation of belligerent occupation or similar becomes established. It also happens when a post-conflict situation gives rise to pockets of insurgency that demand a robust local intervention, as has happened in Iraq since 2003. What must be avoided in relation to riot control agents is a clear ban on their use at all times and in all locations when international humanitarian law generally applies. We must be extremely cautious, for example, of the consequences of the ICTY judgement in the *Tadić* case, concerning the applicability of international humanitarian law 'in the whole territory of the warring states . . . whether or not actual combat takes place there'.[21] In so-called 'three block war' situations, there may be quite different operations going on in close proximity to each other. Transition is not just temporal; it may also be spatial, as forces move from one sector to another. The use of riot-control agents is not banned in all circumstances when international humanitarian law applies, or throughout a territory in which an armed conflict is in train but in which conditions may vary from location to location.

The UK position on riot-control agents is that they are not to be assumed to be a 'method of warfare', even when used during an armed conflict or in a theatre in which combat operations are in train, as long as they are used for purely riot-control purposes. The United Kingdom's new international humanitarian law manual might have been more forthcoming in its description of circumstances when use is permitted. All it does state is that the permitted use of chemicals includes 'law enforcement, [and for] domestic riot control purposes'.[22]

The Study attempts to reflect these concerns. For example, it points out the wording of the Chemical Weapons Convention which 'makes a distinction between use during hostilities as a method of warfare, which is prohibited, and use for purposes of law-enforcement, which is permitted'.[23] However, the discussion of Rule 75 is not as clear as it might be; it could be viewed as banning the use of riot-control agents at all times and in all locations that international humanitarian law applies or, in contrast, it could be seen as permissive in the use of such agents for 'domestic riot control'.[24]

Rule 76

The use of herbicides as a method of warfare is prohibited if they:

- **are of a nature to be prohibited chemical weapons;**
- **are of a nature to be prohibited biological weapons;**
- **are aimed at vegetation that is not a military objective;**
- **would cause incidental loss of civilian life, injury to civilians, damage to civilian objects, or a combination thereof, which may be expected to be excessive in relation to the concrete and direct military advantage anticipated; or**
- **would cause widespread, long term and severe damage to the natural environment.**

---

[21] *Prosecutor v. Tadić*, Decision on the Defence Motion for Interlocutory Appeal on Jurisdiction, Appeals Chamber, 2 October 1995, IT-94-1-AR72, para. 65.
[22] *UK Manual*, para. 6.8.3, p. 108.   [23] Study Vol. I, 264.   [24] Study Vol. I, 263.

Each element of the Rule raises questions about the need for it. If a herbicide is 'of a nature to be a prohibited chemical weapon' it is obvious that it is also a prohibited herbicide. The same is true for those herbicides that are also 'prohibited biological weapons'. It also goes without saying that, if vegetation being targeted is not a military objective, it must be a 'civilian object' and should not, therefore, be targeted (under restrictions implicit in Rule 7). This part of the Rule is more correctly regarded as a rule of targeting law, not one of weapons law properly understood. The last two parts merely reflect Rule 14 and 45 of the Study respectively.

Every single element of Rule 76 is, therefore, a repeat of other Rules proposed in the Study. On the basis that it is repetitive of other Rules one should perhaps not be critical of its inclusion. Herbicides were included in this way because they have posed particular problems in the past and have been a concern to a number of States, with the use of defoliants by the United States in South Vietnam being a particular cause of concern. In fact, while on first examination this Rule is by nature prohibitive, it is also permissive, in that it allows for the use of non-poisonous herbicides during conflict.[25]

While stressing that formulating a rule in this way seems to be somewhat unnecessary, in general this author has no particular difficulty with it.

Specific weapons, means and methods of warfare: bullets

Rule 77

The use of bullets which expand or flatten easily in the human body is prohibited.

This Rule, banning the use of expanding bullets in armed conflict, is fairly well supported by the evidence quoted in the Study. The use of such bullets during armed conflict would clearly breach the general rule on superfluous injury and unnecessary suffering. However, the Study itself acknowledged that there might be circumstances in which use might be considered necessary.[26] While the ban on use during armed conflict is largely unsurprising, therefore, there is no ban on possession because the use of such bullets is considered desirable in certain law enforcement situations.

---

[25] See the discussion of this Rule in G.H. Aldrich, 'Customary International Humanitarian Law – an Interpretation on behalf of the International Committee of the Red Cross' (2006) 76 *British Yearbook of International Law* 503.   [26] Study Vol. I, 269.

This Rule is one that causes us to focus on the utility of certain weapons in some military operations, particularly those associated with the international response to terrorism. While traditionally the dividing line between armed conflict and some other condition falling short of it was considered clear and obvious, today there is greater ambiguity at the margins. To maintain a ban on a weapon that has particularly appropriate utility, given the prevailing conditions, might prove to be unwise and the customary rule may be subjected to challenge. The use of expanding bullets to stop suicide bombers has to be considered seriously, given prevailing circumstances. If there is a clear need effectively to 'stop' a suicide bomber, and these weapons are necessary for that purpose, arguably they should be regarded as lawful. It is certainly conceivable that such use may prove attractive, including during armed conflict, if suicide bombing continues to generate particular security concerns. This suggestion is admittedly contentious and would meet with predictable resistance from some quarters but, as one other commentator has pointed out, an interpretation of the supporting material in the Study 'raises some doubt about (the Rule's) long-term viability, particularly in non-international armed conflicts'.[27]

Rule 78

The anti-personnel use of bullets which explode within the human body is prohibited.

This Rule is less contentious than Rule 77 because exploding bullets can cause greater injury and suffering than those that merely flatten or expand. The ban on use is uncontroversial, is well traced in treaty law and is acknowledged widely as having achieved customary status. It is, of course, the case that the Rule itself is strictly speaking superfluous given the existence of general Rule 70 dealing with superfluous injury and unnecessary suffering.

Specific weapons, means and methods of warfare:
Non-detectable fragments

Rule 79

The use of weapons the primary effect of which is to injure by fragments which are not detectable by X-rays in the human body is prohibited.

[27] Aldrich, 'Customary International Humanitarian Law' (note 25 above), with reference to Study, Vol. II, Part 1, 1771–1786.

This Rule reflects the 1980 Protocol I to the 1980 UN Convention on Certain Conventional Weapons. The ban itself is not contentious. However, as with other Rules, a key question to pose is the extent to which the ban is effective because the weapon breaches Rule 70 dealing with superfluous injury and unnecessary suffering or because the specific treaty rule relating to non-detectable fragments has itself been transformed into custom. On balance, one is inclined to conclude that it is the former rather than the latter. Arguably, this Rule is strictly speaking unnecessary given the existence of Rule 70. Given the number of States party to the treaty giving rise to the specific wording of the Rule (only just over a third), we seem to have here a proposed rule of customary law that arguably appears to be posited in the Study in order to extend the application of a treaty. While it is undoubtedly the case that non-detectable fragments would breach customary law, they do so through Rule 70 rather than because the treaty rule has matured into customary law.

Specific weapons, means and methods of warfare: Booby traps

Rule 80

The use of booby-traps which are in any way attached to or associated with objects or persons entitled to special protection under international humanitarian law or with objects that are likely to attract civilians is prohibited.

This Rule reflects the provisions of Protocol II (1980) and Amended Protocol II (1996) to the 1980 UN Convention on Certain Conventional Weapons, although without the detail. These protocols have so far attracted participation by only just over a third of States. Given that the Amended Protocol was also finalised a mere ten years ago and only entered into force in 1998, it may well be premature to regard it as already forming a part of customary law. One might, therefore, challenge the inclusion of the Rule in the Study.

Very clearly, one of the main concerns with booby traps is that they are potentially indiscriminate and that they therefore breach Rule 71. If that is the case, then the obvious comment is that the proposed Rule 80 may be unnecessary given the general principle of weapons law reflected in Rule 71.

Specific weapons, means and methods of warfare: Landmines

Rule 81

When landmines are used, particular care must be taken to minimise their indiscriminate effects.

Landmines are not inherently unlawful, unless they are anti-personnel landmines covered by the provisions of the 1997 Ottawa Convention[28] and the State possessing and using them is a party to that Convention.[29] The need to ensure as far as possible that landmines are not indiscriminate in their effects is a clear reflection of Rule 71 dealing with the principle of distinction. However, this is itself merely a reflection of Rules 1 and 7 – and not strictly speaking weapons law at all.

Rule 82

A party to the conflict using landmines must record their placement, as far as possible.

This Rule is also linked to the need for those laying landmines to ensure as far as possible that they do not have indiscriminate effect. It also leads into the following Rule which deals with the need for those who have laid landmines to bear responsibility for the clearance of minefields once a conflict is over.

Rule 83

At the end of hostilities, a party to the conflict which has used landmines must remove or otherwise render them harmless to civilians, or facilitate their removal.

As the Study acknowledges, 'Until the 1990s, there was little practice indicating a requirement that those laying mines have to remove them.'[30] The original Protocol II to the 1980 Convention on Certain Conventional Weapons did not reflect this Rule and merely urged cooperation to remove minefields or render them ineffective. The Amended Protocol II,

---

[28] 1997 Ottawa Convention on the Prohibition of the Use, Stockpiling, Production and Transfer of Anti-Personnel Mines and on their Destruction.

[29] The authors of the Study did not feel able to make any claim that the provisions of the Ottawa Convention have achieved customary status. As noted above, however, they did comment on the extent to which a customary rule appears to be emerging – though the opposition of some key States is clearly problematic.   [30] Study Vol. I, 285.

dating from 1996 (in force 1998) is the instrument that suggests a shift in the law towards responsibility resting with the State that lays the mines. However, while this appears to make a great deal of sense and few will dissent from this ideal, there is the practical consideration that a defeated party to a conflict may well not be in a position to conduct effective mine clearance operations. There would appear to be little or no evidence of actual practice relative to mine clearance that would support this Rule and, for that reason, it is perhaps somewhat premature to suggest that it has already solidified. If any practice is in evidence it is to do with the requirement for a State laying mines 'to facilitate their removal' as distinct from removing them itself.

Specific weapons, means and methods of warfare: Incendiary weapons

Rule 84

If incendiary weapons are used, particular care must be taken to avoid, and in any event to minimise, incidental loss of civilian life, injury to civilians and damage to civilian objects.

This proposed Rule is entirely superfluous in relation to incendiary weapons since it merely extends to them one of the underpinning principles of weapons law – that of distinction. To be more precise, it is an unnecessary repeat of the proposed customary law Rules 1 and 7 on distinction.[31] If it is appropriate to acknowledge such a rule for incendiary weapons, why is it not also repeated in a separate version for all weapons mentioned specifically in the Study? It is by no means clear why it should be included in the Study, despite the explanation contained therein.[32]

Rule 85

The anti-personnel use of incendiary weapons is prohibited, unless it is not feasible to use a less harmful weapon to render a person *hors de combat*.

This Rule fits within the customary law prohibition of the use of weapons likely to cause superfluous injury or, particularly, unnecessary suffering (Rule 70). What level of suffering is necessary, however? If a less harmful alternative weapon is available, the suffering caused by incendiary weapons would arguably be unnecessary. There is certainly logic in this

---

[31] Study Vol. 1, 237–244.   [32] Study Vol. I, 287–289.

argument, although this is the sort of logic that is likely to be much
clearer in academic terms than it is in the stressful circumstances of
the battlefield in which the choice of weapon used is likely to be based on
a variety of factors. Indeed, generally speaking it is most sensible and
practical to adopt the approach that any weapon deployed in combat is
to be assumed to be lawful by those using it (it presumably having
gone through the legal review process now required under Article 36
of Additional Protocol I). Establishing a hierarchy of lawfulness, by
which one weapon is deemed to be capable of creating more suffering
than another, leading to a requirement that in the presence of both,
the least capable must be the weapon of choice, could well be problematic. As Hays Parks has pointed out, 'the requirement to seek a "less
harmful weapon" than incendiaries was never discussed in the long and
extensive debate resulting in Protocol III of the Conventional Weapons
Convention, and is not a rule contained in that protocol'.[33]

Notwithstanding this apparently sensible approach, there is State practice that applies restrictions of a hierarchical nature. Volume II of the
Study relates the UK position at the CCW Preparatory Commission in
1979.[34] While interesting, this has now effectively been superseded by the
position on incendiary weapons promulgated in the United Kingdom's
new international humanitarian law manual. This states that the use of
incendiary weapons against combatants is not specifically dealt with in
the Protocol (which only deals with the restrictions related to civilians
and civilian objects) but that their use is certainly governed by the unnecessary suffering principle. They should not, as a consequence, be used
directly against personnel but may be used against the likes of armoured
vehicles, bunkers and built up emplacements, even though personnel
inside them may well be burned as a result.[35]

The UK position represents a tighter restriction than that implied in
Rule 85. Rule 85 is weaker than this, in that it makes unqualified
allowance for anti-personnel use when other weapons are not feasible.
However, while the *UK Manual* interpretation may be considered by
some to be a better one than that contained in the Study, it was not available to the Study authors because the *UK Manual* was published too late
to influence them. Furthermore, the authors of the Study had to take
more than the UK position into account when identifying State practice.

[33] W. Hays Parks, 'The ICRC Customary Law Study: A Preliminary Assessment' (2005)
99 *Proceedings of the American Society of International Law* 208, at 210.
[34] Study Vol. II, Part 1, 1949–1950.   [35] *UK Manual,* Para. 6-12-6, p. 112.

One is inclined to agree with Hays Parks's view that the Rule as proposed is rather surprising, but for different reasons. Either incendiary weapons can be used directly against enemy combatants or they cannot. The Study Rule sits between these two positions and is consequently unsatisfactory in relation to them both. It may well be more appropriate to regard incendiary weapons as lawfully directed against enemy combatants, leaving the UK position as a policy deviation from that customary norm.

Specific weapons, means and methods of warfare: Blinding laser weapons

Rule 86

The use of laser weapons that are specifically designed, as their sole combat function or as one of their combat functions, to cause permanent blindness to unenhanced vision is prohibited.

The 1995 Protocol IV to the 1980 Convention on Certain Conventional Weapons is the treaty law on the subject of blinding laser weapons. Less than a quarter of States have so far become parties to Protocol IV. While the Rule is unquestionably highly desirable and the degree of agreement is certainly encouraging, it is arguably premature to declare the Rule as customary law. The Study makes a strong case for the treaty law to be regarded as the initiative that propelled the ban on such weapons rapidly to the status of customary law. The extent to which we accept this view is a matter of judgement. The fact that it is highly desirable that blinding laser weapons should not be developed is not a reason for assuming that customary law can develop at the speed that it would have to do so for this Rule to be sustainable. There is of course a dilemma here. Are such weapons contrary to customary law because the Rule derived from Protocol IV has achieved that status, or is it the fact that they would be the cause of superfluous injury and unnecessary suffering that renders them unlawful – with Rule 70 being the operative one in this case? The answer to this appears to be clear from the Commentary in the Study.

Prior to agreement being reached over the Protocol, a number of States had apparently been developing laser weapons that may well have fallen foul of this proposed customary rule. If that was indeed the case, the principle stated in Rule 70 was having no effect in relation to these weapons – hence the need for treaty law. On this basis, it would appear that treaty law is the more effective. However, it is clearly desirable for customary law to emerge in order that those States not party cannot initiate weapon development outside the legal ban. The decision to identify a solid customary norm hinges on the extent to which one regards the apparent lack of appropriate laser weapon development alongside the treaty ban as constituting sufficient evidence of state practice to justify the custom. Aldrich for one is happy to support the Study position that the customary norm has already formed.[36] The best this author can say, however, is that a norm is emerging, this should be encouraged, but it is not yet possible to say for sure that it has achieved customary status.

3. Final remarks

While the weapons listed above are all the subject of specific treaty law banning or restricting their possession or use, in all cases the treaty rule can appear superfluous when the weapon is considered against the two general Rules (Rules 70 and 71) covering the main principles of humanity and distinction. Given this, one might ponder not only why there is a perceived need to draw up a specific customary norm reflective of the treaty law, but why there is any need for the treaty law at the outset. While Rules 70 and 71 are obvious candidates for inclusion as customary norms, however, neither has of itself led to a globally agreed ban of a specific type of weapon, means or method of warfare. Indeed, while we may well now fully accept the extent to which blinding laser weapons would breach Rule 70, for example, it took particular effort to draft a treaty rule to result in the termination of programmes of laser weapon development.

Treaty law is, on the evidence available, the principal means by which the fundamental principles of weapon law enshrined in customary law are given effect. This suggests an essential relationship between treaty and custom in weapons law development. The fundamental principles that prohibit superfluous injury and unnecessary suffering and establish the need for discrimination are widely accepted and, without any real doubt, constitute norms of customary law. They are the guiding principles and strong evidence of inevitable superfluous injury, unnecessary suffering or inability to discriminate will lead to types of weapons becoming candidates for prohibition. On their own, however, the customary norms in Rules 70 and 71 are neither sufficiently persuasive nor prescriptive enough to lead directly to the banning of specific types of weapons. This is something that seems to require formal agreement in the form of treaty law. This makes good sense. The guiding principles cause the

---

[36] G. Aldrich, 'Customary International Humanitarian Law' (note 25 above).

international community to question the lawfulness of a particular weapon, means or method of warfare. Nevertheless, the nature of the international system, in which States are reluctant to trust each other without formal agreement on particular issues, results in a practical need for treaty agreement before a specific technology is effectively banned.

This should not necessarily mean that the treaty law becomes more important than the customary. It means that there is a vital – almost symbiotic – relationship between the two sources of weapons law, which are mutually supportive. The treaty law is an essential stage in the banning of a weapon but treaty law rests on a foundation of principles enshrined in custom.

The close relationship between treaty and custom means that it should not be assumed that the banning of a weapon through treaty law must be followed as a matter of course by the transformation of the treaty rule into a customary norm. This will not be necessary, except in order to render the treaty rule binding on non-parties to relevant treaties. If State practice is clear and unambiguous, the customary norm can be accepted; if not, we should resist forcing the pace of transformation, as the Study arguably does in one or two cases.

Clearly, there will be specific customary rules relating to weapons once practice has solidified. These Rules might usefully be regarded as 'secondary customary rules' dealing with specific weapons but derived from the fundamental principles enshrined in Rules 70 and 71. It is clearly the case, for example, that the ban on poison-based weapons has solid customary status. But in this particular case we are faced with a generic weapon, in the sense that poison could be delivered in theory by a range of different weapons technologies. In that sense, it might be argued that the customary ban on poison is approaching the status of a fundamental principle of weapons law; almost of the status of those principles enshrined in Rules 70 and 71. A more specifically technology-related weapon such as a laser weapon is arguably less endowed with such generic qualities, with a ban on it less likely over time to take on the appearance of an additional fundamental principle.

Weapons law is extremely closely related to technological development. We do not know what technologies are going to be available to us in twenty, fifty or a hundred years. Who knows, for example, precisely what the impact of nano-technologies will be on weapons development? It may even be possible that such technologies throw into question the longer term wisdom of existing bans or restrictions on biological or chemical weapons. Such an assertion may appear to some to be almost sacrilegious – but we should not make too many assumptions about the legitimacy of particular technologies before we know their full potential and dormant capability, for good or evil. Both treaty law and customary law will need to be able to cope with such considerations over time.

Specific laws relating to particular weapons are, on the evidence of practical developments highlighted in the Study, probably best articulated in treaties reflecting fundamental principles but formally agreed between States in a manner conducive to developing consensus. If we accept this approach, Rules 70 and 71 should be recognised as the true Rules of customary law.[37] Rule 72 banning poison weapons, which the discussion above has accepted as customary law, might then be regarded as a potential additional fundamental principle – already on the boundary between *lex lata* and *lex ferenda*. More specific weapons-related rules will, it seems, tend to owe their emergence to the treaty process.

Modern conditions have provided us with a number of reasons for reviewing the traditional way of looking at armed conflict. There are no longer clear lines of distinction, either between conflict and some other condition (the old distinction between the condition of 'peace' and that of 'war') or between conflict involving two or more States on the one hand and that involving internal factions (i.e. civil war or non-international armed conflict) or other non-State groups, either against each other or against States (including conflict between States and terrorist groups).

The 'three block war' situation can result in the status of operations changing from that of armed conflict to that of internal security and back again. In such potentially fluid circumstances, a military force can find itself applying international humanitarian law in combat operations one day, with a need to shift gear into internal security and law enforcement mode the next. The use of lethal force in combat in accordance with rules of international humanitarian law contrasts with the need to employ minimum force in law enforcement operations. The example of Fallujah outlined at the beginning of this chapter is especially apt here.

Given the shifting sands of modern day operations, one needs perhaps to question the extent to which traditional distinctions can any longer apply. Indeed, if there is any significant emerging customary practice to be identified from recent operations, it is to do with this new reality.

---

[37] This is the principal conclusion reached by D. Turns in 'Weapons in the ICRC Study on Customary International Law' (2006) 11 *Journal of Conflict and Security Law* 201, although this chapter does not go as far as Turns in dismissing weapon-specific Rules.

Could it be, for example, that operations in both Iraq and Afghanistan are providing evidence of new situations of a quality demanding practices involving the use of weapons, means and methods of warfare previously deemed inappropriate or unlawful in armed conflict? Would it necessarily be unlawful to use expanding bullets against suicide bombers within an armed conflict, either international or non-international?[38] The Study provides no substantive comment on these issues of profound contemporary concern and it is a pity that it does not.

The chapters of the Study, together with the supporting materials, provide a great deal of food for thought in relation to weapons law. One can fully understand why the authors chose to reflect treaty law in the Rules proposed. Nevertheless, there is perhaps evidence of too great a willingness to transform specific treaty prohibitions and restrictions into identified customary rules. It was clearly an extremely useful exercise to propose the Study Rules; hopefully, this chapter and subsequent critiques will be equally useful in refining our understanding of the current state of customary weapons law.

[38] Although it had not been produced before the Study was published, one interesting and pertinent reference now available is: M.N. Schmitt, C.H.B. Garraway, Y. Dinstein, *The Manual on the Law of Non-International Armed Conflict*, (San Remo: International Institute of Humanitarian Law, 2006) Two of the three member Drafting Committee for this manual, Schmitt and Garraway, are contributors to this volume. Para. 2.2.2(12) of that manual dealing with Means of Combat seems to endorse the approach adopted in the Study, including the majority of weapons covered by relevant treaty law, with one important exception: expanding bullets.

Fundamental guarantees

FRANÇOISE HAMPSON

1. Introduction

The phrase 'fundamental guarantees' which appears as the title to Chapter 32 of the Study does not appear to be a term of art. Whilst it is to be found in treaty law, it is only in the title to Article 75 of Protocol I of 1977 to the Geneva Conventions of 1949 and in the title of Article 4 of Protocol II. The phrase is not found within the provision itself. This suggests that 'fundamental guarantees' is simply a label and a way of bringing together certain rules which have something in common, something that generally is not found in other rules.[1]

The obvious definition would be rules which apply irrespective of the status of the individual. That would suggest that such rules represent a bottom line. In that case, given that those with a particular status may be protected by other provisions, the concept would need to be further clarified.[2] Fundamental guarantees are those rules which apply irrespective of the status of the individual and where they are not protected by any other provisions of international humanitarian law. As it stands, this definition might still be too broad. It would apply to the treatment of persons both during military operations and also when in the power of the other side. The first situation is regulated by other rules.[3] The second situation needs to be analysed further. Are the rules applicable to those in the *power* or in

---

[1] Some of the other chapters in Part V of the Study, Treatment of Civilians and Persons *Hors de Combat*, might be thought to come within such a principle, for example Chapters 34–39 and especially Chapters 37–38. This chapter is only concerned with Chapter 32 of the Study.

[2] This would be particularly important in international armed conflicts where there are detailed customary rules regulating the treatment of the wounded, sick and shipwrecked, prisoners of war and civilians in the power of the other side, including in occupied territory.

[3] See the Rules on targeting and the general principles on the use of weapons; Part I and Chapter 20.

the *control* of the other side? In many cases, it would make no difference which word was used but not in all cases. A person is in the control of a party when the latter determines the condition in which the individual finds himself and whether he is free to leave that control. That would encompass all forms of detention and many cases of medical care, at least the care of ex-fighters. It would not appear to include those present in a territory over which the party exercised authority but over whom the party did not exercise control.[4]

The Study uses the word 'power', whilst some of the rules identified would appear to be applicable to those in the 'control' of an opposing party. This confusion appears from the outset. The first sentence refers to 'all civilians in the power of a party to the conflict . . . as well as to all persons who are *hors de combat*'.[5] The next sentence speaks of fundamental guarantees as 'overarching rules that apply to *all* persons' (emphasis added).[6] All would appear to include current fighters and former fighters who have laid down their arms. They are not, however, in the same situation as detainees.

The confusion could easily be resolved if some other part of the Study addressed the rules applicable to persons present in territory over which an opposing party exercises authority.[7] In that case, Chapter 32 of the Study would be about those in the control of an opposing party and the

---

[4] A distinction is being drawn between control of territory and control of people. 'Effective control' of territory, as used in human rights law, e.g. *Loizidou v. Turkey*, 15318/89, Preliminary Objections Judgment of 18 December 1996, [1996] ECHR 70, does not imply control, as defined here, over every person in the territory. The nature and scope of the State's obligations are different in relation to territory or persons over whom they exercise control. The confusion is understandable insofar as the international humanitarian treaty law uses power, rather than control, e.g. Geneva Convention IV of 1949. In the context, however, it is clear that what is meant is control as defined in the text. The problem with a study of customary law is that the context is not defined in the same way. A treaty may relate specifically to the military wounded and sick. In that case, it is clear that those to whom it relates are in the control of the other side. A study of customary law, however, has to integrate the context into the content of the rule. For this reason, the word control would, in most instances, be more accurate than power. This distinction may give rise to problems if the Study is translated into other languages.   [5] Study, Vol. 1, 299.

[6] *Ibid.*

[7] The test of the exercise of authority is factual. It is not implying any legitimacy in relation to the exercise of authority. Examples of persons present in territory over which an opposing party exercises authority include foreigners living in the territory of an opposing party at the outbreak of hostilities (e.g. Iraqi students living in the UK in 1990–91), persons living in occupied territories (e.g. the non-settler population of the Israeli Occupied Territories) and those living in an area controlled by a non-State group during a non-international armed conflict (e.g. Colombians living in FARC-controlled areas).

other chapter would be about civilians and those *hors de combat* present in territory over which it exercises power or authority. It should be noted that Chapter 32 is located in Part V, which is entitled 'Treatment of Civilians and Persons *Hors de Combat*'. That suggests that the section will address both those in territory controlled by an opposing party and those in the control of such a party. That is not in fact the case. There is no separate chapter addressing the issue of those in territory controlled by the opposing party. It is submitted that this is at the root of the main problem with Chapter 32. The authors may have merged their consideration of those in the control of the other side and those in the power of the other side. The situations are, however, significantly different. The strict obligations owed to those over whom one exercises control are only possible on account of that control. The scope of the obligations owed to those in territory over which a party exercises authority is different. Many of the issues addressed may be the same but the solutions are likely often to be different. For example, the responsibility owed to detainees includes an obligation to try to keep them alive. The death of a detainee therefore raises questions. In the case of civilians living in territory under the authority of an opposing party, the obligation must be expressed differently. There may be the obligation not to go round killing them and even to ensure that, generally speaking, medical care is available but that is not the same as the obligation to try to keep them alive. Either the authors are only addressing the situation of those in the control of the other side, in which case the question is why they have not dealt with the other situation, or else they are trying to cover both groups in the same set of rules. The problems to which such possible merger gives rise will be considered further below, in the context of particular Rules. The solution is either to create a separate chapter dealing specifically with those in the power, but not the control, of the other side, or else to expand any of the Rules whose application is different in the two situations and to make two rules instead of one.

Before examining the large number of Rules contained in Chapter 32, Fundamental Guarantees, this chapter will first consider two general issues regarding the formation of customary law which raise a difficulty in the case of several of the Rules within the section on fundamental guarantees but not more generally. The matter of the relationship between international humanitarian law and human rights law has already been examined.[8] There are, however, two specific human rights issues which

---

[8] Chapter 3.

need to be considered in this context, the second of which also raises an issue of international criminal law.

The first problem concerns the geographical scope of human rights obligations. If human rights law only applies within national territory, then human rights material would only be relevant in non-international armed conflict and in relation to measures taken within national territory during an international armed conflict. In that case, any reference to human rights material in Chapter 32 would need to make clear that restriction. Unlike the question of the simultaneous applicability of international humanitarian law and human rights law, where the legal principles appear to be clear, subject to the possible existence of two persistent objectors, the legal position with regard to the geographical scope of human rights law is remarkably confused. If one only examined the jurisprudence of international bodies, notably the Human Rights Committee under the International Covenant on Civil and Political Rights, the broad lines of the answer would be clear but the issue would appear to be not yet completely clarified.[9] The case law of the Inter-American Commission on Human Rights appears to be coherent and relatively comprehensive.[10] The confusion stems principally from the case law of the European Court of Human Rights. It appears not to be possible to reconcile the decisions in the cases of *Bankovic and others, Issa*

[9] See for example, General Comment No.31, Nature of the General Legal Obligation Imposed on States Parties to the Covenant, CCPR/C/21/Rev.1/Add.13, 26 May 2004, para. 10; in exercise of its monitoring function when the State in question is in occupation of (part of) the territory of another State, see Concluding Observations, initial report of Israel, CCPR/C/79/Add.93, 18 August 1998, para. 10; Concluding Observations, second report of Syria, CCPR/CO/71/SYR, 24 April 2001, para. 10; Concluding Observations, fourth periodic report of Morocco, CCPR/C/79/Add.113, 1 November 1999, para. 9 and fifth periodic report, CCPR/CO/82/MAR, 1 December 2004, paras. 8 and 18; in an individual case concerning ill-treatment in detention outside national territory, see *Lopez Burgos v. Uruguay*, HRC 29 July 1981, UN Doc.A/36/40, 176; Communication No.52/1979, CCPR/C/13/D/52/1979.

[10] It should, however, be noted that there is no jurisdictional limitation when the Inter-American Commission is exercising its jurisdiction under the Charter of the OAS and the American Declaration of the Rights and Duties of Man. That may be the basis on which it asserted jurisdiction in the cases of *Coard and others v. the United States*, IACHR Report No. 109/99, Case No. 10,951, 29 September 1999, Ann. Rep. IACHR 1999 and *Salas and others v. the United States*, IACHR Report No.31/93, Case No. 10,573, 14 October 1993, Ann. Rep. IACHR 1993, 312. In a case currently before it, the Commission is dealing with the rights of those detained in Guantanamo; Center for Constitutional Rights; http://www.ccr-ny.org/v2/legal/september_11th/docs/3-13-02%20IACHRAdoptionofPrecautionaryMeasures.pdf. It is noteworthy that the two bodies have not yet been asked to address a case involving the acts outside the region of a State located within the region.

and others v. Turkey and *Ocalan v. Turkey.*[11] The question of the scope of human rights obligations arises on account of the definition of the jurisdiction of the treaty bodies. If a human rights body does not have jurisdiction, is that the same thing as saying that human rights law does not apply outside national territory or merely that it cannot be enforced, or do these amount to the same thing? Three propositions do emerge as clearly established from the jurisprudence. First, there are circumstances in which human rights law is applicable outside national territory. Second, where a State is a belligerent occupant, irrespective of whether it became an occupier lawfully or unlawfully, it will be held responsible for the acts of all the authorities within the territory occupied, as it would in its own territory, and not just the acts of its armed forces.[12] It is not clear whether the concept of occupation is defined in the same way in international humanitarian law and human rights law.[13] Third, it seems as though a State is responsible for the extra-territorial acts of State agents where the victim is within the control of those agents.[14] That clearly covers detention but it is not clear what else it might cover. Whilst, under the law of State responsibility, the State is responsible for the conduct of its armed forces, it is not clear whether the control exercised over the forces is sufficient to bring victims of the acts of those forces within the jurisdiction of the State concerned. It should be noted that the International Court of Justice has had no apparent difficulty with the notion that a State can be found in breach of human rights law for extra-territorial acts, without the necessity to establish occupation.[15]

---

[11] *Bankovic and others v. Belgium and 16 other members of NATO*, 52207/99, Admissibility Decision of 12 December 2001, (2002) 41 *International Legal Materials* 517; *Issa and others v. Turkey*, 31821/96, admissibility decision of May 30, 2000; decision of second Chamber, 16 November 2004 [2004] ECHR 629; *Ocalan v. Turkey*, 46221, judgment of 12 March 2003; judgment of Grand Chamber of 12 May 2005, [2005] ECHR 282. English courts have adverted to the difficulty in reconciling these decisions in *R. (on the application of B and others) v. Secretary of State for the Foreign and Commonwealth Office* [2004] EWCA Civ 1344 (unreported), 18 October 2004, para. 59 and in *R. (on the application of Al-Skeini and others) v. Secretary of State for Defence* [2004] EWHC 2911, para. 222 (High Court) and [2005] EWCA Civ 1721, 21 December 2005, Court of Appeal. The case is currently pending before the House of Lords.

[12] *Loizidou v. Turkey*, 15318/89, judgment of 18 December 1996.

[13] *Ilascu and others v. Moldova & the Russian Federation*, 48787/99, judgment of 8 July 2004, [2004] ECHR 318; *R. (on the application of Al Skeini and others) v. Secretary of State for Defence* [2005] EWCA. Civ 1609 (21 December 2005).

[14] *Lopez Burgos* and respondent governments' argument in *Bankovic*, at para. 37.

[15] *Legal Consequences of the Construction of a Wall in the Occupied Palestinian Territory*, Advisory Opinion of 9 July 2004 (occupation) and *Armed Activities on the Territory of the Congo (Democratic Republic of the Congo v. Uganda)*, Judgment of 19 December 2005 (in

Some of the Rules in Chapter 32 concern those within the control of a party to the conflict.[16] Human rights law is clearly applicable extra-territorially in those circumstances. If other rules apply, possibly in different ways, both to those in the control of a party to the conflict and in territory under the authority of a party to a conflict, the position is less clear in the second situation.[17]

The second question relating to human rights law concerns those who are bound by it. International humanitarian law binds the parties to a conflict but human rights law only binds the State.[18] This raises the concern that reliance on human rights material might elevate a principle to the status of a customary law on the basis of evidence not binding on non-State actors.[19] If reliance solely on *State* practice and not that of non-State armed groups is a problem in the establishment of customary international humanitarian law, it is presumably even more of a problem to rely on a body of rules only capable of binding the State. It is difficult to envisage many circumstances in which a non-State armed group would be able to afford detainees the due process guarantees contained in the Study.[20] Would it be possible for customary international humanitarian law to require more, or at least something different, from a State, at least in a non-international armed conflict, than it does of a non-State armed group?[21]

This issue may also give rise to difficulties in another area of law: international criminal law. If the Study identifies something as prohibited under international humanitarian law, possibly on the basis of human

---

relation to Ituri, which it found to be occupied, and other areas in DRC which were not occupied). It is not clear whether there was any argument concerning the extra-territorial applicability of human rights law before the Court.   [16] For example Rule 90.

[17] For example, if the prohibition of murder, Rule 89, applies not only to the killing of those in detention but also to the killing of civilians in territory under the authority of a party (see further below), the problem referred to in the text would arise in the second situation.

[18] See chapter 3.

[19] This is of particular importance in non-international armed conflicts but could also raise a problem in conflicts characterised as international where one of the parties is a non-state actor.

[20] Rule 100. It is difficult to see how any non-State armed group could ensure that a tribunal was established by law without implying some degree of recognition of legitimacy. To require that a group respect a rule that the State makes it impossible to comply with makes a nonsense of the law.

[21] In an international armed conflict there is an important principle of equality of belligerents. It is difficult to see how this could be said to apply in non-international armed conflicts, other than following recognition of belligerency. The State does not recognise the opposing fighters as combatants. If there is inequality in one sphere, could there not also be in others?

rights material, is this sufficient to make it an international crime, that is to say an offence over which any State may exercise jurisdiction on the basis of universal jurisdiction, provided domestic law so permits? A distinction needs to be drawn between international humanitarian law and international criminal law. The former is civil in character. If a State wishes to allege that another State is in breach of its obligations under the Geneva Conventions, it may be able to go to the International Court of Justice but not to the International Criminal Court.[22] International humanitarian law relates to the obligations of States and parties to a conflict. The individual is only addressed indirectly. A party to a conflict is required to prevent foreseeable violations and to punish actual violations of the rules. International humanitarian law is based on the assumption that a person will generally be punished by his own side. It also gives States, at least in international conflicts, the obligation to seek out and try the suspected perpetrators of grave breaches and requires the punishment of the perpetrators of violations. In non-international armed conflict, the State not only can but is likely to be eager to try non-State actors for *any* use of force. Third States are free to try those responsible for war crimes in non-international armed conflicts, which would not appear to include force directed solely against the armed forces of the State.

If the Rules in the Study are rules of international humanitarian law and not of international criminal law, reliance on human rights material would be unlikely to result in the creation of a new war crime but there is a theoretical possibility that it could do so.[23]

The other issue which raises a problem in relation to various Rules in Chapter 32 is the one referred to at the start of this chapter: whether the Rules are applicable to those in the control or in the hands of a party to a conflict or whether they also apply to those in territory under the authority of such a party. In some cases, the Rule is only applicable to a person in the first situation. It is difficult to see how a party could torture an individual not in its control. In many cases, however, the Rule might apply in two different ways in the two situations. Whilst a party to a conflict has the obligation not itself to subject those in its control to enforced disappearance, does it have any obligation, under international humanitarian

---

[22] For example, *Trial of Pakistani Prisoners of War (Pakistan v. India)*, Order of 15 December 1973, [1973] *ICJ Reports* 347; the case was removed from the list by order of 15 December 1973.

[23] It is conceivable that a person could be charged with a crime against humanity for a serious violation of human rights law. That would be by virtue of the application of international criminal law rather than the application purely of human rights law.

law, to protect those in territory over which it exercises authority from enforced disappearance?[24] In some cases, the Commentary makes it clear whether it is only dealing with the first situation or both. Where it only deals with the first situation, it leaves unaddressed the second. Where the Commentary attempts to deal with both situations, it becomes clear that the Rule usually needs to be formulated in two different ways in order accurately to reflect the scope of the State's obligations. This issue will be further considered below, in the context of the discussion of individual Rules.

2. The Rules

It should be emphasised that the sub-headings used below do not appear in the text of the Study. They are used for convenience only, as a way of grouping the Rules.

a. General principles

Rule 87

Civilians and persons *hors de combat* must be treated humanely.

Rule 88

Adverse distinction in the application of international humanitarian law based on race, colour, sex, language, religion or belief, political or other opinion, national or social origin, wealth, birth or other status, or on any other similar criteria is prohibited.

The Study identifies two very general principles, a requirement of humane treatment and the prohibition of discrimination. The first is limited to civilians and those *hors de combat*. This raises the problem discussed above. If, by definition, a person in the hands of a party to the conflict is either a civilian or *hors de combat*, the Rule applies to all detainees. If it is possible to submit a population to inhumane treatment without taking direct action against individuals, there could be a difficulty. For example, if it is inhumane to subject people to severe deprivation of food as a collective punishment, then the population affected could include current and former fighters who are not *hors de combat*. Another example

---

[24] This issue is currently before the European Court of Human Rights in the case of *Varnava and others v. Turkey*, 16064-6/90, admissibility decision of 14 April 1998.

might be the use of weapons which cause 'superfluous injury or unnecessary suffering', if this is also regarded as inhumane.[25]

The non-discrimination clause is important. The European Convention on Human Rights permits derogation from Article 14, subject to the usual derogation conditions, and is in any event restricted to discrimination in the exercise of a Convention right.[26] The International Covenant on Civil and Political Rights prevents derogation from the prohibition of discrimination on most but not all grounds.[27] In certain circumstances, the prohibition of discrimination based on foreign origin could be important.[28]

b. Killings

Rule 89

Murder is prohibited.

The treatment of killings raises two problems. The word 'murder' is only very occasionally used in the Geneva Conventions and Protocols.[29] In the context in which it is used in the treaty provisions, it appears to be referring to intentional killing. There are, however, other circumstances in which a party and even an individual may be found responsible for a killing. The objection to the use of intentional killing is that it would be too restricted. It is not, however, clear what is meant by 'murder'. To say that it covers intentional unlawful killings is, first, again too limited and, second, of no guidance to a soldier. A rule on conduct resulting in death ought to indicate in what circumstances the death will be regarded as wrongful. That would not be an easy rule to draft but it would have the benefit of being useful. Chapter 3 deals with indiscriminate attacks during the course of a military operation. That still leaves the question of unlawful deaths in territory controlled by a party to the conflict but outside the context of military operations, for example when manning a road block. The obligations of the party in that situation may be

---

[25] See also Chapter 20 of the Study and chapter 10 above.
[26] Protocol 12 to the Convention provides a free-standing prohibition of discrimination but is potentially derogable. It has entered into force but, to date, only 14 States have ratified it.
[27] Compare Arts. 4.1 and 2.1 of the International Covenant on Civil and Political Rights.
[28] Where foreign fighters take part in a conflict for ideological reasons, there may be a temptation to punish foreign fighters in a way different from local ones. This assumes that they do not come within a workable definition of mercenary, if such exists in customary international humanitarian law.
[29] Geneva Conventions of 1949, Common Art. 3; I – Art. 12; II – Art. 12; IV – Art. 32; Protocol I – Art. 75; Protocol II – Art.4.

significantly different from those owed to detainees. Even in relation only to detainees, a party to a conflict may be responsible for the death of a detainee where a charge of murder could not be sustained. It is submitted that the evidence cited in the Commentary and in Volume II would have enabled the authors to go beyond merely prohibiting murder. A further difficulty with the use of the word murder is that it is a common domestic law concept. There is a danger that soldiers, presented with a list of the Rules, will assume that murder means whatever it means in their domestic law.[30] They might conclude that manslaughter was not prohibited.

If the rule is supposed to address both deaths in detention and deaths in territory controlled by the party, separate rules are needed. Furthermore, it might be necessary to distinguish between international and non-international armed conflicts.[31]

c. Ill-treatment

Rule 90

Torture, cruel or inhuman treatment and outrages upon personal dignity, in particular humiliating and degrading treatment, are prohibited.

Rule 91

Corporal punishment is prohibited.

Rule 92

Mutilation, medical or scientific experiments or any other medical procedure not indicated by the state of health of the person concerned and not consistent with generally accepted medical standards are prohibited.

Rule 93

Rape and other forms of sexual violence are prohibited.

Rules 90–93 illustrate the advantage of using human rights material to clarify what is meant by torture, cruel, inhuman and degrading treatment.

---

[30] Whilst 'murder' is one of the grounds on which a person can be charged with a crime against humanity under Art.7 of the Statute of the International Criminal Court, it is only used in relation to war crimes in Art. 8(c)(i), which reproduces common Art. 3 of the Geneva Conventions. In other contexts, the Statute refers to killings.

[31] See chapter 3, p. 63.

Whilst generally the cross-referencing between Rules in this chapter and those in other chapters is very good, there is one omission with regard to Rule 90, the prohibition of torture etc.[32] Some discussion as to whether weapons which cause 'unnecessary suffering or superfluous injury' automatically cause inhuman treatment, or worse, would have been helpful.[33] It is striking that Rule 90 prohibits various forms of ill-treatment but not punishment. It could be argued that the material relied on prohibits both inhuman treatment and inhuman punishment. This raises the question of whether collective punishment, proscribed in both international and non-international armed conflicts, constitutes inhuman punishment.[34]

Rule 91 again raises the question of whether it is limited to those in the control of the other side. If so, it is a useful complement to Rule 90, insofar as it clearly includes punishment, as opposed to treatment. If, on the other hand, it applies to those in territory under the authority of the other side, the Rule is potentially problematical. Not only might this bring within the Rule judicial and educational corporal punishment but it raises the question of the responsibility, under international humanitarian law, of the party in authority to protect individuals from harm at the hands of third parties.[35]

Rule 92 should be uncontroversial. It might have been helpful to make specific reference to the fact that the voluntary donation of blood for the medical benefit of others is not precluded by the prohibition of medical procedures not for the benefit of the person concerned.

The most important aspects of the prohibition of rape and other forms of sexual violence are, first, the definition of rape in international criminal law and, second, the fact that the prohibition is not limited to rape.[36] The

[32] Whilst cross-referencing is good, the work as a whole suffers seriously from the lack of an index. It is to be hoped that this will be corrected in any reprint or second edition.
[33] Rule 70.
[34] This argument was advanced in the case of *Ayder and others v. Turkey*, 23656/94 but neither the Commission Report, 21 October 1999, nor the Court judgment, 8 January 2004, [2004] ECHR 3 addressed the issue. Rule 103 addresses collective punishment; its position in the text suggests that it is viewed as an element of due process.
[35] In international occupation, the occupying power is required to respect, unless absolutely prevented, the laws in force in the country, according to Art. 43 of Hague Convention IV of 1907 respecting the Laws and Customs of War. The position in non-international armed conflicts is unclear and may be politically a very sensitive issue. The ethnic Albanians in Kosovo, for example, did not want to recognise any Serb law passed after the revocation of Kosovo's autonomy.
[36] See generally, Sub-Commission on the Promotion and Protection of Human Rights, Working Paper on the Criminalization, Investigation and Prosecution of Serious Acts of Sexual Violence, E/CN.4/Sub.2/2004/12, 20 July 2004.

definition has implications for States party to the Statute of the International Criminal Court, particularly if their domestic law definition of rape goes back a long time. Given the speed with which certain elements of international humanitarian law established by the case law of international or hybrid criminal courts have allegedly become customary law, it is possible that the definition of rape established by the International Criminal Tribunals for the former Yugoslavia and Rwanda has already acquired that status, particularly given its inclusion in the Elements of the Crime relating to the Rome Statute.[37]

Whilst this is a study of international humanitarian law rather than international criminal law, it might have been helpful to signal in the commentary the wide range of ways in which rape can be charged.[38]

d. Slavery and forced labour

Rule 94
Slavery and the slave trade in all their forms are prohibited.

Rule 95
Uncompensated or abusive forced labour is prohibited.

There is no problem with the Rule on the prohibition of slavery but the reader might have expected the issue of trafficking at least to be mentioned in the Commentary, if only to explain why it was not being addressed. This raises the question of how to characterise trafficking rules when it occurs out of or into an area of conflict. Factually, trafficking may be prevalent in conflict zones but does this make the relevant rules ones specifically applicable in armed conflict.[39]

The essence of Rule 95 is clear but it is ambiguously worded and the material in the Commentary does not reflect the rule. As currently worded, it is not clear whether what is prohibited is uncompensated labour and abusive forced labour or whether the first should be read as uncompensated forced labour. The material in the Commentary addresses the circumstances in which detainees can be compelled to work, restrictions on the work they may be required to perform, deportation to slave labour and compelling persons to serve in the forces of a hostile power. Nowhere in the Commentary is there material on the lack of compensation or abusive force labour, other than as indicated.

[37] For example Art. 7(1)(g)1. [38] Working Paper, note 46. [39] See chapter 3.

Interestingly, the practice of certain States goes beyond the Rule as formulated, prohibiting the use of forced labour even where international humanitarian law would allow it.

e. Hostages and human shields

Rule 96

The taking of hostages is prohibited.

Rule 97

The use of human shields is prohibited.

Much of the practice referred to uses a different phrase from that in the Rule, for example 'using the presence of civilians or other protected persons to render certain military objectives/forces immune from attack'. There is no objection in principle to using a different form of words, on condition that the prohibition is identical or virtually identical as appears to be the case here. The State practice overwhelmingly addresses the situation in which a party to a conflict forces people to act in such a way. There appears as yet to be no evidence to support the obligation of a party to prevent people from so acting, even if voluntarily.[40]

f. 'Enforced disappearances'

Rule 98

Enforced disappearance is prohibited.

The use of the term 'enforced disappearances' may strike an unfamiliar note to experts in international humanitarian law. They will, however, be used for all the constituent prohibitions comprised in the term. The expression refers to detentions where the detaining authority refuses to acknowledge the detention or conceals the fate or whereabouts of the disappeared person, as a result of which the victim is placed outside the protection of the

---

[40] For example, it appears that residents of Belgrade voluntarily went and stood on the bridges over the Danube in an attempt to protect them from attack during the conflict over Kosovo. More recently, it has been said that women in Gaza went voluntarily to act as human shields to protect besieged gunmen in a mosque in Beit Hanoun on 3 November 2006. It should be noted that the facts are confused and disputed.

law.[41] This is not the same as but is related to the phenomenon of the missing in war. The latter concept is broader, referring both to those whose detention has not been acknowledged or communicated to the party on which they depend and also to those missing for some other reasons. Those other reasons could include death on a battlefield or hospitalisation as a result of injury where the party in control of the territory has not notified the party on which the victim depends of his death or injury. An explanation of the relationship between these different concepts would be helpful.[42] Instead, the obligation of notification of the wounded is contained in Chapter 34, of the dead in Chapter 35, of the missing in Chapter 36 and of persons deprived of their liberty in Chapter 37. This illustrates again the need for an index. Under human rights law, including in situations of conflict, there is a continuing obligation to investigate a disappearance.[43] An enforced disappearance is not only a violation of the rights of the disappeared person but also of the next of kin. The reference[44] to the case law establishing that an enforced disappearance constitutes, as a matter of law, inhuman treatment of the next of kin may be an over-simplification. Whilst it is true of the case law of the Human Rights Committee and the Inter-American Commission and Court of Human Rights, under the European Convention on Human Rights, the next of kin have to be able to show that they have been treated in an inhuman way by the authorities.[45]

Rule 98 is a good illustration of the importance of including evidence of customary human rights law in situations of conflict. Had the Study only included the other related rules, identified above, an important dimension of the protection against going missing would have been missed.

g. Detention

Rule 99

Arbitrary deprivation of liberty is prohibited.

---

[41] International Convention for the Protection of All Persons from Enforced Disappearance, adopted by the General Assembly of the UN on 20 December 2006 (A/61/443/Add.3, draft res. IV), Art. 2.

[42] The question of the obligations of a State with actual control of territory in which individuals in a life-threatening situation go missing is currently before the European Court of Human Rights in the case of *Varnava and others*, 16064-6/90.

[43] For international armed conflict, see *Cyprus v. Turkey*, 25781/94, Judgment of 10 May 2001 [2001] ECHR 331; for arguably non-international armed conflicts, see, for example, *Bazorkina v. Russia*, 69481/01, Judgment of 27 July 2006; *Akdeniz and others v. Turkey*, 23954/94, judgment of 31 May 2001 [2001] ECHR 353.   [44] Study, Vol. I, 343.

[45] For example, *Cakici v. Turkey*, 23657/94, judgment of 8 July 1999, ECHR 1999-IV.

The Rule is in two parts, the first dealing with the grounds of detention and the second procedural guarantees relating to the detention. At first sight, it seems strange to include a discussion of detention here, given the existence of a separate chapter on persons deprived of their liberty.[46] In fact, however, that chapter does not deal with *deprivation* of liberty but with the Rules applicable to the treatment of detainees. There is no overlap, beyond that with Rule 123 regarding the recording of the personal details of persons deprived of their liberty.

The formulation of the Rule covers many types of deprivation of liberty: detention without any grounds at all; detention on security grounds but without the requisite threshold of risk having been satisfied; detention without the requisite means to challenge the necessity for the detention; and detention without the other procedural requirements having been satisfied. The result is that the Rule on its own conveys nothing as to when detention will be regarded as arbitrary. Again, this means that the Rule needs to be read in conjunction with the Commentary.

i. Grounds of detention   Given the connection between the issue of detention and the status of an individual, it is perhaps not surprising that this question gives rise to some of the greatest divergence between the rules applicable in international and non-international armed conflict. It is not that the rules are different. It is rather that detention in international armed conflicts is very closely regulated whereas international humanitarian law is virtually silent as to the grounds of detention in non-intentional armed conflicts. It may be the case that this range of provision can be accurately encapsulated in the formula that detention must not be arbitrary but that calls into question the value of any formula so broad as to cover such a range of situations. By virtue of being classified as a combatant in an international armed conflict, an individual is vulnerable to being detained as a prisoner of war. The grounds for the detention or internment of an individual either in territory controlled by the other side or in occupied territory is provided for in detail in the fourth Geneva Convention.[47] Even in relation to a person not benefiting from other protection, Article 75 of Protocol I provides:

---

[46] Chapter 37.
[47] Arts. 41, 42 and 68. See generally, F. Hampson, 'Detention, the 'War on Terror' and International Law', in H.M. Hensel (ed.), *The Law of Armed Conflict: Constraints on the Contemporary Use of Military Force* (Aldershot: Ashgate, 2005).

Except in cases of arrest or detention for penal offences, such persons shall be released with the minimum delay possible and in any event as soon as the circumstances justifying the arrest, detention or internment have ceased to exist.

By contrast, there is nothing at all on the grounds of detention in common Article 3 or Article 4 of Protocol II. The evidence cited with regard to State practice as to non-international armed conflicts may establish that unlawful confinement or detention is prohibited in non-international conflict but the practice does not indicate what *constitutes* unlawful detention.[48]

Most human rights law also prohibits arbitrary detention. That would appear to be capable of applying in different ways in peace time and in situations of conflict. In other words, it may be possible to introduce new grounds of detention in situations of conflict without the need to derogate, except with regard to the European Convention on Human Rights.[49] Furthermore, the provision is potentially derogable, although it may have a non-derogable core, notably with regard to *habeas corpus*.[50] Human rights bodies have developed a coherent body of case law as to what constitutes arbitrary detention. This raises the question discussed in chapter 3 as to whether evidence of customary human rights law applicable in situations of conflict is the same as evidence of customary international humanitarian law and whether the distinction matters. There are no equivalent bodies to the human rights bodies in the field of international humanitarian law.[51] It therefore appears to be left to States to determine what constitutes arbitrary detention in non-international armed conflict.

ii. Procedural guarantees Possible procedural guarantees include the right to be told why one is being detained and, most importantly, the right promptly to challenge the lawfulness of detention. The evidence of State practice is predominantly that of human rights bodies. This raises,

[48] Study, 347–349; see also the discussion of Rule 89 above.
[49] The European Convention on Human Rights in Art. 5 lists exhaustively the only permitted grounds of detention. In order to add to those grounds, it appears to be necessary to derogate.
[50] Human Rights Committee, General Comment No. 29 on States of Emergency, CCPR/C/21/Rev.1/Add.11.
[51] Even if it had ever been called upon to discharge its functions, the International Fact-Finding Commission, under Art. 90 of Protocol, is not there to monitor compliance but to investigate alleged violations.

first, the question of whether that constitutes *State* practice. Is it sufficient to show what the body has said or is it also necessary to show that that has not been opposed by the State in question? Second, it gives rise to the question of whether it is legitimate to place reliance exclusively on human rights materials, where international humanitarian law is silent. It is one thing to use human rights material to provide additional support to international humanitarian law material but quite another to rely exclusively on such material to establish the existence of a customary norm of humanitarian law.[52] It is submitted that it is legitimate to do so where the human rights material relates specifically to situations of conflict and where there is no conflict with humanitarian law. It is simply that humanitarian law appears to be silent. It may be particularly appropriate to do so when a rule appears to exist in international armed conflict and the doubt arises in the field of non-international armed conflict. Article 75 of Protocol I provides certain procedural and due process guarantees. It would not be surprising to find that similar rules exist in non-international conflicts, even if the evidence is to be found in human rights materials.[53]

h. Due process guarantees

Rule 100

No one may be convicted or sentenced, except pursuant to a fair trial affording all essential judicial guarantees.

Rule 101

No one may be accused or convicted of a criminal offence on account of any act or omission which did not constitute a criminal offence under national or international law at the time it was committed; nor may a heavier penalty be imposed than that which was applicable at the time the criminal offence was committed.

Rule 102

No one may be convicted of an offence except on the basis of individual criminal responsibility.

---

[52] See generally chapter 3.
[53] A particular example would be the ability to challenge the lawfulness of detention. The last paragraph in this section (p. 352) appears to be a reference to recognition of belligerency. If so, one might have expected to see some reference to the fact that it has not been claimed since 1945.

Rule 103

Collective punishments are prohibited.

The Rules in this field raise some of the problems discussed at the start of this chapter, such as the difficulty for non-State armed groups in complying with due process requirements both for practical reasons and also because it is difficult to see how any courts could be lawfully constituted. As in the last sub-section, considerable reliance is placed on human rights material. In addition, in certain contexts, the Study refers to the practice of domestic legal systems.[54] As noted at the start of the chapter, State practice in relation to non-international armed conflicts will be found in material not normally examined when looking for evidence of State practice in international conflicts, particularly with regard to the administration of justice. This does, however, raise the broader issue of whether such material can be considered as State practice for the purposes of international law. It is difficult to see why, in principle, it could not constitute such evidence. Most of the particular elements of due process appear to be uncontroversial but it is worth noting how few States in fact afford such guarantees in practice in peacetime, never mind in situations of conflict.

Rule 101, which prohibits retroactive criminal penalties, is straightforward. One issue which can be a problem is not discussed and that is the removal, with retroactive effect, of a barrier to prosecution. One example would be removing the political offence exception to extradition in relation to a particular type of offence. This would have the effect of making an individual vulnerable to extradition, and therefore prosecution, who might not have been subject to the criminal jurisdiction of the requested State. It is submitted that this is not an example of a retroactive criminal penalty. The only test is whether the act was criminal at the time of its commission in the place where it was committed.

There is a useful cross-reference in the discussion of Rule 102 on individual criminal responsibility to the principle of command responsibility. Given the number of States in which military officers appear to be genuinely bewildered at the idea that they can be held responsible for the conduct of others, this is an important connection to make.

---

[54] For example, p. 359, fn. 380.

i. Personal rights

Rule 104

The convictions and religious practices of civilians and persons *hors de combat* must be respected.

Rule 105

Family life must be respected as far as possible.

Given the mass of evidence with regard to respecting convictions and religious practices in international armed conflicts and given the weight of evidence based on human rights material arising out of situations of non-international conflict, it is not surprising that the authors of the Study conclude that the requirement is part of customary law. Human rights law distinguishes between freedom of thought, conscience and religion, which in the nature of things is not susceptible to limitations, and the manifestation of such beliefs, which may be. It must be assumed that the obligation to respect refers to the manifestation of the beliefs, particularly given the reference to practices.

Rule 105 on respect for family life raises the same problem as certain other Rules in this section. In an attempt to cover a wide range of issues, the authors have had to draft the Rule in so vague a way as to make it virtually meaningless, beyond signalling that the authorities should take account of family life. In fact, certain very specific issues arise in situations of conflict with regard to family life. They include the problem of keeping families together during forced movement, evacuation and detention. It might have been preferable if the Rule had been expressed in such a way as better to reflect these precise issues and the practice, rather than being drafted in such a general way. This would have left less 'wriggle room' for States. There is again a useful cross-reference to the specific rules on contact with family members by detainees and to the provision of information with regard to those reported as missing.

3. Final remarks

The authors were confronted with a mass of material on the issues addressed in Chapter 32, much of it human rights material. It is submitted that the way in which the human rights material is used is not inappropriate, even where there is very little evidence of specifically international humanitarian law State practice in non-international armed conflicts. It is likely that States will not dispute the content of the Rules but only, on occasion, their customary law status. There are three inter-related concerns with Chapter 32. First, there is confusion as to whether it only addresses the situation of those in the control of the opposing party or whether it also addresses the treatment of those in territory under the authority of that party. If it is attempting to deal with both, some of the Rules might be better expressed by addressing the two situations separately. If it is only dealing with the first situation, there should be a separate chapter dealing with the second. This contributes significantly to the second problem. Some of the Rules are expressed in such general terms as to make them virtually meaningless, unless read in conjunction with the commentary. That might have been avoided if the authors had either produced more separate Rules or else expressed the existing Rules in greater detail. Third, and perhaps the most striking examples of the second problem, Rule 89 (murder is prohibited) and Rule 99 (arbitrary deprivation of liberty is prohibited) need to be 'unpacked'. It is not surprising that these should be the Rules presenting the greatest difficulty since they are addressing the issues which probably cause the most difficulty in non-international armed conflict. It is surely not without significance that the two areas where the European Convention on Human Rights is most different from the other general human rights treaty texts are Articles 2 and 5. Other treaty texts prohibit the arbitrary deprivation of life and the arbitrary deprivation of liberty. The European Convention, on the other hand, lists the only permissible grounds on which there may be resort to potentially lethal force where absolutely necessary. To modify those grounds, it is necessary to derogate and the only permitted derogation is with regard to lawful acts of war, which begs the question. Similarly, other treaty texts also prohibit arbitrary detention but the European Convention lists exhaustively the only permitted grounds of detention. It is necessary to derogate to modify those grounds. It may be that the authors of the Study thought that the material available to them did not permit them to clarify in what circumstances a killing would be murder or a deprivation of liberty would be arbitrary. Given, however, that other Rules are expressed generally, the concern is that the simplification in the two Rules was the result of a decision to make each Rule apply to as wide a range of situations as possible. The problem with simplification is that it can strip the meaningful content out of a Rule.

12

Status and treatment of prisoners of war and other persons deprived of their liberty

AGNIESZKA JACHEC-NEALE

1. Introduction

One may wonder how the authors of the Study would have approached the topic of detention during armed conflict if they were to analyse it today, nearly three years since the research for the Study was completed. By the end of December 2002, the conflict in Afghanistan was fully underway, where the massive arrests of the members of the Taliban and Al-Qaeda supporters were made. They were then transferred to the military detention facility in Guantánamo Bay. The invasion of Iraq was looming on the horizon. We were yet to hear of the abuse of prisoners in Abu Ghraib prison and other detention centres in Iraq, and the numerous incidents involving torture and inhumane treatment of both combatants and non-combatants by the forces involved in these conflicts.

The mistreatment of individuals deprived of their liberty has occurred probably in every war that has ever been fought, yet the recent practice is particularly shocking as it appears to be directed at diminishing or depriving an individual of dignity and humanity.[1] These practices, which in many cases have been supported by State policy, strike at the very heart of international humanitarian law, the spirit of humanitarian values and respect for a human being during war, the most cruel of all times. The law as we know it has not changed but the fighters and the goals of the fight may have done so. In this era when the rules of war with the limitations they impose are perceived as a hindrance to defeat of the enemy and ultimate victory, they are of utmost importance.

---

[1] 'Detainee Positive Responses', US Federal Bureau of Investigation records of misconduct released only in early Jan 2007, available at: http://foia.fbi.gov/guantanamo/detainees. pdf; see British Parliamentary Intelligence and Security Committee *Report on the Handling of Detainees by UK Intelligence Personnel in Afghanistan, Guantanamo Bay and Iraq*, 1 March 2005.

Detention is the most severe form of restriction on the personal liberty of individuals during an armed conflict and it may be instituted against various groups of persons to suit different purposes. Detention is administered by judicial authority, which orders the detention as a result or in the course of judicial proceedings against the person. Detention should be clearly distinguished from another form of deprivation of liberty, namely internment (otherwise referred to as administrative detention), which is instituted by the executive branch and does not involve judicial process. Internment, the qualified forms of which are assigned residence or confinement, is a measure of control prescribed in exceptional cases for security reasons in armed conflict. Internees or 'security detainees' as they are sometimes referred to, consist primarily of civilians. Prisoners of War (POWs) on the other hand constitute a *sui generis* group of individuals deprived of liberty in international armed conflicts. Such internees will be considered in this chapter separately from other categories of persons deprived of liberty, in accordance with the particular legal regime, relating both to the status and the associated treatment. This approach follows a traditional way of presenting this issue both in the literature[2] and through the treaty development.[3] This, however, is not the approach the authors of the Study took. This will be discussed in detail below.

Treaty development or codification of custom?

Prisoners of War

POWs' status and treatment are commonly discussed in the context of the principle of distinction and the combatancy requirements. There is a conceptual relation between these two terms in that one has to qualify as a combatant to be entitled to POW status upon capture. Enemy soldiers, who surrender or are *hors de combat*, no longer pose a threat to the captors, as they are unable to fight effectively. In the past, captured soldiers were considered the property of the captor and not that of the

---

[2] Most commentators and scholars usually reserve a separate chapter wholly dedicated to POWs. This flows from a fundamental distinction in the legal status afforded to POWs on one hand and to detained or interned civilians, i.e. chiefly but not exclusively non-combatants, on the other hand. These two are perceived as separate bodies of law although they may in some areas have similar norms.

[3] A number of contemporary military manuals follow this distinction too, e.g. United Kingdom Ministry of Defence, *The Manual of Law of Armed Conflict* (Oxford University Press, 2005) (hereafter: *UK Manual*).

hostile State and subject to death at worst and enslavement at best. This practice started changing throughout the eighteenth and nineteenth century, when it was realized that it was militarily more beneficial to exchange each others prisoners.

One of the first records of an agreement between parties regulating treatment of captives was in the Treaty of Amity and Commerce between His Majesty the King of Prussia and the United States of America of 1785. Article 24 of the Treaty provided a set of basic treatment rules, including conditions for confinement (provision of comfortable quarters), remuneration for work and parole conditions. This aimed at highlighting the unique status of POWs, who were not to be considered as criminals nor treated as such. The 1863 Instructions for the Government of Armies of the United States in the Field, prepared by Francis Lieber contained a comprehensive set of protections for POWs.[4] The rules codified therein were developed in subsequent codifications relating to inter-State conflicts.[5] Articles 21 and 22 of the 1880 Oxford Manual of The Laws and Customs of War on Land referred to the status of POWs and Articles 61–80 embodied a more elaborated set of protections, including basic principles of humane treatment. These regulations were drawn nearly verbatim from an earlier final declaration of the Brussels Conference of 1874, a non-binding document signed by fifteen European States.[6] These regulations confirmed the non-penal character of internment, the principle of humane treatment, the possibility of employment of POWs in

---

[4] Approved by Congress of the Confederate States of America 1861 Act Relative to Prisoners of War contained a rather important requirement imposed on the Confederate commanders to 'provide for the safe custody and sustenance of prisoners of war', who later were subject to transfers. It furthermore guaranteed that 'the rations furnished prisoners of war shall be the same in quantity and quality as those furnished to enlisted men in the army of the Confederacy' (Section 1). Section 2 of this Act established that no officers, crew or the passengers of any unarmed vessels, unless they were employed in the public service of the enemy, were to be treated as POWs.

[5] Art. 49 of Lieber Code proposed a formidable definition of Prisoners of War:

A prisoner of war is a public enemy armed or attached to the hostile army for active aid, who has fallen into the hands of the captor, either fighting or wounded, on the field or in the hospital, by individual surrender or by capitulation.

Arts. 50 and 51 of the Code indicated that POW status should be afforded to civilians accompanying armed forces as well as the members of the legitimate *levée en masse* (i.e. civilians uprising in opposition to armed invasion before the occupation is established). Immunity from prosecution was secured in Article 56.

[6] Arts. 11 and 23–34 of the Brussels Declaration regulated both the status and treatment provided for POWs.

public or private works, which had no direct connection to military operations with remuneration for such labour and for the reciprocal nature of
these conditions. It was understood that all these protections could be
afforded to both combatant and non-combatant members of the armed
forces as well the individuals accompanying the army such as correspondents, contractors or traders. Both documents also envisaged that spies
could not expect to be afforded POW protections unlike citizens rising
against invaders (*levée en masse*).

All these documents, at the time of their adoption, reflected evolving
customary practice. They formed the foundations of subsequent treaties
in this field, starting with the 1899 Hague Convention with respect to the
Laws and Customs of War on Land[7] followed by the 1907 Hague
Convention respecting the Laws and Customs of War on Land.[8] Although
18 States ratified the 1899 Convention, they failed to accept the 1907
Convention and so remained bound by the provisions of the earlier
treaty, which proved to be important in the outbreak of World War I.[9]
The Hague Regulations proved to be insufficient and to some extent
inadequate.[10] Meanwhile Germany signed specific bilateral agreements
regarding POWs with Great Britain in 1917 and a year later with France.[11]

Efforts by the ICRC led to the adoption of the first international treaty
solely dedicated to POW matters, the 1929 Geneva Convention Relative
to the Treatment of Prisoners of War.[12] In its ninety-seven Articles the
Convention embodied a fairly comprehensive code covering the status
and treatment of prisoners during the entire period of their captivity
from capture up to release and repatriation. The Convention also secured
the prohibition of reprisals (Article 2) and collective punishments
(Article 46).[13] The Convention, as ratified by forty-six States, constituted
a legal basis for the conduct of belligerents in World War II with the
exception of the Soviet Union which failed to ratify. This resulted in the

---

[7] Arts. 2–20 and 29–31 in Annex to the Convention (IV) Respecting the Laws and Customs
of War on Land, 18 October 1907 (hereafter: Hague Regulations IV).

[8] *Ibid.*, Arts. 2–20 and 31.

[9] D. Schindler and J. Toman (eds.), *The Laws of Armed Conflict* (Leiden: Martinus Nijhoff
Publishers, 2004), p. 55.

[10] H. Levie, 'Enforcing the Third Geneva Convention on the Humanitarian Treatment of
Prisoners of War' (1996/97) 7 *U.S. Air Force Academy Journal of Legal Studies* 259.

[11] *Ibid.*, Howard Levie mentions an agreement with the US in 1918.

[12] Convention Relative to the Treatment of Prisoners of War, 22 July 1929 (hereafter: 1929
Geneva Convention).

[13] The Convention also introduced the institution of Protecting Power, which designation
was non-mandatory. See extensively on this matter, H. Levie 'Prisoners of War and the
Protecting Power' (1961) 55 *American Journal of International Law* 374.

application of the 1907 Hague Regulations and customary rules in relations between Germany and Soviet Union during that conflict.[14] Unfortunately, the 1939–1945 war brought disregard of the existing rules on all sides; for example there was a denial of POW status to Werhmacht members upon their surrender to the Allies in May 1945 and to political commissars of the Red Army following the German *Kommissar Dekret* of 1941, not to mention the gross mistreatment both of Soviet prisoners in German camps and the equally horrendous abuse of German POWs by the Soviets and the Katyn massacre of mainly Polish POWs.[15]

Bearing in mind the Soviets' legal position, the holding in the 1946 Nuremberg Judgment that the Hague Regulations were 'declaratory of the laws and customs of the war', and not the 1929 Geneva Convention, did not come as a surprise.[16] Soon the 1929 Geneva Convention became the subject of judicial scrutiny. The United States Military Tribunal in Nuremberg in the *High Command*[17] trial clarified that despite the customary character of the majority of Hague or Geneva provisions, 'certain detailed provisions pertaining to the care and treatment of prisoners' could not be accepted as the enunciations of the customs of war.[18] The Tribunal went on to review the provisions of both the Hague Regulations and the 1929 Geneva Conventions that were pertinent. While a number of the provisions were assessed as undoubtedly customary,[19] the judges struggled to arrive at the same conclusion regarding Article 31 on the employment of prisoners of war in work directly connected to the operations of war.[20]

---

[14] H. Fischer in D. Fleck (ed.), *The Handbook of Humanitarian Law in Armed Conflicts* (Oxford University Press, 2004), p. 323.   [15] *Ibid.*, p. 324.

[16] International Military Tribunal (Nuremberg) Judgment and Sentences, reprinted in (1947) 41 *American Journal of International Law* 172, at 232.

> The Geneva Convention for the treatment of prisoners of war is not binding in the relationship between Germany and the U.S.S.R. Therefore only the principles of general international law on the treatment of prisoners of war apply. Since the 18th century these have gradually been established along the lines that war captivity is neither revenge nor punishment, but solely protective custody, the only purpose of which is to prevent the prisoners of war from further participation in the war. This principle was developed in accordance with the view held by all armies that it is contrary to military tradition to kill or injure helpless people.

[17] *US v. von Leeb et al.* (US Military Tribunal, Germany, 1948) 12 *LRTWC* 1.

[18] *Ibid.*, p. 89.

[19] For example Arts. 2–4, 7, 9–13, 25–29, 32, 46, 50, 56 of the 1929 Geneva Convention, *ibid.*, pp. 90–91. In the subsequent *Krupp Trial* Art. 30 was added to this list.

[20] Other post-WWII war crimes cases all found violations of this prohibition without taking a position on its disputed customary status *US v. Milch* (US Military Tribunal,

Geneva Convention III of 1949[21] enlarged the scope of categories of persons entitled to POW status[22] as well as specifying the particularities of the conditions of internment. The provisions displayed in greater detail the modalities of the employment and financial rewards to prisoners and it clarified the issues relating to judicial proceedings against them. An essential new guarantee was introduced by Article 5 which required a competent court to determine the status of all persons who had committed a belligerent act and had fallen into the hands of the enemy if there was doubt as to whether they would qualify as a POW under one of the categories stipulated in Article 4.

The status determination standard was further reaffirmed, clarified and supplemented by Article 45 of Additional Protocol I[23] to the 1949 Geneva Conventions.[24] Article 45 not only reiterated the Convention's requirement of POW treatment of such individuals in the predetermination period; it also introduced a presumption of POW status in instances when the person claimed or the Party upon whom s/he depended claimed such entitlement on his or her behalf to the Protecting Party. More controversially, a person who appeared to be entitled was also to be granted POW status and treatment until a competent tribunal made a decision. In all such cases, in addition to any other situations of doubtful status, the captors were obliged to establish a competent tribunal to decide on this matter. Commentary to this Protocol elucidates that the use of the rather vague term 'competent tribunal' meant to encompass not only military tribunals, but also civilian ones as well as administrative bodies vested with determination powers, such as military commissions.[25]

In cases of persons not detained as POWs (following the initial

---

Nuremberg, 1947) 7 *LRTWC* 27; *US v. Krausch et al.* (*I.G. Farben Trial*) (US Military Tribunal, Nuremberg, 1948) [1948] *Annual Digest* 668; *US v. Krupp et al.* (US Military Tribunal, Nuremberg, 1948) [1948] *Annual Digest* 620; *US v. Flick et al.* (US Military Tribunal, Nuremberg, 1947) [1947] *Annual Digest* 266; *Tanabe Koshiro* case (Netherlands Temporary Court Martial, 1947) 11 *LRTWC* 1.

[21] Convention (III) Relative to the Treatment of Prisoners of War of 12 August 1949 [hereafter: Geneva Convention III].   [22] *Ibid.*, Arts. 4 A.(1), (2) and (3), 4B and 33.

[23] Protocol Additional to the 1949 Geneva Conventions of 12 August 1949, and Relating to the Protection of Victims of International Armed Conflicts, 8 June 1977.

[24] M. Bothe, K. Partsch and W. Solf, *New Rules for Victims of Armed Conflicts: Commentary on the Two 1977 Protocols Additional to the Geneva Conventions of 1949* (The Hague: Martinus Nijhoff, 1982), p. 260.

[25] Y. Sandoz, C. Swinarski and B. Zimmermann (eds.), *Commentary on the Additional Protocols of 8 June 1977 to the Geneva Conventions of 12 August 1949* (ICRC Geneva and The Hague: Martinus Nijhoff, 1987), p. 1745.

determination in accordance with Paragraph 1 of Article 45) and who are to be tried for offences arising out of hostilities, the Protocol designates a 'judicial tribunal' as the relevant body to adjudicate when such persons wish to assert their POW status. It requires a public adjudication procedure (except when the interests of State security prevail), which can be attended by the representatives of the Protecting Power.[26] The Article also offers a guarantee of protection for all those who do not benefit from the combatant privilege but who join the fighting. Those who fall into this group (like mercenaries, spies, civilians who do not benefit from protections of Geneva Convention IV or members of armed forces who forfeit their entitlement to POW status and treatment[27]) are entitled at all times to the protections of Article 75 of Additional Protocol I.[28]

While reiterating a number of prohibitions (e.g. murder, torture of all kinds, or outrages upon personal dignity) and reinforcing the obligation of humane treatment without discrimination, Article 75 specified two detention-related requirements. The first refers to prompt information about the reasons for arrest, detention or internment; the second imposes a duty to release an individual as soon as 'the circumstances justifying the arrest, detention or internment have ceased to exist'. There seems to be consensus that Article 75 could apply both as a treaty obligation and as customary norm.[29] Finally, note that Additional Protocol I introduced new conditions in respect to combatant status; these are considered elsewhere in this book.[30] Although the Protocol deprives a certain group of combatants (notably only combatants) of their POW status, it nevertheless affords them 'the protections equivalent in all respects to those accorded to prisoners of war' whether by Geneva Convention III or Additional Protocol I.[31] This means there should not be *de facto* any differences in their treatment.

Other persons deprived of their liberty

'The protection of civilians in time of armed conflict, whether international or internal, is the bedrock of modern humanitarian law'

---

[26] Additional Protocol I, Art. 45(2).
[27] For example those described in Additional Protocol I, Art.44(3) Protocol I, following interpretation in M. Bothe, K. Partsch and W. Solf, *New Rules for Victims of Armed Conflicts*, pp. 261 *et seq.*   [28] Additional Protocol I, Art. 75(3).
[29] K. Dörmann, 'The Legal Situation of "Unlawful/Unprivileged Combatants"' (2003) 85 *International Review of the Red Cross*, 45 at 67 and 71.
[30] Chapter 5, pp. 102–103.   [31] Additional Protocol I, Art. 44 (4).

declared the ICTY in one of their judgments[32] over fifty years after the first treaty aimed at legally securing such protection was adopted.[33] The antecedents of the Convention protections can be found in the Lieber Code (Article 37) and the Hague Regulations (Article 46).

The basic principle is based on the nationality criterion introduced in Article 4 of Geneva Convention IV, which defines persons protected by the Convention to be those who find themselves in the hands of the belligerent party or Occupying Power of which they are not nationals.[34] There are three types of situations in which any of the protected persons' liberty may be restricted. First, protected persons in the territory of a party to the conflict may be confined pending proceedings or serving a sentence involving loss of liberty.[35] They should be treated humanely in accordance with minimum of safeguards enshrined in Articles 27–34 of the Convention.

Second, protected persons in the occupied territory may be subjected to detention as a result of penal proceedings for violation of the penal provisions promulgated by the Occupying Powers in accordance with Article 64–65 cases of espionage or sabotage. Such civilian detainees are subject to special judicial proceedings, which may involve non-political military courts sitting in the occupied country[36] and possibly imposition of the death penalty. Articles 69–77 safeguard the minimum treatment during their detention. In contrast, protected persons who do not commit a serious penal offence but one solely intended to harm an Occupying Power are subject to either imprisonment or internment proportionate to the offence committed (Article 68).

Third, the personal liberty of protected persons may be restricted as a matter of exceptional measures of control and security necessary as a result of war.[37] Aliens in the territory of the belligerent party may be

[32] *Prosecutor v. Kupreškić and others* (ICTY) Judgment of Trial Chamber, 14 January 2000, IT-95-16 at para. 521.

[33] Convention (IV) Relative to the Protection of Civilian Person in Time of War of 12 August 1949.

[34] The Convention concerns itself with 'protected persons', who are de facto civilians. Additional Protocol I uses a notion of civilians, see its Art. 50 (1) for a definition.

[35] Geneva Convention IV, Art. 37.

[36] *Ibid.*, Arts. 66–68 and 71–77. Confinement may also be instituted as a form of disciplinary punishment imposed on internees who commit offences during internment including disciplinary violations (Arts. 119 and 122–123). Art. 126 indicates that Arts. 71–76 are applicable by analogy to internees.

[37] See also *Prosecutor v. Delalić et al.,* (ICTY) Judgment of Trial Chamber, 16 November 1998 IT-96-21, at paras. 572, 583. See also J. Pejic, 'Procedural Principles and Safeguards for Internment/Administrative Detention in Armed Conflicts and Other Situations of Violence' (2005) 87 *International Review of the Red Cross* 375, at 380.

subject to assigned residence or internment only 'if the Security of the
Detaining Power makes it absolutely necessary'.[38] Similarly, civilians in
the occupied territories may be interned or assigned residence 'if the
Occupying Power considers it necessary, for imperative reasons of security'.[39] The ICTY acknowledged the vagueness of a notion of 'security'
and indicated that 'subversive activity carried on inside the territory of a
party to the conflict, or actions which are of direct assistance to an opposing party, may threaten the security of the former, which may, therefore,
intern people or place them in assigned residence if it has *serious and
legitimate reasons* to think that they may seriously prejudice its security
by means such as sabotage or espionage'[40] [emphasis in original]. In the
case of a British-Iraqi national contesting his continued internment by
forces in Iraq, the Court of Appeal stated that the concept of internment
for imperative reasons of security

> creates a high threshold test, and it is available in the ordinary way to a bel-
> ligerent power both during a war and for up to a year during any period of
> occupation that follows the end of the war. International law obliges those
> states who are parties to Geneva IV to treat their internees in the humani-
> tarian way prescribed by that Convention and to afford them the rights of
> review and appeal that are prescribed by Article 78.[41]

Geneva Convention IV imposes restrictions on protection if the protected persons are definitely suspected of or engaged in activities hostile
to the security of that State or Occupying Power. The fundamental obligation of humane treatment as well as fair trial guarantees, remain applicable. Derogation from full protection lasts as long as the 'security
imperative' remains valid.[42]

The confinement of 'security detainees' or 'civilian internees' (these
terms tend to be interchangeably referred to in the legal literature) is
subject to periodic reviews.[43] Failure to respect the procedural safeguards

---

38 Geneva Convention IV, Arts. 41–42, see also *Prosecutor v. Delalić et al.,* (ICTY) Judgment
    of Appeals Chamber, 20 February 2001, IT-96-21-A (2001), at paras. 327–8.
39 Geneva Convention IV, Art. 78.
40 *Prosecutor v. Delalić et al.,* Judgment of Trial Chamber, at para. 576.
41 *R. (on the application of Al-Jedda) v. Secretary of State for Defence* [2006] EWCA Civ 327
    (29 March 2006) at 85. The applicant's claim that his continued detention on security
    grounds and the failure to return him to United Kingdom were unlawful was rejected.
42 Geneva Convention IV, Article 5. Such formulation indicates not only the exceptional
    character of such derogation but also its temporal limitation.
43 Every six months – Geneva Convention IV, Arts. 43 and 78 respectively. For example,
    reviewing continued detention by British forces is conducted on more frequent

may render the internment unlawful.[44] The weakness of the Convention results from a lack of specificity as to the shape of the regular and appeal procedures, whether it is possible to challenge the lawfulness of detention as well as the legal capacity of the competent (whether administrative or judicial) bodies designated to decide upon internment or detention. Shedding some light in that respect the ICTY indicated that it is necessary for such bodies to be equipped with powers to make a final decision regarding a release of prisoners, whose detention cannot be justified by any serious reason, as well as powers to be able to affect the treatment of the detainees, in particular to remedy any abuse or procedural shortcomings.[45]

Civilian internees should be released if the reasons for detention cease to exist or, by the latest, at the close of hostilities, except for those internees in the territory of the belligerent Party who are facing criminal charges or who are serving a sentence.[46]

In recent decades there have been numerous examples of restricting civilians' personal liberty on the grounds of security such as the ongoing Israeli-Palestinian conflict or the 1991–92 Gulf War during which Iraqi nationals living in the United Kindgom, Italy and France were interned from the outset of the war. Detention camps established in the course of the 1990s ethnic conflicts in former Yugoslavia should also be mentioned, predominantly in the context of malpractice.[47]

The distinction of protected persons based on the nationality criterion and the explicit exclusion of certain categories of nationals from Geneva Convention IV coverage posed legal problems in its application to the situations occurring during recent armed conflicts. The issue of nationality of the victims and the belligerent parties (very often the same) in the 1990s conflicts in former Yugoslavia was of tremendous importance.

intervals – first after six days, then after 28 days and thereafter every three months. Expert Meeting on the Supervision of the Lawfulness of Detention During Armed Conflict, The University Centre for International Humanitarian Law, Geneva, 24–25 July 2004, p. 42.

[44] 'An initially lawful internment clearly becomes unlawful if the detaining party does not respect the basic procedural rights of the detained persons and does not establish an appropriate court or administrative board as prescribed in Art. 43 of Geneva Convention IV. The court took a same view in respect of the Art. 78 procedure. *Prosecutor v. Delalić et al.*, Judgment of Trial Chamber, at paras. 582–3.

[45] *Ibid.*, at 581, 1137–1140. The camp commander, who has an authority to release civilian detainees if he has grounds to believe they do not pose any security risk or they have not been afforded the requisite procedural guarantees and fails to do so, commits an offence of unlawful confinement. *Prosecutor v. Delalić et al.*, Judgment of Appeals Chamber, at paras. 378–9.   [46] Geneva Convention IV, Arts. 132–134.

[47] See 'Lawsuit against Serbia over Vojvodina camps', B 29 News, 17 November 2006.

In its first case the ICTY addressed this by concluding that the protected status of the victims was based on the substance of relations (the existence of effective diplomatic protection) rather than its legal characterisation reflecting the spirit and meaning of Article 4.[48] The Court found that the formal bond of nationality was less decisive than allegiance based on ethnicity.[49]

Realities of modern wars bring even more problems. What about those who fulfil the conditions of protected persons but are not aliens in the territory of the party to conflict or are not civilians in occupied territory? Such situations may particularly occur after invasion but before the occupation is fully established (for example in 2001 in Afghanistan). The application of the general protection norms (Article 27–34 of Geneva Convention IV and Article 75 (3) of Additional Protocol I) in these circumstances seems most plausible. Any transfer of captured civilians to the territory of the belligerent party would then trigger the procedure in Articles 42–43.

A further question is raised as regards the nationals of a neutral State or nationals of a co-belligerent State, which maintains normal diplomatic relations with the State in whose hands they are. The Convention explicitly deprives them of protection. What about those who engage in fighting? It is reasonable to assert, based on the literal interpretation of Article 50 of Additional Protocol I in relation to Article 4 of Geneva Convention III, that such individuals clearly fail to satisfy all of the conditions prescribed for recognition of combatancy and should not be classified as combatants (and afforded POW status) but as civilians. Their civilian status (unless they satisfy all the conditions in Article 4 of Geneva Convention III and Articles 43 and 44 of Additional Protocol I[50]) will therefore remain unaffected even if they participate in fighting; however, unlike combatants they can be prosecuted for the mere fact of participation in hostilities, unlike combatants.[51] Upon capture such individuals retain their civilian status but their protection may be restricted to that of Article 75 of Additional Protocol I or the customary norms reflecting this

---

[48] The ruling rejected the earlier Trial Chamber interpretation, which denied application of the Fourth Geneva Convention to this conflict. *Prosecutor v. Tadić* (ICTY) Appeals Chamber, Judgment of 15 July 1999, Case IT-94-1-A, at paras. 164–169. See also L.C. Green, *The Contemporary Law of Armed Conflict* (Manchester University Press, 2000), pp. 232–234   [49] *Ibid.*, pp. 160, 162.

[50] The customary character of the norms in Art. 4 of Geneva Convention III and Additional Protocol I, Art. 43 is undisputed.

[51] Israeli Supreme Court *The Public Committee against Torture in Israel v. The Government of Israel*, HCJ 769/02, Judgment of 13 December 2006, at 24–26 and 31.

provision. A restriction imposed by paragraph 3 of the Article 51 excludes the applicability of the Protocol protections during such time as the individual takes a direct part in hostilities, without prejudice to an overarching operation of Article 72 and consequently Article 75.[52] In other words, they do not lose their civilian status but may be deprived of their full civilian protection.[53]

The procedural and judicial safeguards covered by Article 75 of Additional Protocol I as well as a much more extensive set of the provisions regulating treatment of all civilian detainees or internees will be discussed in more detail in the section analysing the Study Rules relating to the treatment of all persons deprived of liberty.

Non-international armed conflicts Two preliminary observations are necessary here. First, POW status does not arise in non-international armed conflict unless otherwise agreed or declared by one or more parties to the conflict.[54] Thus no difference emerges in treatment of all those deprived of liberty due to their status.

Second, international humanitarian treaty law is silent on the lawful grounds or the review procedures for detention or internment of individuals.[55] Instead it refers to the actual treatment of persons deprived of liberty. Common Article 3 to the 1949 Geneva Conventions imposes more general requirements of humane treatment without adverse discrimination. It prohibits violence to life, health and physical or mental well-being of the person. A more specific but limited set of measures applicable in all situations involving restriction of personal liberty, whether internment or detention, is laid out in Article 5 of Additional Protocol II. Accordingly all

---

[52] On the customary status of Art. 51(3) of the Additional Protocol I see Israeli Supreme Court, *ibid.*, at 30.

[53] Also in the same sense Dörmann, 'The Legal Situation of "Unlawful/Unprivileged Combatants"', at 50–51; H.P. Gasser in D. Fleck (ed.), *The Handbook of Humanitarian Law in Armed Conflicts*, p. 501. According to the *UK Manual* they should be treated the same way as nationals of the host State, referring to the British declaration at the 1907 Conference (presumably in relation to Art. 23 (h)): *UK Manual*, p. 224, fn. 49.

[54] For example the Algerian War of Independence or the 1989 conflict in Eritrea: H. McCoubrey, *International Humanitarian Law: The Regulation of Armed Conflicts*, (Dartmouth: Aldershot Publishing Company, 1990), p. 181.

[55] International law does not preclude the application of the relevant national law as well as international human rights regulations: *UK Manual* at 15.30.3; also J. Pejic, 'Procedural Principles and Safeguards'. See also *R. (on the application of Al Skeini and Ors) v. Secretary of State for Defence* [2004] EWHC 2911 (Admin) Court of Appeal, Judgment of 21 December 2005, and the High Court decision of 14 December 2004 in the same case containing a comprehensive review of relevant case law.

persons deprived of liberty should be provided with sufficient food, drinking water, health and hygiene facilities as well as shelter from the weather and the dangers of conflict and they should be allowed to practise their religion and to receive relief. Paragraph 2 of the same provision imposes additional obligations in respect to the conditions of the place of internment or detention as well as facilitation of the exchange of correspondence and medical assistance.[56]

Released in 2006, the *Manual on The Law of Non-International Armed Conflict*,[57] whilst highlighting the key principles of law applicable in non-international armed conflicts, follows the Additional Protocol II formula entrenched in Article 5 and specific to treatment of persons whose liberty has been restricted.[58]

Many sources indicate that Common Article 3 is declaratory of existing customary international humanitarian law.[59] On the contrary, Additional Protocol II as a whole is not universally recognised as reflective of customary international law.[60] Some argue that only those provisions of Additional Protocol II which supplement and expand the common Article 3 may be considered as customary norms, which would include Article 5 by virtue of its material proximity with common Article 3.[61] This however requires some further evidence, which will be scrutinised under the relevant Rules.

---

[56] A set of fundamental and absolute guarantees reiterating these of Common Article 3 is enshrined in Article 4 of Protocol II whilst Article 6 embodies some indispensable judicial safeguards. Sandoz, Swinarski and Zimmermann, *Commentary on the Additional Protocols*, pp. 1383–1395.

[57] M.N. Schmitt, C.H.B. Garraway and Y. Dinstein *The Manual on The Law of Non-International Armed Conflict with Commentary* (hereafter: the *Manual*) (San Remo: International Institute of Humanitarian Law, 2006).

[58] *Ibid.*, at 3.6 and more generally at 1.2.4.

[59] *Case concerning Military and Paramilitary Activities in and against Nicaragua (Nicaragua v. United States of America)*, Merits, Judgment of 27 June 1986 [1986] *ICJ Reports* 14 at paras. 218, 255; *Prosecutor v. Tadić* (ICTY) Decision on the Defence Motion for Interlocutory Appeal on Jurisdiction, Appeals Chamber, 2 October 1995 (1995) Case No. IT-94-1-AR72 paras. 98, 117; *Prosecutor v. Akayesu* (ICTR) Judgment of Trial Chamber, 2 September 1998, ICTR-96-4-T at paras. 608–609, 618. Similarly H.P. Gasser, 'A Measure of Humanity in Internal Disturbances and Tensions : Proposal for a Code of Conduct', (1988) 262 *International Review of the Red Cross*, 44; but compare with a critique of such approach in T. Meron, *Human Rights and Humanitarian Norms as Customary Law* (Oxford: Clarendon Press, 1989), pp. 25–27.

[60] In *Tadić* and *Akayesu* rulings as indicated. Similarly *UK Manual*, at 15.5.

[61] R.K. Goodman and B.D. Tittemore 'Unprivileged Combatants and the Hostilities in Afghanistan: Their Status and Rights under International Humanitarian and Human Rights Law', The American Society of International Law, Task Force on Terrorism, Dec. 2002, p. 37.

2. The Rules

The authors did not include a chapter specifically dedicated to POWs (status or treatment), yet various Rules in different chapters refer directly or implicitly to issues related to POWs. The subject matter pertaining to POWs is dispersed over a number of Rules in various chapters of the Study. This review of all the relevant materials would have been greatly assisted by a terminological index, with which, regrettably, this book was not equipped.

Starting with the problem of status, Chapter 33 'Combatants and prisoner-of-war status' with its three Rules (Rules 106–108) appears to embody some useful discussion in that respect.[62] At the outset of Chapter 33 (Volume II) the authors stated that they had decided not to present any further references in relation to the treatment of POWs.[63] Therefore one should not expect certain areas covered by Geneva Convention III to be included in the Study, such as determination of status by a competent court, employment, financial regulations, etc. The Study does contain a significant amount of reference to the treatment of POWs but in other parts. It is to be found in Chapter 37 'Persons deprived of their liberty' (Rules 118–128) and Chapter 32 'Fundamental guarantees' (Rules 87–105). Review of the Commentary in these chapters reveals an extensive amount of material directly and sometimes exclusively referring to POWs. This material is often hidden in the subsections, whose titles may suggest some other content – some examples will be provided in the discussion on the Rules below. In particular Chapter 37 includes references in the Commentary to treatment of both POWs and civilian detainees or internees. These Rules will be analysed in more detail below.

Rule 87 (Humane treatment) and Rule 88 (Non-discrimination) from Chapter 32,[64] deserve special attention. The Commentary to both Rules contains subsections entitled 'Civilians' and 'Persons deprived of their liberty'. It must be observed that although the practice contained under 'Civilians' has no special reference to interned or detained civilians (presumably the intention was to cover this in Chapter 37), the practice

---

[62] Rules in Chapter 33 focus on issues of combatancy, which are separately discussed by Rogers in chapter 5 above. The present author will not repeat his valid comments relative to POWs.

[63] Study, Vol. II, Part 2, Introductory Note to Chapter 33 at 2537. In fairness the authors do imply that the Study does not encompass the entirety of customary international humanitarian law, especially those parts of it which benefit otherwise from their nearly universal acceptance as a matter of treaty law (Study, Vol. I, Introduction, xxx).

[64] This issue is dealt with by Hampson in chapter 11.

included in the second subsection (i.e. 'Persons deprived of their liberty')
is largely dedicated to the treatment of POWs in respect of humane treatment and the prohibition against discrimination.[65] These two Rules
undoubtedly reflect customary norms in so far as POWs are concerned,
in the context of international armed conflicts. The practice presented
with regard to Rules 89–95, 97–98 and 100–103 to a lesser extent comprises a mixture of sources including also those applicable to POWs. Rule
99 (Prohibition of arbitrary deprivation of liberty) should probably be
more appropriately placed in Chapter 37.

Finally, a reference should be made to Rules 46–47 (pertaining to
denial of quarter and persons placed *hors de combat*) and Rule 146
(dealing with belligerent reprisals), which are discussed by other authors,
yet they contain a substantive amount of commentary associated to POW
treatment.[66]

It must be noted that this brief review of the relevant Rules cannot be
taken as complete. It merely aims to highlight some research difficulties
resulting from such a particular approach to the topic of POWs.
Reflecting the Study structure the following analysis will provide supple-
mentary comments regarding Rules 106–108 and a comprehensive
review of Rules 118–128, which bear particular relevance to the issues
discussed above.

A. Prisoner of War status

Rules 106–108

**Combatants must distinguish themselves from the civilian popula-
tion while they are engaged in an attack or in a military operation
preparatory to an attack. If they fail to do so, they do not have the right
to prisoner-of-war status.**

[65] Out of about 100 examples of State practice relative to Rule 87 in this subsection, only about fifteen could be interpreted as concerning 'prisoners' or 'detainees' or 'captured combatants'. Strictly speaking these terms cannot be understood to have the same legal meaning as they encompass potentially different groups of individuals though there may be some overlap between these groups, for example captured combatants may be detained only if they are suspected or convicted of the commission of crime. Two excep-tional references to civilian internees are contained in the Study, Vol. II, Part II, paras. 248 and 249 at 2012. The issue is presented in the same manner in the Commentary to Rule 88, the difference being much less in the overall examples of practice included. Therefore it is difficult to see how these examples may provide evidence of uniform or even consis-tent practice, not only with regard to POWs/combatants but also, more broadly, to all persons deprived of liberty.   [66] For example, see Study, Vol. II, Part 2, 3360–3374.

Combatants who are captured while engaged in espionage do not have the right to prisoner-of-war status. They may not be convicted or sentenced without previous trial.

Mercenaries, as defined in Additional Protocol I, do not have the right to combatant or prisoner-of-war status. They may not be convicted or sentenced without previous trial.

Setting aside the potential shortcomings of the requirements relating to the distinction between combatants and civilians, which are expressed by other commentators,[67] the Rule in its current formulation differs from Geneva Convention III, not to mention the Protocol wording of POW entitlement. The latter requires at least a provision of '*the protections equivalent in all respects to those accorded to prisoners of war by the Third Convention and by this Protocol*' in case the combatant forfeits his right to POW status.[68] The protections include those related to judicial proceedings against such individuals.

As far as regular armed forces are concerned the Study itself admits that none of the treaty provisions sets out the requirements of what might be detrimental to POW status.[69] In relation to resistance and liberation movements, however, the Study considers Article 44 (3) of Additional Protocol I, the customary status of which is doubtful.[70] The Commentary goes further and concludes with a brief reference to Article 45(3) of Additional Protocol I by stating that combatants who fail to distinguish themselves as a result are not entitled to POW status and should be afforded the protection of Article 75 Additional Protocol I unless the combatant can benefit from more favorable treatment under Geneva Convention IV.[71] This is a potentially misleading interpretation of this provision in the context of international armed conflicts to which this Rule applies. Paragraph 3 of Article 45 Additional Protocol I does not

---

[67] G. Aldrich, Statement at the Conference to Mark the Publication of the ICRC Study on 'Customary International Humanitarian Law', The Hague, 30–31 May 2005, p. 3. See also the discussion in chapter 5.   [68] Additional Protocol I, Art. 44 (4).

[69] Study, Vol. I, 385. See chapter 5 for more discussion on this issue.

[70] Dörmann, 'The Legal Situation of "Unlawful/Unprivileged Combatants" ', 45, at 46.

[71] Study, Vol. I, 389. *Operational Law Handbook* of the US Army states that the US views among others Arts. 45 and 75 of Additional Protocol I as customary international law. (*Operational Law Handbook*, JA 422 , 1997 at 18-2). This statement was however qualified by the 2002 edition of the same *Handbook*, which declares Art. 45 'acceptable practice though not legally binding.' Judge Advocate General's School, *Operational Law Handbook*, Ch. 2 (2002); but consult M. Matheson, 'Remarks: The US Position on the Relation of Customary Law to the 1977 Protocols Additional to the 1949 Geneva Conventions' (1987) 2 *American University Journal of International Law & Policy* 419, at 427.

condition entitlement to POW status by a requirement of distinction and it does not limit the scope of application to combatants only.[72]

The Commentary to Rule 106 is divided into three subsections, of which only one, *Levée en masse*, contains some reference to POW status, whilst the rest of the material predominantly, if not exclusively, reflects what may be called 'conditions for combatant status', i.e. what conditions need to be satisfied for an individual to qualify as combatant.[73] Unfortunately, the evidence provided therein and in the Commentary (pp. 384–389) contains no pertinent sources in support of this particular formulation of the Rule. Wrestling with these ambiguities and not enough evidence, the present author asserts that the second sentence of this Rule cannot be regarded as reflective of customary international law.

One must agree with the general assertion that spies are not entitled to POW status as a matter of customary international humanitarian law. Neither the Hague Regulations, which undoubtedly embody customary law (Article 29, referring to 'persons') nor the provisions of Additional Protocol I (Article 46, mentioning 'any member of the armed forces') refer to combatants as the only group of persons deprived of POW status due to their engagement in espionage. In legal terms 'any member of the armed forces' encompasses a wider group of subjects (i.e. non-combatant members of armed forces), not to mention a broad application of Hague Regulations Article 29 to any 'person', which naturally may include combatants as much as other persons, including civilians.[74] Articles 5 and 68 of Geneva Convention IV presuppose certain instances where civilians would be involved in espionage. State practice provided in the Commentary does not seem to settle this matter conclusively. Similarly the second sentence of Rule 107 displays a noticeable departure from the established wording of the Hague Regulations, which demands that a spy shall not be 'punished' without a trial. The punishment may entail an

---

[72] In the same sense *UK Manual*, at 4.6 and Sandoz, C. Swinarski and Zimmermann, *Commentary on the Additional Protocols*, at 1761.

[73] The statement by Israel at the CDDH, as cited in Study, Vol. II, Part 2 at para. 124, 2558 provides the only reference to conditions for POW status. The document stresses two '*sine qua non* conditions' for such status (as opposed to combatant status) – respect for laws of armed conflict and distinction between the combatants and the civilians. If relied on for this interpretation, the Study clearly addresses only the latter without looking into the former.

[74] Citing *Flesche* case – Y. Dinstein, *The Conduct of Hostilities under the Law of International Armed Conflict* (Cambridge University Press, 2004), pp. 211–212. The *UK Manual* follows the Hague Regulations reference to 'a person' engaged in espionage, while making an exception for members of armed forces who gather intelligence in uniform at 8.13 in relation to para. 4.9.

imposition of an administrative measure, which the adverse party may decide to impose, whilst 'conviction or sentencing' is clearly associated with judicial proceedings. The explanatory note in the Study also uses the word 'punished' and State practice points to such wording. The reasons behind this terminological departure remain unclear.

Finally, the Rule relative to mercenaries is based entirely on Article 47 of Additional Protocol I, incorporating its definition of mercenaries, which was subject to controversy in 1977.[75] Article 47, the customary status of which has not been confirmed in its entirety, deprives mercenaries not only of POW entitlement but also of combatant privilege. When deprived of liberty Article 45(3) provides for them the minimum standards of treatment in accordance to Article 75 of the same Protocol.[76] The sources gathered in support of this Rule, perhaps not the most extensive, show that there might be a uniform practice in denying POW status to mercenaries, with only one exception. The United States vigorously objects to it, contrary even to the positions of Israel and Iraq, two other States not bound by Additional Protocol I. In conclusion, so far as the status of mercenaries is concerned the customary humanitarian law norm might be developing but some further evidence would assist in consolidation of such claim.

B. Treatment – Persons deprived of liberty

The Rules contained in Chapter 37 'Persons deprived of their liberty' do not deal with the issue of deprivation of liberty as such; instead they address the treatment of those deprived of liberty for reasons related to hostilities, and referred to by the Study as 'detainees'.[77] POWs are traditionally regarded as internees, so are civilians under Geneva Convention IV unless they are detained on criminal charges (common law detainees with the exception of cases regulated by Article 68).[78] The authors consider that the term 'detainees' in the context of international armed conflict encompasses combatants who have fallen into the hands of the adverse party (though not POWs, who are strictly speaking a broader category of individuals), civilian internees and security detainees. It

---

[75] Sandoz, Swinarski and Zimmermann, *Commentary on the Additional Protocols*, p. 1792 and Study, Vol. II, Part 2, 2588 at 321; H. Levie, 'The 1977 Protocol I and the United States' (1993) 38 *Saint Louis University Law Journal* 469.　　[76] *UK Manual* at 8.23.

[77] Study, Volume. I, 428.

[78] J. Pejic, 'Procedural Principles and Safeguards', 375 *et seq.*; slightly differing, Gasser in D. Fleck (ed.), *Handbook of Humanitarian Law*, p. 591.

seems the authors effectively excluded from the coverage non-combatant detainees who are nevertheless afforded POW status (in relation to Article 4 (A) (4–5) of Geneva Convention III) unless they are to be regarded as 'civilian internees' for the purposes of this Chapter.

Under treaty law civilian internees are considered to constitute the same group of individuals as security detainees; thus an additional distinction was probably unnecessary. Having said that, the experiences of modern conflicts show that there may be a group of individuals, who do not satisfy a nationality criterion to qualify as 'protected persons' under Geneva Convention IV and who, whilst directly participating in hostilities, find themselves in the power of a party to the conflict. Most of them remain in the hands of an adverse party, confined on security grounds.[79] It may well be that due to the security grounds of detention they may be 'security detainees'; if so a clarification should be made. It is not clear from the formulation in the Study if the norms presented in Chapter 37 factor in such a group of detainees.

In respect of non-international armed conflict the Study lists three categories of 'detainees': (a) persons who have directly participated in the hostilities and have fallen into the power of the adverse party, (b) persons detained on criminal charges, and (c) persons detained for security reasons. It must be noted that the related treaty law does not categorise detainees in this fashion; there are no specific provisions concerning security detainees, nor does the Study contains any references in the Rules. There is further confusion in the content of State practice and the interpretation of it as far as the first mentioned group is concerned. 'Captured combatants' often mentioned in the relevant parts of Volume II is interpreted to encapsulate the personal scope of this group.[80] In other words, according to the Study the term 'captured combatants' should be read as meaning persons who have directly participated in the hostilities and have fallen into the power of the adverse party. Bearing in mind Common Article 3, it appears logical that 'captured combatants' would only refer to members of the armed forces rendered *hors de combat* by detention.

Rule 118

Persons deprived of their liberty must be provided with adequate food, water, clothing, shelter and medical attention.

---

[79] Compare with discussion regarding civilian detainees under the section 'Other persons deprived of liberty'.

[80] See also discussion in note 71 and the remarks attached to Rule 106.

Provision of adequate food (and water), accommodation, clothing and medical care or otherwise 'maintenance' (see Hague Regulations) of the persons deprived of liberty is a well-established international rule. In relation to international armed conflicts Geneva Convention III imposes these obligations on the Detaining Power in Articles 25–32 and Article 98 (with regard to POWs) as does Geneva Convention IV in Article 81 and in more detail Articles 85, 87, 89–92 (with regard to security detainees) and in particular Article 76 (in respect of detainees facing the criminal charges). Evidence provided in the State practice Commentary supports (in at least sixty-six examples[81]) the customary status of the norm insofar as POWs are concerned. Note that these include examples that mention only 'captured combatants'.[82] Surprisingly in only sixteen instances is there a reference to the provision of needs for 'captured civilians', (civilian) 'internees' or 'all detainees'.[83] One would expect that in light of the universal acceptance of Geneva Convention IV this norm would have a wider implementation than as evidenced in the Study, yet little doubt arises as to its customary status.

In respect of securing maintenance of persons whose liberty is restricted in non-international armed conflicts, the Study correctly points to Article 5(1) of Additional Protocol II. State practice included here illustrates at best ten examples of national implementation either through the domestic military codes and other legislation or in certain factual situations. The Study seems to add to that number all the examples containing the formulation 'captured combatants'. Out of context references create a significant uncertainty in its interpretation.[84] The customary Rule in non-international armed conflicts might be well advancing in that respect but should be substantiated with additional materials.[85]

The most interesting and deserving of greater attention are the actual examples of State conduct in situations of armed conflict. This practice

---

[81] Study, Vol. II, Part 2, 2778–2786.

[82] *Ibid.*, paras. 23, 24, 30–32, 37, 40, 48–49, 53. All these examples are considered as evidence towards the customary nature of the Rule also in non-international armed conflicts, see Study, Vol. I, note 11, 429–430. The only omitted example is here that of Croatia – see Study, Vol. II, Part 2, 2779 para. 30.

[83] *Ibid.*, paras. 26, 28, 30–31, 35, 37, 45, 49–51, 54, 56, 61, 66, 77, 84.

[84] The Study mistakenly (as they refer solely to POWs) points to military manuals in support of this Rule in non-international conflicts: at 22, 36, 39, 41 and 46. Vol. I, 429–430, fn. 11.

[85] Compare section 3.6 in Schmitt, Garraway and Dinstein, *The Manual on The Law of Non-International Armed Conflict.*

should be extended to all other Rules as clearly supporting domestic
legislation or official statements.[86] Perhaps an updated version of the
Study could include examples of conduct of the States involved in conflicts in Kosovo, East Timor, Afghanistan or Iraq. The ICTY for instance,
considered in the *Limaj et al.* case the detention conditions in the
Llapushnik/Lapusnik prison camp and found that the deplorable conditions – water and food were not provided regularly, there was no cleaning
or sanitary facilities, the cowshed and the storage room, where the
detainees were kept were overcrowded and not ventilated – imposed
deliberately for a prolonged time, constituted the offence of cruel
treatment.[87]

Rule 119

**Women who are deprived of their liberty must be held in quarters sep-
arate from those of men except where families are accommodated as
family units, and must be under the immediate supervision of women.**

The requirement of separate dormitories for female POWs (whether
detained awaiting charges or generally interned) is clearly established in
the treaty law.[88] The families of civilian internees, on the other hand,
should be housed together, whenever practicable providing in all other
cases female and male internees are separated. The Rule as proposed neatly
grasps the conditions reflected otherwise in the Geneva Conventions or in
both Additional Protocols. It is also incorporated in the *Code of Conduct for
Military Operations during Non-International Armed Conflict.* Is it supported by State practice?

There seems to be less evidence to support this Rule than Rule 118,
discussed above. Compared with Rule 118, probably only one third of
the amount of material is included. In terms of quality or value, the documents relied upon are of the same type as in the previous Rule (i.e.
mainly military manuals and some legislation), yet as a novelty the Study
enlists national legislation of a couple of countries, which appear to be
applicable to situations of peace and not armed conflict of whichever

---

[86] It must be recognised that some ICRC archived documents may have only a partial value
as they cannot be attributed to any particular State, as further discussed in chapter 3. See
also chapter 2, p. 38.

[87] *Prosecutor v. Limaj et al.* (ICTY) Judgment of Trial Chamber, 30 November 2005,
IT-03-66 at paras. 288–289.

[88] Already in 1929 the belligerents were required to treat women POWs with 'all consideration due to their sex'. Art. 3 of 1929 Geneva Convention.

type.[89] Clearly these refer to domestic human rights protections, and thus have to be carefully assessed.[90]

Significantly less reference appears in respect of non-international conflicts, with only six examples given; half of these examples specifically refer to Additional Protocol II protections.[91] Other examples, which loosely mention 'prisoners', should have a supporting role here.[92] As mentioned above, the meaning of this particular term is not sufficiently clarified in the Study and without access to the documents referred to the present writer finds it difficult fully to accept the proposed evidence. Finally, the assertion that a lack of resources rather than a lack of willingness on the part of the detaining power could have hampered the practice in this field sheds even more doubt as to the customary status of this norm.[93]

Again, as with the previous Rule, it is recommended to consider the actual conduct of States, for instance in the numerous past or ongoing conflicts in Africa or during the 1990s conflicts between the former Yugoslav States. This would certainly add considerable value to the possibly weaker evidence.

Rule 120

Children who are deprived of their liberty must be held in quarters separate from those of adults, except where families are accommodated as family units.

This Rule is very similar to the one above, except that it focuses on children. The Rule should be considered in relation to persons deprived of liberty other than POWs and predominantly in international armed conflicts. When considering the treaty law here one must rely entirely on the appropriate provisions of Geneva Convention IV (Article 82) and Additional Protocol I (Article 77(4)). State practice is less than representative. There are, at best, eight examples of State practice referable to the law of international armed conflict in support of this Rule.[94] There are a

---

[89] Study, Vol. II, Part 2, 2794, paras. 130–134.

[90] The basic human rights documents can be of supporting or clarifying value; see statement in Study, Vol. I, 299.

[91] Study, Vol. II, Part 2, 2792–2794, paras. 115, 117, 118, 128, 129 and 137.

[92] Study, Vol. I, 432, fn. 29. Note the footnote incorrectly lists the Italian IHL Manual, which in the Study, Vol. II, Part 2, 2792, para. 116, refers only to POWs.   [93] Study, Vol. I, 433.

[94] These include agreements mentioned in paras. 160 and 161, which are more likely considered as evidence of State practice: Study, Vol. II, Part 2, 2798.

few more human rights treaties listed, in the majority of cases related generally to situations of peace, though they may also apply in time of conflict. There seems to be a lack of uniformity also in determining the age limit under which a child will be subject to this Rule.[95]

One must therefore conclude that the Rule is supported by rather weak evidence as to its customary nature in respect to armed conflict between States and certainly insufficient evidence with regards to non-international armed conflicts. This is unfortunate as the protection of children, especially those deprived of liberty in armed conflict, is of fundamental importance. It may well be that the predominance of the respective human rights standards in national and international law has already overshadowed the practice in relation to humanitarian law and that customary human rights law will develop more rapidly than customary humanitarian law. Therefore although this is a much-desired customary norm in non-international armed conflicts, it must not be assumed without further evidence.

Rule 121

Persons deprived of their liberty must be held in premises which are removed from the combat zone and which safeguard their health and hygiene.

This Rule incorporates two specific requirements for the accommodation of internment and detention centres, one addressing their location and the other one specifying the obligation for provision of safety from harm/danger of combat and healthy and hygienic conditions of internment. The Rule is reflected in the relevant treaties applicable both to POWs and civilian internees. The 1929 Geneva Convention, although not mentioned in the Study, already embodied the same regulation for POW camps. Geneva Convention III (Articles 22–23) and IV (Articles 83 and 85) followed in a similar fashion. So does the practice, although far more examples focus on the safe location outside a combat zone rather than hygiene and health conditions of camps or detention centres.[96]

There is a useful mention of a report on the military operations in the 1990–91 Gulf War. Elaboration as to the mistreatment of coalition POWs

---

[95] This is indeed acknowledged by the authors: Study, Vol. I, 435.

[96] The author counted nine out of thirty-four examples of State practice in that respect. Yet the Study enumerates a number of other examples, which do not correspond with the relevant content in the Study's Volume II, Part 2 (see Study, Vol. I, 436, fn. 51). Similarly, the matter is treated in respect of non-international armed conflict (see Study, Vol. I, 436, fn. 57).

by Iraqi authorities could have been added in the context both of this Rule and of others, such as Rule 87 (Humane treatment), in a subsection discussing POWs. What comes as a surprise is that no international case law of judicial bodies is cited. The *Krnojelac* or *Aleksovski* cases before the ICTY, mentioned elsewhere in the Study would certainly be relevant.[97] Considering the materials collated in the Study this writer agrees with the authors' recognition of this Rule as customary international law applicable to international armed conflicts.

For non-international armed conflicts the evidence provided does not permit a similar conclusion. Insofar as treaty provisions are concerned Additional Protocol II in Article 5(1)(b–c) contains the safeguards regarding health and hygiene as well as localisation of the places of detention. Out of the wealth of evidence provided in support of this Rule, only six sources relate to non-international conflicts, which include one example of actual practice during armed conflict (1985–86 conflict in Nicaragua) and only in respect to localisation of places of detention. This cannot be accepted as evidence of uniform and widespread practice.

Rule 122

Pillage of the personal belongings of persons deprived of their liberty is prohibited.

This Rule appears to be a qualified version of the general prohibition of pillage contained in Rule 52 earlier in the Study. Prohibition of pillage (or plunder) is indeed long settled not only in treaty provisions but also a customary norm. Whether the same can be said about this prohibition of pillage of the personal belongings of persons deprived of liberty is another matter.

The prohibitory nature of this Rule is very well illustrated by the supporting State practice, where the majority of evidence comes from military justice legislation. As far as the individual victims of the plunder are concerned, some penal provisions relate to POWs only, some more widely to 'prisoners' or 'anyone captured', some to 'protected persons' (including the wounded, shipwrecked and those placed *hors de combat*?) – there does not seem to be much consistency and uniformity in terminology.

Moreover, treaty law takes into consideration situations when POWs or civilian internees' valuables are deposited, mainly for security

---

[97] Study, Vol. II, Part 2, 2787–88. *Prosecutor v. Aleksovski*, Judgment of the Trial Chamber, 25 June 1999, IT-95-14/1; *Prosecutor v. Krojelac*, Initial Indictment, 17 June 1997, IT-97-25.

326 AGNIESZKA JACHEC-NEALE

reasons.[98] These regulations are duly noted in the Study[99]; however, there is a lack of mention of the existence of similar practice under customary international law.

Lastly, a comment is required about the potentially misleading statement contained in the explanatory comments to the Rule in respect of non-international armed conflicts. The comment claims that pillage of persons whose liberty has been restricted is a war crime under the Statutes of the ICTY, the ICTR and the Special Court for Sierra Leone,[100] which is not entirely correct. What is true is that plunder prohibited by these Statutes is used in a general sense (i.e. may involve pillage of the places or property)[101] and not particularly to persons whose liberty has been restricted in accordance with the formulation provided in Additional Protocol II.[102]

Although State practice appears to be mainly directed towards situations of international conflicts, elsewhere the Study suggests that it is supporting its customary relevance to non-international conflicts because it is not excluded from application to non-international conflicts.[103] This legal interpretation does not come across as a valid one since non-exclusion does not automatically imply inclusion.

Rule 123

The personal details of persons deprived of their liberty must be recorded.

This Rule is undoubtedly a customary international norm in relation to POWs and the materials included in the Commentary to this Rule prove that.[104] With regards to civilian internees, although there is a strong

---

[98] Art. 18 of Geneva Convention III and Art. 97 of Convention IV and Art. 4(2)(g) of Additional Protocol II contain only a general prohibition of pillage.

[99] Study, Vol. I, 439.   [100] Study, Vol. I, 438.

[101] Pillaging a town or place, but no personal belongings of detainees, is considered a serious violation of laws or customs in non-international armed conflicts under Art.8(2)(e)(v) of the Rome Statute of the International Criminal Court.

[102] The court elucidated further on this issue in several of their judgments, in particular in *Prosecutor v. Kordić and Cerkez* (ICTY) Judgment of Appeals Chamber, 17 Dec. 2004, IT-95-14/2 at 79, 84; *Prosecutor v. Simić, Tadić, and Zarić* (ICTY) Judgment of Trial Chamber, 17 October 2003, IT-95-9-T at 98–99, as well as in an earlier cases of *Prosecutor v. Blaskić* (ICTY), Judgment of Trial Chamber 3 March 2000, IT-95-14-T at 184, *Prosecutor v. Kordić and Cerkez* (ICTY), Judgment of Trial Chamber, 26 February 2001, IT-95-14/2-T at 352 and in *Prosecutor v. Jelisić* (ICTY), Judgment of Trial Chamber, 14 December 1999, IT-95-10-T at 49.   [103] Study, Vol. I, 438, fn. 74 after semi-colon.

[104] The 1899/1907 Hague Regulations (in Art. 14) contained the relevant protections later included in Arts. 122–123 of Geneva Convention III.

prohibition in treaty law,[105] the evidence of State practice is less extensive; thus there may be a temptation to include the human rights documents to support or strengthen the customary nature of this norm. This
Rule may overlap with Rule 98 (prohibition of enforced disappearances) as well as to some extent with Rule 99 (prohibition of arbitrary
deprivation of liberty), comprehensively discussed elsewhere in this
book.[106] The Rule must also be considered in the context of the search
for missing persons. It is expected that National Information Bureaux
would be established in event of war; these normally feed the relevant
data into the ICRC's permanently running Central Tracing Agency, pro-
cessing information at the international level. In that respect, an interesting account of the procedures employed in the process of registration
of Iraqi POWs during 1990s Gulf War can be found in one of the ICRC's
publications.[107]

One must agree that the practice in this field appears to be well established in respect of POWs and quite possibly of other deprived persons in
international armed conflicts. As far as non-international armed conflicts
are concerned there is nothing in treaty law in this field, except for prohibition of enforced disappearance of persons under the Article 7 of the
Rome Statute. As to the customary character of this norm practice presented in support by the authors fails to convince that the customary
humanitarian rule in this field has matured in non-international armed
conflicts.

Rule 124

A. **In international armed conflicts, the ICRC must be granted
    regular access to all persons deprived of their liberty in order to
    verify the conditions of their detention and to restore contacts
    between those persons and their families.**
B. **In non-international armed conflicts, the ICRC may offer its ser-
    vices to the parties to the conflict with a view to visiting all persons
    deprived of their liberty for reasons related to the conflict in order
    to verify the conditions of their detention and to restore contacts
    between those persons and their families.**

For the first time in this Chapter, the Rule is clearly divided into two parts
depending on the type of the armed conflict. The wording of Rule 124 A

---

[105] Geneva Convention IV, Arts. 136–137 and 140.   [106] See chapter 11.
[107] *The Gulf 1990–91, From Crisis to Conflict, The ICRC at Work* (Geneva: ICRC, 1991)
     chapter 11 in general on the issue, in particular pp. 24–26, 39–40.

is inspired by Article 126 of Geneva Convention III and Article 143 of Geneva Convention IV. Although both treaty provisions mention the verification of the conditions for detention, none of them specifically provides for restoration of contacts between the persons deprived of liberty and their families. While the former is indeed supported fully by the State practice gathered in the Commentary, where most of the materials mention access to POWs camps rather than to both civilian internees and prisoners of war, the essential evidence for the latter is more likely to be found in the Commentary to the subsequent Rule 125.

Notwithstanding its roots in common Article 3 of the Geneva Conventions and Article 18(1) of Additional Protocol II, it is difficult to regard Rule 124B as a customary international law norm as such. The making of an offer by ICRC to visit the persons deprived of liberty and its acceptance or lack of it by the parties to the conflict are both entirely optional. Even though the Study does not generally provide much support in respect of that Rule, it is useful to see some examples of State practice of acceptance of the ICRC services in non-international armed conflicts.

Rule 125

Persons deprived of their liberty must be allowed to correspond with their families, subject to reasonable conditions relating to the frequency and the need for censorship by the authorities.

The right to correspondence or communication is one of the most important privileges of persons whose liberty is restricted or taken away. The ability to inform family or friends about the detainees' whereabouts and their well-being as well as to receive information back from those closest to them can sometimes be life-saving. ICRC efforts as the intermediary are extremely valuable.

The Rule unquestionably must be regarded as customary in international conflicts. Its normative status is sufficiently illustrated by the provisions set out in the numerous military manuals and national legislation as well as some examples of actual conduct of States. The most logical interpretation of 'reasonable conditions' with respect to the frequency of correspondence would be that the volume of the correspondence could be limited in certain circumstances. This interpretation ensues from the collected State practice; to avoid the need to elaborate upon 'reasonable conditions' the Rule could have simply indicated the limitation.

Again, in respect of non-international armed conflict certain doubts arise. Military manuals[108] and domestic legislation[109] are not particularly helpful in establishing a trail of strong evidence supporting this Rule's customary status. If nothing else, supporting material is contained in the accounts of the Red Cross experiences as intermediary in non-international armed conflicts. Particularly interesting are brief comments noting conflicts in Sri Lanka, Liberia and Colombia included in Volume I, but not recalled in Volume II.[110]

Rule 126

Civilian internees and persons deprived of their liberty in connection with a non-international armed conflict must be allowed to receive visitors, especially near relatives, to the degree practicable.

The explanation to this Rule states that State practice establishes this Rule as a norm of customary international law without the usual specification in respect of both types of conflict.[111] It must be inferred from the text that the relevant parts of the evidence in support of this Rule would refer to civilian detainees with regard to international conflicts and to persons deprived of liberty in non-international conflicts. In fact not much practice at all is advanced in support of this Rule irrespective of the application. It is reasonable to think that the authors wanted to differentiate this particular norm from others in that it may well be a developing custom as opposed to an established one. The present writer would be compelled to accept such an approach, bearing in mind the significant accounts again drawn from ICRC experiences in recent non-international armed conflicts.[112]

---

[108] There seems to be an underlying approach of stretching the application of military manuals to non-international conflicts despite a lack of any specific indication to that end therein. See Study, Vol. I, 447, fn. 124 pointing to, for example, the military manuals of Australia, Benin, Croatia, Germany, Madagascar, Nicaragua, Senegal and Togo. The logic seems to be that if the regulation mentions in broad terms the 'captured combatants' or 'civilians', or 'detainees', then by analogy it is regarded as applicable in non-international armed conflicts. Even if we were to accept such approach, the inconsistency here remains visible; for instance the Romanian 'Soldiers Manual' is not listed, despite its similar provision, yet the Nicaraguan military code appears but it seems to refer to POWs only.

[109] A similar problem as in the note above surfaces here too. Azerbaijan's law (para. 506) relates to POWs in a given example whereas Rwanda's Prison Order (para. 510) resembles a protection drawn from human rights law applicable in the ordinary prisons.

[110] Study, Vol. I, 447.   [111] Study, Vol. I, 448.   [112] Study, Vol. I, 449.

Rule 127

The personal convictions and religious practices of persons deprived of their liberty must be respected.

Religious freedom of POWs was incorporated in the 1899 and 1907 Hague Regulations,[113] set out in both Geneva Prisoner of War Conventions[114] and confirmed in the trial of Tanaka Chuichi and two others before an Australian Military Court, where the accused were found guilty of ill-treatment of POWs by cutting the prisoners' hair and beards and forcing them to smoke.[115] The prisoners were Sikhs, whose religion prohibited such behaviour. Enforcing such treatment clearly amounted to infringement of their religious beliefs. These days we would most likely classify it under inhuman treatment subject to prosecution for grave breaches of the Geneva Conventions.

A modern-day example of abuse of this guarantee is the 2005 desecration of the Koran at the Guantánamo Bay detention facility. Following initial media reports and public acknowledgment from the ICRC, the US military conducted an investigation, which confirmed at least five incidents of gross mishandling of the Koran by US personnel.[116] Further allegations of maltreatment were made in relation to cross-gender searches performed on detainees as well as a use of female interrogators to sexually torment prisoners while referring to their religion.[117] Deprivation of religious items might have been inflicted as a form of punishment.[118]

Respect for religious practices and convictions of all those who found themselves in occupied territory was already protected by Article 46 of the Hague Regulations. Article 93 of Geneva Convention IV expanded this protection but only with regard to security detainees, whether in occupied territories or in the territory of the party of

---

[113] Art. 18 in Hague Regulation IV. Obligations to respect religious convictions of all persons were also provided in Art. 46.

[114] Art. 16 of 1929 Geneva Convention and Art. 34 of Geneva Convention III.

[115] *Tanaka Chuichi et al.* case (Australian Military Court at Rabaul, 1946), 11 *LRTWC* 62. Reference to the case is included only in the Commentary to Rule 104, which deals with the fundamental guarantee of respect for convictions and religious practices of civilians and persons *hors de combat*: Study, Vol. I, 377.

[116] 'Red Cross 'raised Koran concerns', BBC News, 19 May 2005. See also US Southern Command Press Release, 3 June 2005, available at: www.voanews.com/mediaassets/english/2005_06/Other/pdf/PR050603.pdf.

[117] Report on Torture and Cruel, Inhuman and Degrading Treatment of Prisoners at Guantánamo Bay, Cuba, Centre for Constitutional Rights, New York, July 2006, pp. 24–29.

[118] *Ibid.*, p. 27.

conflict if the person was not a national of that State. Spiritual assistance to detained or interned individuals in non-international armed conflicts is also secured by treaty law (Article 4.1 and Article 5.1(d) of Additional Protocol II). The significant majority of State practice, however relates to armed conflicts of international character and as such certainly supports the existence of the customary humanitarian law norm.

Rule 128

A. Prisoners of war must be released and repatriated without delay after the cessation of active hostilities.

B. Civilian internees must be released as soon as the reasons which necessitated internment no longer exist, but at the latest as soon as possible after the close of active hostilities.

C. Persons deprived of their liberty in relation to a non-international armed conflict must be released as soon as the reasons for the deprivation of their liberty cease to exist.

The persons referred to may continue to be deprived of their liberty if penal proceedings are pending against them or if they are serving a sentence lawfully imposed.

This Rule concerns an area which has been the subject of heightened controversy throughout the decades and most recently in the context of the so-called 'War on Terror'. With a few hundred detainees entering the sixth year of their captivity in Guantánamo Bay and the United States Supreme Court abstaining from addressing the issue in its *Hamdan* opinion[119] the need for clarification of the law is urgent.

The Rule is divided into three separate Rules, each pertaining to a different group of persons deprived of liberty; the first two are in the context of international armed conflict whilst Rule C concerns armed conflicts of non-international character. The evidence in support of this Rule as a whole is divided into subsections dealing with various elements of the release and return of persons deprived of liberty. These elements include issues pertaining to non-delayed or unconditional release and exchange of prisoners. They also deal with the voluntary nature of return, responsibility for safe repatriation and the role of neutral intermediaries in that process.

---

[119] *Hamdan v. Rumsfeld*, United States Supreme Court, 29 June 2006, 548 U.S. (Supreme Court Reports) 196.

Rules A and B are both strongly rooted in treaty law. Both the Third and Fourth Geneva Conventions have similar formulations. In case of POWs, similar obligations had already been incorporated in the Lieber Code and the Oxford Manual; Article 20 of the 1899/1907 Hague Regulations required speedy repatriation of POWs after the conclusion of peace. The 1929 Geneva Prisoners of War Convention specified that repatriation should take place as soon as an armistice had been concluded. Neither of these formulations proved sufficient in situations when an armistice is never concluded and when a peace is reached long after the end of hostilities. The 1949 Geneva Conventions provisions aimed to rectify these inadequacies; however, whilst securing the right of the detainees or internees to be released and repatriated, they failed to take into account the consent of individuals to be repatriated.[120] This proved to be historically a contentious issue, both in theory and in practice.

Captivity may be terminated by death, successful escape or release in the course of exchange, parole or simply repatriation. As a general rule civilian internees should be released without delay at the end of hostilities or the end of active hostilities in relation to POWs (or occupation, which is omitted in the Rule formulation), except those against whom criminal charges are pending. During hostilities however, civilians must be released as soon as the reasons necessitating the internment cease, while POWs may be subject to direct repatriation or neutral transfer only in compelling medical cases.[121] The Conventions foresee special repatriation agreements to be signed by the parties to the conflict, of which there is renewed use in recent conflicts.[122]

Since the end of World War II two aspects of release and repatriation have been particularly debated, one related to the delays of repatriation and one to the involuntary nature of the return. Some German and Austrian POWs were not released by the Soviets until 1956; India kept Pakistani POWs for over two years in the early 1970s, while some prisoners during the Vietnam and Iran–Iraq conflicts were kept captive at least for seven years.[123] Criticism and condemnation started to surface in relation to such prolonged captivity, which could be considered in terms of inhumane treatment. In 1977 Additional Protocol I provided

[120] The wider issue of forcible return of all displaced persons is discussed in chapter 13.
[121] Arts.132–134 Fourth Geneva Convention, Arts.109–110 and 118–119 of Third Geneva Convention.
[122] See Study Vol. I, 455; but compare H. Levie, 'Violations of Human Rights in Time of War as War Crimes' (1995) 24 *Israel Yearbook of Human Rights* 119.   [123] *Ibid.*

STATUS AND TREATMENT OF PRISONERS OF WAR 333

that an unjustified delay in repatriation was a grave breach of the Protocol.

The problem with a delay in repatriation is closely linked to the notion of 'end of hostilities' and in the case of POWs 'end of active hostilities'. There is an ongoing discussion as to how these terms should be interpreted, especially in light of the recent controversial Security Council resolutions in the context of the 2003 conflict in Iraq (like resolution 1546 (2004)) or certain official statements declaring the end of war.[124] The Study does not provide any assistance in this context.

The issue of enforced repatriation of detainees involves other problems. Quickly repatriated by United Kingdom at the end of World War II, Russian prisoners were treated as traitors, faced charges of 'aiding the enemy' and were sent to Gulags for years of forced labour, or were shot on arrival. Desperate to avoid such a fate, some detainees awaiting repatriation against their wishes committed suicide. During the armistice negotiations following the end of the Korean War, the United Nations Unified Command resisted the position of North Korea, China and the USSR demanding the repatriation of all POWs, even against their wishes. The argument evolved around the interpretation of the right of the prisoner to be repatriated. In the USSR view it was the State's right to have the prisoners repatriated and thus the corresponding duty to repatriate rested on the State of origin.[125] This interpretation failed, since the UN General Assembly affirmed the Unified Command position, allowing voluntary repatriation exercised by the prisoners and based on freedom to return home. This soon transformed into the more stringent principle of no forced repatriation, based on the freedom of choice ascertained by the prisoners, as exemplified in the Iran–Iraq conflict, the Gulf Wars and in the Dayton Peace Agreement. In 2006, a group of Muslim Uighurs, Chinese nationals and former Guantánamo Bay detainees were granted asylum by Albania upon their release from detention. After four years of continued incarceration with no charges pressed, the United States refused to return them to China due to human rights concerns, which was in accordance with the prisoner's preferences too.

Professor Meron notes that interpretation based on human rights influenced practice has effectively remodelled Article 118 of Geneva Convention III in the past years.[126] It is a pity that the Study does not

---

[124] 'President Bush Announces Combat Operations in Iraq Have Ended', White House, 1 May 2003, at www.whitehouse.gov/news/releases/2003/05/iraq/20030501-15.html.
[125] T. Meron, *The Humanization of International Law* (Leiden: Martinus Nijhoff, 2006), pp. 41–45.   [126] *Ibid.*

address these important issues in the Commentary to the Rule as it does through a wealth of sources in Volume II. This is probably the most substantiated Rule in this chapter and the authors must be commended for gathering this truly impressive record. Two separate sections deal with the issue of undue delay and voluntary return. The authors rightly view Rules 128A and B as customary international law norms; however a qualification should be made in the text of the Rule to incorporate the problem of involuntary repatriation by, for example, adding the following: *Prisoners of War objecting to repatriation to their country of origin should be offered an alternative destination.*

Searching for examples substantiating the customary nature of Rule 128C is not easy, and upon closer examination is slightly disappointing, perhaps because of the volume of evidence accompanying Rules 128A and B.[127] It is submitted that although perhaps not yet fully matured, this customary norm may well be developing.

3. Final remarks

Although the present writer may not agree with the authors of the Study regarding some of the Rules' applicability in non-international armed conflicts, the assessment of the customary law status is not the most troublesome issue in her view. More disconcerting is the lack of some pertinent issues related to POWs in particular and to other persons deprived of liberty: for example, those who cannot benefit from the protection of the Geneva Conventions. These include: presumption of POW status under Article 45 of Additional Protocol I (or otherwise Article 5 of Geneva Convention III); special protections during interrogations (namely the right not to answer questions); and judicial safeguards especially for those who are accused of committing offences prior to hostilities (Article 85), to name a few. In light of current developments it is unfortunate that the Study does not contain any reference to the practice of States in this field.

These provisions are specific to POW status and treatment and it is not clear that the decision not to include a separate chapter dedicated to POWs was a correct one. The Study invokes treaty law as justification in so far 'the Third Geneva Convention is considered to be part of

---

[127] One has to review all 350 paragraphs to extract the relevant sources. It could have been more practicable to organise the State practice in accordance with the structure of the Rule itself, namely to have two parts, one relating to Rules A and B and the other to C.

customary international law and, in any event, binds almost all States as a matter of treaty law.' It difficult to accept this as sufficient reasoning behind (a) the non-inclusion of some of the rules and practice relative to POWs in the Study and (b) the customary status of norms confirmed by the existence of the appropriate treaty and not because of State practice supported by *opinio iuris*. The very origins and the overwhelming wealth of the norms relative to POWs are placed in the customs of war. The many protections listed above might have been incorporated in the Study, had the structure of the book made allowance for at least some of the specifics of the POW legal regime in a separate part.

The Rules relative to persons deprived of liberty are as general as they could be to encompass all the categories of detainees, whether in international or non-international armed conflict. All eleven Rules, except for Rule 124A and Rules 128A and B presented in Chapter 37 of the Study ('Persons deprived of their liberty'), are indicated to apply as customary rules in non-international conflicts. There is a strong tendency in the commentary to support the Rules' customary status by a reliance on the relevant parts of Additional Protocol II. If this approach is followed, we are left with the very basic minimum of protections, which are correct as they stand but fail to accommodate certain particularities of treatment afforded otherwise to protected persons or POWs and that should not be neglected. Admittedly some of these are considered in the context of Fundamental Guarantees, like prohibition of pillage or religious safeguards, but this does not assist with clarity on the matter. Furthermore, the general impression from the review of the Rules deemed to be applicable to non-international armed conflicts is that the majority of sources relied upon by the Study derive from international human rights law. This indeed may be a likely result, as even the original treaty norms are inspired by the appropriate human rights standards[128] and undoubtedly certain human rights norms are applicable in the situation of armed conflict.[129] Nonetheless, as discussed elsewhere, doubt arises whether human rights law should be considered as evidence (and if so, to what extent and bringing what value) in support of the customary status of international humanitarian law rules.

A final point to note is that the Rules must not be taken on their own. The Commentary that follows each of the Rules can be helpful in

---

[128] Sandoz, Swinarski and Zimmermann, *Commentary on the Additional Protocols*, p. 1365 in particular para. 4509.

[129] J. Pejic, 'Procedural Principles and Safeguards', at 377–379, 382–383 *et seq.*

understanding its full framework, with possible exceptions. Due to its great assistance in this respect the Commentary might be further expanded to accommodate some additional comments, in line with the position set out in Volume II on a particular matter, such as in the case of Rule 128.

13

Displacement and displaced persons

RYSZARD PIOTROWICZ

1. Introduction

The displacement of people from their homes, regions and even their countries is a common feature of armed conflicts. Indeed the manner in which armed conflicts are conducted makes it almost inevitable: battles are fought not apart from the civilian population but frequently amongst it and even against it. This means that civilians may be forced to flee a conflict simply in order to save their own lives, leaving their homes and often their possessions unattended, at the mercy of those who remain behind or of incoming combatants and civilians. The picture is, however, even bleaker when one considers that civilians may be deliberately displaced by the threat or use of force, either as a means simply of weakening the other side, or else as part of a wider, longer-term strategy to alter the ethnic composition of a particular territory.

Displacement occurs during both international and non-international armed conflicts. In either case those affected may find themselves either outside the territory of their own State (in which case they may be considered refugees in the wider sense of the term),[1] or else in another area of their own State, in which case they are generally referred to as internally displaced persons (IDPs).

Displaced persons (DPs) and IDPs may be seen as victims twice over in the sense that, having been present on a territory where armed conflict is taking place, they are subject to the usual risks attached to such conflicts but the situation is exacerbated because they have had to flee their homes. They may well be destitute and are certainly very vulnerable. On the other hand their new location may be less vulnerable to the immediate threats arising out of the conflict.

---

[1] That is, they are not necessarily refugees within the meaning of the Convention Relating to the Status of Refugees 1951 as amended, which requires that the individual have a well-founded fear of persecution based on a rather narrow range of grounds.

The needs, and vulnerabilities, of DPs and IDPs may vary considerably. Those evacuated from a territory and given temporary refuge in a prosperous State where no conflict is taking place, and where they may receive substantial social benefits, are in a significantly better position than those who may have been housed in some temporary location not far from the conflict. Furthermore, not every IDP is a victim of an armed conflict: as the Guiding Principles on Internally Displaced Persons[2] make clear, one can become an IDP as a consequence of an armed conflict but also due to natural (e.g., floods and earthquakes) or man-made disasters (e.g., nuclear fall-out), or situations of generalised human rights violations which have not reached the threshold required to be considered a non-international armed conflict.

Whether the displacement has been caused by an international or a non-international armed conflict, obligations arise under international humanitarian law but may also exist, significantly, under human rights law and refugee law. A variety of scenarios is possible, giving rise to obligations on the part of the State where the DPs or IDPs are located:

- international armed conflict: civilians are displaced within their own country, within the territory of another party to the conflict (either opposing the State of nationality or allied to it), or within a third State not party to the conflict;
- non-international armed conflict: civilians are displaced within their own State or in another State.

From these scenarios it may be seen that various legal regimes may be relevant. In the case of an international armed conflict the 1949 Geneva Conventions will apply, as will Additional Protocol I of 1977 to those States that have ratified or acceded; States which are not parties to the conflict but which have DPs on their territory are obliged to 'ensure respect' for the Conventions (by virtue of common Article 1) and will thus also be bound to apply the relevant provisions of the Conventions. In a non-international armed conflict, at least common Article 3 will apply, as well as Protocol II for those States that are bound by it. Displacement is prohibited by the Geneva Conventions and Protocols, as well as the Rome Statute of the International Criminal Court.

Also relevant in either type of conflict may be the law of international protection, which indicates whether the displaced are entitled to refugee

[2] UN Doc. E/CN.4/1998/53/Add.2.

status or some form of complementary (subsidiary) protection. In addition, States with IDPs and DPs are of course bound by their human rights obligations towards those under their jurisdiction, whether they are nationals or not.

The relationship of international humanitarian law to human rights law is considered in detail elsewhere.[3] However, it should be noted here that human rights law appears to play a large role in the treatment at least of IDPs in the Study. This aspect will be considered further below.

The Rules do not suggest how they might apply to military forces engaged in peace operations. This is part of a wider issue of how international humanitarian law applies to peace operations and it is potentially problematic here, for example where forces with a limited international mandate are confronted with the reality of people in flight.

Sources used

Chapter 38 of the Study contains the Rules proposed for forced displacement of civilians for reasons related to an armed conflict. The chapter is striking for its reliance on sources derived from human rights law (including refugee law) to substantiate rules of international humanitarian law. This might appear to strengthen the notion that the protection of human rights during armed conflicts is not the monopoly of international humanitarian law. Nevertheless there is a risk here: whereas derogation is not permitted from international humanitarian law it is of course sometimes allowed with regard to human rights. There is no doubt that human rights law is relevant to the protection of DPs but that does not mean that it can necessarily be used to substantiate the customary status of rules of international humanitarian law.

Frequent reference is made to the Guiding Principles on Internal Displacement (Principles).[4] The Principles are said to 'reflect and [be] consistent with international human rights law and international humanitarian law'.[5] There is a problem of circularity here, in that the Rules derive (partially) from the Principles, which are said in part to reflect international humanitarian law. Furthermore, the Principles have not received widespread or unequivocal acceptance by States. To the extent that they reflect existing international humanitarian law or human

---

[3] Chapter 3.
[4] See Study, Vol. I, 461, 465, 467 (footnotes 66, 69), 468–470, 472.   [5] *Ibid.*, para. 3.

rights law they are of course binding but that is the point: to what extent do they reflect the law?

This problem may be addressed by considering what other practice is cited with regard to the asserted Rules. In each case that the Principles are cited, Volume II of the Study lists substantial other practice. In other words, reliance is not placed on the Principles alone. On the other hand, some of that other practice includes human rights instruments, the relevance of which to the establishment of customary rules of international humanitarian law is arguable. There are indeed human rights obligations that *apply* during armed conflicts, but their relevance is founded first of all on the fact that States have accepted them as human rights obligations. That is something quite different from asserting that they are relevant to the elucidation of customary rules of international humanitarian law, which in the first place are derived from the practice of States in the context of armed conflicts. Accordingly, it can be problematic to rely on human rights law as such to establish customary rules of international humanitarian law, unless States, in their practice, have evinced a belief that such rules are relevant to the way in which they apply humanitarian law.[6]

A second potentially problematic aspect of reliance upon human rights law and refugee law concerns what entities are bound by the law. While it is widely accepted that non-governmental armed groups are bound by international humanitarian law (even not taking into account recent developments in international criminal law), it is not necessarily the case that they are bound by human rights law. There has been substantial debate on whether human rights may be owed directly by one individual to another.[7] The obligation frequently found in human rights instruments for States not only to respect the relevant rights but to *ensure* their protection, suggests that they may be breached by non-State actors. Even if so, the consequences for breach lie with the State rather than the perpetrator, whose accountability remains confined to criminal law and perhaps tort.

---

[6] This issue, which is addressed more fully in chapter 3 above, is dealt with at p. xxxi, Introduction to the Study.

[7] See, for example, S. McInerney, 'The European Convention on Human Rights and the Evolution of Fundamental Rights in the Private Domain', in C. Harding and C.L. Lim (eds.), *Renegotiating Westphalia* (The Hague/Boston/London: Martinus Nijhoff Publishers, 1999) pp. 307–315. See also United Nations Human Rights Committee, General Comment No. 31 [80], The Nature of the General Legal Obligation Imposed on States Parties to the Covenant, 26 May 2004, CCPR/C/21/Rev.1/Add.13, para. 8. On the interface with human rights, see further, chapter 3.

If indeed only States are bound by human rights law, questions arise again about the reliance on such human rights sources to establish rules of international humanitarian law that purport to bind non-governmental armed groups. There is no doubt that human rights law remains applicable during armed conflicts. But the fact that human rights law on the face of it places obligations on States only means that it is problematic to use it as evidence of customary rules of international humanitarian law which may be binding on non-State actors.

2. The Rules

Rule 129

A. **Parties to an international armed conflict may not deport or forcibly transfer the civilian population of an occupied territory, in whole or in part, unless the security of the civilians involved or imperative military reasons so demand.**
B. **Parties to a non-international armed conflict may not order the displacement of the civilian population, in whole or in part, for reasons related to the conflict, unless the security of the civilians involved or imperative military reasons so demand.**

Rule 129A prohibits the deportation or forcible transfer of the civilian population of an *occupied* territory, one of the few Rules related to occupation. The purpose of the prohibition is to minimise the disruption of the lives of civilians in the first place, but also to prevent deportations motivated by a policy of exploitation (for example, deportation for forced labour) or by the desire to alter the ethno-geographic configuration of the population.

Substantial recent authority is cited, though some of the State practice cited refers to 'illegal' or 'unlawful' deportations, suggesting that at least some deportations may not be prohibited.[8] However, one must be careful not to misrepresent the position: most of the practice, in referring to illegal or unlawful deportations, is simply accepting that they may sometimes be permissible to protect the security of the civilian population or for imperative military reasons. To that extent the practice supports the Rule, which is clearly aimed at protecting the civilian population *during* an armed conflict.

---

[8] For example, Study, Vol. II, Part 2, Chapter 38, paras. 41–42 (Australia).

Under Article 49(1) of Geneva Convention IV, 'individual or mass forcible transfers, as well as deportations of protected persons from occupied territory to the territory of the Occupying Power or to that of any other country, occupied or nor, are prohibited, regardless of their motive'. Evacuation of the civilian population is only permitted under that Article if its security or imperative military reasons so demand, and then subject to strict conditions. The notion of evacuation is different from deportation; it is intended to protect the population being evacuated rather than to allow removal as such.[9] Deportations and forced transfers are always unlawful; evacuations may be permissible. In this respect the wording of the Rule is unfortunate because it suggests that *deportations* or *forcible transfers* may in fact be lawful if they can be justified by the need to ensure the security of those affected, or else due to imperative military reasons. Unlawful deportations or transfers are a grave breach (Article 147).[10]

Given the accepted customary international law status of the Conventions,[11] Article 49(1) strongly supports the accuracy of Rule 129A as an expression of custom. While the precise wording is not identical, the crucial elements are repeated, that is, the prohibition on deportations and forcible transfers. The one difference is the reference to the 'civilian population' rather than 'protected persons'. Much more recent recognition of the illegality of forced transfers is found in the Statute of the International Criminal Court, which recognises that unlawful deportations may be a war crime[12] and a crime against humanity.[13]

The one example of State practice cited against the prohibition on deportations is that of Israel, a State which might be deemed a partial persistent objector,[14] on the basis that the Supreme Court of Israel has maintained on several occasions that Article 49 of Geneva Convention IV was not intended to apply to the deportation of selected individuals for reasons of public order or security, or else that Article 49 was not part of customary international law: two quite different justifications, the

---

[9] S. Jaquemet, 'The Cross-fertilization of International Humanitarian Law and International Refugee Law' (2001) 83 *International Review of the Red Cross* 651, at 670.

[10] *Ibid.*, Art. 147.

[11] *Legality of the Threat or Use of Nuclear Weapons*, Advisory Opinion of 8 July 1996, [1996] *ICJ Rep.* 66, para. 81: 'The part of conventional international humanitarian law which has beyond doubt become part of international customary law is the law applicable in armed conflict as embodied in: the Geneva Conventions of 12 August 1949'; but see discussion of this issue in chapter 2 above, p. 32.

[12] Rome Statute, Art. 8(2)(a)(vii), Art. 8(2)(b)(viii), Art. 8(2)(e)(viii).

[13] *Ibid.*, Art. 7(1)(d).   [14] Study, Vol. I, 458–459.

former contesting the substance of the rule, the latter its status. The Rule as stated does not (perhaps deliberately) distinguish between citizens and non-citizens. Normally a State is not obliged to permit non-citizens to remain on its territory in the absence of some specific entitlement, such as refugee status or a permanent residence permit. However, an occupying State is in a different position: it does not have sovereignty over the territory and it has no authority as such to remove non-citizens or citizens. Furthermore, Article 4 of Geneva Convention IV is clear that non-citizens in occupied territory may be protected persons and hence covered by Article 49.[15] The Israeli objection to the customary status of the rule is difficult to justify; furthermore the legality of Israel's actions has been consistently challenged as a breach of Article 49 of Geneva Convention IV.[16] The vast majority of the State practice appears to accept both the customary status of the rule as well as its applicability to both individual and mass deportations.[17] Accordingly, the objections of the Israeli court both to the status and the substance of the rule do not appear sustainable.

However, international humanitarian law does not necessarily cease to operate immediately a conflict is over. At least some of the rules of occupation may apply for a long time afterwards.[18] This is relevant because in the period after the close of hostilities there may be significant population movements. The Study does not take account of the expulsion of the German and Polish populations towards the end, and in the aftermath, of World War II. These expulsions occurred at roughly the same time that the Nuremberg Tribunal, which is cited as authority in the Study,[19] was preparing to prosecute German nationals for, *inter alia*, forced deportations and transfers. Poland was factually, if not legally, occupying

---

[15] Geneva Convention IV, Art. 4 states: 'Persons protected by the Convention are those who, at a given moment and in any manner whatsoever, find themselves, in case of a conflict or occupation, in the hands of a Party to the conflict or Occupying Power of which they are not nationals.'

[16] See, for example, Study, Vol. II, Part 2, Chapter 38, para. 186: Note from the Swiss Government protesting against Israel's deportation from the West Bank of the Jordan of Palestinian activists.

[17] There is, however, contrary practice from 1945 that does not appear to have been taken into account in the Study.

[18] Geneva Convention IV, Art. 6(3) provides that, for twelve months after the close of military operations, GCIV continues to apply to occupied territory after which core obligations remain valid for the period of occupation (including Art. 49).

[19] Study, Vol. I, 457–458, referring to Article 6(b) of the Charter of the International Military Tribunal at Nuremberg, which makes 'deportation to slave labour or for any other purpose of civilian population of or in occupied territory' a war crime.

344   RYSZARD PIOTROWICZ

territory that was under German sovereignty at the time. Germany had been subjugated and placed under occupation (and remained so for several years). Poland controlled territory containing millions of Germans and expelled them under the instructions of the countries that ran the Nuremberg trials.[20]

Nor is there mention of the 1952 study of this matter by the *Institut de Droit International,*[21] which recognised the possibility of lawful transfer in some situations, particularly in the case of implacable opposition to the State by individuals.[22] If the 1945 practice is not seen as an exception, then it potentially weakens Rule 129A. It is most unlikely, however, that the expulsions of 1945 would be regarded as lawful today, particularly given the widespread revulsion to ethnic cleansing and the legal response through the development of international criminal law that clearly condemns this practice. If so, a clear repudiation in the Study would have helped. In the *Simić*[23] case, for example, the International Criminal Tribunal for Yugoslavia issued a very clear condemnation of deportation and forcible transfer, suggesting that it could only be lawful, even if justification were claimed under Geneva Convention IV, Article 49, 'in the gravest of circumstances and only as measures of last resort'.[24] Furthermore, transfer based on agreements concluded by others, such as 'military commanders or other representatives of parties in a conflict cannot make a displacement lawful'.[25] Individuals must give genuine, i.e. free, personal consent to be moved for it not to be a forced displacement.[26]

---

[20] At Potsdam it had been agreed that 'the transfer to Germany of German populations, or elements thereof, remaining in Poland, Czechoslovakia and Hungary, will have to be undertaken'. Potsdam Protocol, Paragraph XII, *Selected Documents on Germany and the Question of Berlin 1944–1961*, Cmnd. 1552, Doc. No.7, 38.

[21] (1952) 44 *Annuaire de l'Institut de Droit International*, Vol. II, at 138–199.

[22] 'Nous n'avons pas nié toute possibilité de transfert et nous le reconnaissons particulièrement utile dans les cas où l'opposition des individus à l'État est irréductible', *ibid.*, p. 149. There were decidedly mixed and ambivalent conclusions about the legality of the transfers authorised by the Potsdam Agreement: see pp. 180, 190 and 192 of this Institut report. Brownlie has argued, admittedly long ago, that '[e]xpulsion . . . of populations may occur by agreement and are lawful provided certain conditions are observed', citing the Potsdam Agreement as a case in point: I. Brownlie, 'The Relations of Nationality in Public International Law' (1963) 39 *British Yearbook of International Law* 284, at 324. The same writer suggested, around the same time, that 'measures of security intended to prevent future threats to the peace may include movement of populations': I. Brownlie, *International Law and the Use of Force by States* (Oxford University Press, 1963), p. 408. The Potsdam Agreement is cited as an example.

[23] *Prosecutor v. Simić, Tadić, and Zarić*, Judgment of Trial Chamber, 17 October 2003, No. IT-95-9-T.   [24] *Ibid.*, para. 125, fn 218.   [25] *Ibid.*, para. 127.   [26] *Ibid.* para. 128.

Not all of the practice cited is quite on point. Article 3 of the Convention Against Torture, which prohibits expulsion or return of a person to another State where there exist substantial grounds to believe that the person is at risk of being tortured there, prohibits the deportation of people at risk of being tortured, not deportation *as such*, which is what Rule 129A suggests.[27] In fact, that provision is better seen as an aspect of the wider prohibition of *refoulement*. The Study's reliance on the Convention Against Torture could suggest that the expulsion is legitimate so long as the person is unlikely to be tortured.

A further inconsistency is the citation (in paragraph 2) of Article 45(4) of Geneva Convention IV in support of Rule 129. This provision deals with aliens in the territory of a party to an armed conflict. It provides a rather generous protection against *refoulement* of foreigners during international armed conflicts:

> In no circumstances shall a protected person be transferred to a country where he or she may have reason to fear persecution for his or her political opinions or religious beliefs.

On the face of it this is a more stringent requirement than the equivalent provision of the Refugees Convention, which requires a 'well-founded' fear of persecution in the State of nationality to exist before an entitlement to asylum may arise.[28] Some element of reasonableness ought perhaps to be read into this. While the text refers merely to the individual 'having reason' to fear persecution, it is suggested that such reasons must be coherent and relevant in that they would indicate that the individual might face a real chance of persecution if deported. On the other hand the provision is narrower than the Refugees Convention definition in that it does not include fear of persecution based on race, nationality or membership of a particular social group.

That substantive matter aside, there is an issue of the relevance of Article 45(4) to Rule 129. Article 45(4) addresses the treatment of foreigners located on the non-occupied territory of a State at conflict, who may be settled there or present temporarily. Such persons would not be covered by Rule 129A, which relates to the civilian population of occupied territory. Furthermore, the tenor of Article 45 is that aliens on non-occupied territory of a party to an international conflict may be transferred, subject to certain restrictions. However, aliens present on

---

[27] Study, Vol. II, Part 2, 2910, para. 12.
[28] Convention relating to the Status of Refugees 1951, Art. 1A(2).

territory that is subsequently occupied would be entitled to the protections contained in Section III of Geneva Convention IV.

Despite this inconsistency, there is nevertheless much support for the customary status of the prohibition of *refoulement*, where the forced return of an individual would expose them to a real risk of being subjected to torture or cruel, inhuman or degrading treatment or punishment as well as for a strong, but not absolute, prohibition where the individual would face a threat of persecution or a threat to life, physical integrity or liberty.[29] This has also been recognised to apply during armed conflicts.[30]

Rule 129B prohibits displacement of the civilian population 'for reasons related to the conflict'. The question arises whether there could be a displacement for a reason that is *not* related to the conflict, such as owing to natural disaster. The way that the Rule is phrased suggests that if displacement is caused for some other reason, the rules of non-international armed conflict are irrelevant because it has nothing to do with the conflict and is therefore not covered by international humanitarian law. The range of the prohibition therefore depends on how widely the phrase 'for reasons related to the conflict' is interpreted.

The wording of the Rule is very similar, though not identical, to the first sentence of Article 17(1) of Additional Protocol II.[31] The

---

[29] E. Lauterpacht and D. Bethlehem, 'The Scope and Content of the Principle of *non-refoulement*: Opinion', in E. Feller, V. Türk and F. Nicholson (eds.), *Refugee Protection in International Law* (Cambridge University Press, 2003) 87, p. 149ff, and p. 163.

[30] Recent practice that reflects this includes core components of the European Union common asylum policy. Council Directive 2004/83/EC of 29 April 2004 on minimum standards for the qualification and status of third country nationals or stateless persons as refugees or as persons who otherwise need international protection and the content of the protection granted (OJ L 304/12), provides that an entitlement to international (subsidiary) protection arises if an individual is at risk of serious harm, which is defined to include 'serious and individual threat to a civilian's life or person by reason of indiscriminate violence in situations of international or internal armed conflict' (Art. 15(c)). Council Directive 2001/55/EC of 20 July 2001 on minimum standards for giving temporary protection in the event of a mass influx of displaced persons and on measures promoting a balance of efforts between member states in receiving such persons and bearing the consequences thereof (OJ L 212/12), provides for temporary protection to be given to those who have 'fled areas of endemic violence or armed conflicts' (Art. 2(c)(i)) as part of a mass influx. That protection shall be applied by Member States 'with due regard for human rights and fundamental freedoms and their obligations regarding *non-refoulement*' (Art. 3(2)).

[31] Additional Protocol II, Art. 17(1) states: 'The displacement of the civilian population shall not be ordered for reasons related to the conflict unless the security of the civilians involved or imperative military reasons so demand.'

prohibition, on the face of it, is on the 'ordering' of displacement rather than the displacement itself. These are clearly different things. To order the commission of an act may be a war crime but so too is its perpetration. Even if it is not carried out the order is itself a breach of international humanitarian law. Yet the two appear to be treated as synonymous.[32] Substantial practice is cited in support of the Rule; in particular its acceptance as a war crime and a crime against humanity in the Rome Statute demonstrates a high degree of acceptance. Overall, there is widespread recognition of the illegality of the ordering of the displacement of the civilian population, particularly in recent practice, that suggests it may have customary status.

Rule 130

States may not deport or transfer parts of their own civilian population into a territory they occupy.

This is stated to be a norm of customary international law with regard to international armed conflict. It would have been clearer had Rules 129 and 130 been regrouped, since, with regard to non-international conflict, Rule 129B (the prohibition of displacement) appears to address the situations envisaged in both Rules 129A and in Rule 130. If, in the course of a non-international conflict, one side moves parts of its population into an area hitherto occupied by a different ethnic group, the situation would appear to be covered by Rule 129B which is the non-international conflict equivalent of Rule 129A, prohibiting the non-deportation of the civilian population from occupied territory during international conflict. It might be clearer to express these prohibitions as three separate Rules:

- Prohibition of deportation or forcible transfer *from* occupied territory during international armed conflict (Rule 129A);
- Prohibition of transfer of civilian population *into* occupied territory during international armed conflict (Rule 130);
- Prohibition of displacement of civilian population during non-international armed conflict (Rule 129B).

---

[32] Study, Vol. I, 459. The same treatment occurs in UK Ministry of Defence, *The Manual of the Law of Armed Conflict* (Oxford University Press, 2004), p. 409, para. 15.53 with regard to Art. 17, although the distinction is noted elsewhere in the same chapter, where, in referring to displacement as a war crime, reference is made to the prohibition of the ordering of displacement rather than the displacement itself: p. 392, para. 15.14.

The Rule restates Article 49(6) of Geneva Convention IV.[33] Such transfers are also a grave breach of Additional Protocol I[34] and a war crime under the Rome Statute.[35] The International Court of Justice relied upon Article 49(6) to find Israel's establishment of settlements in the Occupied Palestinian Territory to be in breach of international humanitarian law.[36] The Court focused on the conventional obligation rather than asserting any customary rule.[37]

Irrespective of the order of presentation of the prohibitions in Rules 129 and 130, they reflect a fundamental value that predates the Geneva Conventions. While the Hague Regulations did not specifically outlaw deportations,[38] it has been suggested that this is because the silence on the matter was 'evidence of a self-understood rule'.[39] The problem with taking something as read is that there may then be problems in addressing the matter after the event. The Rules reflect the reality that forced transfers and deportations have been very widely condemned by several international tribunals; they clearly reflect international customary law.

Rule 131

In case of displacement, all possible measures must be taken in order that the civilians concerned are received under satisfactory conditions of shelter, hygiene, health, safety and nutrition and that members of the same family are not separated.

The Rule is arguably expressed too narrowly. It refers simply to the obligation to 'receive' displaced civilians under satisfactory conditions. But sometimes the reception part is just the end of a very long and arduous journey. If States are indeed displacing civilians, surely the obligation should be not only to make sure that reception conditions are adequate, but also that the actual manner and conditions of the displacement also

---

[33] Geneva Convention IV, Art. 49, (6) states: 'The Occupying Power shall not deport or transfer parts of its own civilian population into the territory it occupies.'

[34] Additional Protocol I, Art. 85(4)(a).   [35] Rome Statute, Art. 8(2)(b)(viii).

[36] *Legal Consequences of the Construction of a Wall in the Occupied Palestinian Territory*, ICJ Advisory Opinion of 9 July 2004, at para. 120.

[37] However, in the *Legality of the Threat or Use of Nuclear Weapons*, para. 81, the ICJ made a more general statement regarding the customary status of the Geneva Conventions; this is discussed in chapter 2 above, p. 32.   [38] Hague Regulations IV 1907.

[39] G. Schwarzenberger, *International Law as Applied by International Courts and Tribunals*, *Vol. II, The Law of Armed Conflict* (London: Stevens & Sons Limited, 1968), p. 228.

meet these standards. This is required by Geneva Convention IV[40] and is indeed noted in the Study.[41]

This Rule refers to *any* displacement, both during international and non-international armed conflicts, but the summary and practice there cited refer to displacement that is carried out for security of the civilian population or for imperative military reasons, i.e., lawful displacement.[42] The purpose of the Rule is to promote the humane treatment of those who have been displaced. What about those who are illegally displaced? An illegal displacement will not be legitimised just because it is carried out humanely. Displacement that is not justified by the security needs of the civilian population or imperative military needs will be a war crime.[43] Clearly it is desirable that all displacement, lawful or otherwise, be carried out as humanely as possible. Logic suggests that if lawful displacements must respect certain standards then unlawful ones must also. But customary international law is not required to be logical. The practice does not make this clear, but general principles of international and domestic criminal law demonstrate that the manner in which a crime is committed may exacerbate the offence and lead to a more severe punishment for the perpetrator.[44]

The possibility that the conduct of unlawful displacements might be problematic as far as the attribution of humanitarian responsibilities to the perpetrator is concerned appears to be at least partially recognised in the Study. The Study, rather tentatively, *suggests* that the assistance of the international community may be sought to assist IDPs, and that this might also apply to illegal displacements.[45] In other words, there appears to be some recognition that the rules on how lawful displacements are conducted might not automatically extend to unlawful displacements.

Rule 132

Displaced persons have a right to voluntary return in safety to their homes or places of habitual residence as soon as the reasons for their displacement cease to exist.

---

[40] Geneva Convention IV, Art. 49(3): parties 'shall ensure, to the greatest practicable extent, that proper accommodation is provided to receive the protected persons, that the removals are effected in satisfactory conditions'.

[41] Study, Vol. I, 464–465.   [42] Study, Vol. I, 464.

[43] Rome Statute, Art. 8(2)(b)(viii) and Article 8(2)(e)(viii), regarding international armed conflicts and non-international armed conflicts respectively.

[44] One writer asserts, though without explaining why, that the obligation of protection during displacement applies 'a fortiori' to unlawful displacement: E.C. Gillard, 'The Role of International Humanitarian Law in the Protection of Internally Displaced Persons' (2005) 24 *Refugee Survey Quarterly* 37, p. 41.   [45] Study, Vol. I, 468.

The Rule refers to the right to return; the Practice, rightly, also stresses that return may not be forced where it would cause the breach of certain rights, such as Article 3 of the Convention Against Torture.[46] But that is already to rely on a rule that is not part of international humanitarian law. If there is an obligation under international humanitarian law not to return displaced people it cannot be founded on the Convention Against Torture. In any case, the obligation not only to respect, but to ensure respect, for the Geneva Conventions could include an obligation on States that are not parties to an international or non-international armed conflict not to return individuals to a territory where their basic rights under international humanitarian law might be breached.

The language used in the Rule is that of individuals' rights, rather than States' obligations, but Geneva Convention IV, which is mentioned in the commentary, puts the obligation on States.[47] This apparent shift of emphasis is actually substantive because it purports to create a right that is not found in the Convention itself.

One question raised by this Rule concerns the meaning of 'homes or places of habitual residence'. Is this some kind of *Recht auf die Heimat*? Obviously, most people will want to return to their actual homes if they can – i.e. the very dwellings they used to inhabit, if these dwellings are still standing. In that sense Rule 132 is closely linked to Rule 133. But some of the authority cited[48] is referring to a right to return to one's State of citizenship or nationality. This right certainly exists but is not so specific as the right to return to one's actual home. In some situations it will simply be impossible to return to the actual location where one used to live, even though return to the country, or particular part of the country, itself may be feasible. For IDPs, it may no longer be possible to return to the place from which they fled. The rule stresses not just the country (which would in any case be irrelevant to IDPs) but the place of residence. This might, however, be limited where sovereignty over the territory has changed hands. In that case there is no *Recht auf die Heimat*. If the reference to 'home or place of habitual residence' means the actual home, then clearly there are going to be clashes of law and reality, either because the home does not exist or because others (voluntarily or otherwise) may have moved in.

[46] Study, Vol. II, Part 2, 3010, para. 689.
[47] Geneva Convention IV, Art. 49(2): 'persons . . . evacuated shall be transferred back to their homes as soon as hostilities in the area in question have ceased'.
[48] For example, Study, Vol. II, Part 2, 3010, the human rights treaties at paras. 684–689.

How long do people remain 'displaced', in particular for those in a foreign country where they have integrated? The Rule simply suggests that there is a right to return as soon as the reasons for displacement have ceased to exist. This is most likely to mean after a conflict has finished. A potential problem arises with regard to those who choose to remain, if permitted, in the foreign State: does the right to return subsist indefinitely? This is potentially very problematic because one of the principal political objectives at the end of a conflict is to achieve a settlement of outstanding issues that might give rise to a recurrence. If there is to be an indefinite right to return this could prove highly destabilising. The Rule as stated aims to facilitate speedy return for those who have been displaced. This responds to a humanitarian objective and requires States not to hinder return, but it should arguably apply both ways: where return is objectively feasible, displaced people should be obliged to do so or else to indicate their wish not to return so that greater certainty may be achieved. This is not of course a reference to forced return that puts the individual in danger, as with Cossacks returned forcibly to the USSR after World War II. The Rule, as expressed, is correct but does not tell the whole story: the right of voluntary return, at least where the displaced person is in another country, may also entail a *duty* to return at some point. It is highly debatable whether the host State is obliged to allow aliens to remain on its territory in the absence of an international protection obligation.[49]

One objection to this point could be that the Rule is only setting out the rights of displaced people in this particular situation. It is therefore not necessary to deal with compulsory return as that is not (necessarily) an international humanitarian law issue if the conflict is over or the conditions for their displacement no longer exist. However, it is very clear from the Practice that the Rules have been substantiated frequently by reference to other sources, including human rights law. In other words there is a context, which arguably should include the duty to return, since there is no obligation *as such* on the part of States to permit aliens to remain on the

---

[49] For example, because the individual qualifies for refugee status under the 1951 Convention Relating to the Status of Refugees or can demonstrate an entitlement to subsidiary protection in the sense of the 2004 European Union Council Directive on minimum standards for the qualification and status of third country nationals or stateless persons as refugees or as persons who otherwise need international protection and the content of the protection granted. Art. 15(c) of that instrument recognises 'serious and individual threat to a civilian's life or person by reason of indiscriminate violence in situations of international or internal armed conflict' as a basis for entitlement to protection.

national territory. International humanitarian law clearly is interested in the right of displaced people to return but that is only part of a bigger picture once the conflict is over. If individuals decline to cooperate with reasonable attempts to facilitate speedy and safe return, there should be consequences. The Rule does not appear to take account of this aspect. The relevant practice cited does not address it.[50]

Rule 133
The property rights of displaced persons must be respected.

For this Rule to be effective it must include effective rights of reparation for those whose property has been destroyed or in some way taken over by others, for example by confiscation (officially sanctioned or otherwise), squatting (with housing) or even good faith purchase. Much of the (limited) practice cited seems to support this but the Rule, as expressed, is perhaps too vague. It requires that the term 'property rights' be interpreted to include an effective right to compensation for property of which the individual has been permanently deprived.

3. Final remarks

The principles behind the Rules in Chapter 38 of the Study are firmly established in customary international law. There is in particular a strong prohibition on deportations and forced transfers, which is substantiated by the relevant practice cited in the Study.

On points of detail, the wording of Rule 129A is unfortunate because it may be seen as allowing (wrongly) for the possibility of deportation or forced transfer in limited circumstances; the term 'evacuation' should have been used to clarify the extent of the obligation. The right of voluntary return for displaced persons, as set out in Rule 132, raises different problems. The general principle is clearly stated. However, a number of ancillary issues might have been usefully addressed.

The heavy reliance on human rights law and the Guiding Principles on Internally Displaced Persons is problematic and was not necessary to support the Rules in the light of the existence of other relevant State practice. There is substantial recourse to treaty practice to support Rules; that may be difficult to justify in every case, given that the treaties may have been concluded precisely because the parties wished to engage in specific

---

[50] Study, Vol. II, Part 2, 3009ff, paras. 681–785.

obligations outside general international law. More reliance might have been placed on specific State practice extracted exclusively from the field of international humanitarian law. The Rules are correct as far as they go, but they do not address all the problems that might arise in this area.

14

Implementation and compliance

DAVID TURNS

1. Introduction

Of all the topics in international humanitarian law, arguably none is of more importance than securing compliance with the law's provisions and enforcing the law. Given that armed conflict by its very nature occasions violence, destruction and death, all too often to innocent people, there is little point in having an elaborate system of detailed rules for the conduct of hostilities and the protection of victims in war if there is no corresponding effective system for securing compliance and enforcing those rules. It is all very well having a doctrine of individual criminal responsibility for violations of humanitarian law but criminal proceedings by definition may be brought only after the crime has been committed and the damage done.[1] While war crimes trials are undoubtedly considered more interesting and newsworthy by the media and the public at large, it cannot be doubted that adequate prevention – the task primarily of States, acting through military command hierarchies – is in many respects even more essential to a credible system of legal rules.

Thus, compliance with and enforcement of international humanitarian law at the State level of civil (as opposed to criminal) responsibility, obligations to disseminate the legal rules and incorporate them in domestic legal systems, and ensuring that armed forces are adequately

---

[1] The usefulness of criminal law is aptly demonstrated by the court-martial proceedings in which Corporal Donald Payne of the Duke of Lancaster's Regiment made military legal history by becoming the first British soldier to admit to a war crime under the International Criminal Court Act 2001. Cpl. Payne was one of seven British servicemen facing court-martial on charges related to the death of an Iraqi civilian in British military custody in Basra in September 2003. He pleaded guilty to inhumane treatment of civilians but not guilty to manslaughter and perverting the course of justice under the Army Act 1955. He was sentenced to one year's imprisonment and dismissed from the Army for the 2001 Act charge and acquitted of the other charges, as were the other defendants in the case, for lack of evidence.

instructed in their content, are crucial.[2] By attaining these objectives, States can encourage the observance of the law in armed conflict and ensure that there is a workable system for obtaining enforcement. It follows that the sections of Part VI of the Study that do not deal with individual criminal responsibility and war crimes are at the intersection of the *lex specialis* of international humanitarian law and the *lex generalis* of which it forms a distinct part, namely public international law. In particular, the public international law doctrine of State responsibility is of great importance to this part of the Study – almost to the point where it might be said that Rules 139–150, insofar as they are wholly or partly derived from the 1949 Geneva Conventions, can be characterised as an 'interpretative guide' to those Conventions in the light of the general international law rules on State responsibility.[3] The content of some of the Rules may be found in other treaty instruments that are acknowledged as having crystallised into customary law: Rule 149 on State responsibility, for example, derives in the context of humanitarian law from the 1907 Hague Convention IV.[4]

To the extent that any of the Rules of this Part of the Study are derived more or less verbatim from the Geneva Conventions, such Rules are generally unproblematic. With the recent accession of the last two States in the world that were not previously parties to the Conventions, the latter can now genuinely be said to have attained the status of universal acceptance in international law.[5] The customary law status of the Geneva Conventions as a whole had already been declared a decade earlier by the International Court of Justice when it described the rules therein as, 'fundamental rules [which] are to be observed by all States whether or not they have ratified the conventions that contain them, because they constitute intransgressible principles of international customary law'.[6] Another

---

[2] This was acknowledged by Jean-Philippe Lavoyer, Head of the ICRC Legal Division, in his Official Statement of 22 September 2006, available at: www.icrc.org/web/eng/siteeng0.nsf/html/geneva-conventions-statement-220906?opendocument: 'Certainly, one of the main weaknesses of [humanitarian law] as a whole is the lack of viable enforcement mechanisms', accessed 23 December 2006.

[3] On the law of State responsibility generally, see the International Law Commission's 2001 Draft Articles on Responsibility of States for Internationally Wrongful Acts, adopted by the United Nations General Assembly in Resolution 56/83 of 12 December 2001, UN Doc. A/RES/56/83, (hereafter ILC Draft Articles).

[4] Convention IV Respecting the Laws and Customs of War on Land, The Hague, 18 October 1907, in force 26 January 1910 (hereafter Hague Convention IV).

[5] Nauru acceded to the Conventions on 27 June and Montenegro on 2 August 2006.

[6] *Legality of the Threat or Use of Nuclear Weapons*, Advisory Opinion of 8 July 1996 [1996] *ICJ Rep.* 257, para. 79.

decade before that, the same court opined that, 'the Geneva Conventions are in some respects a development, and in other respects no more than the expression, of such [fundamental general] principles [of humanitarian law]'.[7] The notion of the Geneva Conventions as customary international law is therefore uncontroversial in itself,[8] but the question, a crucial one for the purposes of the present discussion, remains: *which* provisions of the Conventions are rules of customary law? Did the Court mean that the Conventions are customary law *in toto*, or that only certain provisions rise to the level of custom – and if the latter, which ones?

A final comment by way of introduction to Rules 139–150 of the Study needs to address the feasibility and realism of these Rules, especially as regards the responsibility of non-State actors. With the proliferation since 1945 of armed conflicts that are either clearly non-international or at least not strictly of an international character, it is axiomatic that such actors as guerrilla or insurgent movements and other irregular armed groups of all kinds play a major role in the contemporary armed conflict paradigm. Such groups have neither the structure nor the reciprocity-derived incentive to observe humanitarian law in their military operations, and also lack the attributes of sovereignty and equality that would enable them to be held to account in public international law generally. In this sense it is not only 'asymmetric warfare' that is a problem, but 'asymmetric law': the example of Israeli military operations against Hezbollah in Lebanon in July and August 2006 demonstrates the difficulties perfectly. Actions of the Israel Defence Forces, where considered to breach humanitarian law, resulted in Israel incurring international opprobrium as well as threats of securing legal accountability;[9] yet violations committed by Hezbollah (often similar in style and intent, if admittedly not in scale, to the IDF violations) attracted substantially less condemnation – and there is certainly no international legal mechanism to hold them to account for their actions, since they neither represent a State authority as such nor are transparently accountable to or directed or controlled by any other State to the extent that responsibility can be imputed to the latter.[10]

---

[7] *Case concerning Military and Paramilitary Activities in and against Nicaragua (Nicaragua v. United States of America) (Merits)*, Judgment of 27 June 1986 [1986] *ICJ Rep.* 14, para. 218.

[8] But see Scobbie, chapter 2, pp. 32–33.

[9] Reuters, 'Lebanon to Sue Israel for "Barbaric Destruction"', *The Scotsman*, 26 July 2006, http://news.scotsman.com/latest_uk.cfm?id=1086762006, accessed 23 December 2006.

[10] The example of the conflict in Lebanon in summer 2006 is perhaps more complicated than would be ideal. Hezbollah is represented as a political party in the Lebanese Government, and thus would appear to be part of the State; but the movement's fighters who were engaged in hostilities with the IDF are not part of the Lebanese Government

While this may be a problem of practicalities based on political atti-
tudes, rather than a problem of legal doctrine as such,[11] some of the
Rules posited by the Study in Chapters 40–42 may be of comparatively
little effective service to the cause of humanitarian law, since they are
arguably unrealistic and unenforceable in relation to non-State actors.
Although this is in principle no more so than in the case of recalcitrant
States, and there might thus be an argument that these Rules are not
unrealistic and unenforceable as such, non-State actors are less susceptible to international condemnation than States. Non-State actors are not
members of organisations where they have to endure criticism of their
actions and the threat of sanctions by the international community, and
they are generally less dependent on the reciprocal goodwill of others for
their external relations. While there are many ways in which the ICRC
may engage with an armed opposition group, for example, it will generally be by the goodwill of the armed group rather than out of any sense of
legal obligation (which underpins most States' dealings with the ICRC).
The Study may not be wrong in formulating such Rules as part of customary law. But the Study might usefully have discussed more fully the
difficulties and benefits of extending their application to non-State
actors.

2. The Rules

Compliance with international humanitarian law

Rule 139

**Each party to the conflict must respect and ensure respect for interna-
tional humanitarian law by its armed forces and other persons or
groups acting in fact on its instructions, or under its direction or
control.**

Army. The Expert Legal Inquiry into Possible Violations of International Humanitarian
Law, established by the International Commission of Jurists in August 2006, is investigat-
ing violations by Hezbollah as well as by the IDF; so in theory, at least, a member of
Hezbollah could be accountable before an international or national tribunal. See
International Commission of Jurists Press Release, 10 October 2006, available at:
www.icj.org/news.php3?id_article=4029&lang=en, accessed 15 January 2007.

[11] See S. Sivakumaran, 'Binding Armed Opposition Groups' (2006) 55 *International and
Comparative Law Quarterly* 369; M. Mack, 'Compliance with International Humanitarian
Law by Non-State Actors in Non-International Armed Conflicts', International
Humanitarian Law Research Initiative Working Paper, November 2003, available at:
www.ihlresearch.org/portal/ihli/alabama.php, accessed 29 January 2007.

There can be no objection in logic to the assertion that States are under a general duty to respect humanitarian law, in particular to the extent that such a duty can be said to derive from common Article 1 of the Geneva Conventions. In its derivation the obligation is a treaty-based one, and since all parties to any treaty are bound in good faith to respect the treaty and carry out its provisions according to the maxim *pacta sunt servanda*,[12] it might be said that this is a general principle of law rather than a rule of customary international law.[13] It is also a logical corollary of the doctrine of State responsibility, whereby all States are legally responsible for the acts of their officials (including regular armed forces).[14] States are under a general duty to respect the entirety of applicable public international law, and in the specific context of humanitarian law this Rule is certainly welcome in its emphasis on the universality of application of the law in armed conflicts. There may be a doctrinal difficulty in that public international law generally does not deal with non-State actors in the same way as it does with States; the Study is perhaps insufficiently clear as to the strictly legal (as opposed to humanitarian) basis for asserting a customary law extension, to non-State actors, of States' duty to respect and ensure respect for the law.

The Study cites three ICJ decisions to support its assertion of this principle as a customary rule,[15] but a close reading of the relevant decisions reveals that they are being cited as authority for more than they can bear. In its Orders for Provisional Measures in the *Case Concerning the Application of the Genocide Convention*[16] and the *Case Concerning Armed Activities on the Territory of the Democratic Republic of the Congo*,[17] the ICJ ordered the parties to ensure respect for humanitarian law (in the former case the injunction was much more specific and phrased to the effect that the Federal Republic of Yugoslavia was to

---

[12] As encapsulated by Art. 26 of the Vienna Convention on the Law of Treaties, Vienna, 23 May 1969. In its commentary to the draft of what was then Art. 23, the ILC consistently characterised the rule of *pacta sunt servanda* as a 'principle', albeit one of a 'fundamental nature': *Yearbook of the International Law Commission, 1966*, vol. II, p. 211.

[13] A position which is also maintained by G. Fitzmaurice, 'Some Problems Regarding the Formal Sources of International Law', in *Symbolae Verzijl* (The Hague: Martinus Nijhoff, 1958), p. 153, at 174.   [14] See below, discussion of Rules 149–150.

[15] Study, Vol. II, ch. 40, 129–131.

[16] *Application of the Convention on the Prevention and Punishment of the Crime of Genocide (Bosnia and Herzegovina v. Yugoslavia)* Order of 8 April 1993 [1993] *ICJ Rep.* 3, para. 52(A)(2).

[17] *Armed Activities on the Territory of the Congo (Democratic Republic of the Congo v. Burundi)*, Order of 1 July 2000, [2000] *ICJ Rep.* 111, para. 47(3).

ensure that its forces did not commit, incite or become complicit in any acts of genocide – not violations of humanitarian law generally); however, in both cases the statement cited is from the *dispositif* of the Order on Provisional Measures and in neither case did the Court state the legal basis or source of the obligation.[18] In the *Nicaragua* case, the Court noted that the USA's obligation to respect and ensure respect for the Geneva Conventions derived, 'not only from the Conventions them-selves, but from the general principles of humanitarian law to which the Conventions merely give specific expression'.[19] This again uses the term 'general principles of . . . law' as the only non-conventional source of the obligation. Notwithstanding the Court's use of the word 'humani-tarian', it is clear that the source of law being referred to, in terms of the ICJ Statute, was general principles of law rather than custom.[20] Since it is necessary for custom to be strictly proved rather than assumed, and notwithstanding the view that the Geneva Conventions generally have passed into customary law, it is arguable that the Study fails to make a convincing case that this particular principle of law has attained the status of a customary norm.

The aspect of ensuring respect for 'other persons or groups' acting on the instructions or under the direction or control of the State is logical enough *per se*, depending on the exact circumstances of the case, and this again derives from general rules of State responsibility.[21] It is also consis-tent with the International Court of Justice's findings.[22] A State would not be responsible for ensuring respect by armed opposition groups within the same State. It is accepted in the general law of State responsibility that a State will be responsible for acts of an armed opposition group on its territory, but only if the group in question subsequently becomes the gov-ernment of that State or succeeds in forming a new State.[23] Although certain 'special circumstances' are foreseen, in which the conduct of an

---

[18] This might be viewed as more in the nature of a general exhortation to the parties to respect and ensure respect humanitarian law, with a view to not exacerbating the dispute, rather than a statement of specific legal obligation. The various declarations by interna-tional conferences cited in Study, Vol. 2, Part 2, Chapter 40, 117–128) appear similarly exhortative in nature.   [19] *Nicaragua* case, Judgment, para. 220.

[20] As listed separately from custom, in Article 38(1)(c) of the Statute of the ICJ, as a source of law to be applied by the Court. See H. Waldock, 'General Course on Public International Law' (1962-II) 106 *Recueil des Cours* 1, at 54 *et seq.*

[21] See below, discussion of Rules 149–150.

[22] *United States Diplomatic and Consular Staff in Tehran (United States of America v. Iran)*, Judgment of 24 May 1980, [1980] *ICJ Rep.* 3, paras. 171–174; *Nicaragua* case, paras. 86 and 109.   [23] ILC Draft Articles, Art. 10.

unsuccessful rebel movement may be attributed to the State, foremost among those circumstances is that, 'the group must be performing governmental functions'.[24] It is submitted that contemporary understandings of the concept of governmental functions cannot admit of the possibility that they would extend to violations of international humanitarian law, by virtue of the principle propounded by the House of Lords in *Reg. v. Bow Street Magistrates' Court, ex parte Pinochet Ugarte (No.3)*.[25] In respect of groups covered by Article 10 of the ILC Draft Articles on State Responsibility, further exceptional cases may result in responsibility for the State resisting the insurrection where 'the State was in a position to adopt measures of vigilance, prevention or punishment in respect of the movement's conduct but improperly failed to do so';[26] an armed conflict between a State and an opposition group is likely to be the very antithesis of such a situation.[27]

Rule 140

The obligation to respect and ensure respect for international humanitarian law does not depend on reciprocity.

There can be little dissent from the substance of this Rule. It has long been accepted that the rules of humanitarian law are unconditional and universal, and the Vienna Convention on the Law of Treaties (which itself encapsulates customary law) expressly excludes the possibility of terminating or suspending the operation of a treaty because of its breach by another party, in respect of 'provisions relating to the protection of the human person contained in treaties of a humanitarian character'.[28] The other evidence which the Study cites to support the assertion of this Rule

---

[24] *Ibid.*, Commentary to Art. 9, *Yearbook of the International Law Commission, 2001*, vol. II, Part Two, p. 110.

[25] *R. v. Bow Street Magistrates' Court, ex parte Pinochet Ugarte (No.3)*, House of Lords [1999] 2 All ER 97.

[26] Commentary to Art. 9, *Yearbook of the International Law Commission, 2001*, vol. II, Part Two, p. 118.

[27] Commentary to Art. 10 of the Draft Articles asserts that, 'The general principle in respect of the conduct of [rebel] movements, committed during the[ir] continuing struggle with the constituted authority, is that it is not attributable to the State under international law . . . Diplomatic practice is remarkably consistent in recognizing [this]': Commentary, *ibid.*, p. 112.

[28] Above n.12, Art. 60(5). Note, however, the position in relation to the Protocol for the Prohibition of the Use of Asphyxiating, Poisonous or Other Gases, and of Bacteriological Methods of Warfare, Geneva, 17 June 1925. Of the 133 States Parties to the Gas Protocol, twenty-three currently have reservations in force indicating their interpretation of the

– apart from the initial comment that common Article 1 of the Geneva Conventions requires States to respect and ensure respect for the Conventions 'in all circumstances' – is largely taken from the very specific context of war crimes trials and the rejection of arguments that individual defendants were entitled to violate the law by violations of the adverse party.[29] This practice goes to the criminal responsibility of individuals who violate the law, not to the civil responsibility of States for respecting and ensuring respect for that law; these are two quite different aspects of legal liability.

The substantive content of Rule 140 is undoubtedly a general principle of law applicable to obligations of a humanitarian nature (indeed, the Study itself, referring to case law in support, specifically uses the term 'general principle of law' rather than 'rule of customary international law'),[30] but in addition it may be accepted as a customary rule, in the specific context of humanitarian law, to the extent that it derives from the Vienna Convention.

The next two Rules are concerned with securing compliance by the armed forces.

Rule 141

Each State must make legal advisers available, when necessary, to advise military commanders at the appropriate level on the application of international humanitarian law.

The Study correctly states that this is a corollary to several other rules of humanitarian law.[31] This implies that it is a logical supplement to those other rules; again there is no difficulty with its substance, but it is unclear whether the Rule rises to the level of customary international

---

Protocol as forbidding only the first use of the weapons with which it is concerned, and that they reserve the right to use such weapons in reprisal against any other party using them. E.g. China expressly states that it is bound by the Protocol 'under the reservation of reciprocity as from all other contracting and acceding Powers' (source: www.icrc.org/ihl.nsf/ WebSign?ReadForm&id=280&ps=P). It is true that most such reservations predate the 1949 Conventions and it is possible that subsequent treaties banning similar weapons, which do not allow such reservations, have the effect of rendering such reprisals of dubious legality; nevertheless, the fact remains that the non-reciprocity principle is not uncontroversial in humanitarian law. See also the discussion of reprisals, below, Rules 145–148.

[29] Cf. S. Yee, 'The *Tu Quoque* Argument as a Defence to International Crimes, Prosecution or Punishment' (2004) 3 *Chinese Journal of International Law* 87.   [30] Study, Vol. I, 499.

[31] *Ibid.*, 501.

law. States provide legal advisers to their armed forces either as a treaty
obligation under Article 82 of Additional Protocol I[32] or as a matter of
operational practicality, since it is self-evident that commanders in the
field are going to need legal advice as to the correct application of the
rules of humanitarian law. While the provision of legal advisers may
be viewed as flowing from the obligation to respect and ensure respect
for the law, the fact that the first obligation may be customary does not
in and of itself make the second one so. Although some States not
party to Additional Protocol I follow the practice stipulated in Article
82, it is not clear whether they do so as a matter of operational practicality or because they feel that they are under a customary legal obligation
to do so.

Rule 142

**States and parties to the conflict must provide instruction in inter-
national humanitarian law to their armed forces.**

This is a specific treaty obligation under the Geneva Conventions and is
also supplemented by commanders' duty to instruct armed forces under
their command pursuant to Article 87(2) of Additional Protocol I.[33] As a
positive injunction in a set of treaties of universal acceptance – at least
insofar as concerns the 1949 Conventions – there can be little objection to
the customary status accorded it by the Study. However, its extension to
armed opposition groups, implied by the phrase 'States *and parties to the
conflict*', as a matter of customary law seems rather unrealistic. To the
extent that any such groups may have allowed dissemination of humanitarian law among their forces by the ICRC, it is unlikely that it is because
those groups regard themselves as being under a legally binding obligation to do so, although they may find that it makes for good public
relations. This part of the Rule, therefore, appears aspirational rather
than practical and is unlikely to reflect an actual rule of customary international law.

---

[32] The Study itself acknowledges this point: Study, Vol. I, 500 n.36.
[33] The duty to provide instruction to armed forces also exists in relation to specific topics like
cultural property. For an example of State practice in this regard during the belligerent
occupation of Iraq in 2003–2004, see A. Jachec-Neale, 'International Humanitarian Law
and Polish Involvement in Stabilizing Iraq', in S. Breau and A. Jachec-Neale (eds.), *Testing
the Boundaries of International Humanitarian Law* (London: British Institute of
International and Comparative Law, 2006), p. 221 at pp. 240–242.

Rule 143

States must encourage the teaching of international humanitarian law to the civilian population.

This is a laudable aim but it probably represents wishful thinking to assert that it is a rule of customary international law. Notwithstanding the Study's citation of the *Pictet Commentary* to Article 47 of Geneva Convention I[34] as evidence that the words 'if possible' in the Article were 'not included to make civilian instruction optional',[35] it is submitted that the inclusion of this Rule can primarily be considered an aspiration. The *Pictet Commentary* and the Study explain the words 'if possible' by reference to the decentralised control of education in federal States, but even in countries like the UK, international humanitarian law is not taught in schools and is offered as a specialist option at only a handful of the approximately 100 university law schools in the country. Universities in the UK are independent of any governmental authorities as regards their curricula and the nature of their response to any outside attempts to influence subjects of study must be a matter of some uncertainty. The UK Government does little or nothing to encourage the teaching or dissemination of humanitarian law, although there are other countries that do.

The ability to teach international humanitarian law, as a highly specialised area within public international law, depends not only on available staff interest and expertise, but also on resources which are not available in large parts of the world. Are all States in such a position, or States which (for whatever reason) do not play a proactive role in the dissemination of humanitarian law, to be considered legally responsible in international law for the breach of this putative customary law obligation? The answer must be no, inasmuch as the Rule does not impose an absolute obligation to teach humanitarian law, but merely an obligation to encourage its teaching. As such, it clearly reflects an aspiration in that it is an exhortation to a vague and undefined amount of activity and effort rather than quantifiable result. There are many initiatives in all parts of the world that are designed to encourage the teaching of humanitarian law, including moot court competitions, simulations, ICRC 'Exploring Humanitarian Law' projects,[36] and dissemination to youth workers and Red Cross/Red Crescent volunteers. However, most of these

---

[34] Study, Vol. I, 506 n.65.
[35] J. Pictet *et al.* (eds.), *Commentary on the First Geneva Convention* (Geneva, ICRC, 1952), p. 349.   [36] For details of which, see www.ehl.icrc.org.

are actually carried out by agencies other than State authorities, albeit often with the indirect support or encouragement of the State. Even in such cases, it is not sufficiently clear whether States support these initiatives out of a feeling of legal obligation, or for more mundane or practical reasons.

Enforcement of international humanitarian law

Rule 144

States may not encourage violations of international humanitarian law by parties to an armed conflict. They must exert their influence, to the degree possible, to stop violations of international humanitarian law.

This is very much a statement of two halves, the first clearly correct and the second less obvious. There is little problem with the first sentence: it derives at least in part from common Article 1 of the Geneva Conventions ('respect and ensure respect') and as such constitutes an obligation arising under a set of treaties to which all States in the world are now parties. In the *Nicaragua* case, the ICJ held that the USA was 'under an obligation not to encourage persons or groups engaged in the conflict in Nicaragua to act in violation of the provisions of [common Article 3 of the Geneva Conventions]' and that this obligation '[did] not derive only from the Conventions themselves, but from the general principles of humanitarian law'.[37] It might also be argued that the obligation not to encourage violations of humanitarian law is implicit in the notion of complicity in State responsibility (as a matter of general international law doctrine).

As to the latter point, whilst Articles 16–18 of the ILC Draft Articles do not refer to mere encouragement of violations as a basis for international responsibility, such action by a State might be viewed as a corollary of Article 41(2).[38] If serious violations of humanitarian law are *ipso facto* serious breaches of international legal obligations (as they ought to be and as the Study suggests they may be in its allusions to its Rules as possibly constituting *ius cogens*),[39] encouragement of such violations might in and of itself constitute a violation. The Study also cites case law from the ICTY

---

[37] *Nicaragua* case, para. 220.
[38] Art. 41(2) of the Draft Articles reads: 'No State shall recognize as lawful a situation created by a serious breach [of an international legal obligation], nor render aid or assistance in maintaining that situation.'   [39] Study, Vol. I, Introduction, xxxix.

to the effect that norms of humanitarian law constitute rules *erga omnes*.[40] On the other hand, the Draft Articles do not specify encouragement of violations as a form of complicity engaging legal responsibility,[41] and the accompanying Commentary makes it clear that 'incitement' (the closest reference to encouragement that can be found in the Draft Articles) 'is generally not regarded as sufficient to give rise to responsibility on the part of the inciting State, if it is not accompanied by concrete support or does not involve direction and control on the part of the inciting State'.[42] In the *Nicaragua* case, the Court found that the USA was bound by '*general principles* of humanitarian law'[43] not to encourage violations of common Article 3, but did not go so far as to impute State responsibility for any such violations to the USA. Judge Schwebel expressly held that, 'Customary international law does not know the delict of "encouragement"', although he acknowledged that, 'it may reasonably be maintained that a State which encourages violations of [the Geneva Conventions] fails to "ensure respect" for [them], as by their terms it is obliged to do'.[44] Overall, the balance of arguments suggests that it would be hard to ground this part of the Rule in a general notion of complicity in customary international law: the better basis for it is Article 1 of the Geneva Conventions.

The second part of the Rule is more germane to cases of violations of humanitarian law and is certainly evidenced by (attempts at) State practice. The crux is the qualification 'to the degree possible': is such possibility to be gauged as a matter of practical feasibility or political desirability? In the 2006 armed conflict between Israel and Hezbollah in Lebanon, for example, it was clear that the UK repeatedly sought to exert its influence on Israel to moderate some of its operational practices that were alleged to violate humanitarian law.[45] It was equally clear that Israel did not pay any attention at all to such attempts to exert influence. In respect of the Occupied Palestinian Territories, the ICJ in 2004 specifically stated that all

---

[40] *Ibid.*, p. 512.

[41] Art. 16 of the Draft Articles deals with States aiding or assisting in the commission of a wrongful act; Art. 17 with directing or controlling such acts; and Art. 18 with cases of coercion. None of these refer, even obliquely, to encouraging.

[42] ILC Commentary, p. 154.   [43] *Nicaragua* case, para. 255 (emphasis added).

[44] *Ibid.*, Dissenting Opinion of Judge Schwebel, p. 259, para. 259. He nevertheless went on to vote in favour of the relevant provision in the Court's Judgment, holding that, 'what is beyond discussion is that no government can justify official advocacy of acts in violation of the laws of war': *ibid.*, para. 260.

[45] For official UK criticism of Israeli actions in Lebanon, the West Bank and Gaza, see *Hansard*, HC, vol. 449, cols. 21–22, 28 and 32, 17 July 2006; *ibid.*, col. 525, 20 July 2006; *ibid.*, col. 730, 25 July 2006; Foreign Affairs Committee, *Foreign Policy Aspects of the War against Terrorism – Fourth Report of Session 2005–06* (2006 HC 573), para. 206.

States Parties to Geneva Convention IV are under an obligation to ensure respect for the Convention by Israel;[46] in reaction to this, the 10th Emergency Special Session of the UN General Assembly passed, on 2 August 2004, a resolution which expressly calls upon States to comply with that obligation.[47] No action has been taken in conformity with the resolution. The report to the General Assembly in June 2005 by Switzerland,[48] in its capacity as the depositary of the Geneva Conventions, shied away from any concrete measures aimed at securing the enforcement of humanitarian law vis-à-vis Israel, and merely called for 'a mechanism promoting dialogue [to] be envisaged'.[49] The suggestion that a conference of High Contracting Parties to Geneva Convention IV be convened, to take measures to force Israel's compliance with the Convention, was deemed 'inadvisable'.[50]

The cold reality is that very few States in the contemporary world are in a position to bring much influence to bear on other entities – whether governments or non-State actors – that are determined to pursue their politico-military-strategic objectives, irrespective of any violations of humanitarian law that may occur along the way. Even the court of world opinion has very limited influence in such scenarios. Perhaps a more realistic adjustment of this Rule might work, to the effect that the obligation to stop violations of humanitarian law is only applicable when States are actually in a position to do so by virtue of directing or controlling armed forces (whether regular or irregular) in another State, or being in alliance with another State that is committing violations.[51] To the extent that the second sentence of Rule 144 contains the words 'to the degree possible', there can be little objection in principle to the aspiration to which it gives voice. From that aspiration to asserting it as a customary rule, however, is a far from easy path to tread: it is submitted that the vagueness and unquantifiable nature of 'the degree possible', and the fact that it will

---

[46] *Legal Consequences of the Construction of a Wall in the Occupied Palestinian Territory*, ICJ Advisory Opinion of 9 July 2004.   [47] UN Doc. A/RES/ES-10/15, para. 7.

[48] UN Doc. A/ES-10/304.   [49] *Ibid.*, para. 59.

[50] *Ibid.*, para. 17. Such a conference had previously been convened on 15 July 1999 in response to UNGA Resolution ES-10/6 and reconvened on 5 December 2001, but the resulting Declaration merely called upon parties to the conflict in the Middle East to respect the Convention and urged them to settle their dispute in accordance with international law (available at: http://domino.un.org/UNISPAL.nsf/eed216406b50bf6485256ce 10072f637/8fc4f064b9be5bad85256c1400722951!OpenDocument). See also P.-Y. Fux and M. Zambelli, '*Mise en œuvre de la Quatrième Convention de Genève dans les territoires palestiniens occupés: historique d'un processus multilateral (1997–2001)*' (2002) 84 *International Review of the Red Cross* no. 847, 661.

[51] See below, discussion of Rule 149.

differ from one situation to another, depending largely on political considerations, render this too uncertain to be admitted as a norm of customary international law.

Reprisals

Rules 145–148 of the Study deal with the 'controversial and intractable'[52] problem of belligerent reprisals as a method of forcing compliance with the law in armed conflict. The general consensus among most modern commentators seems to be, as Hampson has put it, that 'reprisals have a useful part to play in deterring and/or preventing the recurrence of breaches of humanitarian law, on condition that they are kept within defined limits';[53] in other words, although reprisals have during the twentieth century been increasingly restricted and curtailed in the scope of permissible objects of such action, the doctrine as a concept remains a valid part of the law of armed conflict, particularly in respect of methods and means of warfare against combatants and military objectives.[54] It is also important to bear in mind, however, that 'reprisals, far from enforcing the law, can produce an escalating spiral of atrocities completely undermining respect for the law'.[55]

Rule 145

Where not prohibited by international law, belligerent reprisals are subject to stringent conditions.

This statement would seem to be consistent with the general consensus. The Study correctly points out that there has been a conspicuous decline in the use of reprisals, especially in international armed conflicts, vis-à-vis the increased use of alternative methods of securing compliance. That notwithstanding, many States (including the UK) do have sets of

[52] F. Hampson, 'Belligerent Reprisals and the 1977 Protocols to the Geneva Conventions of 1949' (1988) 37 *International and Comparative Law Quarterly* 818.   [53] *Ibid.*, 843.

[54] See L. Green, *The contemporary Law of Armed Conflict* (Manchester University Press, 2nd edn, 2000), pp. 123–124; Y. Dinstein, *The Conduct of Hostilities under the Law of International Armed Conflict* (Cambridge University Press, 2004), pp. 220–227; A Mitchell, 'Does One Illegality Merit Another? The Law of Belligerent Reprisals in International Law' (2001) 170 *Military Law Review* 155; S. Darcy, 'The Evolution of the Law of Belligerent Reprisals' (2003) 175 *Military Law Review* 184; *contra*, F. Kalshoven, *Belligerent Reprisals* (Sijthoff, Leiden, 1971), p. 377.

[55] C. Greenwood, 'The Twilight of the Law of Belligerent Reprisals' (1989) 20 *Netherlands Yearbook of International Law* 35, at 36.

368 DAVID TURNS

conditions – often stringent, as the Study says – within which they reserve the right to resort to belligerent reprisals. As noted by more than one recent commentator, the scope for reprisals in maritime and air warfare remains relatively broad.[56]

Most commentators seem to agree that in any situation where reprisals are contemplated, customary international law will place the reprisal in one of two categories: either it will be forbidden or, if permitted, it will be severely restricted by a series of conditions. Greenwood identifies four conditions and summarises them as: (1) the need for a prior violation of international law imputable to the State against which the reprisal is to be directed; (2) the need for reasonable proportionality; (3) the purpose of the reprisal must be to stop the adverse party's unlawful conduct and deter future illegalities, rather than to seek revenge; and (4) the lack of any other effective means of redress in the situation.[57] The Study identifies five conditions, the first three of which include and subsume all four of Greenwood's. The Study's fourth condition is that the decision to resort to reprisals must be taken at the highest level of government, and its fifth is that reprisal action must cease as soon as the adverse party's illegal conduct is terminated. Although a minor criticism could be made to the effect that the fifth condition is a logical corollary of the second and third conditions as identified by Greenwood and as such does not require separate articulation, there is no harm in striving for completeness in an area of law as controversial as reprisals. In any event, both the fourth and fifth conditions identified in the Study are in accordance with the practice of the United Kingdom, which actually exceeds the Study's requirements as regards conditions for the legality of reprisals: the UK *Manual of the Law of Armed Conflict* identifies no fewer than nine separate conditions.[58]

Overall the Study's basic view of reprisals is undoubtedly correct and well thought out. Given the controversy that attaches, for instance, to environmental reprisals,[59] it was wise not to have attempted formulation of a general prohibition of belligerent reprisals.

Rule 146

Belligerent reprisals against persons protected by the Geneva Conventions are prohibited.

---

[56] Mitchell, 'Does one illegality merit another?', at 169; Darcy, 'The Evolution of the Law of Belligerent Reprisals', at 210–211.
[57] Greenwood, 'The Twilight of the Law of Belligerent Reprisals', at 40.
[58] UK Ministry of Defence, *The Manual of the Law of Armed Conflict* (Oxford University Press, 2004), § 16.17, (hereafter *UK Manual*). [59] See generally Karen Hulme, chapter 8.

The most notable set of treaty-based restrictions on the right to resort to belligerent reprisals enacted in the last 100 years has been those contained in the 1949 Geneva Conventions. This prohibition is uncontroversial insofar as there is universal acceptance of those substantial provisions of the Geneva Conventions that are recognised as customary in nature. Insofar as the Geneva Conventions pertain to reprisals, they unequivocally forbid reprisals against the categories of persons protected by the Conventions.[60] A variation on this theme, although not stated expressly in the wording of Rule 146, is the question of whether reprisals may be permitted against civilians during the conduct of hostilities (as opposed to civilians in occupied territory or otherwise in the power of an adverse party, against whom reprisals are illegal by virtue of Article 33 of Geneva Convention IV). This proposition is derived largely from Article 51(6) of Additional Protocol I,[61] which the Study interestingly says 'codified' such a prohibition, thereby suggesting that it already existed in customary international law at the time of the drafting of the Additional Protocol.[62] It is also referred to as merely a 'trend' originating in General Assembly Resolution 2675 (XXV) in 1970.[63] The Study also attaches considerable weight, in its discussion of this point, to obiter dicta by the ICTY in *Prosecutor v. Kupreškić*,[64] which has been subject to very severe (and justified) criticism by several authoritative commentators.[65]

The Study's discussion of the last major instance of reprisals in an international armed conflict (during the 1980–1988 Iran–Iraq War)[66] is a helpful illustration of the evolution of the suggested 'trend'. Nevertheless, the Study rightly concludes that to assert such a 'trend' as having attained the status of a customary rule is controversial, to the extent that 'it is difficult to conclude that there has yet crystallised a customary rule specifically prohibiting' such reprisals.[67] The British position is that such reprisals may be taken by British forces but only in response to 'serious deliberate attacks in violation of Article 51' by the adverse party and with

---

[60] Geneva Convention I, Art. 46; Geneva Convention II, Art. 47; Geneva Convention III, Art. 13; Geneva Convention IV, Art. 33.

[61] 'Attacks against the civilian population or civilians by way of reprisals are prohibited.'

[62] Study, vol. I, p. 520.   [63] *Ibid.*

[64] *Prosecutor v. Kupreškić and others*, Judgment of Trial Chamber, 14 January 2000, IT-95-16 paras. 521–536.

[65] A point which has been succinctly and effectively made in R. Cryer, 'Of Custom, Treaties, Scholars and the Gavel: The Influence of the International Criminal Tribunals on the ICRC Customary Law Study' (2006) 11 *Journal of Conflict and Security Law* 239, at 255–256.   [66] Study, vol. I, pp. 521–522.   [67] *Ibid.*, p. 523.

clearance by the Ministry of Defence at Cabinet level.[68] Overall, the Study's caution on this particular point, as elsewhere in relation to reprisals, is warranted.

Rule 147

Reprisals against objects protected under the Geneva Conventions and the Hague Convention for the Protection of Cultural Property are prohibited.

This is again unobjectionable, insofar as it covers objects protected by the Geneva Conventions. The Hague Cultural Property Convention, on the other hand, is less widely ratified,[69] but taken in conjunction with the provisions in Article 53 of Additional Protocol I[70] it is arguable that, at the very least, a norm of customary international law could be emerging in respect of reprisals against cultural property. The comments made above in respect of Rule 146 are also applicable in relation to reprisals against civilian objects during hostilities, and the Study is equally ambivalent – again, correctly – in its conclusions on this point.[71]

Rule 148

Parties to non-international armed conflicts do not have the right to resort to belligerent reprisals. Other countermeasures against persons who do not or who have ceased to take a direct part in hostilities are prohibited.

This, the last of the Study's Rules on reprisals, is the most controversial. Belligerent reprisals were not included in Additional Protocol II, nor are they mentioned as such in common Article 3 of the Geneva Conventions. As one commentator has put it: 'However undesirable reprisals may be from a humanitarian perspective, a strictly legal interpretation of [common Article 3 and Additional Protocol II] would show that their

---

[68] *UK Manual*, above n.56, § 16.19.1.

[69] There are currently 116 States Parties, according to the ICRC: www.icrc.org/ihl.nsf/ WebSign?ReadForm&id=400&ps=P.

[70] 'Without prejudice to the provisions of the Hague Convention . . . of 14 May 1954, and other relevant international instruments, it is prohibited:
    (a) to commit any acts of hostility directed against the historic monuments, works of art or places of worship which constitute the cultural or spiritual heritage of peoples;
    (b) to use such objects in support of the military effort;
    (c) to make such objects the object of reprisals.'

[71] Study, vol. I, 525–526.

use during a non-international armed conflict is not completely proscribed.'[72]

Given the lack of treaty provision in this respect, it is not too difficult to sympathise with the Study's insistence that customary law must prohibit reprisals in non-international armed conflicts. However, the reliance placed on what even the Study characterises as merely an inference in *The Prosecutor v. Martić*,[73] to the effect that such reprisals are prohibited, seems somewhat overstated[74] given that, in the *North Sea Continental Shelf* and *Nicaragua* cases, 'the [ICJ] has adopted and maintained a high threshold with regard to the overt proving of the subjective constituent of customary law formation'.[75] In other words, the existence of a custom – particularly as regards *opinio iuris* – cannot be presumed or inferred from the practice of States: it must be strictly proved. Similarly, the provisions of common Article 3 are too general and vague to be the origin of a prohibition of such a specific concept as reprisals, although the Study is correct to say that any reprisal that infringes common Article 3 will be illegal; but the source of the prohibition is common Article 3 itself, rather than a separate rule on reprisals in non-international armed conflicts. The prohibition of collective punishments could include belligerent reprisals within its scope, in certain circumstances.[76] But since collective punishments are the subject of another rule in the Study (Rule 103), which is stated to apply equally in non-international armed conflicts,[77] it might be concluded that Rule 148 is redundant. The Study concludes, probably correctly, that '[t]here is insufficient evidence that the very concept of lawful reprisal in non-international armed conflict has ever materialised in international law'.[78] The *UK Manual*,[79] in its discussion of reprisals, does not mention non-international armed conflicts at all. Rule 148 could be viewed as redundant on that ground also.

The use of the term 'other countermeasures' is curious: it seems to be based on various proposals submitted at the 1977 Diplomatic Conference by half a dozen States which wanted to secure a prohibition of reprisals in non-international armed conflicts without using the term 'reprisals', on the basis that if that term were used in the treaty it

---

[72] Darcy, 'The Evolution of the Law of Belligerent Reprisals', at 219.
[73] ICTY Trial Chamber I, Review of Indictment Pursuant to Rule 61, 8 March 1996.
[74] Cryer, 'Of Custom, Treaties, Scholars and the Gavel'.
[75] M. Shaw, *International Law* (Cambridge University Press, 5th edn, 2003), p. 82.
[76] F. Hampson, 'Belligerent Reprisals and the 1977 Protocols to the Geneva Conventions of 1949' (1988) 37 *International and Comparative Law Quarterly* 818, at 825.
[77] Study, Vol. I, 374–375.   [78] *Ibid.*, 527.   [79] *UK Manual*, § 16.17.

would create the impression that there was scope for a concept of reprisals in such conflicts.[80] It is hard to see how something that does not even exist as a concept can be the subject of a specific customary rule prohibiting it: normally such prohibitions arise because a particular practice has existed in the past, but there can be no State practice against something which does not exist. This apparent logical gap might be countered by the suggestion that, where there is (non-) practice by States apparently implying a rule that does not necessarily exist because of the lack of *opinio iuris*, the practice is just that: an 'inconclusive' practice of States that does not in itself give rise to a rule of customary international law.

State responsibility

Chapter 42 is the last part of the Study to be considered here; it is headed 'Responsibility and Reparation' and contains two Rules.

Rule 149

A State is responsible for violations of international humanitarian law attributable to it, including:

(a) **violations committed by its organs, including its armed forces;**
(b) **violations committed by persons or entities it empowered to exercise elements of governmental authority;**
(c) **violations committed by persons or groups acting in fact on its instructions, or under its direction or control; and**
(d) **violations committed by private persons or groups which it acknowledges and adopts as its own conduct.**

This is a restatement of the basic rule of State responsibility as it relates to armed conflicts; in those specific terms it is derived from Article 3 of the 1907 Hague Convention IV[81] (reiterated in Article 91 of Additional Protocol I), but as a proposition of general public international law it is unexceptionable. The various forms of State responsibility are summarised by the Rule in line with the ILC Draft Articles. Thus, there is responsibility based on acts committed by: organs of the State (including its armed forces);[82] persons or entities empowered by the State to exercise elements of governmental authority;[83] persons or groups acting in fact on

---

[80] Study, Vol. I, 528–529.   [81] Hague Convention IV, Art. 3.
[82] Rule 149(a); ILC Draft Art. 4.   [83] Rule 149(b); ILC Draft Art. 5.

the State's instructions or under its direction or control;[84] and private persons or groups acknowledged and adopted by the State as its own conduct.[85] Although these permutations of the Rule are consistent with the equivalent Draft Articles as approved by the ILC, there is an internal inconsistency between Rule 149(d) and Rule 139: the wording of the latter does not include the former in its requirement that States respect and ensure respect for international humanitarian law. Rule 149 also does not mention organisational responsibility for actions by military forces of States members of an organisation; thus, the presumption would be that those States remain responsible for the actions of members of their armed forces, irrespective of organisational affiliation.

The Study makes surprisingly heavy weather of the difference between the *Nicaragua* (civil responsibility) and *Tadić*[86] (individual criminal responsibility) tests for cases where violations are committed by persons or groups acting in fact under the direction or control of a State (Rule 149(c)).[87] As the import of Rule 149 is State responsibility rather than individual criminal liability, the Study would have done better to have used the *Nicaragua* test rather than letting the discussion of this point tail off somewhat inconclusively.

Although the Rule here is concerned only with the responsibility of States for conduct that is attributable to them, the last section of the discussion of Rule 149 states that while legal responsibility for armed opposition groups could be asserted, the consequences of such responsibility are not clear.[88] To claim otherwise would seem to be doctrinally flawed in that the classical doctrine of responsibility in public international law attaches to *States* only (except where an armed opposition group subsequently becomes the Government of a State or successfully forms a new State).[89] Absent the possibilities envisaged in Article 10 of the ILC Draft Articles, such groups are unlikely ever to be in a position to provide reparation or even to be susceptible to a legal forum where such reparation could be awarded (other than symbolically, for example as in civil lawsuits brought under the US Alien Tort Claims Act of 1789).[90] This is a point on which the individual criminal liability of perpetrators, whatever their organisational affiliation, is likely to prove more useful than any general assertion of civil responsibility.

---

[84] Rule 149(c); ILC Draft Art. 8.   [85] Rule 149(d); ILC Draft Art. 11.
[86] *Prosecutor v. Tadić*, (ICTY) Appeals Chamber, Judgment of 15 July 1999, Case IT-94-1-A.
[87] Study, Vol. I, 534–535.   [88] *Ibid.*, 536.
[89] According to Art. 10 of the ILC Draft Articles. See above, text accompanying nn.23–27.
[90] 28 USC § 1350.

Rule 150

A State responsible for violations of international humanitarian law is required to make full reparation for the loss or injury caused.

This Rule is unexceptionable in principle, given that a general consequence of State responsibility is the requirement to make reparations
(which may take the form of restitution, compensation or satisfaction).[91]
In principle the reparations must be made to States. The Study comments
on numerous instances of claims being made by individuals in national
courts[92] but it should be noted that these are invariably made under
national legislation rather than under the international law doctrine of
State responsibility, and that in many instances the proceedings were ultimately unsuccessful due to claims of State immunity. Although it is easy
to agree with the Study's assertion that there is 'an increasing trend'
towards this kind of litigation,[93] it is submitted that it does not form part
of the customary law rules on State responsibility; still less of those relating to armed conflicts.

There may be similar doubts about the Study's arguments that the Rule
applies in non-international armed conflicts.[94] First, as regards the State's
liability to pay reparations in such conflicts: since the actions giving rise
to the claims would have been committed in a non-international armed
conflict vis-à-vis the State's own citizens, this would fall outside the parameters of the doctrine of State responsibility, wherein the State's liability
is engaged only vis-à-vis other States, not its own nationals. Although the
Study cites a considerable number of precedents on this point, it is worth
noting that very many of them are human rights cases: obligations under
human rights law (entirely based on treaty obligations) are not the same
as obligations under customary international humanitarian law. Indeed,
the two bodies of law are quite separate from each other and it is submitted that there must be some doubt over the use of authorities drawn
largely from human rights law as primary support for the assertion of a
customary right under humanitarian law.[95]

On the other hand, it must be noted that the principle that victims
of gross violations of human rights and serious violations of international humanitarian law are entitled to remedies and reparations
has, since the Study's publication, been endorsed by the UN General

---

[91] ILC Draft Articles, above n.3, Arts. 31 and 34–37.   [92] Study, Vol. I, 541–545.
[93] *Ibid.*, p. 541.   [94] *Ibid.*, pp. 545–550.
[95] But see Hampson, chapter 3, pp. 59–72.

Assembly.[96] Although the resolution does not specify the extension of the principle to non-international armed conflicts, the broad and general nature of its language infers that all conflicts are referred to. To the extent that the resolution was adopted without a vote,[97] it may be viewed as reflecting the *opinio iuris* of the entire international community, thereby giving rise to a strong presumption in favour of customary international law status. The very diverse precedents cited therein, encompassing human rights instruments and international criminal law treaties as well as humanitarian law treaties, suggest that this may be a customary rule of general public international law rather than one specific to international humanitarian law.

3. Final remarks

The Rules under consideration in this chapter lie at the intersection, not only of humanitarian law and general international law, but, perhaps even more importantly, at the intersection of aspirations and reality. It is submitted that not all of Rules 139–150 are actually substantive rules of customary law: some are technical or procedural rules only, others are aspirational (i.e. they indicate emerging trends or desirable outcomes that have not yet, in the present author's opinion, satisfied the requirements for the establishment of custom in international law), whilst others yet are arguably not even rules of customary law at all, but merely general principles of law. This conflation of actual custom with 'something else' (asserted Rules that do not, it is submitted, rise to the level of custom) is particularly in evidence in Rules 139–143. Rules 144–150, which deal primarily with more substantive rules of humanitarian and general international law in the form of belligerent reprisals and State responsibility, are less problematic in this context.

While the formulation of customary rules is to be welcomed, it is a truism that the rules of international humanitarian law may sound fine in theory but fall short in practice. Where the Rules in question derive from treaties, the matter is comparatively simple: States are required to respect and implement treaties to which they become party, and failure to do so incurs the responsibility of the delinquent State. The enforceability of the Study's Rules, as customary law rules, will be quite a different matter. It is

---

[96] Basic Principles and Guidelines on the Right to a Remedy and Reparations for Victims of Gross Violations of International Human Rights Law and Serious Violations of International Humanitarian Law, 16 December 2005, UN Doc. A/RES/60/147.

[97] See UN Doc. A/60/PV.64, p. 10.

for this reason that it is important, in the present author's opinion, to
separate the customary rules that are feasibly enforceable as such from
the aspirational principles that, no matter how strongly one agrees with
them, will generally be difficult if not impossible to enforce as general
rules. That is not to say that they will never be enforceable; only that more
time will be required for them to attain general recognition as norms of
customary international law.

15

War crimes

CHARLES GARRAWAY

1. Introduction

What is a 'war crime'? Traditional definitions such as 'violations of the laws of war that incur individual criminal responsibility'[1] ask more questions than they answer, as the test of individual criminal responsibility has varied down the ages. Whilst it was long understood that domestic courts could deal with 'crimes of war' within their jurisdiction, it was only the advent of international criminal justice in the twentieth century that brought the issue back into the public consciousness. The London Charter,[2] at the end of World War II, gave the Nuremberg Tribunal jurisdiction over 'violations of the laws or customs of war' and provided an illustrative list, drawn primarily from the Hague Regulations of 1907.[3] This gave considerable discretion to the judges themselves in deciding what fell within their jurisdiction and what did not. The Geneva Conventions of 1949[4] drew a distinction between 'grave breaches' of the Conventions, specified in the text, against which States were required to enact legislation on the basis of obligatory universal jurisdiction, and other acts contrary to the Conventions where States were only required to 'take measures necessary' for their suppression.[5] The grave breaches were clearly defined to include the most heinous acts. However, they were committed only in international armed conflict.

It was in effect the Nuremberg definition, with an expanded list of crimes, which was adopted by the International Criminal Tribunal for the Former Yugoslavia.[6] This included those offences classified as grave

---

[1] See Categories of War Crimes, in R. Gutman and D. Rieff (eds.), *Crimes of War* (London: W.W. Norton, 1999), p. 374.

[2] See the Charter of the Nuremberg Tribunal of 8 August 1945.

[3] *Ibid.*, Art. 6, and The 1907 Hague Regulations.

[4] Geneva Convention I, Geneva Convention II, Geneva Convention III and Geneva Convention IV.   [5] Geneva Convention III, Art. 129.

[6] See Art. 3, Statute of the International Criminal Tribunal for the Former Yugoslavia.

breaches under the Geneva Conventions. However, a new problem came to light when consideration was being given to a Tribunal for Rwanda. To what extent did individual criminal responsibility, in the international sense, extend to non-international conflicts? The International Committee of the Red Cross had taken the line, as late as 1993, that 'according to international humanitarian law as it stands today, the notion of war crimes is limited to situations of international armed conflict'.[7] However, the Rwandan atrocities were clearly committed within a non-international armed conflict and the United Nations Security Council granted express jurisdiction to the Tribunal over violations of common Article 3 to the Geneva Conventions and Additional Protocol II, to which Rwanda was a party.[8] This caused the Yugoslav Tribunal to revisit its own jurisdiction and it came up with two major decisions in the same case.[9] First, it confirmed that its own jurisdiction extended to violations of the laws of war in both international and non-international armed conflict. This in itself caused difficulties in that the differing treaty regimes meant that it became necessary in each case to have an extensive discourse about the nature of the armed conflict before it could be decided which crimes fell within the jurisdiction. In order to ameliorate this difficulty, the Tribunal fell back on customary law and held, secondly, that many of the offences that were crimes in international armed conflict were, under customary law, also crimes in non-international armed conflict. In reverse, the Tribunal also held, in agreement with the International Court of Justice, that the principles enunciated in common Article 3 to the four Geneva Conventions of 1949 were so fundamental as to apply in all types of conflict, both international and non-international.

The Rome Statute of the International Criminal Court took a slightly different line. States were not prepared in a treaty of general application to adopt the open-ended approach taken at Nuremberg. It was argued that this went against the principle of legal certainty and so it was decided to adopt a specific list of offences, covering both international and non-international armed conflict. These included both grave breaches and 'other serious violations of the laws and customs applicable in' armed

---

[7] Preliminary Remarks of the ICRC, 25 March 1993, unpublished, but cited in Christopher Greenwood, 'International Humanitarian Law and the Tadić Case' (1996) 7 *European Journal of International Law* 265.

[8] Statute of the International Criminal Tribunal for Rwanda, Art. 4.

[9] *Prosecutor v. Tadić*, Decision on the Defence Motion for Interlocutory Appeal on Jurisdiction, Appeals Chamber, 2 October 1995, Case No. IT-94-1-AR72.

conflict.[10] The list is, however, a compromise, and should not be taken as exhaustive of all serious violations. Furthermore, the Statute does not go as far as the Yugoslav Tribunal did, in that whilst many of the crimes listed under the section on international armed conflict are replicated in that on non-international armed conflict, the divide between the two types of conflict is maintained. In particular, common Article 3, as in the treaty, is limited to non-international armed conflict. It should perhaps be noted that the Statute for the Iraq Special Tribunal (now the Iraq High Criminal Court) followed the line of the Yugoslav Tribunal and extended the scope of the principles of common Article 3 across the whole spectrum of conflict.[11]

The Rome Statute is perhaps an example of where the international community considered the law had reached in 1998, which was exactly the time that the authors of the Study were working on their *magnum opus*. One would expect therefore to find a degree of correlation between the Rome Statute and the Rules contained in the Study and this is indeed the case.

Linked with the subject of war crimes – and preceding it in the Study – is the issue of individual responsibility. It was stated in the Nuremberg judgment that 'crimes against international law are committed by men, not by abstract entities, and only by punishing individuals who commit such crimes can the provisions of international law be enforced'.[12] Individual responsibility, in the context of war crimes, raises two important issues – superior orders and command responsibility. Both have been hotly debated over the years.

In relation to superior orders, the accepted view at the turn of the century was that expressed by Oppenheim when he stated: 'In case members of forces commit violations ordered by their commanders, the members may not be punished, for the commanders are alone responsible, and the latter may, therefore, be punished as war criminals on their capture by the enemy.'[13] By the time of Nuremberg, the wheel had turned full circle with the Charter providing that superior orders could not be a defence.[14] However, this led to a debate in academic circles as to the

---

[10] Rome Statute, Art. 8.
[11] See Art. 13, Iraqi High Criminal Court Law, 18 October 2005, accessed at http://www.law.case.edu/saddamtrial/documents/IST_statute_official_english.pdf.
[12] International Military Tribunal (Nuremberg) Judgment and Sentences, reprinted in (1947) 41 *American Journal of International Law* 172, at 221.
[13] L. Oppenheim, *International Law: A Treatise*, Vol. 2 (London: Longmans, Green & Co., 1906) p. 264.   [14] Charter of the Nuremberg Military Tribunal, Art. 8.

absolute nature of this rule. The Rome Statute does allow superior orders as a defence in very limited circumstances.[15] The ICC provision has not been without criticism.

In so far as command responsibility is concerned, the doctrine developed primarily after World War II and has been the subject of extensive jurisprudence from the Ad Hoc Tribunals for Former Yugoslavia and Rwanda. Indeed, it can be argued that the doctrine is still in a process of development. The views of the authors of the Study will undoubtedly contribute towards that development.

2. The Rules

Individual Responsibility

Rule 151

Individuals are criminally responsible for war crimes they commit.

This Rule is in principle unexceptionable and follows the line adopted by the Nuremberg Tribunal in its judgment.[16] The extension of the Rule to non-international armed conflicts, in so far as international jurisdiction is concerned, is however of more recent origin though the Statutes and jurisprudence of the Ad Hoc Tribunals for Former Yugoslavia and Rwanda have placed it beyond doubt.

It should be noted that the Rule as drafted does not preclude the possibility of an individual running a defence which may exclude criminal responsibility in the particular circumstances of the case. The Study deliberately avoided going into detail on international criminal law which the Group of Experts considered, rightly, as being outside their specific remit.

Rule 152

Commanders and other superiors are criminally responsible for war crimes committed pursuant to their orders.

That the ordering of a crime entails criminal responsibility is not in doubt. There is ample authority for this proposition, as stated in the Study. Contrary to what is maintained in the Study, however, this is normally considered as a principle of primary responsibility, rather than an

---

[15] Rome Statute of the International Criminal Court, Art. 33.
[16] International Military Tribunal (Nuremberg) Judgment and Sentences.

example of 'command responsibility'. The doctrine of command responsibility in its purest terms, as outlined in Rule 153 below, provides for criminal responsibility of commanders for their *omissions* and failures to act.[17] Rather than setting out a principle of command responsibility, Rule 152 merely confirms that the person who orders a crime is as responsible for that crime as the person who carries out the order.

Rule 153

Commanders and other superiors are criminally responsible for war crimes committed by their subordinates if they knew, or had reason to know, that the subordinates were about to commit or were committing such crimes and did not take all necessary and reasonable measures in their power to prevent their commission, or if such crimes had been committed, to punish the persons responsible.

This Rule seeks to enunciate the classic doctrine of 'command responsibility'. This developed from the Yamashita Case at the end of World War II where it was held that:

> where murder and rape and vicious, revengeful actions are widespread offences, and there is no effective attempt by a commander to discover and control the criminal acts, such a commander may be held responsible, even criminally liable, for the lawless acts of his troops, depending upon their nature and the circumstances surrounding them.[18]

It should be noted that the phrase used is 'responsible, even criminally liable'. Not every failure by a commander will necessarily lead to criminal liability and, in that sense, it is necessary to examine the modern-day doctrine to see if it reflects its origins. Whilst it originated in international armed conflict, there is now clear authority, as outlined in the Study, that it applies equally to non-international armed conflict.

Three specific issues arise: the temporal aspect of the offences, the question of knowledge, and the issue of punishment. In so far as the first is concerned, the Rome Statute,[19] following Article 86 of Additional Protocol I,[20] limits the application of the rule to crimes that subordinates 'were committing or about to commit'. Past offences, dealt with in Article 87 of Additional Protocol I,[21] are treated differently. It is therefore at least

---

[17] Study, Vol. 1, 558.   [18] *United States of America v. Tomoyuki Yamashita*, 327 US 1.
[19] Rome Statute, Art. 28.   [20] Additional Protocol I, Art. 86(2).
[21] Additional Protocol I, Art. 87.

arguable that the commander who fails to prevent crimes is in a different position from the commander who only learns of the crimes after the event but fails to take appropriate action to deal with the perpetrators. Under the doctrine of command responsibility, the commander is held responsible for the crimes themselves (murder, rape, genocide etc.). Whilst this may be appropriate in relation to the commander who has actual or constructive knowledge of the offences *prior* to their commission, it seems somewhat severe on the commander who only learns of the offences later and had no means of stopping them. There is a move today towards recognising this difference and treating the latter case as an example of neglect of duty, rather than pure command responsibility. This distinction is to be found in the 2003 Crimes and Elements for Trials by Military Commissions, issued by the United States Department of Defense, which stated that:

> A commander or superior charged with failing to take appropriate punitive or investigative action subsequent to the perpetration of a substantive offense triable by military commission should not be charged with the substantive offense as a principal. Such commander or superior should be charged for the separate offense of failing to submit the matter for investigation and/or prosecution as detailed in these elements.[22]

It follows that there may be some dispute as to whether the latter part of the Rule truly reflects customary international law as it is currently drafted.

On the question of knowledge, the Rule is sound. It is accepted that actual knowledge of commission of the offence is not required and the Commentary deals at some length with the differing formulations of the constructive knowledge test. That adopted here – 'had reason to know' – is acceptable though it will be subject to the glosses imposed by jurisprudence.

The latter part of the Rule deals with the responsibility to punish. Whilst this is a traditional feature of the doctrine, it sits ill with current pressures to remove the power of discipline from the chain of command on the basis that the commander cannot be 'independent' within human rights definitions. The ICC wording, 'to submit the matter to the competent authorities for investigation and prosecution',[23] sought to avoid this particular problem without lessening the effect. Although the Commentary refers to a 'failure to *investigate* possible crimes and/or failure to

---

[22] Para. 6.C.(4)(b)(2), Military Commission Instruction No.2, dated 30 April 2003.
[23] Rome Statute, Art. 28.

report allegations of war crimes to higher authorities',[24] it does not deal with this specific point.

This is a difficult time to seek to formulate a customary rule on command responsibility and it may be that the current version is not fully in line with recent developments. This is hardly surprising in a field that has been the subject of extensive study in recent years by practitioners and academics alike. What is beyond challenge is that there is indeed a doctrine of command responsibility which can hold commanders to account, though the full extent of that doctrine may not be fully established.

Rule 154

Every combatant has a duty to disobey a manifestly unlawful order.

This Rule is held to be applicable in both international and non-international armed conflict though the wording and the Commentary appear to apply it in an uneven manner. Whilst there is some domestic authority to the contrary, the existence of a duty to disobey a manifestly unlawful order is not really in doubt. However, the Rule limits that duty to 'combatants'. Referring back to Rule 3,[25] this would seem therefore to cover members of the State armed forces in both international and non-international armed conflicts but not to bind armed opposition groups. This goes against the principle of equal application of the law. The Commentary fairly points out the lack of specific practice in relation to armed opposition groups but it is, to say the least, unfortunate that the implication is given that such groups are not under a similar duty.

Rule 155

Obeying a superior order does not relieve a subordinate of criminal responsibility if the subordinate knew that the act ordered was unlawful or should have known because of the manifestly unlawful nature of the act ordered.

In this Rule, the authors have sought to cut the Gordian knot between those who believe that superior orders can never be a defence and those who believe that it can be except where the order given is manifestly unlawful. The line adopted here is similar to that contained in an ICRC draft submitted to the Diplomatic Conference which negotiated

---

[24] Study, Vol. 1, 562.   [25] Study, Vol. 1, 11.

Additional Protocol I, a draft that was ultimately not accepted by the Conference.[26] It differs from the provisions of the Rome Statute[27] but not dramatically so. In the latter, there is included a requirement that the subordinate must be under a duty to obey orders. This would distinguish an 'order' given in a military environment, from a civilian command, however forcibly given. It may be that the authors of the Study consider that the word 'order' itself implies in principle an obligation to obey but this was not considered sufficient during the ICC negotiations.

Secondly, in the Rome Statute, the requirement is simply that the order was not manifestly unlawful. Here, the manifest unlawfulness test is turned into a definition of constructive knowledge. Whilst, in principle, this seems to make sense, it does raise separate issues. For example, is this the only reason that would justify a 'should have known' finding? What if the accused knew it was illegal to attack cultural property but was given target coordinates which, if he had checked on the map readily available to him, would have identified a cultural object of considerable significance? It is correct that he might have a defence under the terms of the Rome Statute in that he did not know that the order was unlawful and it was not manifestly unlawful. However, in that case there is no 'should have known' test. In the Study, such a test has been introduced but only in the limited circumstances where the order was itself manifestly unlawful. The effect would be the same but it would seem a strange result as there could be little doubt but that the subordinate 'should have known' of the manifest illegality of the order, not because of 'the manifestly unlawful nature of the act ordered' but because he should have checked the coordinates; it was that checking that would have revealed the nature of the act ordered. Such anomalies tend to bring the law into disrepute and it may therefore have been safer to stick with the ICC wording which, whilst raising the same issue, is more consistent in its reasoning.

This is a contentious area and the Commentary has gone to some pains to explain why the particular formulation was chosen.[28]

War Crimes

Rule 156

Serious violations of international humanitarian law constitute war crimes.

---

[26] Study, Vol. 1, 565.   [27] Rome Statute, Art. 33.   [28] Study, Vol. 1, 566.

The problem with this Rule, as with so many others, is that the devil is in the detail – and the detail is to be found not in the Rule but in the Commentary. The Rule itself is to some extent a platitude but in order to ascertain what is meant, it is necessary to read carefully the thirty-five pages of explanatory comment. It is here that problems arise.

The Rule recognises that not all 'violations of international humanitarian law' are necessarily war crimes. It clarifies this by including the word 'serious'. But what exactly does this mean and can it be interpreted differently in different contexts? The Commentary seeks to provide a definition of 'serious', namely 'that they [the violations] endanger protected persons or objects or if they breach important values'.[29] However, 'serious' can cover two situations. First, is the violation by its nature 'serious'? It may be assumed that all 'grave breaches' of the Geneva Conventions are by definition 'serious'. However, there may be other violations that may depend for their 'seriousness' on the nature of the infraction itself. Whilst 'pillage or other taking of property contrary to international humanitarian law' is listed,[30] it is acknowledged that the ICTY has found that 'the appropriation of a loaf of bread belonging to a private individual by a combatant in occupied territory . . . would not amount to a "serious" violation of international humanitarian law'.[31] It follows that the word 'serious' may be being used in two separate contexts, the first referring to the nature of the prohibition itself and secondly to the manner in which the prohibition is broken. This is not made sufficiently clear. To be fair, a similar ambiguity can be found in the Rome Statute where the offences themselves appear to be the subject of the adjective 'serious' in Article 8, but the Elements of Crimes introduce elements that require the act to be sufficiently serious to justify international condemnation. An example is in the requirement for the improper use of a flag of truce to result in death or serious personal injury before the International Criminal Court has jurisdiction.[32]

This is linked with the failure to deal adequately with the fact that 'war crimes' may have a different meaning in a domestic or international environment.[33] Two particular issues arise here. First, even where a breach is insufficiently 'serious' to justify international condemnation, that does not mean that it should necessarily not be subject to domestic

---

[29] Ibid., 569.   [30] Ibid., 575.   [31] Ibid., 570.
[32] See Elements of Crimes, Article 8(2)(b)(vii)–1: War Crime of Improper Use of a Flag of Truce, reprinted in R. Lee (ed.), The International Criminal Court, Elements of Crimes and Rules of Procedure and Evidence (Ardsley, NY: Transnational Publishers, 2001), p. 754.
[33] There is a brief reference to this in the Commentary, see Study, Vol. 1, 569 and 571.

criminal prosecution. A misuse of the flag of truce is serious in all circumstances and should be prosecuted in a domestic tribunal whether or
not death or serious personal injury has resulted. Similarly, there may be
breaches of the law of armed conflict which do not themselves qualify as
sufficiently 'serious' in nature to justify international condemnation but
which still should be the subject of domestic proceedings. There is a risk
that, by concentrating on the international definitions, particularly those
contained in the Rome Statute and the Elements of Crimes, the definition
of war crimes will be seen to be being narrowed in an unfortunate
manner. This may have an unfortunate effect on domestic prosecutions.

An area in which the domestic sphere is particularly important is in the
field of prohibited weapons. The text here is delightfully vague, talking
simply of 'prohibited weapons'. However, there are comparatively few
weapons that are 'prohibited' under international customary law, as is
apparent in Part IV of the Study (and even some of those listed there,
such as the use of expanding bullets in non-international armed conflict,
are open to challenge). What is much more important here are the treaty
obligations of different States. This is illustrated by the lengthy debates
during the negotiations on the Rome Statute. The Study acknowledges[34]
that the Ottawa Convention,[35] introducing a ban on anti-personnel landmines, cannot yet be said to represent customary international law,
though later[36] the text could be read as implying that it does. The reference to the UN Secretary General's Bulletin[37] here is also misleading as
some of the weapons prohibited under that document (booby traps and
incendiary weapons for example – see para. 6.2 of the Bulletin) are not
banned under treaty law but merely restricted. This does not necessarily
mean that the law has not moved on so that a treaty restriction has now
become, under customary law, a prohibition but no attempt is made to
argue that point and it would almost certainly run into serious difficulties
in the light of State practice. Most weapons treaties do now require
domestic courts to take jurisdiction over breaches and it is perhaps in the
domestic sphere that much of the activity in relation to this aspect of war
crimes will take place.

---

[34] Study, Vol. 1, 282.
[35] The Ottawa Convention on the Prohibition of the Use, Stockpiling, Production and
Transfer of Anti-Personnel Mines and on their Destruction, 18 September 1997.
[36] Study, Vol. 1, 600.
[37] Secretary General's Bulletin: Observance by United Nations Forces of International
Humanitarian Law, 6 August 1999, reprinted in A. Roberts and R. Guelff, *Documents on
the Laws of War* (Oxford University Press, 3rd edn, 2000), p. 725.

It is perhaps unfortunate that the Study chooses to reopen a number of issues that were raised in New York and Rome on behalf of the ICRC but lost in the debates! For example, the wording of Article 8(2)(b)(iv) of the Rome Statute was the subject of intense debate and the word 'overall' was included quite deliberately to reflect the statement made by the United Kingdom on ratification of Additional Protocol I (and in similar terms by other States) that 'the military advantage anticipated from an attack is intended to refer to the advantage from the attack *considered as a whole* [my emphasis] and not only from isolated or particular parts of the attack'.[38] For many States, that wording was critical. For example, a feint attack may carry little military advantage *in itself* except that it distracts the enemy forces from the point where the real attack is to come. It is unrealistic, as was argued in Rome, to treat each individual attack in isolation; it has to be looked at in context. It is interesting that the Study does not comment on the word 'clearly' in its commentary on the same provision. This word also does not appear in the text of Additional Protocol I but it would seem that here the change of wording contained in the later treaty is accepted. No reason is given why the two additions are treated differently.[39]

The 'other crimes' listed in the Study[40] but which do not appear in the Rome Statute are mostly crimes that the ICRC tried to insert into the Statute but did not succeed for various reasons. In some cases, it was felt that the acts themselves were already covered under other provisions and thus there was no need to identify them separately as war crimes; in others, they failed to satisfy the assembled delegates that they were sufficiently 'serious'. For example 'collective punishments' are indeed prohibited[41] but where the acts would be sufficiently serious to amount to a war crime, as in the *Priebke* case cited,[42] they would be covered under

---

[38] See United Kingdom Statement made on ratification of Additional Protocol I to the Geneva Conventions of 1949, reprinted in Roberts and Guelff, *ibid.*, p. 511. Accordingly, the reference to K. Dörmann, *Elements of War Crimes under the Rome Statute of the International Criminal Court* (Cambridge University Press, 2003) in footnote 45 on page 577 of the Study is incomplete. This is made plain in Lee (ed.), *The International Criminal Court*, p. 148 and is dealt with by Dörmann in later parts of his commentary pp. 170–173 though not in such concise terms.

[39] See also chapter 6 above, p. 156. But for criticism of this approach see R. Cryer, 'Of Custom, Treaties, Scholars and the Gavel: the Influence of the International Criminal Tribunals on the ICRC Customary Law Study' (2006) 11 *Journal of Conflict and Security Law* 239, at 259.   [40] Study, Vol.1, 586.

[41] Additional Protocol I, Art. 75(2)(a)(iii), and Additional Protocol II, Art. 4(2)(b).

[42] *Prosecutor v. Erich Priebke*, Military Tribunal of Rome, 22 July 1997, subsequently in the Military Appeals Court, 7 March 1998 and the Supreme Court of Cassation, 16 November 1998. The case is summarised on the ICRC website at http://www.icrc.org/ihl-nat.nsf/46707 c419d6bdfa24125673e00508145/0370fc27370b3776c1256c8c0055e44d!OpenDocument.

other provisions. In the case of unjustifiable delay in the repatriation of prisoners of war or civilians, this was debated but it was considered that, despite its inclusion as a 'grave breach' in Additional Protocol I, this was not a violation that attracted individual criminal responsibility under customary international law. Indeed, it was a conscious decision in Rome not to include grave breaches of Additional Protocol I in a separate section as was done with the grave breaches of the four Geneva Conventions themselves, because it was not considered that all had gained customary law status.[43] A similar attempt to include crimes omitted from the Rome Statute in relation to crimes in non-international armed conflict can be found elsewhere in the Study.[44] This is not necessarily wrong. As has already been pointed out, the Rome Statute was itself a compromise and does not give an exhaustive list of crimes. There is jurisprudence from international tribunals to the effect that the list of war crimes in non-international armed conflict, recognised under customary law, is growing. However, it is difficult to ascertain at any given time exactly where the boundaries lie.

In relation to crimes in non-international armed conflict, the authors might have gone further than they have done. Common Article 3 is applied only to non-international armed conflict, which is how it appears in the Rome Statute. However, as has been already mentioned, the judgments of the International Criminal Tribunal for Former Yugoslavia and the International Court of Justice make it plain that common Article 3 provides a baseline for *all* armed conflicts. It is correct that, as a matter of treaty law, it is confined to non-international armed conflict though this view appears to have been challenged by the United States Supreme Court in *Hamdan v. Rumsfeld*[45] which considered that it covered all conflicts other than those of an international character listed in common Article 2 of the Geneva Conventions. Nevertheless, it would appear to be subject to growing acceptance that, regardless of the position under treaty law, the principles contained in common Article 3 have a much wider ambit.

The final section relating to 'composite war crimes' may be misleading. 'Enforced disappearances' are not necessarily war crimes though they are listed as crimes against humanity in the Rome Statute.[46] Similarly, 'ethnic cleansing' is more of a euphemism to describe a series of criminal acts.

---

[43] Personal knowledge of the author who was involved in the negotiations in both New York and Rome.   [44] Study, Vol. 1, 599.

[45] *Hamdan v. Rumsfeld*, United States Supreme Court, 29 June 2006, 548 U.S. [Supreme Court Reports] 196.   [46] Rome Statute, Art. 7(1)(i).

I do not consider that there is yet a 'composite' crime of 'ethnic cleansing' under customary international law.

It should be mentioned that in the early drafts put forward as discussion papers for the Rome Statute – some based on ICRC position papers – there was an attempt to include every possible crime that appeared in any treaty. This led to inevitable overlap – cultural property is protected in different language under three separate treaties[47] – and the drafters preferred to look at actions and then find wording to ensure that the actions were criminalised, thus avoiding duplication as far as possible. The 'composite' crimes tend to do the reverse by rolling a number of crimes together. From the point of view of a prosecutor, this can create additional complications as became apparent when it was sought to identify elements of crimes in the ICC negotiations for the classic composite crime of enforced disappearances.[48] The linkage between the different actors was the most difficult part to express and will always be the most difficult part to prove.

The Rule also leaves out a requirement referred to[49] in the above quotation from the *Tadić* case that the violation 'must entail, under customary or conventional law, the individual criminal responsibility of the person breaching the Rule'.[50] There may be some 'serious violations' of an administrative nature that do not necessarily incur criminal responsibility and thus do not amount to war crimes. A post orderly who, through pressure of work, destroys capture cards rather than forwarding them on to the ICRC is committing a serious violation but not necessarily one that incurs criminal liability. However, there is considerable argument as to whether the *Tadić* requirement is indeed a correct element. The authorities referred to in the judgment itself concentrate mainly on the issue of individual criminal responsibility in non-international armed conflict rather than looking at the proposition in the round. Again there may be a difference between international criminal responsibility and domestic. In the same way as grave breaches of the Geneva Conventions involve international individual criminal responsibility, other breaches of the Convention may not, though that does not necessarily exclude criminal

[47] Hague Regulations 1907, Art. 7(1)(i); Hague Cultural Property Convention 1954, Art. 1, Additional Protocol I, Art. 53.
[48] See Elements of Crimes, Art. 7(1)(i), Crime against Humanity of Enforced Disappearance of Persons, reprinted in Lee (ed.), *The International Criminal Court*, p. 746.
[49] Study, Vol. 1, 571.
[50] *Prosecutor v. Tadić*, Decision on the Defence Motion for Interlocutory Appeal on Jurisdiction, Appeals Chamber, 2 October 1995, IT-94-1-AR72, para. 94(iv).

responsibility under domestic law. The Conventions require High Contracting Parties to 'enact any legislation necessary to provide effective penal sanctions for persons committing, or ordering to be committed, any of the grave breaches' but, in relation to other 'acts contrary to the provisions [of the Conventions]' only require States to 'take measures necessary' for their suppression.[51] That may not necessarily require penal sanctions but may include administrative penalties.

It is unclear why the authors decided to leave out this requirement but it may be that the phrase is so vague as to provide no added value to the Rule. It is mentioned in the Commentary.[52]

Rule 157

States have the right to vest universal jurisdiction in their national courts over war crimes.

This Rule does not give rise to discussion other than as regards the definition of 'war crimes' and the question of a link with the prosecuting State. It refers to a 'right', not an obligation, though as the Commentary points out,[53] there is such an obligation in respect of 'grave breaches' of the Geneva Conventions and Additional Protocol I in so far as States Parties are concerned.

It has been accepted for many years that States may exercise universal jurisdiction over war crimes under customary international law. It was recognised by the International Law Commission in the 1996 Draft Code of Crimes.[54] This used to be seen as applying purely to crimes committed in international armed conflict in accordance with the prevailing interpretation of the definition of war crimes. As the definition has changed, the Study maintains that the right now extends to crimes committed in non-international armed conflict. Whilst once controversial, there is a growing body of State practice in support, primarily arising out of the Rwanda genocide, and the lack of objection would seem to confirm that it has now been accepted as legitimate. The Study discusses[55] whether there is any need for a link between the alleged offender and the prosecuting State, such as presence or residence of the offender. Practice is not uniform, and it would be difficult to argue that any such link is required as a matter of law. For the obligations to prosecute grave breaches no such link is required.

---

[51] *Ibid.*   [52] Study, Vol. 1, 571.   [53] Study, Vol. 1, 606.
[54] International Law Commission, Draft Code of Crimes Against the Peace and Security of Mankind, 1996.   [55] Study, Vol. 1, 605, 606.

Rule 158

States must investigate war crimes allegedly committed by their nationals or armed forces, or on their territory, and, if appropriate, prosecute the suspects. They must also investigate other war crimes over which they have jurisdiction and, if appropriate, prosecute the suspects.

This Rule is more controversial. It can be split into a number of parts. The first sentence imposes a duty on States but it is what is not said that is important also. If this duty is indeed imposed under customary international law, there must be a corresponding duty to legislate so that States have jurisdiction over all war crimes committed by their 'nationals, armed forces, or on their territory'. This is not stated here but it is an inevitable consequence. It is arguable whether the duty goes so far. Whilst there may be a duty to 'take measures to ensure the punishment of all persons guilty of war crimes' (General Assembly Resolution 2840 (XXVI), 18 December 1971),[56] that resolution goes on to refer to the possibility of 'extradition to those countries where they have committed such crimes'.[57] Bringing people to justice may not necessarily require prosecution in a State's own courts. The Preamble to the Rome Statute is also cited[58] but this is not normally considered to have imposed an obligation on States to legislate to allow for domestic prosecution of all ICC crimes, though they would be well-advised to do so if they wish to take advantage of the complementarity regime.[59]

Certainly, under the Geneva Conventions, there is the mandatory obligation to introduce penal sanctions for grave breaches and both the Conventions and other treaties require States to take action to 'suppress' other violations.[60] However, as has been examined in relation to Rule 156, this may not necessarily involve criminal prosecution. It is correct that if the violation rises to the status of a 'war crime', it normally requires criminal action but that might not necessarily be best conducted in the

---

[56] Study, Vol. 1, 609, footnote 217.

[57] See para.1, General Assembly Resolution 2840 (XXVI), 18 December 1971.

[58] Study, Vol. 1, 608.

[59] The Preamble reads 'Affirming that the most serious crimes of concern to the international community as a whole must not go unpunished and that their effective prosecution must be ensured by taking measures at the national level and by enhancing international cooperation' (para. 4).

[60] The Prosecutor v. Tadić Decision on the Defence Motion for Interlocutory Appeal on Jurisdiction.

investigating State. Whilst the Rule only requires prosecution 'if appropriate', it is silent on what happens if it is felt 'not appropriate'.

'Appropriate' is undefined, probably wisely; if it is supposed to refer to an evidential test, that in itself may be too strict. There may be other reasons why, even in a case that passes the evidential test, it is felt inappropriate to prosecute. The classic example might be where prosecution would be more appropriately conducted in another country and that country is prepared to undertake the prosecution. It might have been better if the Rule was phrased in more general terms requiring States to ensure that, where appropriate, such persons were prosecuted, thus giving the option of prosecution in another jurisdiction. It should, however, be made clear that 'appropriate' does not give *carte blanche* to prosecuting authorities to avoid prosecutions for political reasons. For example, the fact that a potential accused is a member of the Government would not be an 'appropriate' reason for denying prosecution.

It is interesting that the requirement is limited, in terms of individual responsibility for crimes committed outside national territory, to 'nationals or armed forces'. With the increasing civilianisation (for better or worse) on the battlefield, should States not also take some responsibility for others who may be Government servants or even contractors? The United Kingdom was criticised for limiting jurisdiction in its International Criminal Court Act to nationals, residents and those subject to Service jurisdiction but even this is broader than the Rule, covering those who have established residence in the country as well as those civilians who are made subject to Service jurisdiction by the Service Discipline Acts.[61] What would be the position where a war criminal has permanent residence in a country but not nationality? In some circumstances, extradition to his or her own country may be impossible, particularly in European countries which are prevented by human rights law from transferring persons to jurisdictions where they might face capital punishment.[62]

The second sentence is even broader. The ICJ *Arrest Warrant* case[63] was mentioned under Rule 157[64] but is even more apposite here. If this is a rule of customary international law in relation to non-international

---

[61] See s.51(2), International Criminal Court Act 2001, applying to England and Wales. Similar provisions apply to Scotland and Northern Ireland.

[62] See for example *Soering v. United Kingdom*, European Court of Human Rights, Judgment 7 July 1989, [1989] ECHR 14.

[63] *Arrest Warrant* case (*Democratic Republic of Congo v. Belgium*), Judgment of 14 February 2002, [2002] *ICJ Reports*, 3.   [64] Study, Vol. 1, 606.

armed conflict, then it runs into severe difficulties. How does a State which has taken on universal jurisdiction over war crimes committed in a non-international armed conflict carry out its duty to investigate such crimes committed in another territory without breaching the sovereignty of that territory? To impose an obligation in these circumstances seems to be going too far. It would almost inevitably lead to conflicts of jurisdiction between States. It must perhaps be understood that these Rules are to be read in the wider context of international law and thus cannot in themselves authorise something that would be unlawful under another provision of international law.

Rule 159

At the end of hostilities, the authorities in power must endeavour to grant the broadest possible amnesty to persons who have participated in a non-international armed conflict, or those deprived of their liberty for reasons related to the armed conflict, with the exception of persons suspected of, accused of or sentenced for war crimes.

This is one of the few Rules to apply only in non-international armed conflict. It must be questioned whether it has yet become a norm of customary international law, certainly in this form. There is a slight contradiction in the Commentary in that the text states: 'This shows that authorities are not absolutely obliged to grant an amnesty at the end of hostilities but are required to give this careful consideration and to endeavour to adopt such an amnesty.'[65] The phrase 'careful consideration' is important here and would seem to be a more appropriate standard than that given to the Rule.

Non-international armed conflicts are amongst the most difficult to resolve because they usually involve divisions within a community. It is in these situations that the conflict between peace and justice may be most marked. Whilst this section of the Study is devoted to war crimes, it should be noted that the generally recommended exception to any amnesty includes not only war crimes but other international crimes such as genocide and crimes against humanity.[66] However, there does seem to be a clear discrepancy between national and international practice. It may be in the national interest to grant total amnesty, because

[65] Study, Vol. 1, 612.
[66] Seventh Report of the Secretary General on the United Nations Observer Mission in Sierra Leone, UN Doc. S/1999/836, 30 July 1999, para 54.

without it there can be no peace and it is therefore felt that this is a price worth paying to end the conflict or abuse of power.

Yet, on the international scale, it is frequently made clear that amnesties on the domestic level cannot include international crimes. An example was the Lome Accord of July 1999 in Sierra Leone. Under this, the Government of Sierra Leone undertook to grant 'absolute and free pardon to all combatants and collaborators in respect of anything done by them in pursuit of their objectives'.[67] This was rejected by the United Nations Secretary-General in his report to the Security Council where he confirmed the instruction given to his Special Representative 'to enter a reservation when he signed the peace agreement stating that, for the United Nations, the amnesty cannot cover international crimes of genocide, crimes against humanity, war crimes and other serious violations of international humanitarian law'.[68] Subsequently the Appeals Chamber of the Special Court for Sierra Leone in the case of *Prosecutor v. Kallon and Kamara*[69] held that whilst the amnesty was binding on the Government of Sierra Leone as a matter of domestic law, it was not binding on the Special Court by virtue of Article 10 of its own Statute. It went on to rule that an international tribunal cannot be deprived of its jurisdiction to prosecute an offender by the grant of amnesty.

Sierra Leone is but one example of many where domestic amnesties of wide scope have been granted. It would seem therefore that, in practice, amnesties are indeed granted but their effect is limited to the domestic jurisdiction. Whilst this too has been challenged in many South American countries and immunity agreements in some cases have been lifted, as noted in the Commentary, the tendency seems to be towards recognising the jurisdiction of third party States to try cases even if the host State itself is precluded under domestic law.

Recent research indicates that only a minority of national amnesties appear to comply with the suggested Rule by excluding all international crimes.[70] There has been an increase in the trend to exclude

---

[67] Peace Agreement Between the Government of Sierra Leone and the Revolutionary United Front of Sierra Leone, (Lome Accord), 7 July 1999, Art IX(2).

[68] Seventh Report of the Secretary General on the United Nations Observer Mission in Sierra Leone, S/1999/836, 30 July 1999, para. 7.

[69] *Prosecutor v. Morris Kallon and Brima Bazzy Kamara* (Special Court for Sierra Leone) Appeals Chamber Judgment, 13 March 2004, Case No.SCSL-2004-15-AR72(E), and Case No.SCSL-2004-16-AR72(E).

[70] Research carried out at Queen's University, Belfast discloses that in a study of 419 amnesties, only 94 excluded international crimes though it was acknowledged that this might be an underestimation because of differing wording.

international crimes after the Lome Accord, but the conclusion reached by the research is that it is 'too early to say that a State practice has developed for the purpose of identifying a rule of customary international law'.[71]

Rule 159 does not deal in depth with Truth and Reconciliation Commissions, though they are touched upon in the Commentary. The difficulty that faces any State emerging from a period of internal conflict is that efforts to provide 'judicial' justice cannot solve all the problems. In many cases, Rwanda being one in point, the sheer number of participants makes the use of judicial processes to deal with them all simply not feasible. In such circumstances, some form of truth-revealing process may be required and this will often involve some degree of 'amnesty'. It should be born in mind, however, that revelation of the truth is itself a measure of reparation to victims. How that amnesty is granted and on what terms will depend very much on the particular situation but this should not necessarily be seen as a contradiction with this Rule. It may also be that the Rule should, at present, be limited solely to international tribunals where it is fully accepted that domestic amnesties for international crimes can have no effect.

Rule 160

Statutes of limitation may not apply to war crimes.

The two main relevant treaties are the 1968 United Nations Convention[72] (now with forty-nine parties) and the 1974 European Convention[73] (still only three parties, Belgium, Netherlands and Romania). Neither is widely accepted. Many civil law countries have severe difficulties with this issue as was apparent in the debates on the International Criminal Court and whilst they were, sometimes reluctantly, prepared to accept a prohibition in relation to international jurisdiction, they were not so willing to accept that this applied to national jurisdictions, in spite of the problems that this might raise in the matter of complementarity. Examples are given in the Commentary of States who have adopted such a rule, in some cases in their constitution, but the

---

[71] L. Mallinder, 'To Forgive but not Forget? Amnesties, Transition and the Price of Peace', unpublished doctoral thesis on file with the author.

[72] Convention on the Non-applicability of Statutory Limitations to War Crimes and Crimes Against Humanity, 26 November 1968.

[73] European Convention on the Non-applicability of Statutory Limitations to Crimes Against Humanity and War Crimes, 25 January 1974.

paucity of such examples is a telling factor and, each, to a certain extent, was in response to a specific situation.

Whilst this Rule may be at least on its way to becoming an accepted norm in relation to 'the most serious crimes of international concern' as they apply to international prosecutions, it may not be such for those that fall within domestic rather than international jurisdiction. This may account for the apparent contradictions in the French position outlined in the Study.[74]

Rule 161

States must make every effort to cooperate, to the extent possible, with each other in order to facilitate the investigation of war crimes and the prosecution of the suspects.

In principle, there should be no objection to this Rule. The only concern is in its wording. The requirement to 'make every effort to the extent possible' is a high one and one must ask whether the obligation goes quite so far. The United States is quoted as supporting 'good faith efforts', a position taken from remarks made by Michael Matheson, then Deputy Legal Adviser to the State Department, in 1987.[75] Although the current Administration seems to have distanced itself from those remarks in recent years as a statement of official policy, maintaining that these were personal views,[76] the standard of 'good faith efforts' seems a more realistic one. States have to manage limited resources and whilst it may be 'possible' to transfer large numbers of staff across to a war crimes investigation arising from an incident in another country, it may not be realistic in the light of domestic pressures, particularly if similar evidence can be obtained as easily elsewhere. What is 'possible' may not be 'feasible' taking into account all other circumstances.

---

[74] Study, Vol. 1, 617.
[75] See The Sixth Annual American Red Cross – Washington College of Law Conference on International Humanitarian Law: A Workshop on Customary International Law and the 1977 Protocols Additional to the 1949 Geneva Conventions, Session One: The United States Position on the Relation of Customary International Law to the 1977 Protocols Additional to the 1949 Geneva Conventions, Remarks of M. Matheson (1987) 2 *American University Journal of International Law and Policy* 415, at 418.
[76] Errata Sheet, 2005 *Operational Law Handbook*, published by the International and Operational Law Department, The Judge Advocate General's Legal Center & School, US Army, 27 September 2004.

3. Final remarks

The field of international criminal law is still to an extent in its infancy. It took nearly fifty years from Nuremberg to the establishment of the 'Ad Hoc' Tribunals for Former Yugoslavia and Rwanda. Since then there has been a move away from such 'Ad Hoc' international courts with a primary right to jurisdiction, towards hybrids with a greater role given to domestic jurisdictions. This follows the example of the International Criminal Court where the Court has no primacy. The relationship between international courts and national courts is now seen as 'complementary' though the exact relationship is sometimes difficult to work out and may depend very much on local factors. There is a growing awareness that there is no 'one size fits all' solution. It follows that, in examining the Rules contained in this part of the Study, care needs to be taken not only to differentiate between different types of conflict but also between different types of jurisdiction. It is not entirely clear that that requirement has been fully met. Some of the Rules are drafted in a way that may impact differently on the international and domestic jurisdictions and thus may, or may not, be equally applicable to both.

The basic principles themselves are comparatively non-controversial. However, the difficulties lie in the exact wording and it may be thought that, at times, the standards imposed by the Rules as stated are the ideal and go somewhat beyond what States in the real world would be prepared to accept, certainly in their own domestic arenas. Indeed, as has been seen, the Commentary in some cases tempers the absolutism of the Rules themselves. Codified international law is the subject of agreement amongst States after lengthy negotiations. It is inevitably subject to compromise and practical reality, which may water down the desirable to the feasible. If States find that customary law is being used to 'raise the bar' so that requirements are being imposed which States would not be prepared to accept at the conference table on grounds of practicality, then the whole structure of customary law, as providing a foundation for treaty law and underpinning the legal system, may be cast in doubt.

There is at present a nervousness about the increasing reliance on international criminal law as a means of controlling warfare. The conduct of warfare creates problems that are simply not to be found in the types of situation that domestic legal systems operate within. Whilst this should not be taken as suggesting that criminal law has no role to play in this field, care must be taken not to over emphasise the part it can play. The law of armed conflict has always been a mix of humanity and pragmatism and that same pragmatism needs to be reflected in the way in which criminal law governs the conduct of warfare. Not all soldiers are embryo war criminals!

PART 4

Conclusions

16

Conclusions

ELIZABETH WILMSHURST

The invitation given by Dr Yves Sandoz in his foreword to the Study to read, discuss and comment upon its contents[1] has been taken up with enthusiasm by the contributors to this book. They have written from their personal perspectives, relying on their different areas of expertise; in commenting on the Rules they have put the law into its historical context and added to the discussion about application and implementation of the law. They have welcomed the Study as a very valuable resource, while identifying various issues as deserving of further consideration by both the authors and the readers of the Study. These issues concern both the methodology used by the Study and the Rules themselves.

The methodology

The Study gives fresh impetus to the debate about the nature of customary international law and the manner of its formation. Some of the issues the authors of the Study had to grapple with apply to any attempt to ascertain custom: what is the relevant State practice, when can practice in relation to treaties be regarded as evidence of custom, what evidence is available for *opinio iuris* and is there always a need to seek it? Because so much of international humanitarian law is regulated by treaty, the second of these issues is particularly relevant. There are other issues relating solely to the assessment of custom for the purpose of international humanitarian law. They include the problem that practice in non-international conflicts may be difficult to identify since State practice will frequently be based on domestic law rather than international law, as well as the controversy regarding the exact relevance to this area of the law of human rights, environmental law and other bodies of law.

---

[1] Study, Vol. 1, xvii.

The methods for the collection of research for the Study used by the ICRC command respect and admiration.[2] The description of the assessment of customary law,[3] written with the assistance of Professor Maurice Mendelson, gives a classic, even conservative, statement of the sources and formation of customary law. But in the *application* of the methodology, the evidence of many of the contributors to this book leads to the conclusion that the authors of the Study have sometimes adopted an approach which is less conservative than is claimed.

On the question of the relevance to the formation of custom of *State practice in conformity with treaties*, Iain Scobbie concludes that there 'appears to be too easy an elision from the fact of widespread participation in the Geneva Conventions and Additional Protocols to the normative conclusion of customary status'.[4] He suggests that in considering the existence of a rule supported by a treaty the Study appears to make certain rules of the Protocols presumptively customary rather than merely conventional.[5] There are many examples of this in the book; see, for example, the discussions of Rule 4 (on the definition of the armed forces)[6] and the first sentence of Rule 45 (on damage to the natural environment).[7]

There is of course a problem here, as illustrated throughout the *Nicaragua* case.[8] It is not easy, if at all possible, to ascertain whether practice is in implementation of a treaty rather than of a customary rule. It may be one or the other, or both. Further, if all practice under a treaty were to be ignored, it could be difficult to conclude that any provision of the Geneva Conventions was customary law, except in respect of those provisions which codified pre-existing law. Prior to universal participation in a treaty the practice of the very few non-ratifying States would be given disproportionate weight if the assessment as to custom focused only on them.[9]

---

[2] They are described in the Introduction to the Study at pp. xlv–li. Researchers into national practice were appointed; in addition there were teams of researchers into international practice. The ICRC examined its own archives. A Steering Committee was formed of a group of academic experts in international humanitarian law. A further group of academic and governmental experts gave assessments of draft texts. There were additional readers for each part of the Study.   [3] Study, Vol. 1, xxxi–xlv.

[4] Chapter 2, p. 30.   [5] *Ibid.*, p. 34.   [6] Chapter 5, p. 110.   [7] Chapter 8, p. 232.

[8] *Military and Paramilitary Activities in and Against Nicaragua (Nicaragua v. United States of America)*, Merits, Judgment of 27 June 1986 [1986] *ICJ Reports* 14.

[9] See Jean-Marie Henckaerts, 'Study on Customary International Humanitarian Law: A Contribution to the Understanding and Respect for the Rule of Law in Armed Conflict' (2005) 857 *International Review of the Red Cross* 175, at 184.

The Study has been careful to acknowledge objections and reservations to particular provisions of the Additional Protocols. Examples of analysis of objections include the discussion with respect to the qualification as a civilian in case of doubt,[10] works and installations containing dangerous forces,[11] prisoner-of-war status for members of resistance and liberation movements,[12] and reprisals against civilians.[13] It does however appear to be the general view of the contributors[14] to this book that the Study has on occasion adopted a fairly relaxed view of what is needed to constitute customary law. The Study authors are not alone in their approach, of course. The International Court of Justice determined the customary law status of common Articles 1 and 3[15] and decided on the 'intransgressible principles' of customary law of the Geneva Conventions[16] without a careful analysis of State practice and *opinio iuris*. Nor was the determination of the Sierra Leone Special Court as to the customary nature of the criminalisation of child enlistment[17] sufficiently supported by evidence at the relevant time, as explained by Judge Robertson in his dissent. We appear to be demanding of the authors of the Study a more formalistic approach to the formation of customary law than the courts always provide. But such a demand may be justified, and the authors of the Study themselves do not appear to have claimed a special exemption for international humanitarian law from the ordinary rules as to the formation of customary law.[18]

As regards the *identification of State practice*, the Study has taken a fairly expansive view, relying on both verbal and physical practice; the former includes statements made by representatives of States at treaty conferences and resolutions of international organisations. While some concern is expressed in the preceding chapters about the weight the authors have attached to various kinds of verbal evidence,[19] Iain Scobbie

---

[10] Study, Vol. 1, 23–24. [11] *Ibid.*, Vol. 1, 139–141. [12] *Ibid.*, Vol. 1, 387–389.

[13] *Ibid.*, Vol. 1, 520–523.

[14] From this group there must be excepted the one contributor who is a staff member of the ICRC.

[15] *Military and Paramilitary Activities in and Against Nicaragua (Nicaragua v. United States of America)*, Merits, 218–220.

[16] *Legality of the Threat or Use of Nuclear Weapons*, Advisory Opinion of 8 July 1996, [1996] *ICJ Reports* 66.

[17] *Prosecutor v. Norman* SCSL-2004-14-AR72(E) paras. 18–24. On the general point see T. Meron, 'Revival of Customary International Law' (2005) 99 *American Journal of International Law* 817, at 819, 820.

[18] Although the Introduction at xlii makes reference to Kirgis's 'Sliding Scale' ; and see Scobbie, chapter 2, pp. 27, 28.

[19] See e.g. Bethlehem generally at chapter 1 and Schmitt at chapter 6, p. 134.

considers that 'in principle the Study's use of essentially verbal acts in the construction of its Rules is unimpeachable';[20] he does not agree with claims that battlefield practice should be seen as paramount.[21] He also doubts the validity of criticisms of the Study's use of official manuals and reports, pointing out that it is difficult to see how States can disavow such documents when the State representatives were acting in an official capacity at the time.[22]

There are also criticisms made in this book with regard to the discussion of *persistent objectors and specially affected States* in the formation of custom. An example given by Karen Hulme relates to the objections by nuclear weapon States to the application of the environmental provisions of Additional Protocol I to nuclear weapons. The Study concludes that these States are persistent objectors to the rule of customary law on this point, but this is a wrong conclusion; Hulme explains that the objections from these specially affected States prevent the rule, with regard to nuclear weapons, from becoming custom at all.[23]

Finally, the relationship between *human rights law and international humanitarian law* continues to be a difficult one. The treatment given in the Study will add to the debate. Ryszard Piotrowicz (in relation to the sources of law used for the Rules on displaced persons)[24] and David Turns (in relation to Rule 150)[25] have criticised the use of human rights law in the Study in its derivation of rules of international humanitarian law. Françoise Hampson, however, is of the view that the use of human rights material as additional support for a principle otherwise established by humanitarian law evidence is legitimate. The other use made of human rights material in the Study, she points out, is to clarify the meaning of a rule of humanitarian law and to give examples of its scope. In her view the use of this material by the Study is 'legitimate, necessary and conservative'.[26]

The Rules

The Rules which emerge from the use of this methodology have attracted both commendation and comment in this book. It is by no means surprising that some of the Rules formulated by the Study have given rise to debate. The authors of the Study interpreted the mandate to the ICRC to prepare 'a report on customary rules of international humanitarian law

---

[20] Chapter 2, p. 37.   [21] *Ibid.*, pp. 37–38   [22] *Ibid.*, p. 40.
[23] Chapter 8, p. 233.   [24] Chapter 13.   [25] Chapter 14.   [26] Chapter 3, p. 73.

applicable in international and non-international armed conflicts'[27] as that of providing an 'accurate assessment of the current state of customary international humanitarian law'.[28] While a more cautious approach would have confined the report merely to a collection of the relevant practice – in itself an extremely valuable work – and avoided drawing up suggested rules of law, the ICRC might then have been criticised for failing to fulfil their mandate.[29] But their ambitious objective required them in effect to take a photograph of a moving target. The task of establishing a rule of customary international law in any field is notoriously difficult and the claim for authoritative status for norms across the greater part of international humanitarian law made it almost inevitable that there would be disagreements on the formulation of individual Rules by the authors and on their choice of particular proposals as having the status of customary international law.

The large majority of the Rules in the Study, in particular those regarding international armed conflict, are well established as customary: see for example most of the Rules governing targeting and the protection of persons and objects (discussed in chapters 7 and 8). On the other hand, recurring difficulties are identified regarding some other Rules.

There is criticism of what is seen as an attempt to provide *over-simplified* Rules, some of which are said to bear little resemblance to the actual practice of States and the generally accepted customary law provisions. This is evident in Bill Fenrick's discussion of Rule 54 (attacking objects indispensable to civilians' survival) in chapter 9. In some instances the simplicity of a Rule as formulated is deceptive and renders it open to misinterpretation. Limiting factors may be found only in the Commentary to the Rule, and not in the Rule itself. For example, Charles Garraway points to Rule 156 ('Serious violations of international humanitarian law constitute war crimes'). To ascertain what the Rule means, it is necessary to read carefully the 35 pages of explanatory comment.[30] Chapter 7 contains other examples, including with regard to Rules 35–37. The result is that the Rules should not

---

[27] Mandate from the 26th International Conference of the Red Cross and Red Crescent, Geneva, 3–7 December 1995, Resolution 1, International Humanitarian Law: From Law to Action; Report on the Follow-up to the International Conference for the Protection of War Victims (1996) 310 *International Review of the Red Cross*, p. 58.

[28] Study, Vol. 1, xi.

[29] This is certainly the view of Hampson, chapter 3, p. 50.

[30] Chapter 15 p. 385. See also in the contrary sense R. Cryer, 'Of Custom, Treaties, Scholars and the Gavel: The Influence of the International Criminal Tribunals on the ICRC Customary Law Study' (2006) 11 *Journal of Conflict and Security Law* 239, at 263; he criticises the Commentary for undermining this Rule.

be read on their own, without regard to the Commentary. A publication which contained only the Rules would give a misleading account of customary international humanitarian law, for this reason alone.[31]

Where *treaties* have significantly influenced the formation of customary law, the terms of the treaty have sometimes been changed or simplified in the drafting of the relevant Rule of the Study without adequate explanation. An instance of this is given by Daniel Bethlehem in chapter 1, who points out that Rule 5 relating to the definition of civilians appears to omit certain elements in Article 50 of Additional Protocol I,[32] thus giving rise to normative uncertainty and possibly undermining civilian protection rather than enhancing it. Michael Schmitt, on the other hand, commends the authors for not having formulated Rule 10 as an exact model of the equivalent provision in the Protocol. In other instances the Rules follow the treaty formulation almost exactly, but it is difficult to ascertain sufficient practice as regards the specific detail of the Rule to conclude that that detail now amounts to custom. Michael Schmitt provides an interesting method of contrast throughout his chapter by presenting certain Rules with their direct Additional Protocol I Article equivalents; this demonstrates how the wording in the Articles has in some cases been adopted wholesale to create the Rules, for example, Rule 8. He shows how Rule 6 ('civilians are protected against attack unless and for such time as they take a direct part in hostilities') appears to be based directly on the wording of Article 51.3 of Additional Protocol I even though the United States has rejected the customary status of this Article because of their objection to the phrase 'for such time'.[33] It would be easier in such instances to affirm that there is evidence only for a principle, where there is little evidence for the detail of the formulation.

Another criticism is that the Study elevates proposals or *aspirational goals* to the status of laws. In some instances there is presented as customary law what is either law in the course of development or a matter which is still being contested.[34] Whether or not the contributors to this book

---

[31] However, see J. M. Henckaerts (2005) 87 *The International Review of the Red Cross*, 175, an article on the Study which contains the Rules as an annex, starting at p. 198. There is a short preambular paragraph but it does not refer to the Commentary.

[32] Chapter 1, p. 12.   [33] Chapter 6, p. 144.

[34] See also M. Maclaren and F. Schwendimann, 'An Exercise in the Development of International Law: the New ICRC Study on Customary International Humanitarian Law' (2005) 6 *German Law Journal* 1217 at 1236–1238; G. Aldrich, 'Customary International Humanitarian Law – an Interpretation on behalf of the International Committee of the Red Cross' (2005) 76 *British Yearbook of International Law* 503.

accept the sometimes slender amount of practice as sufficient to substantiate the proposed Rule depends on their attitude to the rigour required in the assessment of custom.[35] This issue is illustrated in particular by many of the Rules which are stated to apply to non-international armed conflict. The attempt by the Study to classify rules as applicable to non-international armed conflict when they have previously applied only to international conflict is criticised.[36] The distinction between the laws applicable in the two kinds of conflict is undoubtedly being blurred and this development is being encouraged or influenced by the jurisprudence of the ICTY and State practice. However the continuing distinction is inevitable, not least by reason of the fact that the entitlement to prisoner-of-war status does not exist in non-international conflict. In view of the fact that one of the objects of the Study was to provide evidence of the applicability of many rules of customary international law to non-international armed conflict,[37] it is to be regretted that, notwithstanding all the care taken by the authors, some of the proposed Rules for non-international conflicts do not have the same degree of evidentiary support as for those in international conflict.

Some comments have been made in the opposite direction, however. In relation to some areas, rules are in the process of crystallisation as new practice emerges. Because of its chosen method of listing only Rules which it characterises as already binding norms, the Study has sometimes omitted what could be useful discussion on areas which are ripe for legal development. There is an ongoing process of rule formation and where the evidence is not yet sufficient it is valuable to record what practice there is. In some areas the Study has done this, for example in relation to the eight Rules which are only 'arguably' customary in relation to non-international armed conflict. Further, on matters where there is widely accepted practice based on ambiguously worded treaty language (usually in Additional Protocol I), it would have been useful had the Study taken the opportunity, instead of keeping to the exact wording of the treaty, to adopt new and clearer wording based on generally accepted practice. Examples of the latter are given by Michael Schmitt as to Rules 1 and 21 (regarding targeting) and Steven Haines as to Rule 70 (with regard to means and methods causing superfluous injury or unnecessary suffering).

---

[35] See chapter 12 for a number of proposed Rules which Jachec-Neale considers not quite to have reached the status of customary law; her approach is to be contrasted with that of Fenrick in chapter 9. [36] For example in chapter 14 in relation to Rule 142.
[37] Study, Vol. 1, xxxix.

Finally, the reader who seeks commentary on today's compelling questions of international humanitarian law will be disappointed for the most part. The so-called global war on terror has given rise to problems of both interpretation and application of international humanitarian law. The Study was ten years in the making and at least at its inception its researchers did not have available practice drawn from the swiftly changing circumstances. The Study cannot perhaps be expected to make a significant contribution to the debate on the identification of the applicable rules or on whether the existing rules are sufficient, in relation to such matters as the length of detention of the prisoners at Guantanamo Bay.[38] Similarly the difficult questions of occupation law raised by the occupation of Iraq following the military intervention in 2003 cannot be addressed in a volume which deals only incidentally with that body of law. In this context it is disappointing that the Study has not dealt with the question of the status of a conflict, and whether or not there is a conflict at all: the problems of the characterisation of a conflict have bedevilled the search for the rules applicable, for example, to detainees at the close of the main international conflict in Afghanistan in 2001. Jelena Pejić in chapter 4 does something to fill the gap, but the gap in the Study remains a real one. Further, there might very usefully have been discussion of the Martens clause and its impact in the formation of custom.[39] In these circumstances the plea is for the Study to have been more, not less, ambitious.[40]

Some of the chapters in this book draw attention to developments relating to what some describe as the new reality, including cross-border operations, differing uses of weaponry, and pressures on humanitarian law coming from 'humanitarian' occupation and the growing use of human rights law by domestic and international courts in conflict situations. What can be described as missed opportunities in the Study can also be used as an invitation to the ICRC to revise and add to the Study in the future.

The value of the Study

The focus of a large part of the discussion in this book has been those Rules the status of which as customary law is the most controversial. Less attention has been given, on the whole, to Rules with which the contributors are

[38] See for example discussion of Rule 128 in chapter 12 above.
[39] See chapter 2, p. 18.
[40] But as J.M. Henckaerts points out in 'Customary International Humanitarian Law – a Rejoinder to Judge Aldrich' (2005) 76 *British Yearbook of International Law* 525, at 526, the Study is not intended to be a handbook of international humanitarian law.

in full agreement. The resulting critical nature of some of the contributions should not be allowed to detract from the overall merit of the Study. As was said in the preface, it is the unanimous view of the contributors to this book that the Study represents a valuable work of great service to international humanitarian law. It is undoubtedly the case that the answer to the question 'what is customary international humanitarian law?' is now, thanks to the Study, very much easier to provide.

The Study has already achieved a remarkable success in the short time following its publication in 2005. Its use, as a matter of course, by international and national courts and tribunals can be confidently expected. This will be particularly likely for the ICTY, having as it does a duty to apply, as regards crimes within its own jurisdiction, only rules of international humanitarian law which are 'beyond any doubt part of customary international law'.[41] Use of the Study is likely to be regarded as easing the tribunals' task of determining the rules applicable at the time of an offence; as the former President of the Yugoslav Tribunal has written, the Study 'will be a significant aid to international tribunals in exercising their functions consistently with the legality principle.'[42]

The Study has already had an impact in judicial decisions.[43] It was cited, for example, in the ICTY interlocutory appeal decision in *Prosecutor v. Hadžihasanović*.[44] To support a finding that the 'wanton destruction of cities, towns or villages' and 'devastation not justified by military necessity' in non-international armed conflict were criminalised under customary international law, the Appeals Chamber looked to the Study's evidence, collected in Volume II, of examples of States' military manuals

---

[41] Report of the Secretary-General pursuant to paragraph 2 of Security Council Resolution 808, S/25704 (3 May 1993), para. 34.

[42] T. Meron, 'Revival of Customary International Law' (2005) 99 *American Journal of International Law* 817, at 833.

[43] The Study has also been cited in two reports of UN Rapporteurs: *Human Rights in Lebanon*, Report of the Special Rapporteur on the right to food, Jean Ziegler, on his mission to Lebanon, A/HRC/2/8, 29 September 2006, para. 8, footnote 3; and Report of the Special Rapporteur on extrajudicial, summary or arbitrary executions, Philip Alston; the Special Rapporteur on the right of everyone to the enjoyment of the highest attainable standard of physical and mental health, Paul Hunt; the Representative of the Secretary-General on human rights of internally displaced persons, Walter Kälin; and the Special Rapporteur on adequate housing as a component of the right to an adequate standard of living, Miloon Kothari, Mission to Lebanon and Israel (7–14 September 2006), UN Doc. A/HRC/2/7, 2 October 2006, para. 22, footnote 22.

[44] *Prosecutor v. Hadžihasanović*, Appeal of Decision on Acquittal, No. IT-01-47-AR73.3, paras. 29–30 (11 March 2005). See also *Prosecutor v. Stakić* Judgment IT-97-24-A, 22 March 2006, para. 296, in relation to Rule 129.

and legislation creating an offence of attacking civilian objects during armed conflict.

The Study has been cited in domestic cases. In the *Adalah*[45] case concerning the tactic of the Israeli Defence Force (IDF) of using civilians as human shields, the Israeli Supreme Court cited first Rule 20 in support of a requirement on the IDF to give effective warning to a wanted person before an arrest could be carried out, and secondly, Rule 97 prohibiting the use of human shields, in support of a prohibition on the IDF to use local residents as human shields. Finally, Rule 24 was cited as evidence of customary international law that civilians must be distanced from hostilities if at all possible, which the Court understood as prohibiting the IDF from involving civilians in conflict and thus the use of civilians as human shields. A later case before the Israeli Supreme Court concerned the legality of 'targeted killings'. The Court considered the customary law status of Article 51(3) of Additional Protocol 1 which provides that civilians are protected 'unless and for such time as they take a direct part in hostilities'. In a careful judgment, the Court referred with approval to Rules 1 (principle of distinction between civilians and combatants), 6 (loss of protection against attack) and 7 (principle of distinction between civilian objects and military objectives) of the Study and decided that the whole of Article 51(3), including the words 'for such time' had customary status.[46]

The US Supreme Court cited the Study in the case of *Hamdan v. Rumsfeld*,[47] ruling that Common Article 3 applied to the detainees captured in the 'conflict' with Al-Qaeda and holding that the military commission regime was in breach of that Article. In considering the requirement that a trial be held before a 'regularly constituted court', the Court cited the Commentary to Rule 100 of the Study to define a regularly constituted court as one which has been 'established and organised in accordance with the laws and procedures already in force in a country'.[48] The newly established military commissions were in breach of

---

[45] *Adalah and others v. GOC Central Command, IDF and others*, Israel Supreme Court, 23 June 2005 (HCJ 3799/ 02) paras. 20, 21 and 24.

[46] *Public Committee against Torture in Israel and another v. Government of Israel and others* (HCJ 769/02, 11.12.05) paras. 23, 29–30 and 41–42; the Court also referred with approval to Rules 11 (indiscriminate attacks) and 14 (proportionality). See also references to the Commentary of the Study in paras. 33–34 and 40 and 46.

[47] *Hamdan v. Rumsfeld*, United States Supreme Court, 29 June 2006, 548 U.S. [Supreme Court Reports] 196.

[48] Rule 100: No one may be convicted or sentenced, except pursuant to a fair trial affording all essential judicial guarantees. Quote from the Commentary to Rule 100, page 355.

this requirement since they were constituted by Congress after the arrest of the detainees.

On the other hand, the Eritrea–Ethiopia Claims Commission in their Partial Award of 2005 appeared to depart from one Rule in the Study. The Commission discussed whether the aerial bombardment of an Eritrean water reservoir by Ethiopian forces was a violation of the applicable humanitarian law prohibiting such targeting and considered whether Additional Protocol 1 Article 54(2) has passed into customary law. In relation to Rule 54, the Study discussed this Article and State practice prohibiting the targeting of objects indispensable to the survival of the civilian population. The Commission noted the Study 'with appreciation' but did not endorse the Study's 'broader conclusion' regarding the scope of the proposed prohibition of targeting indispensable objects[49] and applied Article 54(2) to interpret this customary norm more narrowly than the Study had done.[50]

Reactions to the Study by States are not yet sufficiently numerous to give an indicative picture.[51] But States and their armed forces will undoubtedly be using the Study for reference and guidance – and they will need to do so, in view of the fact that courts, non-governmental organisations, human rights bodies and the ICRC itself will be referring to the Study as their first port of call for the existence of customary international law on a particular issue. The volumes of evidence constitute a unique resource which will, perhaps, be quite as useful as the exact wording of the Rules themselves.[52]

Academic commentary on the Study has been published in journals of international law, defence studies and human rights around the world including in the United Kingdom, United States, France, China, Australia, Israel and Germany. The literature has pointed to, among other things, the relevance of the Study in the development[53] and in the

---

[49] Partial Award, Western Front, Aerial Bombardment and Related Claims, Eritrea's claims 1, 3, 5, 9–13, 14, 21, 25 and 26, note 23.

[50] If, however, the Commission had considered the Commentary to the Rule, rather than simply the Rule itself, they may not have regarded their finding as inconsistent with the Study; this is therefore an example of the fact that it is misleading to consider the Rules themselves in isolation.

[51] The US comments dated 3 November 2006, setting out a number of concerns, have been published at http://www.defenselink.mil/home/pdf/Customary_International_Humanitarian_Law.pdf.

[52] Meron considers that the use by the ICTY of the practice gathered by the Study rather than the 'black letter rule' in the *Hadzihasanović* case may be symptomatic of future practice: T. Meron, *The Humanization of International Law* (Leiden: Martinus Nijhoff, 2006).

[53] M. Maclaren and F. Schwendimann 'An Exercise in the Development of International Law'.

revival[54] of customary international humanitarian law, the relationship between international humanitarian law and human rights law in
the Study,[55] the impact of the Study on customary humanitarian law,[56]
and the influence of international criminal tribunals on the Study.[57]
Conclusions on the Study range from the laudatory: 'The Study will certainly become the leading source of customary international humanitarian law'[58] to the more cautious: 'the Study goes too far in declaring its
proposed rules to be customary law, for in doing so, its credibility crum-
bles.'[59] This debate will, it is hoped, be enriched by the contributions in
this book.

It may be that readers of this book will conclude that some contributors have been altogether too critical of aspects of the methodology of the
Study or of the formulation of individual Rules. They may adopt the
general sentiments expressed by Dieter Fleck:

> Where there are gaps in existing positive law, States should be encouraged
> to use the ICRC Study with a view to closing such gaps, rather than criticis-
> ing progressive statements made in the Study, or taking advantage of legal
> lacunae in a spirit of advocating freedom of operations and even drawing
> short-sighted unilateral advantage at the expense of victims of armed
> conflicts.[60]

Such a view, for which there must be some sympathy, depends upon a
belief that the best way to ensure the protection of victims of war is to use
more 'progressive' methods to assess custom and to encourage imagina-
tive uses of soft law.[61] Further, should not the influence of the Martens
clause persuade acceptance as customary law of 'principles of humanity
and dictates of public conscience', leading to a possibly less formalistic
approach to the assessment of custom?

---

[54] Meron, 'Revival of Customary International law'.

[55] H. Kriege, 'A Conflict of Norms: The Relationship between Humanitarian Law and
Human Rights Law in the ICRC Customary Law Study' (2006) 11 *Journal of Conflict and
Security Law* 265.

[56] D. Fleck, 'International Accountability for Violations of the *Ius in Bello*: The Impact of the
ICRC Study in Customary International Humanitarian Law' (2006) 11 *Journal of Conflict
and Security Law* 179, at 185.

[57] R. Cryer, 'Of Custom, Treaties, Scholars and the Gavel'.

[58] MacLaren and Schwendimann, 'An Exercise in the Development of International Law', at
1240.

[59] Aldrich, 'Customary International Humanitarian Law', at 507; see also Y. Dinstein, 'The
ICRC Customary International Humanitarian Law Study' (2006) *Israel Yearbook on
Human Rights* 1.

[60] Fleck, 'International Accountability for Violations of the *Ius in Bello*', at 181.

[61] See e.g. *ibid.*, at 180.

An alternative point of view, however, is that while State forces and armed opposition groups should be encouraged to act in a humanitarian way and, indeed, to follow the Martens clause, the exigencies of conflict and the powerful interests of belligerents will frequently be such that only firmly established rules of law will be sufficient to constrain battlefield conduct in a direction contrary to military desirability. In such circumstances, those claiming the existence of legal rules, whether treaty or custom, must be able to substantiate them as such. Unsupported rhetoric about the existence of legal norms may cause the law to fall into disrepute with the result that there will be failure to observe such rules as there are. In other words, clarity about the existence of rules of law can assist in securing compliance.

This book has therefore attempted a sympathetic critical scrutiny of the Study, with the aims both of assisting in clarifying the existence of customary law and of contributing to the discussion of State practice in particular areas of international humanitarian law. In the suggestions for reformulation of specific Rules, and in the discussion of areas not covered by the Study, the contributors express the hope that the book will be a catalyst to further work and will represent a contribution to any such work, in particular if there should be a further edition of the Study.

INDEX

Rule numbers refer to the full text of Rules

CPSIA information can be obtained
at www.ICGtesting.com
Printed in the USA
LVHW011718200920
666590LV00004B/40

9 781107 402386